Microsoft .NET:
Architecting Applications
for the Enterprise,
Second Edition

Dino Esposito
Andrea Saltarello

PUBLISHED BY
Microsoft Press
A Division of Microsoft Corporation
One Microsoft Way
Redmond, Washington 98052-6399

Library of Congress Control Number: 2014940680
ISBN: 978-0-7356-8535-2

Printed and bound in the United States of America.

3   16

Microsoft Press books are available through booksellers and distributors worldwide. If you need support related to this book, email Microsoft Press Book Support at mspinput@microsoft.com. Please tell us what you think of this book at http://aka.ms/tellpress.

Microsoft and the trademarks listed at http://www.microsoft.com/en-us/legal/intellectualproperty/Trademarks/EN-US.aspx are trademarks of the Microsoft group of companies. All other marks are property of their respective owners.

The example companies, organizations, products, domain names, email addresses, logos, people, places, and events depicted herein are fictitious. No association with any real company, organization, product, domain name, email address, logo, person, place, or event is intended or should be inferred.

Acquisitions and Developmental Editor: Devon Musgrave
Project Editor: Carol Dilllingham
Editorial Production: Waypoint Press, www.waypointpress.com
Peer Reviewer: Cesar De la Torre Llorente
Copyeditor: Roger LeBlanc
Indexer: Christina Yeager
Cover: Twist Creative • Seattle and Joel Panchot

To my wife Silvia. You make me feel sandy like a clepsydra. I get empty and filled all the time; but it's such a thin kind of sand that even when I'm full, without you, I just feel empty.

—DINO

To Laura, mum, and Depeche Mode. Moved, lifted higher. Moved, by a higher love.

—ANDREA

Contents at a glance

Contents

What do you think of this book? We want to hear from you!

Microsoft is interested in hearing your feedback so we can continually improve our
books and learning resources for you. To participate in a brief online survey, please visit:

microsoft.com/learning/booksurvey

PART III   SUPPORTING ARCHITECTURES

Chapter 8   Introducing Domain Model   191

Chapter 9   Implementing Domain Model   217

What do you think of this book? We want to hear from you!

Microsoft is interested in hearing your feedback so we can continually improve our books and learning resources for you. To participate in a brief online survey, please visit:

microsoft.com/learning/booksurvey

Introduction

Good judgment comes from experience, and experience comes from bad judgment.

—Fred Brooks

We find that the preceding quote contains the essence of software architecture and the gist of the architect's role. Software architecture requires judgment because not all scenarios are the same. To exercise sound judgment, you need experience, and in this imperfect world, experience mostly comes from making some mistakes and bad choices—from bad judgment.

However, the world we live in often doesn't give you the opportunity (or even the time) to form your own experience-based knowledge from which good judgment is developed. More often than not, all that executives want from architects is the right architecture right away.

We've written this book primarily to endow you with a solid, reusable, and easily accessible base of knowledge about software architecture. In past years, we've completed projects using technologies like Microsoft Windows DNA, Distributed COM, multitier CRUD, SOA, DDD, CQRS, and event sourcing. We've used Microsoft Visual Basic 6 as well as C#, C++, Java, and JavaScript. We've seen technical solutions change frequently and perspectives about these approaches also evolve.

In the end, we came to the same conclusion as Fred Brooks. We don't wear white coats, we're not doctors, and we're not writing prescriptions. Our purpose here is to aggregate various positions, add our own annotations and comments to those positions, and generate an honest summary of facts and perspectives.

In these times in which developers and architects are asked to do it right and right away, we offer a snapshot of knowledge—a readymade software architect's digest for you to use as the starting point for further investigation and to use to build up your own judgment. If software architecture were a theorem, this book (we hope) would provide a collection of necessary lemmas.

Organization of this book

Software architecture has some preconditions (design principles) and one post-condition (an implemented system that produces expected results). Part I of this book, titled "Foundation," lays the foundation of software architecture and focuses on the role of the architect, the inherent mechanics of software projects, and aspects—like testability and readability—that turn software into top-quality software.

Part II, "Devising the architecture," focuses on the topmost layers that form a typical enterprise system: the presentation layer and business layer. We left for later the canonical third layer: the data access layer. We push a relatively new approach for designing a system and call it *UX-first*. It is a task-based methodology that leads to commands and domain events starting from agreed-upon mockups and screens. In a task-based design philosophy, the role of the domain model is much less central and the same data access layer is just part of the infrastructure, and it's not necessarily based on canonical relational tables. However, the most forceful chapter in Part II—the one we recommend everybody read—is Chapter 5, "Discovering the domain architecture." In a nutshell, the chapter makes the point that only a deep understanding of the domain can lead to discovering an appropriate architecture. And, maybe more importantly, the resulting architecture doesn't have to be a single, top-level architecture for the entire application. As you recognize subdomains, you can model each to subapplications and give each the most effective architecture. As weird as it might sound, this is the core lesson of Domain-Driven Design (DDD).

Part III, "Supporting architectures," covers three supporting architectures you can use to build the various subdomains you recognized. For each architecture, we have a couple of chapters—an introduction and an implementation. The first supporting architecture we consider is the Domain Model. Next we head to Command/Query Responsibility Segregation (CQRS) and event sourcing.

Finally, Part IV, "Infrastructure," contains a single chapter—it deals with infrastructure and the persistence layer. This is interesting because it's not simply a chapter about SQL, Entity Framework, and relational databases. We primarily talk polyglot persistence, NoSQL data stores, and services used to hide storage details.

So, in the end, what's this book about?

It's about what you need to do and know to serve your customers in the best possible way as far as the .NET platform is concerned. The patterns, principles, and techniques we describe are valid in general and are not specific to complex line-of-business applications. A good software architecture helps control the complexity of the project. And controlling complexity and favoring maintainability are the best strategies we have for fighting the canonical Murphy's Law of technology: "Nothing ever gets built on schedule or within budget." To get there, there's just one thing you're not allowed to fail on: understanding (deeply) the business domain.

Who should read this book

Software architects are the ideal audience for this book, but lead developers and developers of any type of .NET applications will find this book beneficial. Everyone who wants to be an architect should find this book helpful and worth the cost.

Is this book only for .NET professionals? Although all chapters have a .NET flavor, most of the content is readable by any software professional.

Assumptions

Strong object-oriented programming skills are a requirement for using this book. A good foundation in using the .NET platform and knowledge of some data-access techniques will also help. We put great effort into making this book read well. It's not a book about abstract design concepts, and it's not a classic architecture book either, full of cross-references and fancy strings in square brackets that hyperlink to some old paper listed in a bibliography at the end of the book.

This book might not be for you if...

This book might not be for you if you're seeking a reference book to pick up to find out how to use a given pattern. Instead, our goal is sharing and transferring knowledge so that you know what to do at any point. Or, at least, you know what two other guys—Dino and Andrea—would do in an analogous situation. This is (hopefully) a book to read from cover to cover and maybe more than once. It's not a book to keep on the desk for random reference only.

Downloads: Code samples

In the book, we present several code snippets and discuss sample applications with the primary purpose of illustrating principles and techniques for readers to apply in their own projects. In a certain way, we tried to teach fishing but we aren't providing sample fish to take home. However, there's a CodePlex site we want to point you to:

http://naa4e.codeplex.com/

There you find a few Visual Studio 2013 projects, one for each of the supporting architectures we describe in the book. A sample online store system—the I-Buy-Stuff project—is written according to the Domain Model architecture and then ported to CQRS. Two more projects complete the set: a live-scoring application and a mini-ERP system that illustrates event sourcing.

We invite you to follow the project because we plan to add more demos in the future.

The sample code has a few dependencies on common technologies such as Visual Studio 2013 and SQL Server. Projects make use of Entity Framework, ASP.NET MVC, RavenDB, Bootstrap and WURFL. Everything is linked to the project through Nuget. Refreshing the packages ensures you're able to reproduce the demo. In particular, you don't need a full installation of SQL Server; SQL Express will suffice.

Acknowledgments

When Andrea and I wrote the first edition of this book back in the summer of 2008 it was a completely different world. The huge economic downturn that hit the United States and other parts of the world, and still bites Europe, was just on the horizon. And Entity Framework was still to come. We covered patterns and technologies that are much less relevant today, and there was no cloud, mobile, or NoSQL. Still, at several times we caught the book ranked among Amazon's Top 10 in some category as long as four or five years after publication. For a technical book, lifespan of five years is like a geological era. We've been asked several times to work on a second edition, but the right astral conjunction never arrived until the spring of 2014. So here we are. Thanks to Devon Musgrave, Steve Sagman, Roger LeBlanc, and Carol Dillingham—a wonderful team.

As emphatic and partisan as it may sound, in over 20 book projects so far, I never left a lot of work for technical reviewers to do. And I hardly learned much from peer reviewers—for whatever reason. Well, this time it was different. Cesar De la Torre Llorente—our peer reviewer—did a fantastic job. He promptly caught issues with the outline and content, even deep issues that I missed entirely and Andrea just perceived as glitches that were hard to explain in detail and fix. Cesar convinced us to restructure the content several times, reshaping the book to what it needed to be, and leading it to become what, we think, it should be.

Finally, I wish to reserve a word or two for some people that shared—sometimes without even realizing it—insights and remarks as valuable as gold. One is Hadi Hariri for his constantly updated vision of the IT world. Another is Jon Smith for reminding us of the many facets of the architect's role. Yet another is Giorgio Garcia-Agreda for conveying to me some of the innate attitude for problem solving (especially in harsh conditions). Last, but not least, my thanks also go to Roberto Raschetti. He may wonder why he deserves this accolade, but without doubt, he showed me the way, from the time I was a freshly graduated student to that huge project we had in store for months to come.

Finally, Mom, Dad—this is another one for your bookshelf! Sure you don't need a bigger one?

PS: Follow us on Facebook (facebook.com/naa4e) and tweet using #naa4e.

—Dino

This book would not exist without Dino. Dino is the one who caused me to accept the daunting task of writing a sequel to a book that, to my dismay, revealed itself to be a huge hit and applied a lot of pressure on me.

Never again is what you swore the time before.

Dino approached me several times to ask my feelings about writing a second edition, had the patience to accept a bunch of refusals, and then, after getting me committed, understood that this writing had to be a "two-paces process" because it would take time for me to write what he could, in just a few hours, put into elegant, insightful words.

Not only am I slow at writing, but I'm quite fussy. But Dino has always been very supportive in my struggle to make sure that this book would be at least as good as the previous edition, and then some.

I'm taking a ride with my best friend.

Being as fussy as I am, I was really pleased to have Cesar De la Torre Llorente as our peer reviewer because he did a fantastic job, not only at reviewing the contents, but also at giving us valuable advice about how to restructure our content. Thank you Cesar. We really owe you a lot.

He knows where's he's taking me, taking me where I want to be.

But for this book to exist and, in my opinion, be a good one, we still needed a wonderful team behind us, and that's where the support we got from Devon Musgrave, Steve Sagman, Roger LeBlanc, and Carol Dillingham really made a difference. Thank you guys!

This is real fun, this is fun.

Writing a book while being a full-time consultant meant devoting a lot of time to being in front of your PC instead of being free and with the people you love, and that could be quite frustrating for both sides. Nevertheless, Laura and mum understood how important this book was for me and bestowed me with terrific support. And love.

You're like an angel and you give me your love, and I just can't seem to get enough of.

Finally, I want to thank all the guys at Managed Designs: without the experience gained because of all our endeavors, this book would not be half as good.

My secret garden's not so secret anymore!

And last, but not least, thank you Helen and Maruska for having been there when I struggled for words. Thank you from the bottom of my heart, miladies.

Welcome to my world, step right through the door.

PS: Follow us on Facebook (facebook.com/naa4e) and tweet using #naa4e.

—Andrea

Errata, updates, & book support

We've made every effort to ensure the accuracy of this book and its companion content. If you discover an error, please submit it to us via *mspinput@microsoft.com*. You can also reach the Microsoft Press Book Support team for other support via the same alias. Please note that product support for Microsoft software and hardware is not offered through this address. For help with Microsoft software or hardware, go to *http://support.microsoft.com*.

Free ebooks from Microsoft Press

From technical overviews to in-depth information on special topics, the free ebooks from Microsoft Press cover a wide range of topics. These ebooks are available in PDF, EPUB, and Mobi for Kindle formats, ready for you to download at:

http://aka.ms/mspressfree

Check back often to see what is new!

We want to hear from you

At Microsoft Press, your satisfaction is our top priority, and your feedback our most valuable asset. Please tell us what you think of this book at:

http://aka.ms/tellpress

We know you're busy, so we've kept it short with just a few questions. Your answers go directly to the editors at Microsoft Press. (No personal information will be requested.) Thanks in advance for your input!

Stay in touch

Let's keep the conversation going! We're on Twitter: *http://twitter.com/MicrosoftPress*.

The authors will be maintaining a Facebook page at *facebook.com/naa4e*.

Please precede comments, posts, and tweets about the book with the #naa4e hashtag.

Foundation

CHAPTER 1

Architects and architecture today

The purpose of software engineering is to control complexity, not to create it.
—Dr. Pamela Zave

At the very beginning of the computing age, the costs of hardware were largely predominant over the costs of software. Some decades later, we look around and find the situation to be radically different. The industry made incredible progress, and hardware costs have fallen dramatically. Software development costs, on the other hand, have risen considerably, mostly because of the increasing complexity of custom enterprise software development.

This situation has created the need for a set of precepts to guide engineers in the design of such systems. Appropriated from the construction industry, the term *architecture* has become the common way to describe the art of planning, designing, and implementing software-intensive systems. When the two of us were teenagers the "Love Is" comic strip (*http://www.loveiscartoon.com*) was at its peak of popularity. Each installment contained a piece of teenage wisdom about love. One cartoon said something like, "Love is a necessity, not a luxury." Well, that's precisely the point with architecture in software.

In this first chapter, we try to share our vision of architecture and how you figure it out and then implement it. In doing so, we'll touch on the role that architects play in the process and the basic facts we've seen ruling the mechanics of software projects. Needless to say, our experience is just ours. Although we've been working on some interesting projects of various sizes, our experience is still limited to what we've seen and the mistakes we've made. Nonetheless, we like to think of this book as the excuse for you to start a longer and more focused conversation within your team about the way you actually build things that work.

> **Note** Although some definitions you find in this book come from international standards, others reflect our personal opinions, experiences, and feelings. We will cover the well-recognized best practices on architecture, but we will also comment from own experience. We hope this combination will help you relate the, sometime dry, international standards to what you will find in the real world.

What's software architecture, anyway?

One of this book's authors had, in the past, frequent interaction with an architecture studio. One day, a question popped up for discussion: What's architecture? Is it an art? Or is it just building for a client?

In software, the term *architecture* precisely refers to building a system for a client. That's it: no more and no less.

This said, finding a more detailed description of what's involved in building a system for a client is the toughest part. We often wonder whether there's really a point in it. A million times we ask ourselves this question, and a million times we find the same answer. It's hard, but let's give it a try. At worst, it ends up being a brainstorming session, and brainstorming is never a bad thing.

So let's try to clarify what "software architecture" is or, at least, what we intend it to be.

Note The term *architecture* goes hand in hand with the term *architect*. Architect is a role, and we'll discuss later in the chapter the responsibilities we associate with the role of an architect. However, the term *architect* still makes people think of a profession. Unfortunately, the professional figure behind the term is not universal. That title is qualified by adjectives such as enterprise, solution, security, and so forth. Unless we specify otherwise, we mean the professional figure sometimes described as a *software architect* or *solution architect*.

Applying architectural principles to software

Many of us grew up as software experts first thinking that software is somehow related to the world of construction, and later fighting that notion. The analogy was first used in the software industry to express the need to plan and design before building computer programs. However, a fundamental difference exists between designing and building habitable structures and designing and building usable software systems.

Software exists to automate business processes and human actions; civil architecture artifacts exist as a service to the community. Usually, civil architecture services are planned and realized with best intentions and to be useful to the greatest number of people. Their aim isn't to satisfy just a few stakeholders. In addition, civil architecture artifacts are costly and complex enough that nobody ever thinks of making variations to the approved project on the fly. Or, at least, variations occur only occasionally.

Things go differently in software.

Software is typically created for a small group of stakeholders; some of them pay from their own pocket to get something that helps their organization function better. Requirements, therefore, are continuously refined, added, removed, and reprioritized. This approach to software requires agility and doesn't wed well with the idea of a big upfront design like you have in civil architecture.

In a nutshell, today the architectural parallelism between construction and software is not as close as it was a couple of decades ago. However, many dictionaries still list a software-related definition of the term "architecture." And software architecture is described as "the composition, integration, and interaction of components within a computer system." It is certainly a definition everybody would agree on. But, in our opinion, it is rather generic and abstract.

Hence, it doesn't work.

We think that software professionals should agree on a more detailed explanation that breaks down that definition into smaller pieces and puts them into context.

Defining the architecture from a standard viewpoint

Many seem to forget that a standard definition for software architecture exists. More precisely, it's been around since September 2000 when the American National Standards Institute/Institute of Electrical and Electronics Engineers (ANSI/IEEE) standard 1471, "Recommended practice for architectural description of software-intensive systems" was released. Over the years, the document also became International Organization for Standards/International Electrotechnical Commission (ISO/IEC) standard 42010. Those interested in reading the full standard can link to the following URL: *http://www.iso.org/iso/iso_catalogue/catalogue_tc/catalogue_detail.htm?csnumber=45991*.

Software architecture is concerned with the organization of any *software-intensive system* that solves a problem and achieves its mission in full respect of stakeholders' concerns. In extreme synthesis, this is the official definition of the term *software architecture* you get from international standards papers.

Stakeholders are defined as all individuals interested or concerned about the building of the system. The list includes the builders of the system (architects, developers, testers) as well as the acquirer, end users, analysts, auditors, and chief information officers (CIOs).

Concerns are defined as any interests that stakeholders can have about the system and the influence they exercise on the system, whether developmental, technological, operational, organizational, economic, or legal.

Note We know that a lot of people get scared when they run across acronyms like ISO, ANSI, and the like. We also tend sometimes to skip these references because they, well, just sound boring and mindful of the abundant doses of theory we received at university. Anyway, standards papers are full of information we just agree with. In this chapter, we reference standards mostly to say that in some areas (such as, processing user requirements) a lot has been done and it has been done well enough to reuse it.

Diagram of a software-intensive system

Figure 1-1 summarizes the core part of the official diagram that describes software architecture according to papers recognized by the ISO, IEC, and IEEE.

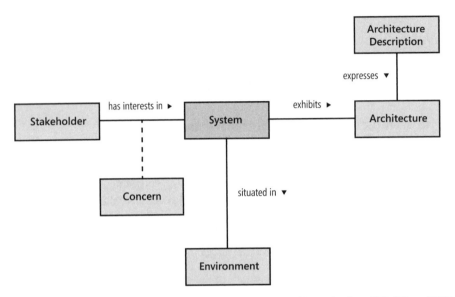

FIGURE 1-1 A diagram summarizing the software architecture viewpoint from ISO, IEC, and IEEE.

A system lives in a context, and this context influences the design of the system by driving some developmental and operational decisions. Although current standards envision the system as a composition of interconnected components, architecture also establishes some firm points that are hard to modify later. In a way, expressing software development in terms of architecture boils down to making some key decisions that affect the development life cycle and, ultimately, the quality of the resulting system.

Our very own blend of software architecture

When new people join our companies, we offer them—regardless of skills and roles—our personal view of software architecture.

We're Italian, and in Italy we're rigidly serious about coffee. When it comes to an espresso, there are not that many different types of coffee. The only recognized categorization is between a good espresso and a not-so-good espresso. But when we enter Starbucks, like everybody else, we have our own favorite blend of coffee.

We like to extend the coffee analogy to software architecture.

As with espresso, in this world we see only good architecture and not-so-good architecture. To keep with the analogy, we're restricted to just architecture that results in a working system. We don't consider here bad architecture resulting in failing systems, just like we don't drink bad espresso!

When served bad espresso, an Italian doesn't complain, he just walks out of the bar and shares the appropriate (and respected) feedback.

When it comes to laying out architecture, just like we do at Starbucks, we have our own vision of it. Our vision can be depicted by a plain graph with nodes and arcs, but we feel it expresses how we think and how we work. (See Figure 1-2.)

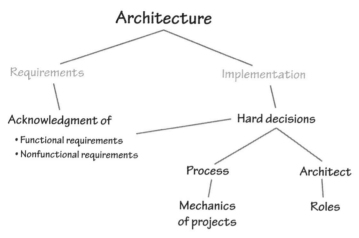

FIGURE 1-2 Our essential vision of software architecture.

Acknowledging requirements

The mission of the system is expressed through a set of requirements. These requirements ultimately drive the system's architecture.

In rather abstract terms, a *requirement* is a characteristic of the system that can be either functional or nonfunctional. A *functional* requirement refers to a behavior the system must supply to fulfill a given scenario. A *nonfunctional* requirement refers to an attribute of the system explicitly requested by stakeholders.

Are the definitions of functional and nonfunctional requirements something standard and broadly accepted? Actually, an international standard to formalize quality characteristics of software systems has existed since 1991.

A quick look at the ISO/IEC 9126 standard

As a matter of fact, failure to acknowledge requirements is one of the most common causes—often, the primary cause—that leads straight to the failure of software projects. The ISO/IEC 9126 standard defines a general set of quality characteristics required in software products. The standard identifies six families of quality characteristics, articulated in 21 subcharacteristics. The main families are functionality, reliability, usability, efficiency, maintainability, and portability. Table 1-1 explains them in more detail and lists the main subcharacteristics associated with each.

TABLE 1-1. Families of quality characteristics according to ISO/IEC 9126

Family	Description
Functionality	Indicates what the software does to meet expectations. It is based on requirements such as suitability, accuracy, security, interoperability, and compliance with standards and regulations.
Reliability	Indicates the capability of the software to maintain a given level of performance when used under special conditions. It is based on requirements such as maturity, fault tolerance, and recoverability. Maturity is when the software doesn't experience interruptions in the case of internal software failures. Fault tolerance indicates the ability to control the failure and maintain a given level of behavior. Recoverability indicates the ability to recover after a failure.
Usability	Indicates the software's ability to be understood by, used by, and attractive to users. It dictates that the software be compliant with standards and regulations for usability.
Efficiency	Indicates the ability to provide a given level of performance both in terms of appropriate and timely response and resource utilization.
Maintainability	Indicates the software's ability to support modifications such as corrections, improvements, or adaptations. It is based on requirements such as testability, stability, ability to be analyzed, and ability to be changed.
Portability	Indicates the software's ability to be ported from one platform to another and its capability to coexist with other software in a common environment and sharing common resources.

Subcharacteristics are of two types: external and internal. An external characteristic is user oriented and refers to an external view of the system. An internal characteristic is system oriented and refers to an internal view of the system. External characteristics identify functional requirements; internal characteristics identify nonfunctional requirements.

The newer ISO/IEC 25010 standard supersedes ISO/IEC 9126 and was issued in March 2011. ISO 25010 has eight product-quality characteristics and 31 subcharacteristics.

Functional requirements

A functional requirement defines a required function in a software system. A *function* is described in terms of input, behavior, and output. The main issue of functional requirements is the description of the expected behavior. Unfortunately, the description often isn't as clear and understandable as it should be.

In the ISO/IEC 9126 document, functional requirements are described as the capability of software to provide functions that meet stated and implied needs when the software is used *under specified conditions*. Software architecture depicts the *what*; software design depicts the *how*. However, we believe we too often forget about the third axis—the *when*.

You might remember the Ariane 5 disaster back in 1996. In brief, during its maiden flight, the Ariane 5 rocket crashed 40 seconds after takeoff. According to the official report, the rocket self-destroyed as the result of a chain-reaction triggered by an unhandled exception—overflow in a number conversion. The unhandled exception bubbled up in an uncontrolled way to presenting incongruent orbital numbers to the self-destroy module. Correctly interpreted as evidence of the rocket being irreversibly lost in space, self-destruction was, in the end, just a savvy choice. The irony was that the module where the exception went unhandled was not supposed to be running, because it was unnecessary, at the time of takeoff. So engineers knew that incongruent numbers could be received during takeoff, but instead of trapping exceptions, they just assumed it would never be necessary because the module would not function at takeoff!

Therefore, the *when* dimension of requirements does matter.

How should your Internet-based client application behave in the case of poor connectivity? Should it fail? Should it try to wait and recover? Should it be nice to users? Should it use cached data and switch silently to offline mode? There's no obvious answer; it all depends on the requirements that fall under attributes like reliability and recoverability. It's your responsibility as an architect to find answers—sometimes asking more questions in a second and more thoughtful pass. Having those answers leads to a better understanding of the system and, subsequently, reduces the likelihood of doing the wrong thing or not coding a required feature.

Ideally, all functional requirements are gathered before development starts and never modified once development has started. More likely, though, many functional requirements are discovered or fully understood only during development sprints. This creates the need for revisiting the implementation and sometimes the architecture of modules and, in tough cases, even subsystems. Failing to do this, starts the notorious "Big Ball of Mud" syndrome we discuss in the next chapter.

> **Important** In the beginning of our careers, we were more prone to mistaking for gold whatever came out of interviews with customers. Like a funny Dilbert cartoon, it was like we were blaming ourselves for not being able to fully deal with requirements, no matter how numerous, disorganized, contradictory, and partial they were. (By the way, check out *http://dilbert.com/strips/comic/2001-04-14*.) "The customer is always right" was our motto, and customer requirements were like the Table of Law. Over the years, we learned that the customer always has the final word on any functional decisions, but it's our responsibility to prospect for a sound range of options. And we build the range of options out of successfully acknowledging raw requirements we get from interviews.

Nonfunctional requirements

A nonfunctional requirement refers to an attribute of the system explicitly requested by stakeholders. Typical attributes are things like scalability, security, or perhaps accessibility. While functional requirements are mostly about code and implementation, nonfunctional requirements are mostly about architectural choices and, subsequently, aspects of the system that are hard to change later. Nonfunctional requirements can affect technologies used in a project as well as technical solutions.

For example, how would you address the need for extreme scalability?

Note We have still not met a customer who doesn't claim that extreme scalability of the contact-list application is vital for the survival of the company and the health of investors' portfolios. Regardless of what's actually being said, and sometimes done, our two cents are that true extreme scalability needs are quite uncommon. Unless, of course, you are really building the next Twitter or Facebook!

Scalability is the ability of a software system to provide the same performance as the number of connected users grows, thus generating a lot more work and traffic. For a system to scale well, reads and writes must occur in the shortest possible amount of time. This could mean, for example, using caching extensively in reading and making use of asynchronous writing.

Similarly, *security* can be effectively addressed by designing the system so that critical modules can be deployed to isolated machines. *Accessibility* is best addressed if you choose ASP.NET MVC rather than, say, ASP.NET Web Forms for the implementation of the site. This is because ASP.NET MVC offers a lot more control over the rendered HTML.

In general, nonfunctional requirements must be acknowledged at the same time as functional requirements. The latter produces software specifications; the former helps with implementation strategies and inspires technological choices. Functional and nonfunctional requirements are inherently linked, and both are subject to change continually. Nonfunctional requirements, though, raise the need to make some hard decisions.

 Note Several friends who helped us write this book had a comment at this point. While they could agree word for word with the previous section, they wanted to clarify that in many cases functional requirements also impact architectural choices and aspects of the system that are hard to change later. Absolutely!

Gathering requirements

There are tons of books that explain how to gather and write requirements. So you can learn that, for example, a good requirement addresses one and only one thing, is not ambiguously written, can be easily traced back to a business or stakeholder requirement, is not obsolete, and so forth.

 Note If you're looking for a book that explains the theory of software requirements, we recommend *Software Requirement Patterns* by Stephen Withall (Microsoft Press, 2007).

What happens in practice, though, is that business people describe what they believe they want and developers build what they believe those business people described. No matter what effort you put in to gathering of requirements, there's always something that was withheld, omitted, forgotten, or just expressed in a way that was clear to some but not to others. At the foundation of this communication issue, there's the fact that business people and developers use different vocabularies.

We are strong believers that architects and developers should speak the same language as the business people.

Regardless of how, say, a voucher is actually coded, to fully implement it you must understand what it is. Even more importantly, you need to understand what the business people mean by it. As an architect, you should not expect that business people understand your language, which is made of things like database tables, services, and protocols. It's you, instead, who should make any necessary effort to know and understand the entities that populate the business domain.

> **Important** The point of having technical people speak the same language as business people is the foundation of a key concept we introduce in Chapter 5, "Discovering the domain architecture." This concept is *ubiquitous language*, and it is one of pillars of the Domain-Driven Design (DDD) methodology.

How we deal with requirements

A simple but effective practice to process functional requirements is grouping them by categories, as described earlier in Table 1-1. What we usually do is create a Microsoft Office Excel document with one tab for each category. Next we go through the actual list of requirements we gathered from interviews and simply map each to an existing category.

When done, we read it back and stop on all those tabs that are either empty or that have just one or two requirements. If no requirements are found, say, under the attribute of *portability*, we stop and wonder if we know enough about it and if we asked enough questions. Having no explicit *portability* requirement might mean that portability is not a requirement, or it could mean we just don't know about it.

In particular, *portability* relates to the software's ability to be used within different environments. Having no such requirements, say, in a service back end should immediately raise the question of whether the back end should be usable only from web clients or whether support also for iOS and Android clients is essential.

What's architecture and what's not

When you think about creating or defining the architecture of a software system, you first try to identify a possible collection of interacting components that, all together, accomplish the requested mission. In international standards, there's no mention for any methodology you can use to decompose the system into more detailed pieces. Let's say in the first step you a get a conceptual architecture and some different views of it. In a second step, you need to get closer to a functional and physical architecture. How you get there is subjective, even though a top-down approach seems to be a reasonable strategy. You decompose components into smaller and smaller pieces, and from there you start building.

The actual implementation of the breakdown process depends on the methodology selected for the project—the more you are agile, the more the breakdown process is iterative and articulated in smaller and more frequent steps. The output of the breakdown process is a set of specifications for the development team. Also, the content and format of the specifications depend on the methodology. The more you are agile, the more freedom and independence you leave to developers when implementing the architecture.

Defining the borderline between architecture and implementation

The constituent components you identified while breaking down the system represent logical functions to be implemented in some way. The design of components, their interface, their responsibilities, and their behavior are definitely part of the architecture. There's a border, though, that physically separates architecture from implementation.

This border is important to identify because, to a large extent, it helps to define roles on a development team. In particular, it marks the boundary between architects and developers. Over the years, we learned that architects and developers are not different, say, types of fruit, like apples and oranges. They are the same type of fruit. However, if they are apples, they are like red apples and green apples—distinct flavors, but not a different type of fruit. And neither flavor is necessarily tastier.

The border between architecture and implementation is recognized when you reach a *black box of behavior*. A black box of behavior is just a piece of functionality that can be easily replaced or refactored without significant regression and with zero or low impact on the rest of the architecture. What's above a black box of behavior is likely to have architectural relevance and might require you to make a hard-to-change decision.

So what's our definition of good architecture? It is architecture in which all hard-to-change decisions turn out to be right.

The science of hard decisions

There are aspects and features of a software system that are hard (just hard, not impossible) to change once you enter the course of development. And there are aspects and features that can be changed at any time without a huge effort and without having a significant impact on the system.

In his book *Patterns of Enterprise Application Architecture* (Addison-Wesley, 2002), Martin Fowler puts it quite simply:

> If you find that something is easier to change than you once thought, then it's no longer architectural. In the end architecture boils down to the important stuff— whatever that is.

To sum it up, we think that under the umbrella of the term *architecture* falls everything you must take seriously at quite an early stage of the project. Architecture is ultimately about determining the key decisions to make correctly as early as possible in the project, but wishing you could make them as late as possible.

Hard decisions are everywhere

When we talk about hard architectural decisions, we are not necessarily referring to decisions about design points that can be difficult and expensive to change later. Hard-to-change decisions are everywhere and range from the definition of conceptual layers to the signature of a constructor.

To illustrate the point, let's go through a few examples of architectural points that can run into budget limits and deadlines if you have to touch them in the course of the project.

The first example is changing the organization of the business logic. There are several approaches for the design of the business logic: Transaction Script, Table Module, Domain Model, Domain Model with separation between commands and queries, and Event Sourcing, just to name a few. Once you have opted for, say, Table Module (which means, essentially, that you'll be putting logic in repository-like components built around database tables like you probably did for years around *DataSet*s and *DataTable*s), moving to a domain model is hardly something you can do in an afternoon. That change of direction requires nontrivial changes in the data access layer and in the application (service) layer, and probably also in the presentation layer.

A second example is switching to a different library for the same task. Suppose you developed some functionality around a given library. One day, the client pops up and lets you know that a new company policy prevents the IT department from buying products from a given vendor. Now you have a new, unexpected nonfunctional requirement to deal with, but at what cost? In the best case, you can get a similar tool from an authorized vendor or, perhaps, you can build a similar tool yourself. Alternatively, you can consider introducing a radical change into the architecture that makes that library unnecessary.

> **Note** If you attended some of the conferences Dino spoke at in the past couple of years, you may have heard about this experience already. In short, Dino's company bid for building a time-sensitive mobile app for four distinct platforms: iOS, Android, Windows Phone, and BlackBerry. The bid was made on the assumption that PhoneGap would be a feasible option. Unfortunately, a prototype built with PhoneGap was rejected by the customer, bringing the team back to square one and with four fewer weeks to get the job done.
>
> The team was left with one of two unpleasant options: doing the work four times in a fraction of the time or inventing something new. The team managed to reuse some of the PhoneGap markup on a mobile site and incorporated web views in the frames of four basic, mostly static and graphic-only native apps. Function-wise, it worked beautifully, and there was even time to survive one silly reject of the app by Apple. Stress-wise, though, it was a pain in the proverbial rear end.

A third, and maybe unusual, example of hard decisions is changing a class member's modifier. In general, when you use the *sealed* and *virtual* modifiers, you take on a not-so-small responsibility. In C#, by default each class is unsealed and each method on a class is nonvirtual. In Java, instead, things go differently for methods, which are all virtual by default. From a design perspective, sealed classes are preferable. In fact, when a class is sealed from the beginning you know it—and you create your code accordingly. If something happens later to justify inheritance of that class, you can change it to unsealed without breaking changes and without compromising compatibility. Nearly the same can be said for virtual methods and the visibility of classes and class members, which are always private by default. The opposite approach doesn't work as smoothly. You often can't seal a class or mark a virtual method as non-virtual without potentially breaking some existing code.

Context makes decisions hard

About four years ago, during a conference , we heard a prominent speaker say a great piece of truth for that moment in time. He proclaimed that mobile and cloud computing were the biggest headache for CTOs as they try to figure out what to do with both.

This little memory introduces a painful type of architectural hard decision. It happens when you know that a given piece of technology, or perhaps a pattern, can be helpful but you have no concrete evidence for that. You look around for case studies and eagerly hope to find them, or just any sort of literature that can help you rule in something or rule out something.

Decisions on well-known best practices are easy to make because there are lots of case studies. However, making decisions about new technologies, like NoSQL, is really rather difficult because case studies of real-life applications are few and far between and sometimes even biased.

The architecture process

Processed by the chief architect, requirements are communicated to the development team and then implemented. Everybody would agree that good architecture and good design speed up the actual development of modules. But how would you actually go about building applications?

In principle, building software is the joint effort of three groups of people: project management, development, and testing/quality assurance (QA). The splitting of tasks is nearly perfect in theory. Project management is responsible for product specifications, the definition of quality standards, and schedule. Development ensures that ideal algorithms are used and code is written according to the most appropriate patterns. Finally, the QA team stresses the behavior of the application, with the declared purpose of breaking it so that it can be updated and made stronger.

The three teams must work together at any point in the process, although some project management needs to be done before development begins and testing can't start until some code has been built. The whole point of software development is defining the engagement rules for the teams and defining how they should interact. A software development *methodology* attempts to do this.

Methodologies fall essentially into two main types: Waterfall and Agile. Waterfall-based projects tend to proceed sequentially across a number of phases, culminating with the release of the software. Agile-based projects tend to be circular and iterate through tasks several times until the application is ready or, sometimes, until the deadline is looming. Choosing the methodology, in a way, determines the type of architectural process.

Upfront architecture

Upfront architecture is when everything must be set in stone before you start. A lot of design work is done before starting to write code. Coding is mostly seen as the actual translation of well-defined ideas into the compiling of instructions.

The Waterfall model dates back to the 1970s. It is a model in which software development proceeds from one phase to the next in a purely sequential manner. Essentially, you move to step N+1 only when step N is 100 percent complete and all is perfect with it. Figure 1-3 shows a sample of the Waterfall model.

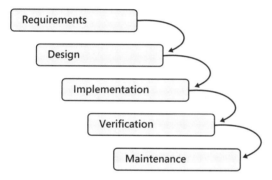

FIGURE 1-3 The Waterfall model

In the real world, some overlap between phases is acceptable, but the emphasis remains on making plans, creating budgets, and arranging the work schedule at one time. This approach is great for clients because it gives them a number of apparent certainties. The reality is different, however. It is not uncommon that projects end up running over the budget and the deadline and sometimes even fail to deliver on expected requirements. This poor result is largely because of the big design effort that is required up front, which just doesn't get along with the actual dynamics of modern software.

The root problem of software design is that requirements change quickly over time to the point that some requirements might be different by the time development ends. No clients are willing to pay for software that they know is not going to satisfy all requirements. At the same time, clients don't like at all to be subject to variable costs that might grow as changes and additions are applied to the artifact.

As a result, the Waterfall model is considered a thing of the past, and you can blame its demise on the whole idea that software development is a form of engineering.

Emerging architecture

Today's view of the architecture process is that any team should start developing as soon as possible to get early feedback and improve the software based on the real code. This means moving things fast, accepting and even embracing change, delivering some value early, and welcoming feedback.

Emerging architecture is a process that results from the incremental building of the software. After the initial startup, the project goes through a series of iterations that include design, coding, and testing. Every iteration produces a deliverable but incomplete version of the system. At each iteration, the team enters design changes and adds new functions until the full set of specifications are met. Figure 1-4 provides a graphical view of the iterative process.

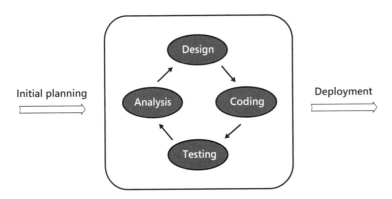

FIGURE 1-4 The iterative model

Iterative development forms the foundation of Agile methodologies. The term *Agile* was deliberately selected to symbolize a clear opposition to heavyweight methods such as the Waterfall model. The principles behind Agile methods are listed in the "Agile Manifesto," which was first published in 2001 and which you can find at *http://agilemanifesto.org*.

When an Agile project starts, only a few requirements might be fully defined, but you know for a fact that many more will show up or need to be clarified between this point and the end of the project. With an Agile mindset, this is not an issue. Development is articulated in iterations. At the start of an iteration, you negotiate with the customer the subset of the existing requirements that should be implemented. During the iteration, you focus on a single requirement at a time and implement it. At the end of the iteration, you deliver a working piece of software. It might be incomplete, but it works. Next you go with another iteration that focuses on another set of requirements. If something changed in the meantime or proved to be wrong, refactoring is in order. And the process continues until there's nothing more to add. The length of an iteration is measured in weeks—often, two weeks. In a word, an *agile process* is agile enough to react to changes. And changes in the business are the rule, not the exception.

Agile methodology is a blanket term. When you refer to an Agile methodology, you aren't talking very precisely. Which methodology do you mean, actually?

The most popular Agile methodology for software development is *Extreme Programming* (XP). In XP, phases are carried out in extremely short iterations that take two weeks to terminate. Coding and design proceed side by side. For more information on XP, visit *http://www.extremeprogramming.org*.

Scrum is another popular Agile methodology, but it is more aimed at managing projects rather than just developing code. Scrum is not prescriptive for any software development model, but it works very well with XP as a method for developing code. For more information on Scrum, have a look at *Agile Project Management with Scrum* by Ken Schwaber (Microsoft Press, 2004).

Important Agile architecture is sometimes presented as an oxymoron, like saying that if you're agile you don't do any architecture analysis, you just start coding, focus on functionality, and completely ignore modeling. Honestly, our take is that although Agile doesn't preclude any such behavior, this vision is mostly mythical. In our experience, Agile mostly means just the opposite and that architecture and modeling concerns are addressed throughout the entire development life cycle.

Emerging architecture with upfront analysis

It may be worth mentioning a third option that sits somewhere in the middle of Waterfall and Agile. It is a process that comprises a good deal of preliminary upfront analysis and then starts with a classic Agile methodology. Some call this a very disciplined Agile approach; some also refer it to as a *sprint zero* thing.

More generally, though, we find that all software development methodologies share a few common attributes: a number of phases to go through, a number of iterations to produce the software, and a typical duration for a single iteration. All phases execute sequentially, and there's always at least one iteration that ends with the delivery of the software. The difference between methodologies is all in the order in which phases are entered, the number of iterations required, and the duration of single iterations. After accepting this premise, the step to adopting Agile methods is much smaller than you might think at first.

Who's the architect, anyway?

As you've seen, architecture is mostly about hard-to-change decisions. And someone has to make these decisions.

The design of the architecture is based on the analysis of the requirements. Analysis determines what the system is expected to do; architecture determines how to do that. And someone has to examine the *whats* to determine the *hows*.

The architect is the professional tying together requirements and specifications. But what are the responsibilities of an architect? And what are the required skills?

An architect's responsibilities

According to the ISO/IEC 42010 standard, an architect is the person, team, or organization responsible for the system's architecture. The architect interacts with analysts and the project manager, evaluates and suggests options for the system, and coordinates a team of developers.

The architect participates in all phases of the development process, including the analysis of requirements and the architecture's design, implementation, testing, integration, and deployment.

Let's expand on the primary responsibilities of an architect: acknowledging the requirements, breaking the system down into smaller subsystems, identifying and evaluating technologies, and formulating specifications.

Acknowledging the requirements

In a software project, a few things happen before the architect gets involved. Swarms of analysts, IT managers, and executives meet, discuss, evaluate, and negotiate. Once the need for a new or updated system is assessed and the budget is found, analysts start eliciting requirements, which are typically based on their own knowledge of the business, company processes, the context, and feedback from end users.

When the list of requirements is ready, in many cases the project manager meets with the architect and delivers the bundle, saying more or less, "This is what we (think we) want; now you build it."

The architect acknowledges the requirements and makes an effort to have them adopted and fulfilled in the design.

> **Important** A moment ago, we mentioned yet another role: the *project manager*. The project manager is a role that may be defined differently in different companies. We think of it as the role responsible for deciding on the methodology, scheduling work, tracking, reporting, and serving as a valuable link between technical and business people. This role can be played by the same individual who plays the role of the architect. When this happens—and it is not unusual—requirements flow directly from the domain experts to the development team. If other people are in the middle, the risk we see is that domain knowledge gets contaminated, like that children's game where one child whispers a phrase into another child's ear. The second kid talks to a third kid and so on, until the sense of the original phrase is irreversibly lost. It is critical that requirements expressed in *Ubiquitous Language* flow from domain experts to the development team with no middlemen or just in a pass-through layer.

Breaking down the system

Based on the requirements, the architect expresses the overall system as a composition of smaller subsystems and components operating within processes. In doing so, the architect envisions logical layers, services, or both. Then, based on the context, the architect decides about the interface of layers, their relationships to other layers, and the level of service orientation the system requires.

Note At this stage, the architect evaluates various architectural patterns. *Layering* is a common choice and the one we are mostly pursuing in this book. Layering entails a vertical distribution of functionality. *Partitioning* is another approach where all parts are at the same logical level and scattered around some shared entities—such as an object model or a database. Service-Oriented Architecture (SOA) and Hexagonal Architecture (HA) are patterns that tend to have components (services in SOA, adapters in HA) operating and interacting at the same logical level. Micro-services is another recent architectural pattern centered on the idea of specialized and isolated components.

The overall design will be consistent with the enterprise goals and requirements. In particular, the overall design will be driven by requirements; it will not lead requirements.

The resulting architecture is ideally inspired by general guidelines, such as minimizing the coupling between components, providing the highest possible level of cohesion within components, and giving each component a clear set of responsibilities.

The resulting architecture is also driven by nonfunctional requirements, such as security, scalability, and technologies allowed or denied. All these aspects introduce further constraints and, to some extent, delimit the space where the architect can look for solutions.

Finally, the architect also strategizes about tasking individual developers, or teams of developers, with each of the components based on the layout of the system.

Important There are no absolute truths in software architecture. And no mathematical rules (or building codes like in structural engineering) to help in making choices. Company X might find architecture A successful at the same time company Y is moving away from it to embrace architecture B. The nice fact is that both might be totally right. The context is king, and so is gut feeling.

Identifying and evaluating technologies

After acknowledging requirements and designing the layers of the system, the next step for the architect entails mapping logical components onto concrete technologies and products.

The architect typically knows the costs and benefits of products and technologies that might be related to the content of the project. The architect proposes the use of any technologies and products that he reckons will be beneficial and cost effective for the project.

The architect doesn't choose the technology; based on his skills, the architect just makes proposals.

The architect might suggest using, say, Microsoft SQL Server 2014 because of its new clustered column store indexes or perhaps opting for Single-Page web application supported by an ASP.NET Web API back end. Similarly, the architect might raise the point of using a local NoSQL document store instead of some cloud-based table storage.

Who does make the final decision about which technologies and products are to be used?

Typically, it is the project manager or whomever manages the budget. The architect's suggestions might be accepted or rejected. If a suggestion is rejected, using or not using a given product or technology just becomes a new nonfunctional requirement to fulfill, and that might influence, even significantly, the architecture.

Formulating specifications

The architect is ultimately responsible for the development of the system and coordinates the work of a team of developers. Technical specifications are the means by which the architect communicates architectural decisions to the developers.

Specifications can be rendered in various forms: UML sketches, Microsoft Word documents, Microsoft Visio diagrams, or even working prototypes.

Communication is key for an architect. Communication happens between the architect and developers, and it also happens between architects and project managers and analysts, if not users. A great attribute for an architect to have is clarity of language.

The interaction between architects and developers will vary depending on the methodology chosen. And also the involvement of project managers, analysts, and users varies based, essentially, on the level of agility you accept.

The role of the architect

Architecture implies a role that is generically referred to as "the architect." According to ISO/IEC, there are not various types of architects. An architect is an architect. Period.

However, if you look around (and examine resumes), you see quite a few definitions of *architect*. In the end, it's an overused word, and it really means very different things depending on the context, the company, or even the country.

How many types of architects do you know?

In the United States, an *enterprise architect* (EA) has almost nothing to do with application development because the person in that role focuses for, say, 90 percent of the time on IT-related business strategy, orchestration, and infrastructure. In an extreme synthesis, EA is the figure that weds business and IT. A candidate for this role is expected to know very little about software architecture subjects and probably nothing about things like layered architecture or DDD.

In many companies, the role responsible for hard decisions, and in charge of proposing approaches and technologies, is not even labeled as an "architect" but gets the title of *lead developer* or something similar.

So you can find labels such as enterprise architect, infrastructure architect (IA), technology-specific architect (TSA), and even solution architect (SA). All these distinctions are kind of misleading because they attempt to break into parts what is ultimately an atomic, yet complex, role. In our opinion, it creates unnecessary categorization and lays the groundwork for confusing, *who-does-what* scenarios.

In this book, we go with the ISO/IEC definition of an architect, which is the "person, team, or organization responsible for the system's architecture." When mapping this concept to the widest possible range of companies, it turns out that what we call *architect* is a software (or solution) architect or even a lead developer.

Architect roles

You might have noticed it already, but if you go to Microsoft TechEd you see that the Architecture track has almost no sessions about real issues related to software development and architecture. For this reason, all the gazillion DDD sessions we submitted in years past have been regularly rejected. Among the Microsoft TechEd events staff, *architect* mostly means a role concerned with enterprise architecture. And all DDD sessions at Microsoft TechEd are under the Development track!

It is fine to have multiple architects on the same project team. Likewise, it is fine, if not desirable, that different architects have slightly different skills. However, as we intend it in this book, and regardless of the official titles, architects have significant exposure to code. They work out the design of the system but then work closely with developers to ensure proper implementation.

As we see things, an architect is, among other things, a better and more experienced developer. We don't believe there's value in having architects who just speak in UML and Visio and leave any implementation details to developers. At least, we've never found it easy to work with these people when we've crossed paths with them.

Common misconceptions about architects

Mostly as a result of the various meanings associated with term *architect*, a set of misconceptions has grown out of the mass of personalized definitions and interpretations. Let's go through a few of them and, we hope, clear up a few.

The architect is an analyst

This is a false statement. An architect is simply not an analyst.

At times, an architect might assist analysts during elicitations to help clarify obscure requirements or smooth out weird and fancy requirements added to the list just for "completeness." At times, an architect might participate in meetings with stakeholders. But that's it.

In general, an analyst is a person who is an expert on the domain. An architect is not (necessarily) such an expert. An analyst shares with an architect his own findings about how the system should work and what the system should do.

This common misconception probably originates from the incorrect meaning attributed to the word *analyst*. If the word simply indicates someone who does some analysis on a system, it is quite hard to deny the similarities between architects and analysts. Some 30 years ago, the term system *analyst* was used to indicate a professional capable of making design considerations for a system. But, at the time, software wasn't as relevant as it is today; it was merely a (small) part of an essentially hardware-based system.

Today, the roles of an analyst and an architect are commonly recognized as being different. And hardly ever does an architect play the role of an analyst.

> **Note** Given that roles are not always neatly separated, especially in small companies, it can happen that the same person serves as an analyst and architect. This simply means there's a person in the company who knows the business and processes well enough to come up with functional requirements and translate them into specifications for developers. The roles and responsibilities are still distinct, but the distinct skills for each are found in the same individual.

The architect is a project manager

Is this another false statement? It depends.

The architect is responsible for the system's architecture, and that person coordinates and guides the development of the system. The project manager represents stakeholders and manages the project by choosing, in the first place, a methodology. The project manager is then responsible for ensuring that the project adheres to the architecture while proceeding within the limits of the timeline and budget.

If we look at the role of the architect and the role of the project manager, we find that they are distinct. Period.

However, it is not unusual that one actor ends up playing two roles. Like in the theater, this hardly happens in large companies, but it happens quite frequently in small companies.

In summary, if you want to be a software architect when you grow up, you don't necessarily have to develop project-management skills. If you have skills for both roles, though, you can try to get double pay.

The architect never writes any code

This is definitely an ongoing debate: Should architects write code? There are essentially two schools of thought.

One school thinks that architects live on the upper floor, maybe in an attic. Architects then step down to the developers' floor just for the time it takes them to illustrate, using diagrams, what they have thought about the system. After this, they take the elevator up, collect their things, and go out to play golf. When on the course, they switch off their cell phones and focus on the game. When done, if they missed a call or two, they call back and explain to dummy developers what was so clear in the diagram that nobody on the developers' floor could understand. According to this school of thought, architects never, ever dirty their hands with even the simplest C# statement. C#? Oh no, the latest language they've been exposed to is probably Pascal while in college and Visual Basic at home.

Another school of thought thinks, instead, that every architect is a born developer. To take the metaphor one step further, we could say that the class *Architect* inherits from the class *Developer* and adds some new methods (skills) while overriding (specializing) a few others. Becoming an architect is the natural evolution in the career of some developers. The basic differences between an architect and a developer are experience and education. You get experience by time on the job; you get education from studying good books and taking the right classes. In addition, an architect has the ability to focus her vision of the system from a higher level than an average developer. Furthermore, an architect has good customer-handling skills.

An architect might not write much production code. But she writes a lot of code; she practices with code every day; she knows about programming languages, coding techniques, libraries, products, tools, CTPs, and she uses the latest version of Visual Studio. In certain areas of programming, an architect knows even more than many developers. An architect might be able to write tools and utilities to help developers be more productive. And, more often than you might think at first, the architect is just a member of the development team. For example, an architect writing production code is an absolutely normal occurrence in an Agile context. It is also a normal occurrence in small companies regardless of the methodology. At the same time, having an architect who writes production code might be absolutely weird to see in some large-company scenarios, especially if a traditional and non-Agile methodology is used.

What about the two of us? To which school do we belong?

Well, Andrea is more of an architect than Dino because he works on the fifth floor. Dino, on the other hand, is closer to development because he has quite a few highly technical ASP.NET books on his record and, more importantly, works on the second floor. We don't play golf, though. Dino plays tennis regularly, whereas Andrea likes squash better. We just have been denied access to the first school of thought.

Note In no other area of engineering is the distinction between those-who-design and those-who-build as poorly accepted as it is in software. The distinction exists mostly through postulation rather than flowing from a public recognition of skills.

The canonical comparison is with civil architecture. Bricklayers have unique skills that engineers lack. No bricklayer, though, will ever dream of questioning designs or calculations simply because they lack the skill to make the decisions themselves. They do their own work the best they can, taking full advantage of having the building work delegated to them.

In software, the situation is different because architects and developers have common roots. The more skilled a developer is, the more he feels encouraged to discuss design choices—and often with reason. The more the architect loses contact with everyday programming, the more he loses the respect of other developers. This generates a sort of vicious circle, which magically becomes better as you switch to an Agile methodology.

Summary

Architecture is a necessity and not a luxury for modern software. Assuming there was ever a time in which architecture was optional, that's no longer today. And the difference is all in the complexity required by modern software.

It is a common perception that software can be compared to civil engineering; however, when civil engineers set out to build, say, a bridge, a bridge gets built. In addition, the bridge almost always functions correctly and is built fairly close to the original budget. You can hardly say the same for many software projects. When it comes to software, it is sometimes very uncertain what stakeholders will eventually get out of their commitment. It is more certain, instead, that the original budget might be exceeded and that any deliverables are likely to be different, to some extent, from expectations.

Why is it so with software?

Overall, we believe that software development can hardly be subjected to fixed and rigid rules as with other disciplines, such as civil engineering. Software development is not pure engineering because it is contaminated by abundant doses of design, plain creativity, and even psychology. In addition, software has a very dynamic nature because it is relatively slow to build but needs to stay in sync with continuously changing business requirements. Software practices change so rapidly that, at any time, it's really hard to capture and store the current state of the art.

In this chapter, we focused on software architecture and the architect role in an attempt to capture the essence of both. In the next chapter, we move the focus toward what architects actually do when they try to apply architecture to a problem domain. In the next chapter, we discuss more of the mechanics of software projects and the scary thing that make projects fail—the big ball of mud.

Finishing with a smile

Here's a humorous twist on some of the topics discussed in this chapter:

- Adding manpower to a late software project makes it later. (*Fred Brooks, "The Mythical Man-Month", Addison-Wesley, 1995*)

- Nothing ever gets built on schedule or within budget. (*http://www.murphys-laws.com*)

- Failure is not an option; it's included with the software. (*http://www.murphys-laws.com*)

CHAPTER 2

Designing for success

How does a project get to be a year late? One day at a time.
—Fred Brooks

We define a *successful software project* as a project that derives a working solution from well-understood business needs. We define *successfully designed software* as software that, in the context of a successful project, is designed reusing existing code and infrastructure (wherever possible) and refined in light of available technologies and known best practices.

The availability of successfully designed software today is critical for any *type* and any *size* of business, but even more critical for any business today is avoiding poor-quality software. Bad software can cause organizations to lose money in various ways—whether it is a slow-responding page that drives traffic away from your website, a cumbersome user interface that turns into a bottleneck and generates queues in the service you provide, or even an unhandled exception that triggers an uncontrolled chain reaction and produces really unpredictable effects.

Software projects rarely live up to expectations. We guess that everybody who happens to hold this book in their hands knows the truth of that statement quite well. So what can impede success in designing software? If we have to go to the very foundation of what makes software projects not fully meet expectations, we would track it back to something called the "Big Ball of Mud" (BBM).

The BBM is a nice euphemism for "a software disaster."

In our definition, a *software disaster* is a system that grows badly and uncontrolled and, just because of that, is really hard to fix. Sometimes, poorly designed line-of-business systems get patched up enough to work and, in the end, become legacy code for others to deal with. In general, we think that teams should always aim at designing software for success even though the proverbial *piece of tape* can help make history. In fact, as reported by Space.com (at *http://bit.ly/1fJW6my*), cosmonaut Yuri Gagarin—the first man to enter space in 1961—was instructed to tear off a piece of tape and adjust some gear right before the launch.

> **Note** A great recent example of a BBM is probably *healthcare.gov*. It was built by a consortium of over 50 vendors under the theoretical control of the US federal government. In the end, and looking at it from the outside, it seems that none of the vendors building the various pieces were responsible and accountable for the overall quality. Integration tests were probably ignored for the most part, and no end-to-end scenarios—the body and soul of such a multivendor system—were tested in a timely manner. Finally, if concerns about the project were ever raised, they were blissfully ignored or withheld in the name of business or looming deadlines. But, in the end, by hook or by crook, the site works.

The "Big Ball of Mud"

The term *Big Ball of Mud* was created years ago to refer to a system that's largely unstructured, padded with hidden dependencies between parts, has a lot of data and code duplication, and doesn't clearly identify layers and concerns—namely, a spaghetti-code jungle. The term was coined by Brian Foote and Joseph Yoder, from the University of Illinois, and discussed in their paper, which is available at *http://www.laputan.org/pub/foote/mud.pdf*.

In this paper, the authors don't condemn the BBM as the worst-ever practice; they just recommend that architects and developers be ready to face the BBM risk and learn how to keep it under control. Put another way, the BBM threat is a constant in nearly any software projects that grow beyond some critical mass. Learning how to recognize and handle a BBM is then the only way to avoid software disasters.

Causes of the "Big Ball of Mud"

There are a few basic facts about the BBM that can invade a software project. First and foremost, the BBM doesn't get formed overnight and isn't that big in the beginning. Second, no single developer can create the BBM from scratch. The BBM is always a product of teamwork.

In an effort to get at the root of things, we identified a few main causes that can lead—often in cooperation—to developing the BBM.

Failing to capture all the client asked for

Architects and developers build software, especially enterprise software, for a clear purpose. The purpose of the software is expressed through high-level statements declaring the objectives the customer intends to achieve and the problems to be solved. There's a full branch of the software engineering science that deals with software requirements and classifies requirements in a variety of levels—business requirements, stakeholder requirements, functional requirements, testing requirements, and maybe more.

The point is how you go from a long list of roughly expressed requirements to concrete features to code in a programming language.

In Chapter 1, "Architects and architecture today," we listed the acknowledgement of requirements among the primary responsibilities of an architect. Requirements often come from various sources and refer to different views of the same system. It is therefore not surprising that some requirements contradict one another or that the relevance of some requirements looks quite different when coming out of interviews with different stakeholders. Analyzing the requirements and deciding which ones really map directly to a feature is only the first phase of the architect's job.

A second phase comes when the list of selected features is submitted for validation. The proposed list of features must address the entire list of requirements for all stakeholders. It is acceptable that some requirements for some stakeholders are just cut off.

Yes, it is acceptable as long as you're able to explain and justify why those requirements have been dropped.

To design a system that solves a problem, you must fully understand the problem and its domain. This might not happen right away, and it might not happen smoothly from a plain reading of requirements. Sometimes you have to say "No." More often, you have to ask why and then discuss the pros and cons of having a new feature to back a given set of requirements.

The lesson we all learned in years past is that a first run of code, which might be written according to a partial and incomplete understanding of needs, helps a lot more than spending days seeking the perfect solution up front. An Agile approach to development in this regard is based more on common sense than methodology.

Acknowledging requirements requires communication and communication skills. And sometimes communication just doesn't work. Sometimes both parties believe the wrong thing, and both parties ultimately try to save their proverbial rear end. So developers find it easy to complain that they didn't get enough details, and business people retort every point by saying that the details were there, written in the documents.

At the foundation of communication issues, there's the fact that business and developers use different vocabularies and use and expect different levels of precision in the description. In addition, nearly everybody—except developers—tends to believe that programming is far easier than it actually is. Adding a new requirement is for business or sales people just as easy as adding a new line to the document. In reality, some adaptation to the system is necessary and comes at an extra cost.

Because software adaptation that results from new or changed requirements does have a cost—and nobody wants to pay for it— some feature adaptation is performed by removing other features, or more likely, by cutting down refactoring, testing, debugging, and documentation. When this scenario happens, which is too often, the Big Ball of Mud is served.

Important In the previous chapter, we discussed how we usually deal with requirements. We want to briefly recall the points here. Essentially, we group raw requirements by categories and use International Organization for Standards/International Electrotechnical Commission (ISO/IEC) categories as a starting point. The actual process of grouping can be as simple as having a Microsoft Office Excel worksheet with one tab per category. We then go through the various tabs and add or remove requirements because it seems to make more sense. We also look carefully at the tabs that remained nearly empty and try to learn more about those aspects. In the end, the process makes us proactively seek more information and clearer information, generating it out of known data or getting it by asking for more details.

Sticking to RAD when the system grows

In the beginning, the project seems quite simple to arrange. The project—the customer says—is not supposed to grow and become a large and complex system. So you might opt for some forms of Rapid Application Development (RAD) and pay little attention to aspects of the design that could scale up well with the size of the application.

If it turns out that the system grows, the RAD approach shows its inherent limitations.

Although a RAD approach might be just right for small and simple data-centric applications (like CRUD applications), it turns out to be a dangerous approach for large applications containing a lot of ever-changing domain rules.

Imprecision of estimates

Business people always want to know exactly what they get before they commit and loosen the purse strings. Business people, however, reason in terms of high-level features and behavior. Once they have said they want the website available only to authenticated users, they believe they have said all there is to say on the topic. They don't feel the need to specify that users should also be able to log in via a long list of social networks. And should this point be raised later, they would swear that it was there, written in the documents.

Developers, instead, want to know exactly what they are supposed to build in order to make reasonable estimates. At this level, developers think in terms of nitty-gritty details and break up business features into smaller pieces. The problem is that estimates can't be precise until all requirements have been clearly defined and acknowledged. And an estimate is subject to change as requirements change.

Uncertainty reigns. Here's a common scenario:

- The business and development teams reach an initial agreement on features and schedule, and everybody is happy. The development team is expected to provide a prototype as the first step.

- The development team delivers the prototype and sets up a demo session.

- The demo session gives some more concrete insight about the system being built. The business people somehow extend their vision of the system and ask for some changes.

- The development team is happy to add more project items but needs extra time. Subsequently, building the system becomes more expensive.

- For the business people, however, it's always the same system, and there's no reason why it shouldn't cost the same. All they did was add a new level of precision!

When you make an estimate, it is extremely important to point out *where* the uncertainty lies.

Lack of timely testing

In a software project, testing happens at various levels:

- You have unit tests to determine whether individual components of the software meet functional requirements. Unit tests are also important to catch any regression in the functionality when code is refactored.

- You have integration tests to determine whether the software fits into the environment and infrastructure and whether two or more components work well together.

- You have acceptance tests to determine whether the completed system, in all of its parts, meets all customer requirements.

Unit tests and integration tests pertain to the development team and serve the purpose of making the team confident about the quality of the software. Test results tell the team if the team is doing well and is on the right track.

For both unit and integration tests, a critical aspect is when tests are written and performed.

As far as unit tests are concerned, there's a large consensus on that you should write tests along with the code and have test runs integrated with the build process. Running unit tests, however, is generally faster than running integration tests. Integration tests also might take much longer to set up and likely need to be reset before each run.

In a project where you bring components together from individual developers or teams, chances are that components won't fit together easily at first. For this reason, it is recommended that integration costs be diluted incrementally throughout the project so that issues show up as soon as possible. Pushing integration tests to the end is painfully risky because it cuts down the margin of time you have to fix things without introducing patches and hacks on top of other patches and hacks.

Unclear ownership of the project

As the *healthcare.gov* case proves, many vendors might be contracted to build the system and clear ownership of the project is a must.

The vendor or individual who owns the project is responsible for the overall quality and lists among her duties checking that every piece is of the best possible quality and fits with the rest of the system. This figure can easily push testing to be done in a timely manner so that integration issues are detected early. At the same time, this figure can mediate schedules and needs between the teams and stakeholders so that every vendor plays on the same team without damaging other players.

When project leadership is not clearly defined or, as in *healthcare.gov*, it is defined but not strictly exercised, taking the project home is left to the good will of individual vendors—except that each vendor has no reason to look beyond their contract. So especially under pressure, it is easy to focus on what just works regardless of the integration and design aspects.

When this happens, in only a few iterations, the spaghetti-code is ready to be served.

Ignoring a status of "crisis"

Technical difficulties are the norm rather than a novelty in a software project.

Whenever such difficulties arise, it makes no sense to stay vague and try to reassure the client. Hiding problems won't gain you any additional rewards if you close the project successfully. If the project fails, however, having hidden problems will certainly cause you a lot of extra troubles.

As an architect, you should aim at being as open and transparent as open-sourced software.

If you recognize a sort of a crisis, let others know about it and tell them what you're doing and plan to do. Providing a detailed calendar of fixes is the hardest part of the job. However, stakeholders just need to be informed about what's going on and feel confident that the teams are moving in the right direction. Sometimes, a detailed calendar of updates and numbers about the work being done is more than enough to avoid pressure increasing on you beyond any bearable threshold.

How is recognizing a status of "crisis" related to the Big Ball of Mud and successful projects?

Again, it is a matter of common sense. Being open and transparent about difficulties sounds an alarm, and there's a chance that bad things can be stopped earlier than when it's too late.

Symptoms of the "Big Ball of Mud"

It should be clear that as an architect, project manager, or both you should maximize your efforts to avoid a BBM. But are there clear and unambiguous symptoms that indicate you're on the trajectory of a rolling ball of mud?

Let's identify a few general signs that make the alarm bells ring if the design is headed down the slippery slope.

Rigid, therefore fragile

Can you bend a piece of wood? And what would you risk if you insist on doing it?

A piece of wood is typically a stiff and rigid matter characterized by some resistance to deformation. When enough force is applied, the deformation becomes permanent and the wood breaks up.

What about rigid software?

Rigid software is characterized by some resistance to changes. Resistance is measured in terms of regression. You make a change in one class, but the effects of your change cascade down the list of dependent classes. As a result, it's really hard to predict how long a change—any change, even the simplest—will actually take.

If you pummel a glass, or any other fragile material, you break it down into several pieces. Likewise, when you enter a change in software and break it in various places, that software is definitely fragile.

Like in real life, fragility and rigidity also go hand in hand in software. When a change in a software class breaks (many) other classes because of (hidden) dependencies, you have a clear symptom of a bad design that you need to remedy as soon as possible.

Easier to use than to reuse

Imagine you have a piece of software that works in one project and you would like to reuse it in another project. However, copying the class or linking the assembly in the new project just doesn't work.

Why is that so?

When you move the same code to another project and it doesn't work, it's usually because of dependencies or because it was not designed for being shared. Of the two, dependencies are the biggest issue.

The real problem isn't just dependencies, but the number and depth of dependencies. The risk is that to reuse a piece of functionality in another project, you have to import a much larger set of functions. At the end of the day, no reuse is ever attempted and code is rewritten from scratch.

This is not a good sign for your design, either. This negative aspect of a design is often referred to as *immobility*.

Easier to work around than to fix

When applying a change to a software class, you often figure out two or more ways to do it. Most of the time, one way of doing things is nifty, elegant, and coherent with the design, but terribly hard and laborious to implement. The other way, conversely, is much smoother and quicker to code, but it is a sort of a hack.

What should you do?

Actually, you can solve it both ways, depending on the given deadlines and your manager's direction about it.

In general, a situation is less than ideal when a workaround seems much easier and faster to apply than the right solution. Sometimes, in fact, there's more to it than plain extra labor. Sometimes, well, you're just scared to opt for more than a basic workaround. Regression, that's what really scares you. If you have good and abundant unit tests, at least you can be sure that regression, if any occurs, will be quickly caught. But then you start thinking that, well, unit tests don't fix code and maybe the workaround is the fastest way to give it another go!

And a feature that's easier to hack than a fix doesn't sound like a great statement about your overall design either. It simply means that too many unneeded dependencies exist between classes and that your classes do not form a particularly cohesive mass of code. So this is enough to scare you away from applying the right solution, which is likely more obtrusive than a quick fix and requires a deeper level of refactoring.

This negative aspect of a design is often referred to as *viscosity*.

Using metrics to detect a BBM

In literature, another common name used to refer to building a software-intensive system on top of poor code is *technical debt* (TDBT).

Created by Ward Cunningham, the metaphor of debt is particularly appropriate because poor code, much like financial debt, can grow over time and accumulates interest to be paid back. In the long run, TDBT becomes a heavy weight to carry and affects, and sometimes prevents, further due actions. Paraphrasing a popular quote from Sir Winston Churchill, one could say, "TDBT, for a development team, is like a man standing in a bucket and trying to lift it up by the handle."

TDBT is an abstract idea and claiming to have tools to measure or even remove it is like claiming you can do magic. However, metrics descend from careful observation of the facts and a bit of analysis. Results are not necessarily pure gold, but at a minimum they help increase awareness.

Let's look into some metrics and tools to help you determine whether a BBM is trying to bite you.

Static code analysis

In general, people on a team know where most problems lie, but sometimes you need to provide evidence of code-related problems instead of just listing them orally. Static code-analysis tools scan and probe the code for you and produce a useful report to bring to the table for discussion.

Microsoft Visual Studio 2013 has its own static-code analyzer that can calculate things such as code coverage and cyclomatic complexity. Other similar frameworks are embedded in the CodeRush and ReSharper products (discussed later in the chapter), or they are available as separate products from the same vendors.

An interesting static-analysis tool is NDepend (*http://ndepend.com*), which also has the capability to create a dependency graph for you to visually spot and easily show the quantity and location of the most troublesome areas.

Important In spite of possible appearances, static code-analysis tools will tell you neither what originated technical debt nor what is necessary to do in order to reduce it. They're all about providing input for making a decision; they're not about making the decision for you.

Knowledge silos

Another interesting set of manual metrics you can use to identify a flavor of TDBT is the number of bottlenecked skills you have on the team. If there's only one member on the team who holds certain skills, or owns a given subsystem or module, that's going to be a big pain if the individual leaves the company or suddenly becomes unavailable.

The term *knowledge silo* or *information silo* is commonly used to refer to a situation where ownership of the code is on an individual's shoulders. It might not be a problem for the individual, but it's definitely a problem for the team.

Terminology We just used a couple of terms whose meaning can be different depending on the team. The terms are *module* and *subsystem*. In this context, we're not giving these terms any special meaning other than being a way to refer to blocks of code. A subsystem generically refers to a subset of the entire system; a module is a part of the subsystem.

Mechanics of software projects

If you ask the question "What makes projects fail?", probably the most common answer you receive will trace failures back to business-related issues such as missing requirements, inadequate project management, incorrect cost estimates, lack of communication, and even incompatibility between people on the various teams. You hardly see the perception that bad code might hurt.

Given all this, we think that an undetected BBM can seriously damage a software project, but an unfought BBM can really kill it.

In the end, it's individuals, and the actual interaction between individuals, that really determines the success or failure of a software project. However, the structure of the organization and the overall culture within it also has an impact on the final result.

Organizational culture

Apple's organization, at least during the Steve Jobs era, looked inspired by the one-man-show idea. One man pushes ideas and strategy, and all the teams work to support and implement the strategy. As long as the idea is a great one and the strategy is appropriate, success comes.

The Microsoft model that Steve Ballmer announced the company was revisiting in the summer of 2013 (which you can read a critical review of at *http://www.mondaynote.com/2013/07/14/ microsoft-reorg-the-missing-answer*) is based on divisions that often compete with one another and hardly talk to each other.

You may remember what happened around 2008 when two groups within Microsoft produced two nearly equivalent frameworks—Linq-to-SQL and Entity Framework. To the outside world, it was hard to make sense which combination of events led to that situation.

Note In the biography of Steve Jobs written by Walter Isaacson, you can read a very interesting opinion about companies organized in divisions. Steve Jobs shares his perspective of why Apple, and not say Sony, was actually successful with the iPod idea. To turn the idea into reality, Apple had to first build hardware and software and then negotiate rights on music. A company like Sony had at least the same experience as Apple with hardware and software and, additionally, already had in-house access to rights for music and movies. Why didn't Sony build the iPod business then?

According to Jobs, it was the culture at Sony deriving from having divisions within the company that each had their own profit/loss account. Probably, the division making profits from the music rights saw the division making money from the MP3 players as a threat. The two divisions might have fought each other instead of working together for the success of the company. The book is *Steve Jobs* by Walter Isaacson (Simon & Schuster, 2011).

Teams and players

There's an old joke about an Italian team and a German team participating in an eight-man rowing race. Composed of one leader and all rowers, the German team wins the race hands down. The Italian team investigates the reasons for the failure and finds out that the team was composed of all leaders and one young rower.

A team is all about having people with complementary skills making a coordinated effort.

Note The joke about rowing teams then continues by discussing how the Italian team made plans for the return race, but that's probably a bit beyond the scope here. Anyway, if you're curious we'll tell you that the Italian team fired the rower and managed to maintain four leaders, two supervisors of leaders, one commander-in-chief, and one new, older (because he was more experienced) rower.

In a software project, both managers and developers pursue their objectives. Managers tend to do that in a more aggressive way than most developers do. Developers report to managers, and this sometimes makes developers more inclined to just take on any tasks and deadlines. It should not be underestimated here that the nature of most developers is that of being a hero. Developers wish to be considered superheroes who come down to earth and save the world.

As an example, suppose a manager plans to show a potential customer a demo on Monday morning. He wants to make sure he has an impressive demo to show. So the manager approaches the development team and asks for the demo to be ready on Monday. That likely breaks the ongoing sprint or, in general, alters the scheduled activity. What's the best way to handle such an inherent conflict of interest on a team or in a company? Here are a few possible scenarios:

- The development team can try to accommodate the new deadline so that the manager can pursue his own legitimate objectives.

- The development team doesn't accept the new deadline and holds on to the current schedule, thus making it problematic for the manager to keep the customer happy.

- The development team and manager work together to find a reasonable goal that fits in both schedules and doesn't prevent anyone from pursuing their respective objectives.

In our experience, the first scenario is the most common and the last one is the most desirable. With regard to developers trying to accommodate any modified schedule, we find particularly valuable again the opinion of Uncle Bob. By promising to *try to accommodate* the new deadline, the development team is making an implicit admission of having held back for a while. It's like saying, "Yes, we could do more, but for some reason we haven't been; now it's about time we squeeze out every bit of energy." But if the team has not been holding back on effort, trying to accommodate a tighter deadline will force members to work extra hours, sacrificing their own personal time. This is not fair to developers, who deserve their own life, and it is not fair to management, who just heard a lie.

How many times have we tried ourselves to accommodate tighter schedules? If we did it, we likely did it to avoid a potentially rude confrontation. The only good rule to be a great team player is being a great communicator who's always honest and never lies.

The keyword here is *negotiation*, with the aim being to share a reasonable goal and find a reasonable compromise between respective needs and schedules. With reference to the previous example, a good compromise could be to fork out some work and create an ad hoc build that is padded with fake code and just works for a demo. This doesn't remove much effort from the main branch, doesn't introduce a significant delay in the ongoing sprint, and doesn't require team members to work extra hours or cut features.

Scrum firefighters

Especially in an Agile environment, every unforeseen event is potentially a crisis and needs to be addressed properly and instantly.

In Scrum, a common way of doing that is giving one or more members of the team the title of *firefighters*.

The Scrum firefighter is responsible for doing any extra work that diverges from the iteration but is still necessary to preserve the efforts of the rest of the team. Just as it is OK for real-world firefighters to be idle sometimes, it is OK for the Scrum firefighters to be idle, or just minimally active on the project, during the iteration.

Because it could be highly annoying to be a Scrum firefighter, it should be a role that all members of the team rotate into and out of. In our experience, 20 percent of the development workforce should be the maximum you concede to firefighting. From this, you might think you're facing a 20 percent cut in productivity; instead, you're actually getting possibly higher throughput.

Leader vs. boss

We all know that costs are the sore point of software projects. Costs are a function of the hours required to code all the requested features, including testing, debugging, documentation, and a number of other side activities. The development team leader takes care of this, usually reporting to a project manager.

Sometimes there's a mutual lack of trust between these two figures: the manager thinks the development team is holding back effort, and the development team thinks the manager just wants to produce more with less.

Needless to say, leadership is a critical skill.

It is not infrequent to see managers who halve the estimates and then complain that the project is late. And then they go to their bosses, blame the development team, and ask for more resources. In this way, they experience the effects of the Brooks' law, which says that "Adding manpower to a late software project makes it later."

There's a profound difference between leaders and bosses.

First and foremost, the boss expects the team to serve them instead of serving the team. Bosses sit on top of the business hierarchy and command others to perform tasks that they are not willing to do or are unable to do. A leader, conversely, focuses on the business and leads development from the trenches. A good way to summarize the difference is by saying that a boss creates followers whereas a leader creates other leaders.

The difference between leaders and bosses is well summarized by a popular picture you might have seen a million times around your Facebook pages; you can find it at *http://www.lolwall.co/lol/264722*.

Helping the team write better code

We've found out that too many developers seem to have the perception that bad code, in the end, doesn't hurt that much.

If you count the number of projects that reportedly failed because of code-related issues, well, we agree that the number is not going to be huge. However, you don't have to create a true disaster to lose a lot of money on a software project.

As an architect, what can you do to help the team write better code?

Bad code is really more expensive than good code

We're not sure about you, but we definitely think that writing bad code is really more expensive than writing good code. At least, we think it is more expensive in the context of a project with a significant lifespan and business impact.

As simple as it may sound, a project dies of bad code when the cost of working with that code—that is, creating, testing and maintaining it—exceeds the cost that the business model can bear. By the same token, no projects would fail for code-related issues if companies managed to keep the cost of code extremely low.

This is the sore point.

How would you define the items that contribute to the final bill for the code? Which actions comprise "writing the code": coding, building, debugging? Should you consider testing as an extra, on-demand feature? What about documentation? And bug fixing?

Sometimes managers just short-circuit the problem and boil it down to cutting development costs by hiring cheap developers or deciding to cut off tests and documentation.

Unfortunately, these managers don't realize they are only lowering the cost of producing code that possibly, but not necessarily, just works. Producing *code that just works* is only one aspect of the problem. In modern times, requirements change frequently, complexity grows and, worse yet, complexity is often fully understood only as you go. In this scenario, producing code is only one item in the total bill of costs. Code maintenance and evolution is the biggest item.

As the good architect knows very well, one can address code maintainability only through well-written code, a good understanding of software principles and language features, well-applied patterns and practices, and testability. This makes coding more expensive than producing *code that just works*, but it is far cheaper than maintaining and evolving *code that just works*.

Using tools to assist coding

We think that a successful project is based on two factors: management that knows about leadership, and development that knows about code quality.

As far as coding is concerned, there doesn't have to be a time for developers to write just code and then a later time to fix it and clean it up. As every developer can swear to, this second pass never happens and even when it happens, it'll never be as deep and profound as it should be.

A significant aid to writing better code the first time comes from code-assistant tools. Typically integrated into the IDE, these tools simplify common development tasks, making developers proceed faster and with a great chance to write much better code. At worst, code is written faster, possibly leaving some time for a second pass.

Services like auto-completion, tips on idiomatic design (that is, writing code in accordance with the language or framework-suggested idiom), code inspections, predefined snippets associated with keystrokes, and having predefined and customizable templates available are all practices that speed up development and ensure consistency and possibly better and cleaner code.

Code-assistant tools make development a sustainable effort and vastly improve the quality of the code you write with a couple of extra clicks. A code-assistant tool can catch duplicated and unused code, make refactoring a pleasant experience, simplify navigation and inspection, and force patterns.

For example, all developers agree in principle that a well-chosen naming convention is key to the readability and quality of code. (See Chapter 4, "Writing software of quality.") However, when you realize that you should change a namespace or a method name, you have the problem of doing that at least throughout the entire codebase you own. It's crazy work that code-assistant tools can conduct for you in a fraction of the time it would take for you to do it yourself.

ReSharper is the most popular code-assistant tool available. For more information, visit *http://www.jetbrains.com/resharper*. Other analogous tools are CodeRush from DevExpress (*http://www.devexpress.com/Products/CodeRush*), and JustCode from Telerik (*http://www.telerik.com/products/justcode.aspx*).

Be sure to keep in mind, however, that code-assistant tools are not magic and all they do is give you a chance to write better and cleaner code at a lower cost and with less effort. Beyond this point, everything else is still up to you. You guide tools in the refactoring process as well as during code editing.

How to tell people their code is bad

Suppose you noticed that some people on the team are writing bad code. How would you tell them about it?

There are psychological aspects involved here. You don't want to be sharp, and you don't want to hurt anybody; at the same time, you don't like it that other people's work can turn on you at some point. Communication is key, isn't it? So you have to find the best way to tell people when their code is bad.

Overall, we believe that the best way to focus attention on some code is by subtly asking why it was written the way it is. You might find out more about the motivation, whether it was misinformation, a bad attitude, limited skills or perhaps constraints you just didn't know about.

Be sure you never judge your coding alternative to be better without first having clear evidence. So you can simply look curious and interested about the real motivation for the offending code and express a willingness to know more because you would have coded it differently.

Make everyone a better developer

We like to summarize the golden rule of having teams write good code:

Address the code, not the coder. But try to improve the code through the coder.

You can have any piece of bad code fixed in some way. When this happens, however, you don't want to blame the coder; you do want, instead, to help the coder to improve his way of doing things. If you're able to do this, you get benefits in at least two areas. You get a better developer on the team, and you possibly have a happier and more motivated developer on the team. You made the developer feel as close to the hero status as possible because he now has the perception of having done his job in the best possible way.

To improve in some areas, everybody needs both training and practice. The most effective way to do this, though, is combining training and practice in an Agile manner. Too often, instead, we see companies that buy training packages, have them squeezed and delivered in a handful of days, and then expect people to be up and running the next Monday. It doesn't work this way—not that effectively, at least.

Let's revive an expression that was quite popular a few years ago: *training on the job*. It refers to doing some actual work while learning. It results from the collaboration of people on the same team with different skills.

Inspect before you check-in code

You can have the best coding standards ever in your company, but how do you enforce them? Trusting developers is nice, but verifying is probably more effective. Peer programming and regular design reviews are concrete ways to check the health of the codebase. In a typical design review, you can take some sample code and discuss it openly and collectively. The code can be a real snippet from the project—that some of the participants actually wrote—or, to avoid emotional involvement, it could even be an aptly written piece of code that illustrates the points you want to make.

To enforce coding standards, you can also consider applying check-in policies to your source control system, whether it is Microsoft Team Foundation Server (TFS), TeamCity, or other system. Can the process be automated in some way?

Today nearly any source-code management tool offers ways to exercise control over the files being checked in. For example, TFS has gated check-ins. A gated check-in is essentially a check-in subject to rules. Files, in other words, will be accepted into the system only if they comply with established rules. When you choose to create a gated check-in, TFS invites you to indicate an existing build script to use. Only if the build completes successfully will the files be checked in.

In TFS, a *build* is just an MSBuild script, and it can be customized with a variety of tasks. TFS comes with a number of predefined tasks that can be integrated. For example, you find code-analysis (formerly FxCop) tasks and a task for running selected test lists. Because an MSBuild task is nothing more than a registered component that implements a contracted interface, you can create new tasks yourself to add your own validation rules.

Note that JetBrains' ReSharper—one of the aforementioned code-assistant tools—features a set of free command-line tools in its latest edition that can be used in a custom MSBuild task to detect duplicated code and apply typical inspections, including custom inspections against custom templates you might have defined. Interestingly, you don't even need a ReSharper license to use the command-line tools. For more information on ReSharper command-line tools, have a look at *http://www.jetbrains.com/resharper/features/command-line.html*.

Happy is the project that doesn't need heroes

Developers tend to have a super ego and, at least in their most secret dreams, wish they could work 80-plus hours a week to save the project, keep customers happy, and be true heroes in the eyes of management and fellow developers.

We like to paraphrase a popular quote from the poet and dramatist Berthold Brecht and say that we'd love to always be in a situation that doesn't need heroism. The need for heroes and the subsequent high pressure comes mostly from inadequate deadlines.

Sometimes deadlines are unfair from the beginning of a project. In other cases, deadlines prove to be wrong along the way.

When this happens, it's emotionally easier to just acquiesce, but being afraid to point out unfair deadlines brings about the need for heroes. Communicating and making troubles clear is a matter of transparency and also an effective way to regain a bit more of control and reduce pressure.

In software, we'd say you experience pressure because of looming deadlines or lack of skills. Both situations can be addressed properly if communicated in a timely way.

We don't want heroes, and although we've been heroes ourselves quite a few times (as most of you, we guess, have been), we think we have learned that heroism is an exceptional situation. And in software, exceptions are mostly something to avoid.

Encourage practice

Why on earth do professional athletes in nearly any sport practice every day for hours? Is there really some analogy between developers and professional players? It depends.

One way to look at it is that developers practice every day at work and don't compete with other developers. Based on this, one can conclude that there's no analogy and, subsequently, no point in practicing.

Another way to look at it is that players exercise basic movements very frequently so that they can repeat them automatically. Going regularly back to the foundation of object-orientation, design patterns, coding strategies, and certain areas of the API helps to keep knowledge in the primary cache and more quickly accessible.

> **Note** After having written ASP.NET books for years and practiced with authentication and membership systems for as many years, Dino lately has felt like he's in serious trouble when having to work on a role-based ASP.NET system. "Man," he recently said to me, "when was the last time that I dealt with roles?" In the end, it took a lot more than expected to create a role-based UI infrastructure and related membership system.

Continuous change is part of the deal

Continuous change is an effective way to describe the dynamics of modern software projects. A software project begins by following an idea or a rather vague business idea. Architects and domain experts face the problem of nailing down some formal requirements to make the original idea or business needs a bit more tangible.

In our experience, most software projects are like moving targets and requirements are what move the target around. Every time a new requirement is added, the context changes and the dynamics of the system—designed and working well without that feature—changes as well. Requirements change because a better understanding of the problem domain is developed, because it is a fast-paced problem domain, or just because of timeline pressure.

Requirements churn is a common term to indicate the rate at which requirements—functional nonfunctional, or both—change in the context of a software project. A high requirements churn contributes to creating an ideal habitat for the BBM.

Reconsidering the entire system architecture whenever a new requirement is processed is the only way to be serious about preventing the BBM. Reconsidering the entire system architecture does require refactoring, and it does have a significant cost. The whole point here is finding ways to keep costs low. Refactoring is one of those things that is hardly perceived as bringing value to the project. It's too bad that failing to refactor takes value away.

Note Twitter went live in 2010 with a web front end full of client-side capabilities. A lot of functions were provided by generating HTML on the fly on top of dynamically downloaded JSON data. In 2012, Twitter refactored the entire system and chose server-side rendering. It was an architectural refactoring, and it was, of course, expensive. But they figured it was necessary, and they kept on serving a few hundred millions users, so right or wrong it just worked.

As an architect, both architectural and design refactoring are key tools. Architects have no control over history and the evolution of the business scenario and the real world. And architects are required to constantly adjust things and never rebuild. This is where refactoring fits in.

Getting out of the mess

Even with all the best intentions, and regardless of the team's efforts, the design of a system at some point might head down the slippery slope. Forming the BBM is generally a slow process that deteriorates the design over a relatively long period. It works by studding your classes with hacks and workarounds up until a large share of the code gets hard to maintain and evolve.

At this point, you're in serious trouble.

Managers face the choice of making a bargain with the devil and calling for more hacks and workarounds or a performing a deep redesign based on reviewed requirements and new architectural choices.

What's the difference between doing a complete system redesign and starting development entirely from scratch? In terms of a call to action, the difference is minimal, if any. The psychological side of the choice, though, is different. By calling for a redesign, management pushes the message that the team is catching up and fixing things quickly. By calling for a rewrite, management admits failure. And very rarely in software projects is failure is an option.

The moment at which management calls for a significant restructuring of the existing codebase certifies that the team completed a software disaster. The existing codebase then becomes a nasty form of *legacy code*.

That odd thing called "legacy code"

In software, you often inherit existing code that you must maintain, support, or just keep *as is* and integrate with the new stuff. This code, too, is commonly referred to as *legacy code*. However, the main challenge for architects and developers is not surviving existing legacy code, but not creating any more.

Legacy code is just what the name literally says it is. It is code; and it is legacy. According to the Oxford Dictionary, the word *legacy* means something left or handed down by a predecessor. Furthermore, the dictionary adds a software-specific definition for the word that goes along the lines of something superseded but difficult to replace because of its wide use.

Our general definition of legacy code is any code you have around but don't want to have around. Legacy code is inherited because it works. There's no difference at all between well-designed and well-written code that works and poorly designed and poorly written code that works. The troubles begin when you have to put your hands on legacy code to maintain and evolve it in some way.

The idea of legacy code is somehow related to the idea of software disasters. However, having legacy code on a project is not a disaster per se. It just starts turning bad when the legacy code you have on the project is yours. How do you turn legacy code—whether it is yours or inherited—into more manageable code that doesn't prevent the project as a whole from evolving and expanding as expected?

Note Michael Feathers wrote a paper a decade ago that neatly wraps up the point of legacy code and strategies around it. The paper is available at *http://www.objectmentor. com/resources/articles/WorkingEffectivelyWithLegacyCode.pdf*. What makes this paper particularly interesting is the relationship the author identifies between legacy code and tests. Legacy code, in other words, is just code without tests.

Note Too many developers have to work with legacy codebases where fundamental principles of software design and testing practices are just nonexistent, turning the code into a software disaster. As we move ahead and outline a general strategy to deal with bad code, we also want to point you in advance to a resource that illustrates how to improve the code through a combination of well-known refactoring techniques and code-analysis tools: *http://blog.jetbrains.com/blog/2013/05/14/recording-refactoring-legacy-code-bases-with-resharper.*

Checkmate in three moves

All in all, recovering from a software disaster is analogous to recovering from an injury. Imagine for a moment that while on vacation you decided to go out running for quite a long time and received some physical damage, such as a strong Achilles strain.

For a very active person, well, that's just a disaster.

You see a doctor and the doctor goes through the steps of a simple but effective procedure. First, the doctor orders you to stop any physical activity, including in some cases walking. Second, the doctor applies some rigid bandage around the injured ankle and maybe around the whole leg. Third, the doctor suggests you try walking again as you feel better and stop again if you don't feel comfortable doing that. That's the way it works, and a lot of people go through that process successfully.

The same procedure can be applied to software injuries, and it mostly works. More precisely, the strategy is reasonably effective but the actual effects depend on the seriousness of the injury.

Stop new development

A strict prerequisite of any strategy aimed at turning badly written code into something much more manageable is stop development on the system. In fact, adding new code can only make a poorly designed system even worse. Stopping development, however, doesn't mean that you stop working on the system. It simply means don't add any new feature until you have restructured the current system to a more maintainable codebase that can receive new features without compromising the existing features.

The redesign of an evolving system is like catching a runaway chicken. You need to be in a very good shape to make it. But is the team who failed on it once really in shape at that point?

Isolate sore blocks

Just as the doctor applies a rigid bandage around sore ankles, the architect should apply layers around badly written blocks of code. However, what does *block of code* mean here specifically? It is probably easier to state what a "block of code" is not.

A block of code is not a class, but it is something that likely spans multiple classes, if not multiple modules. A block of code actually identifies a behavior of the system—a function being performed—and includes all the software components involved in that. It is key to identify macro functions and define an invariant interface for each of them. You define a layer that implements the interface and becomes a façade for the behavior. Finally, you modify the code so that each and every path that leads to triggering that behavior passes through the façade.

As an example, have a look at Figure 2-1. The figure represents a small section of a messy codebase where two critical components, C1 and C2, have too many dependencies on other components.

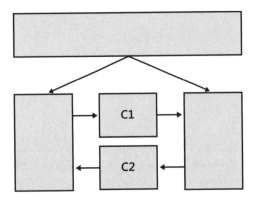

FIGURE 2-1 Representing a section of a messy codebase.

The purpose is turning the layout of Figure 2-1 into something with more separated blocks. You need to understand that you can't claim you'll get the right design the first time. Isolating sore points is just the first step, and you should not be too concerned about the size of the layers you introduce. Turning back to the doctor's analogy, sometimes the doctor applies a bandage to the entire leg even though the problem is mostly around the ankle. After a few days of rest, though, the doctor may decide to reduce the bandage to just the area around the ankle.

Likewise, isolating sore software blocks is an iterative work. Figure 2-2 shows a possible way to isolate the sore blocks of Figure 2-1.

Looking at Figure 2-2 you might guess that C1 and C2 have been duplicated; however, this is just an intermediate step, but it is necessary in order to obtain two neatly separated subsystems invoked by a given caller. Separated subsystems should be like black boxes now.

Note also that block of code might even span layers and sometimes tiers. Like the doctor's bandage, reducing the area covered by isolated blocks is the ultimate purpose of the effort.

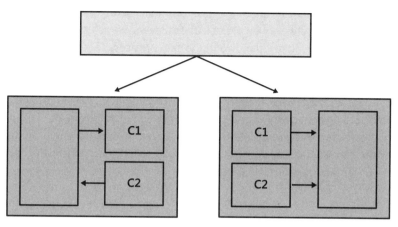

FIGURE 2-2 An intermediate step in the design where the client calls into isolated blocks through a new contracted interface.

 Terminology We're going to cover Domain-Driven Design (DDD) extensively in this book; in particular, starting with Chapter 5, "Discovering the domain architecture." So we rate as highly important relating the concept of isolated blocks as described here with the concept of a DDD *bounded context*. In a DDD project, a *bounded context* can also be a black box of legacy code. In DDD, a bounded context has a unique related model and can be composed of several modules. Subsequently, several modules can share the same model.

Test coverings

Once you refactor the system into a bunch of neatly separated blocks, you should still have a system that works—only it is a little bit better in terms of design. You don't want to stop here, however. So it is highly recommended that at this point you introduce tests that can tell you whether after further refactoring the system still works.

In this context, tests are mostly integration tests—namely, tests that possibly span multiple modules, layers, and tiers. They are tests that can be hard to set up—for example, databases to fill with ad hoc data for simulation, services to connect—and long to run. Yet, they are absolutely necessary to have and run. In his aforementioned paper, Feathers uses the term *test covering* to indicate tests aimed at defining behavior invariants to make further changes against.

 Note Tests play a key role in any refactoring experience. You surely need to end the process with tests that can measure any regression after any future refactoring. However, in some situations you might find it helpful to have tests ready before you even start isolating sore blocks.

Terminology The term *layer* usually refers to a logical boundary. Conversely, a *tier* is a physical boundary. More concretely, when we talk about layers, we refer to blocks of code (that is, classes or even assemblies) that live in the same process space but are logically separated. A tier implies a physical distance and different processing spaces. A tier is usually also a deployment target. Whether some code goes to a layer or tier is a matter of choice and design. Boundaries are what really matters. Once you have clear boundaries, you can choose which is a layer and which one goes to a tier. For example, in an ASP.NET project, you can have some application logic deployed in-process within the same application pool as the core ASP.NET and pages or deployed to a distinct tier hosted, say, on another Internet Information Services (IIS) machine.

Continuous refactoring

After the first iteration of test coverings, you should have stabilized the system and gained some degree of control over its behavior. You might even be able to apply some input values to tests and check the behavior. Next, you enter in a refactoring loop where you try to simplify the structure of the black boxes you created. In doing so, you might be able to take some code out of black boxes and reuse it through new interfaces. Have a look at Figure 2-3.

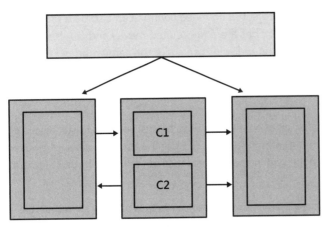

FIGURE 2-3 Another black box added to break the system down into more manageable pieces.

As you can see, now C1 and C2 have been moved out of subsystems and encapsulated in a new black box that is testable itself. By repeating this procedure, you might be able to progressively reduce the size of black boxes. A nice effect is that now existing integration tests may be rewritten to be a lot closer to unit tests.

Deciding whether or not to add manpower

A popular quote from Frederick P. Brooks and his popular book *The Mythical Man Month* (Addison-Wesley, 1995) says that adding manpower to a late project just makes it later. And for sure—this is our addition—doing so has no chance to significantly affect the schedule. Yet, when a project is late, the first thing that springs to mind is just adding to the workforce. However, in the presence of sequential constraints on project activities (for example, debugging taking place after development), adding to the workforce doesn't bring any benefit. According to Brooks, the bearing of a child takes nine months, and nine women will never deliver a baby in one month.

So the question is: what should you do when a project is late? Should you never consider adding manpower? It depends on the results of an honest analysis of the reasons why the project is late.

Need for more time

A project might be late just for the obvious reason that each feature needs more time than estimated in order to be completed. If tasks are sequential in nature, more people on the team is just more management work and probably a less-than-optimal use of the assigned resources.

This reality moves the focus to estimates. Software people are not known to be able to estimate effort carefully. Software people live with the underlying certainty that all will go well in the end and that everything can be fixed by simply working longer hours. This attitude also makes monitoring progress hard. The quote at the top of the chapter says it all—a project gets late one day at a time. If progress is tracked in a timely way, falling behind schedule can be fixed without long hours or with a limited extra time. At worst, the extra time can be diluted over a much longer period of time.

But even when estimates of the technical effort are correct, another aspect is often neglected. Any project has both direct and indirect costs. Direct costs comprise things like salaries and travel expenses. Indirect costs include, for example, equipment and administrative tasks. In addition, there are the costs of the unknown: meetings, revisions, and all those little tasks that haven't been communicated to everyone or fully understood. Estimate omissions are common, and omissions are addressed only by experience—your direct experience or that of subject experts. Obviously, you should always do your best to clearly write out every little task that makes work complete, and count it at least in the time column.

A pragmatic approach is always comparing actual costs to estimates when a project is done. If you determine the delta and turn it into a percentage, under or over, you can use this factor to multiply estimates next time.

In general, there are two main dynamics in software projects depending on the working model: fixed price or time/materials. In the former case, if you realize you need more time, as a project manager you try to find a way to resync with the schedule. You try to lower the quality-cutting development time and testing, limiting documentation and any activity that is not strictly necessary to passing final tests for the iteration. You also try to renegotiate and read carefully back the requirements to see if anything agreed on can be reformulated as a change request. If you are in time/materials mode, you can manage to calculate the delta between estimates and actual time in the past iterations and use that to correct estimates for each new iteration.

Need for more expertise

Another reason why a project might be late is that the implementation of certain features takes longer because some people are not up to the task. If you need more expertise, don't be afraid to bring in the best talent you can find. When you approach talented people, however, it should be clear why you intend to bring them in. You can have experts to train your people or to solve the issue. Neither option is clearly preferable over the other.

Training delivers more added value because the results of training remain within the company and increase assets. At the same time, training—even when tailor-made courseware is delivered—typically addresses topics at a rather general level and might take extra time to be adapted to the ongoing project. On the other hand, calling for consulting is theoretically more effective but requires that you give experts full access to the code, people, and documentation. The more intricate the codebase is, the longer it might take and the less reliable results might be.

Experts don't do magic; magic doesn't exist in software. If an expert does magic, it may be a trick. And so it is in life.

Summary

In spite of the name, software engineering is *not* about engineering; or at least it is not about engineering in the common sense of the word *engineering*. Software is a too dynamic and evolving a matter to be boxed in a set of fixed rules.

The major enemy of software projects is the BBM, and the BBM is strictly related to piecemeal growth and the project lifespan. The piecemeal growth of projects is a matter of fact; having an effective strategy to cope with that is essential. This might require the ability and personality to negotiate with project managers, customers, and stakeholders. Domain experience leads you to sensible judgment about features that most likely will be requested and allows you to better guide the customer to discover what they need.

Not all projects are created equal, and understanding the lifespan of the project is another critical factor. You don't want to put the same effort and care into the design of a short-lived project and a mission-critical system or a line-of-business application. Complexity must be controlled where it really exists, not created where it doesn't exist and isn't supposed to be.

The mechanics of software projects is sometimes perverse, but successful projects are possible. Whatever bad can happen around a software project doesn't happen overnight. If you can catch it in a timely manner and fix it, you spend money on prevention, which is worth much more than any money spent in recovery.

Finishing with a smile

See *http://www.murphys-laws.com* for an extensive listing of computer (and noncomputer) related laws and corollaries. Here are a few you might enjoy:

- All models are wrong, but some models are useful. (*George E. P. Box*)

- Walking on water and developing software to specification are easy as long as both are frozen.

- An oil leak will develop.

CHAPTER 3

Principles of software design

All programming is maintenance programming because you are rarely writing original code.
It's only the first 10 minutes that the code's original, when you type it in the first time. That's it.
—*Dave Thomas and Andy Hunt*

A popular saying in software development is that good architecture is architecture in which all hard-to-change decisions turn out to be right. Software architecture is about implementing behavior around pillars. Changing pillars on the go is obviously problematic, but it might become necessary if the pillars fail to support enough weight, or if you think of a better idea. Ensuring that code can survive changes and extensions is the Holy Grail of software, and it's exactly the theory that all gurus and book authors propound and recommend you do.

The real world is different.

Detecting alarming symptoms of code deterioration is the easiest part; deciding what action to take to fix them is a bit harder. In general, designing a software system is challenging because it requires you to focus on today's requested features while ensuring that the resulting system is flexible enough to support any future fixes, changes, and new features.

How would you code to ensure that fixes and extensions can be applied seamlessly and ideally at the sole cost of their implementation?

Maintainability is the quality characteristic you should give the highest priority to when you design a system. *Maintainability* refers to the degree to which a codebase handles updates without generating regression and new issues. Unfortunately, maintainability is not a one-off feature you can implement; instead, it results from various factors, such as adopting principles and common patterns and paying attention to code cleanliness, readability, and testability.

This chapter provides you with a quick summary of common practices in software engineering. It first outlines some universal principles that should always inspire the design of software and then moves on to discuss principles of object-oriented design and key design vectors such as SOLID.

Note SOLID is now an extremely popular acronym in software development. It's formed from the initials of five design principles: Single responsibility, Open/close, Liskov's , Interface segregation, and Dependency inversion. We'll touch on SOLID principles later in the chapter.

Universal principles of software design

When the two of us started programming, which was long before we started making a living out of it, the old BASIC language was still around with its set of GOTO statements. Like many others, we wrote toy programs, jumping from one instruction to the next within the same monolithic block of code. They worked just fine, but they were only toy programs in the end.

Note Every time we looked at the resulting messy BASIC code we wrote, continually referring to other instructions that appeared a bunch of lines up or down in the code, we didn't really like it and we weren't really proud of it. But, at the time, we just thought we were accepting a cool challenge that only a few preordained souls could take on. Programming is a darned hard thing—we thought—but we are going to like it.

It was about the late 1960s when the complexity of the average program crossed the significant threshold that marked the need for a more systematic approach to software development. That signaled the official beginning of software engineering.

From *spaghetti* code to *lasagna* code

Made of a messy tangle of jumps and returns, GOTO-based code was soon belittled and infamously labeled as *spaghetti code*. And we all learned the first of a long list of revolutionary concepts: *structured programming*. In particular, we learned to use subroutines to break our code into cohesive and more reusable pieces. In food terms, we evolved from spaghetti to lasagna. If you look at Figure 3-1, you will spot the difference quite soon.

FIGURE 3-1 From a messy tangle to a layered and ordered block.

Lasagna forms a layered block of noodles and toppings that can be easily cut into pieces and embodies the concept of structure. Lasagna is also easier to serve, which is the food analogy for reusability.

What software engineering really has been trying to convey since its inception is the need for some design to take place *before* coding begins and, subsequently, the need for some basic design principles. Overall, we think that the target of software engineering has been moving a bit lately.

Design doesn't precede coding, but often it goes side by side with coding. As you code, you learn more about the ideal design and refactor to it as soon as possible—ideally, at the beginning of the next iteration. In this way, design and coding evolve together, creating the need for code that can be easily and safely updated without introducing bugs and regression. This is maintainable code—at least, the modern meaning of it.

At the foundation of maintainable code there are two core principles—cohesion and coupling. These principles were first introduced by Larry Constantine and Edward Yourdon in their book *Structured Design: Fundamentals of a Discipline of Computer Program and Systems Design* (Yourdon Press, 1976).

Important The need for extremely maintainable code also signals a huge shift from methodologies that held the spotlight for many years. Today, a big upfront design is just not affordable and even kind of pointless. Things evolve too fast; companies just need to have their processes improved to catch up with fast-changing business needs. A comprehensive upfront design that is signed-off on at some point and takes ages to be challenged and updated is simply awkward and ill-fitting in today's dynamic computing world. However, extreme dynamism and agility doesn't mean you have to dismiss planning, good practices, effective principles, and numbers. It means, instead, that you should stop pointing at the lack of big upfront design as an excuse for poor code.

Cohesion

Cohesion indicates that a given software module—be it a subroutine, class, or library—features a set of responsibilities that are strongly related. Put another way, *cohesion* measures the distance between the logic expressed by the various methods on a class, the various functions in a library, and the various actions accomplished by a method. If you look for a moment at the definition of cohesion in another field—chemistry—you should be able to see a clearer picture of software cohesion. In chemistry, cohesion is a physical property of a substance that indicates the attraction existing between like-molecules within a body.

Cohesion measurement ranges from low to high and is preferably in the highest range possible.

Highly cohesive classes favor maintenance and reusability because they tend to have no dependencies. Low cohesion, on the other hand, makes it much harder to understand the purpose of a class and creates a natural habitat for rigidity and fragility in the software. Decreasing cohesion leads to creating classes where responsibilities (namely, methods) have very little in common and refer to distinct and unrelated activities. Translated into a practical guideline, the principle of cohesion recommends creating extremely specialized classes with few methods, which refer to logically related operations. If the logical distance between methods grows, you just create a new class.

Ward Cunningham—a pioneer of *Extreme Programming*—suggests that we define cohesion as being inversely proportional to the number of responsibilities a class has. We definitely like this definition.

Important Strongly related to cohesion is the Single Responsibility Principle (SRP). In the formulation provided by Robert Martin (which you can see at *http://www.objectmentor.com/resources/articles/srp.pdf*), SRP indicates that each class should always have just one reason to change. In other words, each class should be given a single responsibility, where a *responsibility* is defined as "a reason to change." A class with multiple responsibilities has more reasons to change and, subsequently, a less cohesive interface.

Coupling

Coupling measures the level of dependency existing between two software modules, such as classes. Two classes, A and B, are said to be coupled when it turns out that you have to make changes to B every time you make any change to A. In other words, B is not directly and logically involved in the change being made to module A. However, because of the underlying dependency, B is forced to change; otherwise, the code won't compile any longer.

Coupling measurement ranges from low to high and the lowest possible range is preferable.

Low coupling doesn't mean your modules are to be completely isolated from one another. They are definitely allowed to communicate, but they should do that through a set of well-defined and stable interfaces. Each module should be able to work without intimate knowledge of another module's internal implementation. Conversely, high coupling hinders testing and reusing code, and it makes understanding the code nontrivial. It is also one of the primary causes of a rigid and fragile design.

Low coupling and high cohesion are strongly correlated. A system designed to achieve low coupling and high cohesion generally meets the requirements of high readability, maintainability, easy testing, and good reuse.

Note Introduced to support a structured design, cohesion and coupling are basic design principles not specifically related to object orientation. However, it's the general scope that also makes them valid and effective in an object-oriented scenario. A good object-oriented design, in fact, is characterized by low coupling and high cohesion, which means that self-contained objects (high cohesion) are interacting with other objects through a stable interface (low coupling).

Separation of concerns

A principle that is helpful to achieving high cohesion and low coupling is separation of concerns (SoC), introduced in 1974 by Edsger W. Dijkstra in his paper "On the Role of Scientific Thought." If you're interested, you can download the full paper from *http://www.cs.utexas.edu/users/EWD/ewd04xx/EWD447.PDF*.

Concerns are different pieces of software functionality, like business logic or presentation. SoC is all about breaking the system into distinct and possibly nonoverlapping features. Each feature you want in the system represents a concern and an aspect of the system. Terms such as *feature*, *concern*, and *aspect* are generally considered synonyms. Concerns are mapped to software modules and, to the extent that it is possible, there's no duplication of functionalities.

SoC suggests you focus on one particular concern at a time. It doesn't mean, of course, that you ignore all other concerns of the system. More simply, after you assign a concern to a software module, you focus on building that module. From the perspective of that module, any other concerns are irrelevant.

> **Note** If you read Dijkstra's original text, you'll see that he uses the expression "separation of concerns" to indicate the general principle but switches to the word "aspect" to indicate individual concerns that relate to a software system. For quite a few years, the word "aspect" didn't mean anything special to software engineers. Things changed in the late 1990s when aspect-oriented programming (AOP) entered the industry. We love to make the reference here to show Dijkstra's great farsightedness.

Isolation

SoC is concretely achieved through using modular code and making large use of information hiding. Modular programming encourages the use of separate modules for each significant feature. Modules are given their own public interface to communicate with other modules and can contain internal chunks of information for private use.

Only members in the public interface are visible to other modules. Internal data is either not exposed or it is encapsulated and exposed in a filtered manner. The implementation of the interface contains the behavior of the module, whose details are not known or accessible to other modules.

Isolating parts of the software that are likely to change, or that might require ad hoc settings (for example, security settings), is a common practice that ensures high levels of maintainability.

Object-oriented design

Before object orientation (OO), any program resulted from the interaction of routines. Programming was procedural, meaning that there was a main stream of code determining the various steps to be accomplished.

OO has been a milestone in software design.

OO lets you envision a program as the result of interacting objects, each of which holds its own data and—at least in theory—behavior. How would you design a graph of objects to represent your system? Which principles should inspire this design? We can recognize a set of core principles for object-oriented design (OOD) and a set of more advanced and specific principles that descend from, and further specialize, the core principles.

To find a broadly accepted definition of OOD, we probably need to look at the Gang of Four (Erich Gamma, Richard Helm, Ralph Johnson, and John Vlissides) and their landmark book *Design Patterns: Elements of Reusable Object-Oriented Software* (Addison-Wesley, 1994). The book is commonly referred to in literature as GoF, which is the universal acronym for "Gang of Four."

The gist of OOD is contained in this sentence:

> *You must find pertinent objects, factor them into classes at the right granularity, define class interfaces and inheritance hierarchies, and establish key relationships among them.*

The basics of OOD can then be summarized in the following three points: find pertinent objects, minimize coupling between interfacing objects, and favor code reuse.

In GoF, we also find another excerpt that is particularly significant:

> *Your design should be specific to the problem at hand but also general enough to address future problems and requirements.*

This brings up some more, and subtler, aspects of object-orientation.

Important Object-oriented design is still a topic that all developers should read about, but it's not strictly related to all aspects of software development. OOD applies mostly to areas where you need modeling. This hardly includes presentation or data access, but it certainly includes the business logic if you choose to represent the entities within the business domain according to the *Domain Model* pattern. In other parts of the system, you just happen to use classes but you hardly spend time identifying pertinent classes and building sophisticated hierarchies. All you do—that mostly works—is create standalone classes and keep them as thin as possible and with as few responsibilities as possible.

Pertinent classes

Nearly everybody who studied computer science heard at some point that the world is full of objects, whether they are cars, buildings, chairs, or even people. Objects are all around you and, just for this reason, OO is a very natural way to design software systems. You also learned that there's quite a formal way to associate real objects you see with software objects (for example, classes) you design.

Requirements and use cases offer the raw material that must be worked out and shaped into a hierarchy of pertinent classes. A common practice for finding pertinent objects is tagging all nouns and verbs in the various use cases. Nouns originate classes or properties, whereas verbs indicate methods on classes. Let's consider the following sample requirement:

> To view all **orders** placed by a **customer**, the **user** indicates the customer **ID**. The program displays an error message if the customer does not exist. If the customer exists, the program displays **name**, **address**, **date of birth**, and all outstanding **orders**. For each order, the program gets **ID**, **date**, and all **order items**.

The sample use case suggests the definition of classes such as *User*, *Customer*, *Order*, and *OrderItem*. The class *Customer* will have properties such as *Name*, *Address*, and *DateOfBirth*. Methods on the class *Customer* might be *LoadOrderItems*, *GetCustomerByID*, and *ViewOrders*.

Note that finding pertinent objects is only the first step. As recommended in the statement that many consider to be the emblem of OOD, you then have to *factor* pertinent objects into classes and determine the right level of granularity and assign responsibilities.

In particular, the placement of the code for the action of *retrieving* data is critical. Does this behavior belong to the *Customer* class or is it part of some additional layer? That mostly depends on the logical context in which the class is being designed, the patterns used to make the design, the level of separation achievable between layers and, why not, the skills and strategic vision of developers and architects.

Program to an interface

Every time you use a class, you establish a deep link between the calling code and the class. You can't use the calling code if the called class is not available. This form of dependency might or might not be tolerable. It all depends on the nature of the called class and the role it has in the design. Let's have a look at the following code:

```
public class SomeComponent
{
  public void DoWork()
  {
    // Get an instance of the logger
    Logger logger = new Logger();

    // Get data to log
    var data = GetData();

    // Just log
    logger.Log(data);
  }
}
```

The class *SomeComponent* is tightly coupled with the class *Logger* and its implementation. The class *SomeComponent* is broken if *Logger* is broken or not available and, more importantly, you can't use another type of logger. If the tightly coupled code belonged to a class that's logically correlated to the caller, it wouldn't be that bad to have coupling. The two classes form a logical unit. In other cases, you get a real design benefit if you can separate the interface from the implementation.

The use of the logger in the example is not coincidental.

Logging is one of the canonical examples of a *cross-cutting concern*. A cross-cutting concern is any functionality you might need to have in a class that's not strictly related to the requirements set for the class. When you implement a class, you might need things like logging, authentication, threading, caching, object pooling, error handling, localization, and validation. Should these aspects be part of the implementation of the class, or are they better placed outside of the caller class? If set to be part of the class, a cross-cutting concern seriously risks the introduction of code duplication. If referenced as in the previous example, instead, the cross-cutting concern leads to tight dependencies.

A clean decomposition of cross-cutting concerns comes with the use of patterns like *Dependency Injection* (DI) or *Service Locator* (SL), where the class is made dependent on an abstraction rather than a truly compiled module. In general, decomposing a cross-cutting concern means programming a class to interfaces rather than implementations.

The *Logger* class needs to undergo an *Extract Interface* refactoring aimed at extracting an interface to express the core functionality of the component. Here's a possible definition for the *ILogger* interface:

```
interface ILogger
{
    void Log(string data);
}
```

The refactoring step also produces the following *Logger* class:

```
public class Logger : ILogger
{
    public void Log(string data)
    {
        ...
    }
}
```

The *SomeComponent* class now receives—in some way—a reference to an *ILogger* component. This makes the *SomeComponent* class able to work with any logger component that implements the interface. The *SomeComponent* class has been successfully decoupled from the logger, and the resulting code is easier to reuse and extend. For example, logging the behavior of *SomeComponent* to, say, a database just requires the development of a specific class that implements the interface and the injection of the reference.

 Important Strictly related to this example and this principle of OOD are the Dependency Injection and Service Locator patterns. Both patterns provide a way to pass classes programmed to interfaces some actual reference to an interfacing instance.

Composition vs. inheritance

Reusability is a fundamental aspect of the object-oriented paradigm and one of the keys to its success and wide adoption. You create a class one day, and you're happy with that. Next, on another day, you derive a new class from it, make some changes here and there, and come up with a slightly different version of the original class.

Is this what code reuse is all about? Well, there's more to consider.

With class inheritance, the derived class doesn't simply inherit the code of the parent class. It really inherits the context and, subsequently, it gains some visibility of the parent's state. Is this a problem?

For one thing, a derived class that uses the context it inherits from the parent can be broken by future changes to the parent class. In addition, when you inherit from a class, you enter into a polymorphic context, meaning that your derived class can be used in any scenarios where the parent is accepted. It's not guaranteed, however, that the two classes can really be used interchangeably. Ensuring that this is what happens is your responsibility as a good object-oriented developer; it doesn't come for free out of the implementation of OO languages. Providing the guarantee that the parent and its derived classes can be used interchangeably is the goal of *Liskov's principle*, which we'll discuss later.

The inherent limitation of inheritance—one of the popular pillars of OO—was recognized quite soon. In fact, in GoF the authors identify two routes to reusability: white-box and black-box reusability. The former is based on class inheritance and suffers from the issues we just mentioned. The latter is based on object composition.

Object composition entails creating a new type that holds an instance of the base type and typically references it through a private member:

```
public RegisteredUser
{
  private User theUser;

  public RegisteredUser()
  {
    // You can use any lazy-loading policy you want for instantiation.
    // No lazy loading is being used here ...
    theUser = new User();
  }

  public object DoWork()
  {
    var data = theUser.DoSomeWork();

    // Do some other work
    return Process(data);
  }

  private object Process(object data)
  {
    ...
  }
}
```

In this case, you have a wrapper class that uses a type as a black box and does so through a well-defined contract. The wrapper class—*RegisteredUser*—has no access to internal members of *User* and cannot change the behavior in any way. It uses the object as it is rather than changing it to do its will. External calls reach the wrapper class, and the wrapper class delegates the call internally to the held instance of the class it enhances. (See Figure 3-2.)

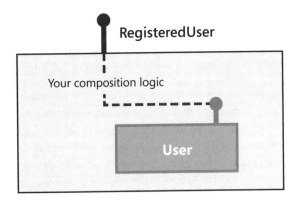

FIGURE 3-2 Object composition in action.

The logic that ties together the wrapper and wrapped class is up to you. You decide which part of the *User* class should be exposed outside and how. Figure 3-3, instead, shows how the diagram should be rendered in the case of inheritance.

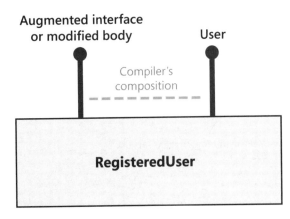

FIGURE 3-3 Relationship between a base class (*User*) and a derived class (*RegisteredUser*).

Composition has one key benefit you don't get with inheritance: it is a form of defensive programming and, as such, it makes it harder to introduce subtle bugs related to object-oriented known bad practices, such as fragile base classes, virtual members, and constructors.

Two classes composed together have no explicit relationships; you can't use the *RegisteredUser* class where an instance of *User* is expected. If this turns out to be a problem, you can have both classes implement some common *IUser* interface.

> **Important** Another point in favor of composition that we like to point out is that it explicitly denies inheritance. In this way, it helps developers—especially junior developers—not to think of objects as a new way to design the world in its entirety. When it comes to object-oriented design, it is key that the model is tailor-made and optimized for the specific problem. Sometimes, instead, we tend to abstract too much, and this can produce a less-than-optimal graph of classes.

A second pass at object-orientation

We believe that nearly everybody would agree that OO is great in theory but that, in practice, it needs some adjustment. And the amount of adjustment might sometimes be quite large and fully wipe out the benefits. OO was originally perceived and pushed as a way to tackle complexity. Because objects are all around us, if only we could model software entities after real-world objects we'd be mostly done. Modeling proved quite hard, though. The net result is that we too often end up adding artificial complexity instead of taming the natural complexity of things.

> **Terminology** The term *anemic domain* refers to a hierarchy of classes that just contain properties and nearly no behavior and internal logic. A rich model, called a *domain model* in DDD, is a model where classes for the most part are made of data (properties) and behavior (methods).

Sometimes some artificial complexity is created by the wrong perspective on things. In general, when you study object-orientation at school, teachers mostly offer an academic perspective of things where the emphasis is on aspects like abstraction, technology neutrality, elegance of design, or even individual creativity. When students become professionals and are called upon to write real-world code in the industry, they are instead forced to focus on other parameters, such as testability, reusability, effectiveness, and especially maintainability.

Inheritance, in particular, is sometimes more pain than gain as the GoF's argument against composition proves. There are safe ways to use inheritance—just adding code to derived classes—but the resulting graph of objects can hardly be the faithful representation of a whole model from some domain in the real world. The effectiveness of OO for the most part has been demonstrated in labs or toy or fortunate projects. Most projects experienced trouble, and it's not really relevant whether such failures were the result of the inherent shortcomings of OO or limited skills. Either way, OO can hardly be seen as the universal paradigm of software development.

In the name of code reuse, OO might sneakily slip gratuitous complexity and subtle bugs into the mix. Experts can probably manage it, but will you have only experts on your team? To really write effective code, we believe that developers should focus on the following three points:

- Isolate parts that likely change.

- Sometimes classes are not required; if all you need is a function, just use a function.

- Be aware that the real world offers events rather than models, and events just carry data.

For some reason, OO represents the mainstream paradigm today because most popular languages are in one way or another object-oriented. Languages—even object-oriented languages—are just tools for expressing a behavior in the most reasonable and maintainable way. In this regard, here are a few remarkable words about OO from Edsger Dijkstra: "Object-oriented programming is an exceptionally bad idea which could only have originated in California."

 Note We like to point you to the following post, which ironically summarizes many of the arguable points about object-orientation: *http://hadihariri.com/2013/11/24/refactoring-to-functionalwhy-class.*

Development and design vectors

Universal principles such as coupling, cohesion, and SoC, along with OOD principles, give us some rather general guidance about how to design a software application. As you might have noticed, all these principles are rather old (but certainly not outdated), as they were devised and formulated at least a couple of decades ago.

In more recent years, some of these principles have been further refined and enhanced to address more specific aspects of the design.

SOLID principles

A ways back, Robert C. Martin identified five fundamental principles for clean and more effective software design. These principles later were shortened to the popular SOLID acronym. The acronym originates from the initials of the names of the principles:

- Single Responsibility (SRP)

- Open/Closed (OCP)

- Liskov's principle (LSP)

- Interface segregation (ISP)

- Dependency inversion (DIP)

Object modeling is neither easy nor is it an exact science. Principles exist for the most part to show you the way to go—to give guidance and possibly to point you in the right direction. The whole point of modeling is finding the right mix of principles. Some of them might even be in conflict. Some SOLID principles (in particular, SRP and OCP) might really be hard to apply extensively in a large codebase. They might lead you to continuous refactoring until you discover that over a certain threshold the curve of effort grows while the curve of benefit starts decreasing. Blind focus on principles— in particular, SRP and OCP—might distract you from the main target, namely producing maintainable code that works.

> **Note** You might want to listen to a podcast by Joel Spolski on the theme of testability, quality of code, and SOLID. Find it here: *http://www.joelonsoftware.com/items/2009/01/31.html.*

Single Responsibility principle

When a class grows big, featuring methods upon methods, there is a chance it is exposing way too many responsibilities. And what's the ideal number of responsibilities for a class? Just one. And what's the definition of a responsibility? A responsibility is a reason to change. The Single Responsibility principle says

There should never be more than one reason for a class to change.

In the end, the whole point of this principle is that each class should be ideally built around one core task. Rather than simplicity in itself, the main point here is that by exposing a very limited number of responsibilities, the class intersects a smaller segment of the system and as requirements change the likelihood that you need to edit the class is lower.

Too often SRP is used as a blind measure of quality for code. By taking SRP to the limit, though, you seriously risk producing a wealth of anemic classes—just properties and little or no behavior. Every class tends to take the smallest possible amount of responsibility, but you still need places to concentrate all the orchestration logic that the system still requires. The resulting model might be less balanced than ideal.

That's why we call SRP a vector—when writing code, keep in mind that classes should be as simple as possible and focus on one main core task. But that shouldn't become religious dogma or a measure of performance and quality.

Open/Closed principle

The Open/Closed principle invites developers to create software entities (whether classes, modules, or functions) that can happily survive changes. The principle says the following:

A module should be open for extension but closed for modification.

Open for extension ultimately means that an existing class should be extensible and usable as the foundation for building other related functionality. But to implement other related functionality, you should not change the existing code which, subsequently, remains closed for modification.

OCP encourages the use of programming mechanisms like composition, interfaces, and generics that can generate a class that can be extended without modifying the source code. For example, if you program a class to log its activity using a generic logging interface, you automatically enable that class to use any logger that exposes the interface. If you use composition, you can build up new functionality on top of existing components without touching them.

Liskov's principle

As discussed earlier, inheritance can be a tricky thing, and composition is definitely a safer way to code classes. In particular, in a derived class you can do things that actually prevent the derived class from being used in any place where the parent class is accepted. This subtle aspect of object-orientation is often the source of bad surprises for developers. For this reason, we suggest you keep it in mind whenever you happen to use inheritance in your codebase. The principle says the following:

Subclasses should be substitutable for their base classes.

Apparently, you get this free of charge from just using an object-oriented language. The reality is different. The essence of the Liskov's principle is that a derived class can't restrict conditions under which a base class executes. Likewise, a derived class can't avoid producing some of the results the parent class guarantees. This fact is often summarized by saying that a derived class should require no more and provide no less than its parent.

The canonical example of the Liskov's principle is the square/rectangle hierarchy.

At first sight, deriving *Square* from *Rectangle* seems like a wise and even elegant idea. Isn't a square just a special type of rectangle? Well, we recommend you consider the expression "special type of" used in the context of class inheritance to be an alarm bell for possible violations of the Liskov principle. If it sounds like it is a special type of some other entity, use inheritance very carefully!

An API designed to receive and handle *Rectangle* objects might fail when it receives a *Square* object that, say, forces height and weight to be equal. In other words, the preconditions set on a *Rectangle* should not be restricted by any derived class with the addition of a new precondition.

Liskov's principle and code-assistant tools

Code-assistant tools help a lot in catching nasty bugs during editing. If you're responsive to suggestions, you can really fix your code quickly and in real time.

In past chapters, we referred to "writing code right the first time" as the most effective way to increase the quality of code in software projects. Augmenting skills is certainly one way of getting to that, but it takes time and a lot of good will, and it is costly too. Using a well-made code-assistant tool costs you much less and makes basic refactoring one or two clicks away. These tools (for example, ReSharper) also let you do a lot more sophisticated things but—trust us—just the bare minimum is good enough.

Another tool to pay attention to is Code Contracts. Introduced with the Microsoft .NET Framework 4.0, Code Contracts is an API you can use to specify preconditions and postconditions on class methods. Interestingly, when you have a derived class that overrides a virtual method and adds a precondition, you get a warning at compile time, as shown in Figure 3-4.

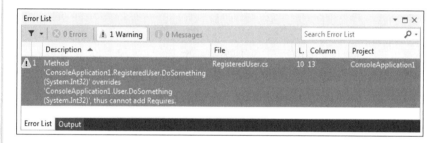

FIGURE 3-4 The Code Contracts tools can catch violations of Liskov's principle at compile time.

The warning message you get from Visual Studio is a bit obscure, but at least it states clearly that the problem is the extra *Requires* precondition. Let's consider the following code:

```
public class User
{
    public virtual void DoSomething(int number)
    {
        return;
    }
}
public class RegisteredUser : User
{
    public override void DoSomething(int number)
    {
        Contract.Requires<ArgumentException>(number > 0);
    }
}
```

It's easy to see that *RegisteredUser* puts an additional constraint on the method *DoSomething* and doesn't provide the same set of services as *User*. An API built around *User* might be used to call the method *DoSomething*, passing a negative value. In the moment in which the API is passed a *RegisteredUser* instance, the code is broken.

Sometimes violations of Liskov's principle generates nasty runtime errors, and the quickest way to fix them is by checking the actual type of the parameter being passed. Here's an example:

```
public class MyApi
{
    public void DoSomething(Rectangle rect)
    {
        if (typeof(rect) is Square)
            return;                    // or whatever is best here

        // Regular code here
        ...
    }
}
```

This is a clear symptom that something is wrong with your code.

Another common code issue that might be traced back to Liskov's principle is the use of virtual methods. Whenever you define a virtual method, you should make sure you're not calling any private member from within it. Doing so would restrict implementors of derived classes from overriding the method having access to the same share of the context of the parent class.

Note that Liskov's principle also applies to interfaces rather than just to derived classes.

Interface Segregation principle

The Interface Segregation principle addresses interface obesity and recommends that interfaces be kept to a bare minimum of functions. The primary point is not that you should have thin interfaces, but that you should not have fat interfaces. The principle says this:

> Clients should not be forced to depend upon interfaces that they do not use.

Correct application of the principle means factoring out interfaces into multiple sets of functions so that it is easier for each client to match just the set of function it is really interested in. In addition, unlike classes, interfaces can be summed up in a class declaration. So there's really no reason for having a single interface with 20 methods instead of two or three distinct and smaller interfaces. Segregation, though, makes sense only if splitting has some functional sense.

The canonical example of segregated interfaces starts with the following interface:

```
public interface IDoor
{
    void Lock();
    void Unlock();
    Boolean IsDoorOpen { get; }

    Int32 OpenTimeout { get; set; }
    event EventHandler DoorOpenForTooLong;
}
```

The *IDoor* interface can be simplified and split in two functional groups: door and timed door.

```
public interface IDoor
{
    void Lock();
    void Unlock();
    Boolean IsDoorOpen { get; }
}
public interface ITimedDoor
{
    Int32 OpenTimeout { get; set; }
    event EventHandler DoorOpenForTooLong;
}
```

Failing to adequately adhere to the Interface Segregation principle leads to implementations that are complex and to having many methods that aren't implemented at all. Furthermore, clients are forced to depend on interfaces they don't use—and still, these clients are subject to changes to such interfaces.

Dependency Inversion principle

DIP is an extremely important principle, and it is the theoretical foundation for common patterns such as Dependency Injection and Service Locator, which we'll address in a moment. DIP says the following:

High-level modules should not depend upon low-level modules. Both should depend upon abstractions.

Dependency inversion is a formal way to express the concept behind the "programming to interfaces, not implementations" principle. When you are writing a method and feel the need to call into an external component, as a developer you should wonder whether the function you're going to call is private to the class or is an external dependency. If it is an external dependency, you just abstract it to an interface and proceed coding against the interface. Next, you're left with the problem of how to turn the interface into some concretely callable instances. That's the realm of patterns such as Dependency Injection.

Patterns for handling dependencies

The idea behind DIP doesn't really need a complex scenario to be effectively illustrated. Just imagine a method that reads bytes from a stream and writes them out to some buffer:

```
void Copy()
{
  Byte byte;
  while(byte = ReadFromStream())
      WriteToBuffer(byte);
}
```

The pseudocode here depends on a couple of lower level modules: the reader and writer. According to DIP, we should abstract the dependencies to interfaces—say, *IReader* and *IWriter*. Subsequently, the method can be rewritten as follows:

```
void Copy()
{
  Byte byte;
  IReader reader;
  IWriter writer;

  // Still need to instantiate reader and writer variables
  ...

  while(byte = reader.Read())
      writer.Write(byte);
}
```

Who really does provide instances of the reader and writer components? To actually solve the issue, you need some further specification. In other words, you need a pattern.

Service Locator pattern

The first pattern used to apply the DIP is the Service Locator pattern, which can be summarized as follows:

```
void Copy()
{
  Byte byte;
  var reader = ServiceLocator.GetService<IReader>();
  var writer = ServiceLocator.GetService<IWriter>();

  while(byte = reader.Read())
      writer.Write(byte);
}
```

You use a centralized component that locates and returns an instance to use whenever the specified abstraction is requested. The service locator operates while embedded in the code that it serves. It acts as a factory and can include discovery and activation logic as complex as you need. It is common to create a service locator as a class that exposes a few static factory methods, as shown here:

```
public class ServiceLocator
{
    public Object GetService(Type typeToResolve) { ... }
    public T GetService<T>() { ... }
    public Object GetService(String typeNickname) { ... }
}
```

You can indicate the type you want to be resolved as a parameter or through a generic prototype. If the same type can be resolved in different ways depending on the context, it is common to pass a plain string nickname for the type to be instantiated. Internally, the *GetService* method can be written along the following guidelines:

```
public Object GetService(String typeNickname)
{
    if (typeNickname == "sometype")
        return new SomeType();
    if (typeNickname == "someothertype")
        return new SomeOtherType();
    ...

}
```

Obviously, the service locator can employ sophisticated forms of instantiation (indirect creation, object pooling, singleton) and read abstract/concrete type mappings from some configuration file.

With regard to the downside of this pattern, we like to mention that it requires you to deeply look into the code to figure out how dependencies are handled. On the other hand, the most compelling scenario for it is when you have to add extensibility to some large legacy code that is hard to redesign in a different way. An excellent example of the Service Locator pattern is the way the ASP.NET MVC team managed to add new extensibility points in the codebase in the transition to version 3 of the framework when they introduced the *DependencyResolver* class.

> **Important** Service Locator is considered, in many cases, an anti-pattern. The reason is that you end up having references to the service locator class spread out in your code. Worse yet, you won't get errors until execution time. The following is a good post to read to understand why Service Locator might be considered an anti-pattern: *http://blog.ploeh. dk/2010/02/03/ServiceLocatorisanAnti-Pattern*. The comments are also pretty good to read.

Dependency Injection pattern

A better alternative is to use the Dependency Injection pattern. (It's also known as the Inversion of Control, or IOC, pattern.) The resulting code looks like this:

```
void Copy(IReader reader, IWriter writer)
{
  Byte byte;
  while(byte = reader.Read())
      writer.Write(byte);
}
```

The list of dependencies is now explicit from the signature of the method and doesn't require you to go down the line to pinpoint calls to a service locator component. In addition, the burden of creating instances for each spot dependency is moved elsewhere.

There are three ways to inject dependencies into a class: using the constructor, a setter property, or an interface. All three techniques are valid, and the choice is up to you. We usually opt for injecting through the constructor because in this way you make it clear from the beginning what the dependencies of a class are.

Dependency injection based on constructors is also a great way to detect if a class "smells." If you spot a class with, say, 20 dependencies in the constructor, chances are good that the class is not taking SRP literally!

The key point of Dependency Injection is that factory code resides outside the class. This code, however, can be repetitive and long enough in nontrivial scenarios. It can be so boring and error-prone that it largely waters down the benefits of the pattern. For this reason, Dependency Injection is often associated with specific productivity tools, known as *IoC containers*.

An IoC container is built around a container object that, bound to some configuration information, resolves dependencies. The caller code instantiates the container and passes the desired interface as an argument. In response, the IoC framework returns a concrete object that implements that interface. Applying Dependency Injection right probably requires that you call your IoC container directly only once, and all it takes is a few lines of code because most of the dependencies usually will be handled by constructors of involved classes.

Microsoft currently provides several IoC choices. One is Managed Extensibility Framework (MEF), which primarily targets extensibility and offers great plugin support in client applications. Next, there are MEF 2 and Unity, which you can discover at *http://unity.codeplex.com*. MEF 2 is available as a NuGet package for .NET 4.5 and Windows Store applications.

Unity and MEF 2 can be considered full IoC containers. MEF, on the other hand, covers only the basic functions of an IoC container.

Note As we see things, Microsoft .NET trends in the server and on the cloud side seem to focus more strongly on Dependency Injection patterns while promoting it as a more fundamental topic. This emphasis by Microsoft will make SOLID principles and DI even more important to be understood and used by architects and developers. Dependency injection nowadays is a fundamental concept.

Important Dependency Injection and Service Locator are also fundamental patterns from a testability standpoint, because these patterns make it natural to inject dependencies into classes as you test them.

Coding vectors

There's another class of software principles that you should definitely be aware of. DRY, KISS, YAGNI and a few others just belong to that category. We like to call principles in this class *coding vectors*.

So what's the difference between vectors and principles?

In physics, a *vector* is a quantity fully described by magnitude and direction. So compared to a plain scalar quantity, a vector adds up to a new level of information—the direction.

Applied to software, we tend to use the term *vector* to point to principles that express both magnitude and direction. In this case, we also consider direction to be predominant to magnitude. The set of principles being described here should be considered for the direction they point at rather than for a concrete pattern to bring into your codebase. These principles apply to the software project as a whole and are not limited to classes and algorithms.

KISS

KISS stands for *Keep It Simple, Stupid* and points at having systems, including software systems, where any level of logic found in the implementation is strictly necessary. The principle considers unneeded complexity to be any layer of logic that can be considered extra given the system requirements. The principle also balks at the Occam's razor principle that suggests the hypothesis with the fewest assumptions should always be chosen.

Is there anybody out there who believes that simplicity is not a virtue? In life, simplicity sometimes has a negative connotation, such as something that is not sophisticated and rich enough in terms of features. In software, too often developers tend to over-engineer things; so KISS is a word to the wise to remind you that bottom-up building with a full perspective on things is the ideal way to create software.

We particularly love to mention a couple of corollaries to the KISS theorem. One is from Antoine de Saint-Exupéry, French poet and pioneer aviator. He used to say that perfection is achieved not when there is nothing left to add, but when there is nothing left to take away. The other quote is from Albert Einstein who was often recommended keeping things simple—specifically, as simple as possible, but no simpler. Because—we add—*simpler than simple* is often simplistic. And simplistic software is definitely a bad thing.

We often like to summarize the "simplicity above all" concept by paraphrasing people's rights in court: everything you write can and will be used against you in a debugging session.

And, worse yet, it will be used in every meeting with the customer.

YAGNI

YAGNI is the acronym of *You Ain't Gonna Need It*, which is a popular principle from Extreme Programming. Related to KISS, the principle blames problems on the implementation of any functionality that is not strictly dictated by requirements. Implementing a function when you foresee you might need it, rather than when you actually need it, exposes you to a number of potential headaches. First and foremost, it means more coding, debugging, and testing. It might also mean more documentation for the rest of the team. Furthermore, if the feature is unnecessary today, just the simple fact it exists could constrain future extensions. Finally, if the feature is not expressly required at a given time, are you sure you know enough about it?

YAGNI, though, is a vector; it has an inherent value (namely, magnitude) and gives you guidance (namely, it shows you a direction). If you blindly apply YAGNI to your project, you might fail to plan features ahead of time. When a relevant feature has to be implemented at the latest possible moment, it might require a lot more work than if it were planned in advance.

YAGNI is not a principle that must be treated like a doctor's prescription. It is a general guideline, and it points you in the right direction.

DRY

DRY is the acronym of *Don't Repeat Yourself*. It is a principle formulated by Andy Hunt and Dave Thomas in the book *The Pragmatic Programmer: From Journeyman to Master* (Addison-Wesley, 1999). Too hastily interpreted as a plain—and fairly obvious, indeed—recommendation to avoid code duplication, DRY in the authors' minds addresses a far grander point. Every aspect of the software development process, and every deliverable, should have just one credible and unambiguous representation.

DRY certainly applies to code duplication, but it also touches on data models, services, storage, tests, and documentation. More than everything else, though, DRY attempts to teach a method. You should avoid the trouble of keeping different parts of the system in sync. If you need to make a change anywhere, you should be able to do it once, and that should be enough.

When just applied to code, DRY becomes a sort of once-and-only-once kind of recommendation. You write the code that accomplishes a given operation within an application only once. Put this way, it is conceptually analogous to normalization in relational data models. Getting only one unambiguous implementation for a piece of code is the primary objective of refactoring; as such, it is much harder to achieve than it might seem at first.

 Note Ironically, the opposite of DRY is WET, an acronym for something like "write everything twice." In accordance with the true meaning of DRY, we suggest rephrasing WET as "wire everything twice."

Tell, don't ask

Overall, *Tell-Don't-Ask* is the inspiring principle of object modeling. At the foundation of OOP, there was Stroustrup's idea of creating software entities that could incorporate data and expose some behavior. That's precisely the point behind *Tell-Don't-Ask*.

When designing an interface, avoid asking for data to be processed in some outermost logical container; instead, tell the interface to perform some action on some explicit data. Bundling together data and behavior helps you with modeling because it more closely represents the observed reality. To fully make sense of *Tell-Don't-Ask*, consider the following everyday scenario:

Your significant other asks something along the lines of this: "Honey, what are you doing right now? Are you busy?"

Your significant other plays the role of the outermost logical container and is planning to orchestrate you in some process she's eager to arrange. The point is that you might or might not be able (or willing) to do the task. But you are requested to provide data about your internal state without knowing the reason that data is required. Your answer might lead your significant other to command you to assist regardless of your situation or to find an alternate way of accomplishing the task.

Wouldn't it be simpler and easier for everybody if she just told you what to do?

Honey, I need you to take the trash out.

The significant other—the orchestrator—only needs to keep track of whether the task has been accomplished or not in the allowed time. All the details of how it happens are delegated to and encapsulated in the object receiving the command.

Use of patterns

When facing a problem, a developer will certainly draw from the well of personal experience for any solutions to similar problems that worked in the past. Such building blocks are nothing more than hints and represent the skeleton of a solution. However, these same building blocks can become more refined day after day and generalized after each usage to become applicable to a wider range of problems and scenarios. Such building blocks might not provide a direct solution, but they usually help you to find your (right) way. And using them is usually more effective and faster than starting from scratch.

These building blocks are known as *patterns*.

The word *pattern* is one of those overloaded terms that morphed from its common usage to assume a specific meaning in computer science. According to the dictionary, a *pattern* is a template or model that can be used to generate things—all kinds of things. In computer science, we use patterns in design solutions at two levels: implementation and architecture.

What's a design pattern, exactly?

We software professionals can attribute the concept of design patterns to an architect—a real architect, not a software architect. In the late 1970s, Christopher Alexander developed a pattern language with the purpose of letting individuals express their innate sense of design through a sort of informal grammar. From his work, here's the definition of a pattern:

> *Each pattern describes a problem which occurs over and over again in our environment, and then describes the core solution to that problem, in such a way that you can use the solution a million times over, without ever doing it the same way twice.*

Nicely enough, although the definition was not written with software development in mind, it applies perfectly to that. So what's a design pattern?

A design pattern is a known and well-established core solution applicable to a family of concrete problems that might show up during implementation. A design pattern is a core solution and, as such, it might need adaptation to a specific context. This feature becomes a major strength when you consider that, in this way, the same pattern can be applied many times in many slightly different scenarios.

Design patterns are not created in a lab; quite the reverse. They originate from the real world and from the direct experience of developers and architects. You can think of a design pattern as a package that includes the description of a problem, a list of actors participating in the problem, and a practical solution.

The primary reference for design patterns is GoF. Another excellent reference we want to recommend is *Pattern-Oriented Software Architecture* by Frank Buschmann et al. (Wiley, 1996).

How to work with design patterns

Here is a list of what design patterns are not:

- Design patterns are not the verb and should never be interpreted dogmatically.

- Design patterns are not Superman and will never magically pop up to save a project in trouble.

- Design patterns are neither the dark side nor the light side of the Force. They might be with you, but they won't provide you with any special extra power.

Design patterns are just helpful, and that should be enough.

You don't choose a design pattern; the most appropriate design pattern normally emerges out of your refactoring steps. We could say that the pattern is buried under your classes, but digging it out is entirely up to you.

The wrong way to deal with design patterns is by going through a list of patterns you might find in books and matching them to the problem. Instead, it works the other way around. You have a problem and you have to match the problem to the pattern. How can you do that? It's quite simple to explain, but it's not so easy to apply.

You have to understand the problem and generalize it.

If you can take the problem back to its roots and get the gist of it, you'll probably find a tailor-made pattern just waiting for you. Why is this so? Well, if you really reached the root of the problem, chances are that someone else did the same in the past 20 years (the period during which design patterns became more widely used). So the solution is probably just there for you to read and apply.

This observation prompts us to mention the way in which all members of our teams use books on design patterns. (By the way, there are always plenty of such books scattered throughout the office.) Design patterns books are an essential tool. But we never read such books. We use them, instead, like cookbooks.

What we normally do is stop reading after the first few pages precisely where most books list the patterns they cover in detail inside. Next, we put the book aside and possibly within reach. Whenever we encounter a problem, we try to generalize it, and then we flip through the pages of the book to find a pattern that possibly matches it. We find one much more often than not. And if we don't, we repeat the process in an attempt to come to a better generalization of the problem.

When we find the pattern, we start working on its adaptation to our context. This often requires refactoring of the code which, in turn, might lead to a more appropriate pattern. And the loop goes on.

Where's the value in patterns, exactly?

Many people would agree in principle that there's plenty of value in design patterns. Fewer people, though, would be able to indicate what the value is and where it can be found. Using design patterns, per se, doesn't make your solution more valuable. What really matters, at the end of the day, is whether or not your solution works and meets requirements.

Armed with requirements and design principles, you are up to the task of solving a problem. On your way to the solution, though, a systematic application of design principles to the problem sooner or later takes you into the immediate neighborhood of a known design pattern. That's a certainty because, ultimately, patterns are solutions that others have already found and catalogued.

At that point, you have a solution with some structural likeness to a known design pattern. It is up to you, then, to determine whether an explicit refactoring to that pattern will bring some added value to the solution. Basically, you have to decide whether or not the known pattern you found represents a further, and desirable, refinement of your current solution. Don't worry if your solution doesn't match a pattern. It means that you have a solution that works and you're happy with that. You're just fine. You never want to change a winning team!

In summary, patterns might be an end when you refactor according to them, and they might be a means when you face a problem that is clearly resolved by a particular pattern. Patterns are not an added value for your solution, but they are valuable for you as an architect or a developer looking for a solution.

Refactoring

Refactoring is the discipline of restructuring existing code in such a way that the external behavior remains unaltered. You refactor your code not because it doesn't work but just to better address some nonfunctional attribute—such as readability, maintainability, testability, or extensibility—or even to improve performance.

Even though the term *refactoring* might lead some people to think of sophisticated practices, for the most part refactoring is the continuous performance of a few micro-operations. In addition, some of these operations are mechanically performed for you by ad hoc tools like ReSharper. Here are a few common refactoring operations:

- **Extract method**   Move a bunch of lines to a newly created method, thus making the original method shorter and promoting readability and code reuse.

- **Extract interface**   Turn the public methods in an existing class into a newly created interface. In this way, you promote interface programming and lower coupling between modules.

- **Encapsulate field**   Wrap a field in a class with a pair of getter and setter methods.

Refactoring also means renaming classes and methods throughout the codebase and moving classes to different namespaces. This is a delicate activity where code assistant tools really shine; without an automatic tool, renaming can really be painful. But renaming is critical to improving code readability, as you'll see in more detail in the next chapter.

In the end, refactoring can be summarized in two points. One is continuous code editing improves readability and design. The other is performing more ambitious restructuring aimed at making the existing code adhere to a specific pattern.

Defensive programming

As Murphy used to say, if something can go wrong, it will. And Murphy was not a software engineer. As developers, we know the pattern very well. We mentioned the Ariadne 5 disaster in Chapter 1, "Architects and architecture today." It all happened because developers didn't write their code defensively. Defensive programming is about making the software work in a predictable manner in spite of unexpected inputs.

Concretely speaking, defensive programming is all about carefully checking input data in each and every method you have and making it clear through documentation and other means what each method actually produces. This can be done in a couple of ways—an old way and a more modern and effective way.

The If-Then-Throw pattern

An old but good practice of software development recommends that you place at the top of each method—before any significant behavior takes place—a barrier of conditional statements. Each conditional statement checks a different condition that input values must verify. If the condition isn't verified, the code throws an exception. This pattern is often referred to as *If-Then-Throw*.

To be honest, we've heard If-Then-Throw labeled as a pattern, but we don't think a formal definition exists for that. Maybe we should simply refer to it as a practice? Anyway, it's not rocket science and is mostly about common sense. The idea is that the first lines of a method should be devoted to checking the validity of method arguments. In this way, if any invalid data is passed, you fail as quickly as possible without proceeding any further in the code. The application of this pattern is particularly important for constructors because it ensures that the state of the object is valid. You don't need to use the pattern for private methods because these methods can be called only from the class itself and likely from the same author. Here's an example: you pass every argument through a Boolean expression that ascertains whether the value is acceptable. If it is not, you just throw an exception:

```
public class Match()
{
    public Match(String id, String home, String visitors)
    {
        // If-Then-Throw implementation
        if (String.IsNullOrWhitespace(id))
            throw new ArgumentException("id");
        if (String.IsNullOrWhitespace(home))
            throw new ArgumentException("home");
        if (String.IsNullOrWhitespace(visitors))
            throw new ArgumentException("visitors");

        ...
    }

    ...
}
```

Extensive use of the If-Then-Throw pattern serves the purpose of evaluating the preconditions for a public method to run. It says nothing about the output generated and invariant conditions. At the end of the day, the If-Then-Throw pattern is a useful little thing especially if you apply it extensively to nearly any piece of data you receive from outbound calls.

For stricter and more effective control over the behavior of a class as a whole, you might want to look into something that Bertrand Meyer called *Design by Contract*. Design by Contract is an approach to programming based on the idea that each piece of software has a contract in which it formally describes what it expects and what it provides. The If-Then-Throw pattern nearly covers the first part of the contract, but it entirely lacks the second part.

Software contracts

Design by Contract describes the interaction between software components as a contract, where obligations and benefits are clearly expressed and enforced. Design by Contract isn't natively supported in any mainstream programming language. However, frameworks exist to let you taste flavors of it in commonly used languages such as Java, Perl, Ruby, JavaScript and, of course, the Microsoft .NET Framework languages. In .NET, you create software contracts via the Code Contracts library added to the .NET Framework 4.

In the implementation of a software contract—regardless of the syntax details—any time you write a class method, you should be sure you can answer the following questions:

- Under which conditions can the method be invoked?

- Which conditions are verified after the method terminates?

- Which conditions do not change before and after the method execution?

These three questions are also known, respectively, as preconditions, postconditions, and invariants. Let's go a bit deeper into software contracts using the .NET implementation—Code Contracts—as a reference.

Preconditions

Preconditions refer to the Boolean conditions that must be verified for the method to start its execution. Typically, preconditions set conditions on input parameters and the current state of the class that exposes the method. Conceptually, preconditions are the same as the If-Then-Throw pattern. Have a look at the following code excerpt. It comes from a class—named *Match*—that describes any team sport game with periods (for example, basketball, football, water polo, and so on).

```
public Match(String id, String team1, String team2)
{
    Contract.Requires<ArgumentException>(id.IsAlphaNumeric(IdLength, IdLength));
    Contract.Requires<ArgumentException>(!team1.IsNullOrWhitespace());
    Contract.Requires<ArgumentException>(!team2.IsNullOrWhitespace());
    ...
}
public Match EndPeriod()
{
    Contract.Requires<ArgumentException>(IsInProgress());
    Contract.Requires<ArgumentException>(IsBallInPlay);
    Contract.Ensures(!IsBallInPlay);

    IsBallInPlay = false;
    if (CurrentPeriod == LastPeriod)
        Finish();
    return this;
}
```

The constructor expressly requires that its *id* argument be alphanumeric and of the specified length. If it is not, it throws an *ArgumentException* exception. Similarly, team names must be neither empty nor null; otherwise, the same exception is thrown. *Contract.Requires<T>* is the .NET way to express a precondition and bind it to a custom exception if the condition fails.

There a few interesting things to notice here. First and foremost, you express Boolean guards in the positive way, whereas you have them in the negated form if you opt for the If-Then-Throw pattern. This works also as a form of documentation and as a guide for testers. Second, the syntax is particularly compact and custom, and if they are aptly named, functions can be used to keep the readability of the code high.

Preconditions on the constructor check only input data, but if you look at the method *EndPeriod*, you see that preconditions can also be applied to the internal state of the object. You can't call a period if game is not in progress and the ball is not in play.

Postconditions

Postconditions refer to the output generated by the method and the changes produced to the state of the object. A postcondition is a Boolean condition that holds true upon exit from the method. Managing postconditions manually can be cumbersome, but .NET Code Contracts really makes it a piece of cake.

Here's a short but illustrative example: the method *Sum* of a calculator class. Without preconditions, the method looks like this:

```
public Int32 Sum(Int32 x, Int32 y)
{
    // Shortcut exit (optimizing  2*x)
    if (x == y)
        return x << 1;

    // Perform the operation and return
    var result = x + y;
    return result;
}
```

The method has two exit points. If you want to manually evaluate a postcondition, you need to save somewhere the value being returned, pass it by the Boolean evaluator, and then decide whether to throw or return. Here's what the final code might look like:

```
public Int32 Sum(Int32 x, Int32 y)
{
    // Shortcut exit
    if (x == y)
    {
        // Perform the operation
        var temp = x << 1;

        // Evaluate postcondition
        if (temp <0)
            throw new ArgumentException();

        return temp;
    }

    // Perform the operation
    var result = x + y;

    // Evaluate postcondition
    if (result <0)
        throw new ArgumentException();

    return result;
}
```

Using Code Contracts the resulting code is surprisingly clean:

```
public Int32 Sum(Int32 x, Int32 y)
{
    Contract.Ensures(Contract.Result<Int32>() >= 0);

    if (x == y)
        return x << 1;

    var result = x + y;
    return result;
}
```

The *Ensures* method captures the value being returned and ensures it is not negative; if the value is negative, the method throws a *ContractFailedException* exception.

Invariants

Invariants refer to a Boolean condition involving members of the class that do not change during the execution of any public methods, including constructors and setters. Invariants are used in all those scenarios where it is essential to avoid leaving objects in a logically inconsistent state. Have a look at the sample *News* class:

```
public class News
{
    public String Title {get; set;}
    public String Body {get; set;}

    [ContractInvariantMethod]
    private void ObjectInvariant()
    {
        Contract.Invariant(!String.IsNullOrEmpty(Title));
        Contract.Invariant(!String.IsNullOrEmpty(Body));
    }
}
```

The *Invariant* method specifies that neither *Title* nor *Body* can be empty or null. Expand this to any set of business rules for a domain class—you have an easy way to ensure that your objects are always in a valid state. If some code that uses *News* sets, say, *Title* to null, immediately an exception for a contract violation will be thrown. More importantly, you don't have to write a single line of code to check invariants after any call of a public method. That's the magic of the .NET Framework Code Contracts implementation.

Note We regularly use preconditions and often postconditions. We find invariants to be sometimes too restrictive with their extremist, strictly no-compromise vision of the code. But that's just our experience, and experience sometimes comes out of the level knowledge of things you have.

Magic of .NET code contracts

In .NET, you express software contracts using a high-level syntax centered on a bunch of static methods out of the *Contract* class. However, the code that actually gets compiled is slightly different. If you use a decompiler (for example, dotPeek or .NET Reflector) to snoop into the code of the *Contract* class, you find that each method is nearly void and just throws an exception. Where's the trick, then?

An additional tool integrated into the build process of Visual Studio—the Code Contracts rewriter—does the trick of reshaping any code of yours that uses contracts, understanding the intended purpose of expressed preconditions and postconditions and expanding them into proper code blocks placed where they logically belong. In the end, the rewriter alters the output of the compiler and expands preconditions in an actual block of If-Then-Throw statements, moves If-Then-Throw blocks for postconditions to each detected exit point, and places If-Then-Throw blocks around invariant conditions past the invocation of each public method. All this work is transparent to you and performed as a post-compile step.

> **Important** For reasons we could never understand completely, the Code Contracts API is a native part of the .NET Framework. However, the rewriter is not part of the .NET Framework download. It is a separate download you can get through the Visual Studio Gallery extension at *http://visualstudiogallery.msdn.microsoft.com/ 1ec7db13-3363-46c9-851f-1ce455f66970*.

Summary

Especially in the past two decades, a lot has been done in the Information Technology (IT) industry to make a systematic approach to software development possible. Methodologies, design principles, and finally, patterns have been developed to help guide architects to envision and build systems of any complexity in a disciplined way.

In the beginning, we chased a disciplined way of coding for the sake of elegance and design. It soon turned into a more serious matter of survival and success-or-fail. We discovered that maintainability is king. If you can favor maintainability over everything else, well, that's the best deal ever and the most beneficial compromise you can get. With maintainability, you can have anything else. But why is software maintenance so expensive?

Maintenance becomes expensive if, for whatever reason, you produced unsatisfactory software, you haven't tested it enough, or both. More often than not, though, maintenance becomes the standard way of working because requirements are not laid out well, requirements are released frequently, and prototypes and frequent builds are requested. Which attributes make software easier to maintain and evolve? At the top of the list is structured design, which is best applied through proper coding techniques.

In this chapter, we outlined principles of software design, cataloguing them in universal principles, object-oriented design principles, and then SOLID principles and coding vectors. While principles address a general point, design patterns represent a more structured solution for a recurring problem. Taking code from its current state to a better state is the goal of refactoring. The ease of refactoring is the measure of how maintainable your code is. Every successful step of refactoring takes your project one step away from the "Big Ball of Mud."

In addition to structured design, code readability is another fundamental asset for code. Readability, as well as testability and extensibility, are aspects of code we address in the next chapter.

Finishing with a smile

Speaking of principles and software attributes, we reserved the spotlight for maintainability. Sometimes it seems that maintainability is used as an excuse to take dependency injection to its extreme: every class is an injectable component. Or any code you write is JavaScript-like.

See *http://www.murphys-laws.com* for an extensive listing of computer (and noncomputer) related laws and corollaries. Here are a few you might enjoy:

- An expert is someone brought in at the last minute to share the blame.

- If it seems too good to be true, it probably is.

- The probability of bugs appearing is directly proportional to the number and importance of people watching.

CHAPTER 4

Writing software of quality

As a system evolves, its complexity increases unless work is done to maintain or reduce.
—Prof. Manny Lehman

Nobody likes debt but, as harsh as it might sound, some level of debt in life is unavoidable. Technical debt in software is no exception. Abstractly speaking, *technical debt* is sort of a mortgage taken out on your code. You take out a mortgage every time you do quick-and-dirty things in your code. Like mortgages in life, technical debt might allow you to achieve an immediate result (for example, meeting a deadline), but that comes at the cost of interest that needs to be paid back (for example, higher costs of further maintenance and refactoring).

In Chapter 2, "Designing for success," we identified the most common causes of technical debt. It's a long list and includes looming deadlines, too early deadlines, and limited understanding of requirements. Sometimes it also includes limited skills, lack of collaboration, and inefficient scheduling of tasks. In addition, lack of awareness of any of these points delays taking proper action on your code and conducting fix-up procedures, thus letting technical debt grow bigger.

Back in the 1970s, Professor Manny Lehman formulated a few laws to explain the life cycle of software programs. At the foundation of Lehman's theory, there's the observation that any software system in development deteriorates over time as its complexity grows. Forty years later, plenty of software architects and developers have found out on their own that software deterioration is really a concrete force and must be addressed with concrete actions to survive software projects.

Lehman's laws and concepts, like the *Big Ball of Mud* and *Technical Debt*, all refer to the same mechanics that can lead software projects down the slippery slope of failure. Lehman formulated his laws a long time ago and mostly from a mathematical perspective. *Big Ball of Mud* and *Technical Debt* emerged more as real bites of life in the trenches.

In the end, we came to realize that all software needs to be maintained all the time it is used. Subsequently, a good piece of software is software that lends itself to being refactored effectively. Finally, the effectiveness of refactoring depends on three elements—testability, extensibility and readability—and a good number of relevant tests to catch any possible form of regression.

The art of writing testable code

For years, .NET developers relied only on debugging tools in Microsoft Visual Studio to ensure the quality of their code. The undeniable effectiveness of these tools made it worthwhile to combine two logically distinct actions: *manual* testing of code, and working around bugs to first reproduce and then fix them.

For years, this approach worked quite nicely.

In the past decade, however, a big change occurred under our .NET eyes: development teams became a lot more attentive to *automated* testing. Somehow developers figured out that automated tests were a better way to find out quickly and reliably what could be wrong and, more importantly, whether certain features were still working after some changes were made. Debuggers are still functional and in use, but mostly they're used to proceed step by step in specific sections of code to investigate what's wrong.

Automated testing adds a brand new dimension to software development.

Overall, we think it was just a natural change driven by a human instinct to adapt. The recognized necessity of testing software in an automated way—we could call it the necessity of applying the RAD paradigm to tests—raised another key point: writing software that is easy to test.

This is where *testability* fits in.

What is testability, anyway?

In the context of software architecture, a broadly accepted definition for *testability* describes it as the ease of performing tests on code. And testing code is just the process of checking software to ensure that it behaves as expected, contains no errors, and satisfies requirements. A popular slogan to address the importance of testing software comes from Bruce Eckel and reads like this:

> If it ain't tested, it's broken.

On the surface, that statement is a bit provocative, but it beautifully serves the purpose of calling people's attention to the ability to determine *explicitly*, *automatically*, and *repeatedly* whether or not some code works as expected.

All in all, we believe there's no difference between *testable code that works* and *untestable code that works*. We used similar phrasing in Chapter 2 while referring to poorly written code. Well, believe it or not, there's a strict relationship between well-written code and testable code: they're nearly the same thing. A fundamental quality of good code, in fact, is that is must be testable. And the attribute of testability is good to have regardless of whether you actually write tests or not.

At the end of the day, testable code is loosely coupled code that uses SOLID principles (Single responsibility, Open/close, Liskov's principles, Interface segregation, and Dependency inversion) extensively and avoids the common pitfalls of object-orientation, as discussed in Chapter 3, "Principles of software design." In particular, the Dependency Inversion principle in one of its two flavors—Dependency Injection and Service Locator—is the trademark of testable code.

Principles of testability

Testing software is conceptually simple: just force the program to work on correct, incorrect, missing, or incomplete data, and verify whether the results are in line with any set expectations. How would you force the program to work on your input data? How would you measure the correctness of the results? And in cases of failure, how would you track the specific module that failed?

These questions are the foundation of a paradigm known as *Design for Testability (DfT)*. Any software built in full respect of DfT principles is inherently testable and, as a pleasant side effect, it is also easy to read, understand, and subsequently maintain. DfT was developed as a general concept a few decades ago in a field that was not software. In fact, the goal of DfT was to improve the process of building low-level circuits within boards and chips. DfT defines three attributes that any unit of software must have to be easily testable:

- **Control**   The attribute of control refers to the degree to which it is possible for testers to apply fixed input data to the software under test. Any piece of software should be written in a way that makes it clear what parameters are required and what return values are generated. In addition, any piece of software should abstract its dependencies—both parameters and low-level modules—and provide a way for external callers to inject them at will.

- **Visibility**   The attribute of visibility is defined as the ability to observe the current state of the software under test and any output it can produce. Visibility is all about this aspect—postconditions to be verified past the execution of a method.

- **Simplicity**   Simple and extremely cohesive components are preferable for testing because the less you have to test, the more reliably and quickly you can do that.

In general, simplicity is always a positive attribute for any system and in every context. Testing is clearly no exception.

Why is testability desirable?

As we see things, testability is much more important than the actual step of testing. Testability is an attribute of software that represents a (great) statement about its quality. Testing is a process aimed at verifying whether the code meets expectations.

Applying testability (for example, making your code easily testable) is like learning to fish; writing a unit test is like being given a fish to eat. Being given a fish resolves a problem; learning to fish is a different thing because it adds new skills, makes you stronger, and provides a way to resolve the same problem whenever it occurs.

When DfT is successfully applied, your code is generally of good quality, lends itself well to maintenance and refactoring, and can be more easily understood by any developers who happen to encounter it. In such conditions, writing unit tests is highly effective and easier overall.

The ROI of testability

The return-on-investment (ROI) of testability is all in the improved quality of the code you get. Writing classes with the goal of making them testable leads you to favor simplicity and proceed one small step a time. You can quickly catch when a given class is becoming bloated, spot where you need to inject dependencies, and identify which are the actual dependencies you need to take into account.

You can certainly produce testable code without actually writing all that many tests for each class and component. But writing tests and classes together helps you to comprehend the ROI.

The final goal, however, is having good code, not good tests.

If you need to prove to yourself, or your manager, the ROI of testability, we suggest you experiment with writing classes and tests together. It turns out that the resulting tests are a regression tool and provide evidence that in all tested conditions (including common and edge cases) your code works. The tests also improve the overall design of the classes, because to write tests, you end up making the public interface of the classes easier to use.

Tests are just more code to write and maintain, and this is an extra cost.

This said, it turns out that testability is a sort of personal epiphany that each developer, and team of developers, will eventually experience—but probably not until the time is right for them.

Note The term *code smell* is often used to indicate an unpleasant aspect of some code that might indicate a more serious problem. A code smell is neither a bug nor a problem per se; it still refers to code that works perfectly. However, it refers to a bad programming practice or a less-than-ideal implementation that might have a deeper impact on the rest of the code. Code smells make code weaker. Finding and removing code smells is the primary objective of refactoring. To some extent, code smells are subjective and vary by languages and paradigms.

Testing your software

Software testing happens at various levels. You have *unit tests* to determine whether individual components of the software meet functional requirements. You have *integration tests* to determine whether the software fits in the environment and infrastructure and whether two or more components work well together. Finally, you have *acceptance tests* to determine whether the completed system meets customer requirements.

Unit tests

Unit testing consists of writing and running a small program (referred to as a *test harness*) that instantiates classes and invokes all defined methods in an automatic way. The body of each method instantiates classes to test and perform some action on them and then checks the results.

In its simplest form, a test harness is a manually written program that reads test-case input values and the corresponding expected results from some external files. Then the test harness calls methods on classes to test, using input values, and compares the results with the expected values. Obviously, writing such a test harness entirely from scratch is, at a minimum, time consuming and error prone. More importantly, it is restrictive in terms of the testing capabilities you can take advantage of.

The most effective and common way to conduct unit testing is to use an automated test framework such as MSTest (the one integrated in Visual Studio), NUnit, or xUnit. Here's a brief example of the code you need to write to test your classes with MSTest in Visual Studio:

```
using Microsoft.VisualStudio.TestTools.UnitTesting;
using MyMath.Model;

namespace MyMath.Model.Tests
{
    [TestClass]
    public class MyMathTests
    {
        [TestMethod]
        public void TestIfFactorialIsCorrect()
        {
            var factorial = new Factorial();
            var result = factorial.Compute(5);
            Assert.AreEqual(result, 120);
        }
    }
}
```

The test harness framework processes the class shown in the preceding code, instantiates it, and runs each of the methods labeled as *TestMethod*. Each test method performs some work on the classes under test. In the example, the test is conducted on the class *Factorial* to see if the method *Compute* produces the expected result when it is invoked with a given argument.

Note that unit tests run repeatedly most commonly as part of the build process. A test passes if the behavior of the tested class is the one you assert. For example, the following is another legitimate test that passes if the sample *BasketMatch* class throws an argument exception, but it fails otherwise:

```
[TestMethod]
[ExpectedException(typeof(System.ArgumentException))]
public void TestIfBasketMatchThrowsIfNullIsPassed()
{
    var match = new BasketMatch("12345", null, null);
    return;
}
```

This example, however, is interesting because it leads to a subtler point. Let's assume the code passes the test; is it guaranteed that it passed because the second or the third parameters were null? In theory, you might have a bug in the constructor that throws an argument exception if, say, the first argument is just 12345. In this case, the test passes but you missed a bug.

To be more precise, you should double the test and check independently whether the second and third parameters are null. Even better than that, you should check the parameter name of the exception being thrown. This feature is not natively supported by MSTest although some extensions exist that support this feature. One is SharpTestex, which you can see at *http://sharptestex.codeplex.com*. Using this syntax, you can rewrite the test as shown here:

```
[TestMethod]
public void TestIfBasketMatchThrowsWhenTeam1IsNull()
{
    Executing.This(() => new BasketMatch("12345", null, "Visitors"))
            .Should()
            .Throw<ArgumentNullException>()
            .And
            .ValueOf
            .ParamName
            .Should()
            .Be
            .EqualTo("Team1");
}
```

There might be various reasons why a test doesn't pass. In the first place, it could just be an error in the test. More likely, though, it's an issue in the class you test. In this case, you arm yourself with the debugger, slay the bug, and fix the code. Finally, it could be a matter of dependencies.

> **Important** How many assertions should you have per test? Should you force yourself to have just one assertion per test in full homage to the principle of narrowly scoped tests? It's a controversial point. Sometimes, the need for multiple assertions often hides the fact that you are testing many features within a single test. However, if you're testing the state of an object after a given operation, you probably need to check multiple values and need multiple assertions. You can certainly find a way to express this through a bunch of tests, each with a single assertion, but it would probably be just a lot of refactoring for little gain. We don't mind having multiple assertions per test as long as the code in the test is testing just one macro behavior.

Dealing with dependencies

When you test a method, you want to focus only on the code within that method. All that you want to know is whether that code provides the expected results in the tested scenarios. To get this, you need to get rid of all dependencies the method might have.

For example, if the method invokes another class, you assume the invoked class will always return the correct results. In this way, you eliminate at the root the risk that the method fails under test because a failure occurred down the call stack. If you test method A and it fails, the reason has to be found exclusively in the source code of method A and not in any of its dependencies.

It is highly recommended that you isolate the class being tested from its dependencies. Be aware, though, that this can happen only if the class is designed in a loosely coupled manner—for example, through dependency injection or a service locator. In an object-oriented scenario, class A depends on class B when any of the following conditions are verified:

- Class A derives from class B.

- Class A includes a member of class B.

- One of the methods of class A invokes a method of class B.

- One of the methods of class A receives or returns a parameter of class B.

- Class A depends on a class that in turn depends on class B.

How can you neutralize dependencies when testing a method? You use test *doubles*.

Fakes and mocks

A *test double* is an object you use in lieu of another. A test double is an object that pretends to be the real one expected in a given scenario. A class written to consume, say, an object that implements the *ILogger* interface can accept a real logger object that logs to Internet Information Services (IIS) or some database table. At the same time, it also can accept an object that pretends to be a logger but just does nothing. There are two main types of test doubles: fakes and mocks.

The simplest option is to use fake objects. A *fake object* is a relatively simple clone of an object that offers the same interface as the original object but returns hard-coded or programmatically determined values. Here's a sample fake object for the *ILogger* type:

```
public class FakeLogger : ILogger
{
    public void Log(String message)
    {
        return;
    }
}
```

As you can see, the behavior of a fake object is hard-coded; the fake object has no state and no significant behavior. From the fake object's perspective, it makes no difference how many times you invoke a fake method and when in the flow the call occurs. Typically, you use fakes when you just want to ignore a dependency.

A more sophisticated option is using *mock objects*. A mock object does all that a fake does, plus something more. In a way, a mock is an object with its own personality that mimics the behavior and interface of another object.

What more does a mock provide to testers? Essentially, a mock accommodates verification of the context of the method call. With a mock, you can verify that a method call happens with the right preconditions and in the correct order with respect to other methods in the class.

Writing a fake manually is not usually a big issue—for the most part; all the logic you need is simple and doesn't need to change frequently. When you use fakes, you're mostly interested in the state that a fake object might represent; you are not interested in interacting with it. Conversely, use a mock when you need to interact with dependent objects during tests. For example, you might want to know whether the mock has been invoked, and you might decide within the test what the mock object must return for a given method.

Writing mocks manually is certainly a possibility, but it is rarely an option you want to seriously consider. For the level of flexibility you expect from a mock, you need an ad hoc mocking framework. Table 4-1 lists a few popular mocking frameworks.

TABLE 4-1 Some popular mocking frameworks

Product	URL
Moq	http://github.com/Moq/moq4
NMock2	http://sourceforge.net/projects/nmock2
Typemock	http://www.typemock.com
Rhino Mocks	http://hibernatingrhinos.com/open-source/rhino-mocks

Note that no mocking framework is currently incorporated in Visual Studio, but you can find most of them easily available via NuGet packages. Here's a quick example of how to use a mocking framework such as Moq:

```
[TestMethod]
public void TestIfMethodWorks()
{
    // Arrange
    var logger = new Mock<ILogger>();
    logger.Setup(l => l.Log(It.IsAny<String>()))
    var match = new Match("12345", "Home", "Visitors", logger);

    // Act
    ...

    // Assert
    ...
}
```

The class under test—the *Match* class—has a dependency on an object that implements the *ILogger* interface:

```
public interface ILogger
{
    void Log(String msg);
}
```

The mock repository supplies a dynamically created object that mocks up the interface for what the test is going to use. The mock object implements the method *Log* in such a way that it does nothing for whatever string argument it receives. You are not really testing the logger here; you are focusing on the *Match* class and providing a quick and functional mock for the logger component that the controller uses internally.

There's no need for you to create an entire fake class; you just specify the code you need a given method to run when invoked. That's the power of mocks (and mocking frameworks in particular) when compared to fakes.

> **Note** Arrange-Act-Assert (AAA) is a common pattern for structuring unit tests. First, you arrange all necessary preconditions and set up input data. Next, you act on the method you intend to test and capture some results. Finally, you assert that the expected results have been obtained.

Integration tests

Unit tests are written by developers for themselves. They exist as a regression tool and to make the team confident about the outgoing quality of the software. Unit tests basically answer questions like "Are we doing well?" or "Are we on the right track?" or "Does it break other components?" The scope of unit tests covers a single functional unit of the system. The unit is likely a class, but not all classes reach the logical level of being considered a functional unit of the system.

Integration tests are the next level of testing—that's when you take multiple functional units and see if they can work well together. Integration tests, then, involve different parts of the system and test them in a scenario that's really close to reality. The goal of integration tests is to get feedback about the performance and reliability of individual components. Often, integration tests cross layers and tiers of the whole system and involve databases and services.

In unit tests, you test just one unit at a time, but how many components should you test together in an integration test? Integration tests take a much longer time than unit tests to be set up and run. And this set-up time is the same every time you run them. For example, imagine a scenario where you need a component to operate on a database. Every time you run the test you must ensure the database is in a coherent state that you must restore (or check at the very minimum) before you can run the test again.

To save time in integration tests, sometimes you take the shortcut of the *Big Bang* pattern.

In this scenario, all or most of the components are connected and tested, all at once. You configure the system in a user-like environment and push a typical workload on it to see how it goes. In this way, you certainly save a lot of time, but if something goes wrong you might be left clueless when investigating the issue. In fact, integration tests can reveal whether parts of the system work well together, but they can hardly tell you why they are not working—and sometimes, if many parts are involved, tests also fail to tell you which specific module actually failed.

As obvious as it might sound, planning integration tests is not easy.

First, you can't start until all involved modules are released, and modules won't be released until they are considered finished and working by respective owners. Typically, with integration testing, you risk starting quite late, at a time in which managers are under pressure and wish to rush, maybe just hoping that it will be OK. A better strategy (if you're allowed to follow it) is doing *bottom-up* integration testing, which basically consists of integrating low-level modules first and as early as possible. Each module might be just a little more than an empty box at this time, but with the help of some preliminary implementation of classes, you can see the big picture quite soon. Issues can be reported early, and fixing them can prevent other similar issues from appearing later.

> **Tip** Preliminary implementation here also means having classes with the right interface but no logic just returning canned data. It is interesting to notice how this is in line with one of the key Test-Driven Development (TDD) prescriptions: start developing your classes, writing enough code to pass the (unit) test first. If you do so, you also position yourself well for integration tests. We'll return to TDD in just a moment.

> **Note** One of the sore points of the *healthcare.gov* problematic startup was the lack of sufficient integration tests, which are highly critical in such as large, variegated, and distributed system. You just witnessed in the Big Bang approach to integration testing one of the most likely causes of the initial troubles. You can read an interesting and short analysis of the *healthcare.gov* story here: *http://bit.ly/1bWPgZS*.

Acceptance tests

Acceptance tests are the contracted tests you run to determine whether the fully deployed system meets your requirements. This is the only sure fact we know about acceptance tests. Who writes and runs the tests varies; therefore, the formulation of such tests also varies.

It's a common thought—mostly absorbed from Extreme Programming—that stakeholders and QA people write acceptance tests together, starting from user stories and picking the relevant scenarios to test. Each user story can have one acceptance test or multiple tests, as appropriate. Stakeholders take care of the positive side; QA takes care of edge cases. Finally, developers review tests to ensure that actual actions make sense within the deployed system.

An acceptance test is a black-box test. All that matters is the actual result you get; no knowledge of the internals is assumed. Acceptance tests should also work as regression tests prior to candidate releases and to detect breaking changes when a newer version is released. Sounds simple? Well, it's probably because there are a few points we left unaddressed.

In particular, how do you write acceptance tests?

In its simplest form, an acceptance test is a set of step-by-step instructions to be repeated against the fully configured system to observe outputs. To run acceptance tests often, you should find a way to automate them. This means that acceptance tests should be coded as programs whenever possible.

But if you expect stakeholders to write acceptance tests, which language should they use? How do you ensure that acceptance tests are in sync with all details of implementation? Should acceptance tests exist before or after the whole system is built? All these questions have no definitive answer, and most teams just follow the recommendation of Extreme Programming and define the implementation details on a per-instance basis.

An Agile methodology, Behavior-Driven Design (BDD) was proposed by Dan North a few years ago with the declared goal of tidying up the chaos surrounding all aspects of project development, including automated acceptance tests.

Behavior-Driven Design

BDD aims to define cyclic interactions between any involved stakeholders leading to the delivery of the final product. One of the pillars of BDD is the production of well-defined outputs from each inter-action. To enforce that guideline, BDD suggests you work around a number of statements that use a relatively high-level language at first. These statements are then further specified by developers up to the point they become actual code and form a concrete implementation of the system.

BDD statements are centered on three points: preconditions, action, and output. You can create these statements manually using any text editor and use them as the basis of acceptance tests. Better yet, you can do your BDD work within a tool integrated with your IDE so that you start with BDD statements and end up with code and all tests—unit and integration—you might need along the way.

A typical BDD statement looks like this:

```
Scenario: User is tracking the score of a water polo match
    Given The user on page /match
      And The match is fully configured
      And The match is started
    When The user clicks on Goal button on the left
      Then The system updates the match scoring one goal for Home
```

A BDD framework can transform such a simple statement into runnable code and tests. In Visual Studio 2013 (and earlier versions), you can use SpecFlow, which is available as an extension from the Visual Studio Gallery Extension. Visual Studio also comes with a few NuGet packages you can use to configure a test project to be BDD aware. For more information, check out *http://www.specflow.org*.

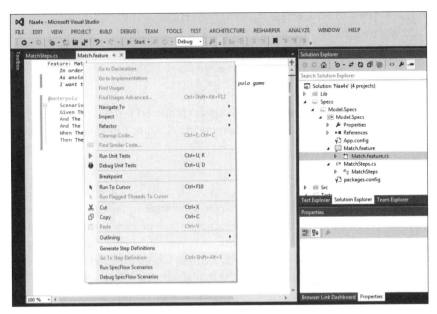

FIGURE 4-1 The SpecFlow extension in action within Visual Studio 2013.

When you're done with all Given/When/Then statements, all you do is run unit tests from the same context menu shown in Figure 4-1. Figure 4-2 shows a possible result.

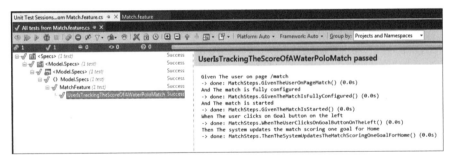

FIGURE 4-2 The results of running unit tests from SpecFlow tests.

Common practices of software testing

While everybody agrees on the importance of having tests in software projects, there are still a number of highly debatable points regarding testing that everybody resolves in their own way. These open points revolve around the role of the test, the time at which you write them, the quantity and location of tests, and more.

Let's briefly address some of them in the hope of clarifying things a bit. Our purpose here is to aggregate different positions, add our own annotations and comments, and generate an honest summary of facts and perspectives.

In other words, we're not doctors, so we won't write prescriptions!

Test-Driven Development

Test-Driven Development (TDD) is a process that leads developers to write their code starting from tests. For each class or method, a TDD developer starts with an initially failing test that represents the expected behavior. Then, iteratively, the developer adds code to the method or class to make the test pass and refactors the code to improve it, whatever that means. This refactoring includes adding more functionality, improving the design, improving readability, injecting dependencies, complying with guidelines of some sort, and so forth.

It turns out that TDD brings a few basic facts to the table:

- Tests are not the primary goal of TDD. Quite the reverse: tests are focused on letting the ideal design emerge naturally out of continuous refactoring.

- The ultimate goal of tests in TDD is not high code coverage but better design.

- Continuous refactoring is not optional. Refactoring is the substance of TDD much more than tests are.

TDD is one of those topics that divides people into two opposite and strongly opinionated (even fighting) camps. Many think that just because TDD is extensively based on tests, unit tests are the ultimate goal (and code coverage along with it). At a second glance, these people wonder where the benefits of TDD actually are, because writing silly tests for a basic method seems, well, just like a lot of overhead. Next, these people form the opinion that, well, tests can be added at a later time and only in the areas of code where you need them to be in order to catch regression. In the end, these people tend to be against TDD and sometimes say it is of little use.

As we tried to summarize in the initial bulleted points of this section, we feel that there's a common misunderstanding regarding TDD. Tests are the means, not the end. TDD, on the other hand, is a plain software developments process that is as good as many others out there. TDD is not a referendum on unit tests. To use the words of Robert C. Martin, "The act of writing a unit test is more an act of design than of verification." In the end, TDD is about design and just uses tests as the means to achieve good design. At the end of the process, though, you hopefully have well-designed code and, as a free premium, a bunch of tests with a high level of code coverage.

You must be well aware of the role of tests if you embrace TDD, and you must be similarly aware of the role of refactoring. You can't claim you're doing TDD if you stop at the code that makes any test pass. Refactoring is the tool you use to get better design.

Like any other process, in any field of the industry, TDD is not perfect. In particular, TDD involves a bit of work and continuous throwing away of tests and code. In a way, TDD never gives you the feeling that a class or a method is well done at some point, but this is the nature of iteration, after all.

Anyway, writing tests on the way to understanding code implies a change of mindset. Some companies force this change on developers.

Our opinion is that if you're looking for a large-scale improvement in code quality and the skills of individual developers, TDD probably is—all things considered—the best option because it gives you a step-by-step procedure: write a failing test, add code, make the test pass, refactor, repeat. Because your code must pass tests, you're led to loosen up its design, handle dependencies carefully, avoid static and global methods, keep classes lean and mean, always choose the simplest option—all things that make code better.

Can I write my tests later?

Because TDD is a plain software-development process, it's not a mandatory choice and is not the only safe way to clean code. You can design your code effectively using other, equally valid, techniques. When you have code, though, it's reasonable to say you need tests. If you don't do TDD—where tests are part of the process—tests become your end at some point. And you just write them when you need them and for the areas of code where you think they are required.

You can sure write tests after you write the code.

That's not necessarily good or bad; it's just a different software-development process. In this case, tests are for validation and regression and represent an additional item and cost in the project workspace. As such, it is an item (and a cost) that can be cut off in the face of looming deadlines or tight budgets.

In TDD, tests are an integral part of the software-development process. If you write code first and tests later when you need them, then tests and code are separate entities.

In the end, tests serve the purpose of validating code and catching regression. And these are fundamental aspects of modern code development. An interesting reading on the test-first vs. test-after debate can be found at the following site: *http://hadihariri.com/2012/10/01/tdd-your-insurance-policy.*

Should I care about code coverage?

The primary purpose of unit and integration tests is to make the development team confident about the quality of the software they're producing. Basically, unit testing informs the team whether they are doing well and are on the right track. But how reliable are the results of your tests?

In general, successful testing seems to be a good measure of quality if tests cover *enough* code; but no realistic correlation has ever been proven to exist between code coverage and actual software quality. And likewise, no common agreement has ever been reached on what "enough" means in numbers. Some say 80 percent of code coverage is good; some do not even bother quoting a figure. For sure, forms of full code coverage are actually impractical to achieve maybe not even possible.

Code coverage is a rather generic term that can refer to quite a few different calculation criteria, such as function, statement, decision, and path coverage. Function coverage measures whether each function in the program has been executed in some tests. Statement coverage looks more granularly at individual lines of the source code. Decision coverage measures the branches (such as an *if* statement) evaluated, whereas path coverage checks whether every possible route through a given part of the code has been executed.

Each criterion provides a viewpoint into the code, but what you get back are only numbers to be interpreted. So it might seem that testing all the lines of code (that is, getting a hypothetical

100 percent statement coverage) is a great thing; however, a higher value for path coverage is probably more desirable because it looks into actual code paths. Code coverage is useful because it lets you identify which code hasn't been touched by tests. At the same time, it doesn't tell you much about how well tests have exercised the code. Want a nice example?

Imagine a method that processes an integer.

You can have 100 percent statement coverage for it, but if you lack a test in which the method receives an out-of-range, invalid value, you might get an exception at run time in spite of all the successful tests you have run.

Code coverage and the Ariadne 5 disaster

As reported, back in 1996 the Ariadne 5 rocket self-destroyed 40 seconds after takeoff because of an overflow exception that went unhandled up through the code until it reached the self-destroy module, which told the rocket it was out of orbit and it was safer to destroy it. (The full story is here: *http://www.around.com/ariane.html*.)

Admittedly, we didn't take any look at the source code of the project. However, if the reports are correct we can easily guess that the code contained a method attempting the conversion of a floating point into an unsigned integer. We also have no idea of the code coverage for the project, but we assume you don't try to launch a $7 billion rocket without a good deal of tests.

No matter what the actual code coverage was, we'd say that a test checking a very large, out-of-range floating point value would have been easy to write and would have warned about the problem. Or such a text was written but its results were blissfully ignored.

Figure 4-3 shows the output of the code-coverage tool in Visual Studio 2013. As you can see, it's just numbers that mean very little without interpretation and context.

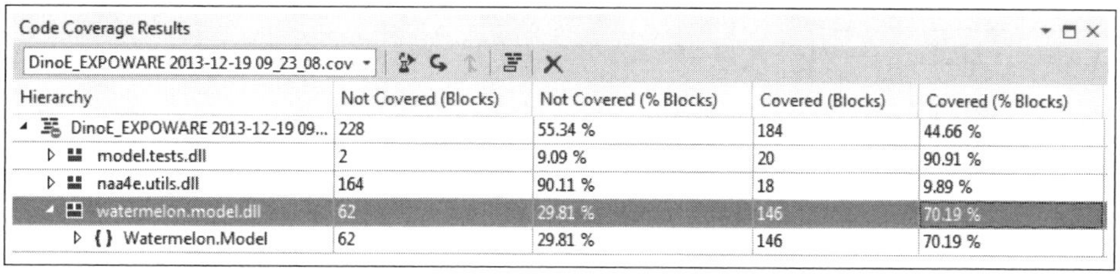

Hierarchy	Not Covered (Blocks)	Not Covered (% Blocks)	Covered (Blocks)	Covered (% Blocks)
▲ DinoE_EXPOWARE 2013-12-19 09...	228	55.34 %	184	44.66 %
▷ model.tests.dll	2	9.09 %	20	90.91 %
▷ naa4e.utils.dll	164	90.11 %	18	9.89 %
▲ watermelon.model.dll	62	29.81 %	146	70.19 %
▷ { } Watermelon.Model	62	29.81 %	146	70.19 %

FIGURE 4-3 The Code Coverage user interface in Visual Studio 2013.

In the end, code coverage is just a number subject to specific measurement. The relevance of tests is what really matters. Blindly increasing the code coverage or, worse yet, requiring that developers reach a given threshold of coverage is no guarantee of anything. A well-tested application is an application that has high coverage of relevant scenarios.

Which part of my code should I test?

In Figure 4-3, you get an average of 44 percent for the project, but coverage is fairly low in a utility library and much higher in a library that implements the model used by the application. Does that mean something?

As we see things, a utility library is a relatively static thing: either it works or it does not. If a function there is found to be buggy, it gets fixed, and that's it. If the utility you write there—say, a function that shortens strings and adds an ellipsis at the end—is quite generic and can be called from various places, you might still want to have some tests to exercise it, especially with edge cases. But unit tests are probably more relevant and extend to common cases and edge cases in the areas where the code does its business.

You can generically call it the *business layer* or, more specifically and in line with the vision of this book, the *domain layer*. You should focus your testing efforts where critical decisions involving the logic of the application are made. Figure 4-4 shows a typical workflow following a user action. The command passes through the application layer and results in a sequence of orchestrated calls to various pieces of the back end, including external services, the domain model, domain services, and the persistence layer. When a response has been produced, it is formatted back for the user interface. The shading in Figure 4-4 indicates the priority of testing, with the darkest shading indicating the items with the highest priority for testing.

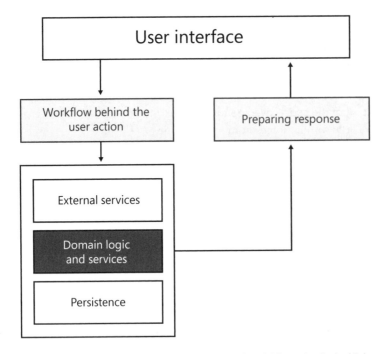

FIGURE 4-4 The darkest colors indicate the items for which testing is the highest priority.

The domain layer is the most complex part and the part most affected by requirements churn. Subsequently, it is the part where most bugs might manifest. Orchestration and adapters to and from presentation formats have the more mechanical parts of the application, and their behavior can be observed in many other ways: by code inspections, reviews, QA testing, and plain debugging.

As a more general rule, we'd say that you should prioritize tests for components consumed by a lot of other components, logical components where a deep understanding of the requirements is essential, and components owned by multiple developers. Don't blindly sit down and write tests, and don't force your developers into that. It's silly to have lots of tests that have no chance to ever fail.

Note When writing a unit test, you should know a lot of details about the internals of the unit you're testing. Unit testing is, in fact, a form of white-box testing, as opposed to black-box testing in which the tester needs no knowledge of the internals and limits testing to entering given input values and expecting given output values.

Automating the buildup of unit tests

Suppose you're not a TDD fanatic. At some point, you might just happen to have a C# class and no unit tests for it. Where would you start getting some? Because you wrote the code, you are the best person to determine what's critical to test. However, it's always too easy for humans to miss, skip, or underestimate an edge case, especially in a potentially large codebase. As a result, all tests might pass, but the code can still fail.

The Microsoft Pex add-in for Visual Studio can come to your rescue because it aims to understand the logic of your code and suggest relevant tests you need to have. Internally, Pex employs static analysis techniques to build its knowledge of the behavior of your code.

In addition, if you have parameterized tests in your test project, Pex can figure out which combination of parameters needs be passed to give you full coverage of possible scenarios. Finally, if you use .NET Code Contracts in your code, Pex will use that information to fine-tune the unit tests it suggests or generates for you.

In summary, Pex is an innovative white-box testing tool that can be used in two ways: as an aid to generate nontrivial unit tests, and as a peer reviewer who can quickly look at your code and find holes and omissions in it. You can download Pex from *http://research.microsoft.com/en-us/projects/pex*.

The practice of code extensibility

As mentioned by Dave Thomas and Andy Hunt, authors of the aforementioned book *The Pragmatic Programmer* (Addison-Wesley, 1999), all programming work is a form of maintenance. Only a few minutes after being typed for the first time, a class enters its infinite maintenance cycle. Most of the time, maintenance entails refactoring the existing codebase to patterns or just to a cleaner design.

However, under the capable umbrella of the term *maintenance* also falls the attribute of code extensibility—namely, extending existing code with new functions that integrate well with existing functions.

We can say for code extensibility nearly the same that Donald Knuth said of optimization: when prematurely done, it can be the root of all software evil. The ego of many developers is strongly stimulated by the idea of writing code that can be extended with limited effort. This might easily lead to over-engineering. A picture is worth a thousand words here: Figure 4-5 shows what we mean. The picture was inspired by the comic strip at *http://xkcd.com/974*.

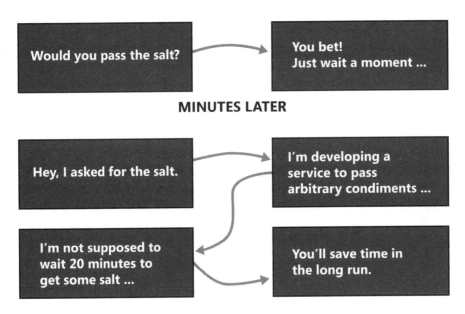

FIGURE 4-5 The general problem of over-engineering.

When the attribute of extensibility is fundamental, you might want to consider the following three aspects in your code: interface-based design, plugin architecture, and state machines.

 Important Most of the time, you need to find evidence that you need a more extensible and flexible design. The need for a more abstract and flexible design is the typical outcome of a refactoring session. A more extensible design can also surface in the early stage of sprints when you're about to implement a new feature.

Interface-based design

Interfaces represent a contract set between two software parties. When a software component—say, a class—declares it can handle a given interface, the net effect is that it can then work with any other component, either one existing today or to be written in the future, that exposes the same interface. This concept is at the foundation of extensible code.

The criticality of this approach is in the number of software components you should design with extensibility in mind. It's highly impractical to have all classes designed to be extensible and receive interfaces for every single piece of strategy they need to deal with. Failing on this point is what leads you right to over-engineering.

The challenge—and trust us, it is really a tough challenge—is just figuring out when extracting an interface from a strategy and sharing it between multiple components is something that really gives you more value.

Plugin architecture

When the word *extensibility* is uttered many just think of plugins. A plugin is an external component that adds a specific feature to an existing application that was not originally part of it. For this to happen, though, the host application must be designed in such a way it detects and handles plugins.

The host application dictates the programming interface of plugins, determines unilaterally what data plugins receive once they are loaded, and specifies when they are invoked and where they must be placed to be recognized. The host application also needs to have a special layer of code that handles the loading and unloading of available plugins.

There are many ways to write a plugin-based architecture. The substance of such an architecture is well summarized by the Plugin pattern as described by Martin Fowler. (See *http://martinfowler.com/ eaaCatalog/plugin.html*.) Your code at some point (called the *extension point*) uses a component to perform a given task. The task is abstracted to an interface or base class. The class uses an ad hoc layer to read from a centralized configuration the registered plugins, and it uses a factory to instantiate them. The canonical example of a plugin-based architecture is a website using an Inversion of Control (IoC) framework and having configuration centralized to a section of the *web.config* file.

When you have a plugin-based architecture, one problem you sometimes run into is sharing the state of the application with the plugins. The problem might not show if all plugins just work with data injected through methods at given extension points. If this plain approach doesn't work, you should consider centralizing the data model for the system so that all plugins have equal access to the data.

State machines

State machines are a common way to break complex tasks into manageable steps that implement some narrowly defined behavior. In its simplest form, a state machine is a *switch* statement. In a switch statement, you can easily add an extra case with related code. It's easy and effective.

Whenever you find an area of code that might expand to incorporate multiple tasks and cases, wrapping it in a state machine, or more generally in a sort of black box, is a good move toward extensibility.

Writing code that others can read

We're both watching our remaining hair turn gray, whichmeans we started writing code at a time when common people looked at developers as weird human beings—half scientist and half magician. We were all pioneers some 20 years ago, and we used to make a point—often just a funny point—of hiding our code from others. Not because we didn't want others to read our code, but just to prove we were smarter. So it was considered smarter to write code in a way that others couldn't read and understand.

This attitude might never have changed much over time if one of the key problems software architects face when working in a team is ensuring that code is understandable and written according to common conventions.

Do you remember the International Obfuscated C Code Contest (IOCCC)? If not, we suggest you visit *http://www.ioccc.org*. IOCCC is an open contest that takes place every year. Participants submit some working C code that solves a problem—any problem. "What's the deal?" you might ask. Well, the funny thing is that the winner is not selected because of an innovative algorithm, performance, compactness, or other common metrics. The only metrics that really matter is how obscure and obfuscated the C code is. You can find the source code of winning programs of past years at *http://www.ioccc.org/years.html*. Figure 4-6 shows the listing of one such program.

FIGURE 4-6 The source code of a program which participated to the IOCCC contest.

The code is guaranteed to work well, but it is quite hard to make sense of what it does.

Well beyond the fun of an obfuscated C contest, readability in programming is critical. If code that gets checked in is perfect and won't be touched anymore at any time, you could accept that it is written in an obfuscated manner. In any other case, other developers (and often the same developer who originally wrote it) might find it hard to understand the code because it was not written with good practices in mind.

We said and heard this a gazillion times; we know it. Yet, readability is often neglected—maybe not always entirely neglected, but neglected just enough to result in some extra waste of time (and money) when the existing code needs to be reworked or new people need to be trained on the internals of the system being built.

Readability as a software attribute

Maintainability is known to be one of the key attributes of software, at least according to the ISO/IEC 9126 paper. For more information, refer to *http://en.wikipedia.org/wiki/ISO/IEC_9126*.

Maintainability, however, results from various factors, one of which is certainly readability. Code that is hard to read is also hard to understand for everybody, including the author. Our friend Kevlin Henney recently wrapped up in the 140 characters of a tweet a juicy piece of wisdom about code readability. Kevlin tweeted that a common fallacy is to assume that authors of incomprehensible code will somehow be able to express themselves lucidly and clearly in comments, as a way to dissolve any lack of clarity about the code.

We couldn't agree more. Comments are part of the code, but it's not comments that significantly augment the readability of a piece of code. Comments are just like icing on the cake; comments are not the cake. Furthermore, comments might not be the type of icing you like to have on the cake.

Toward a commonly accepted definition of readability

If you're not completely convinced of the importance of having readable code, consider that any developers who put their hands on code they don't clearly understand are capable of making the code even worse. It's not simply a matter of aiming for the highest possible level of quality; it's purely a matter of saving money.

Unfortunately, readability is a very subjective matter and arranging some automatic tools to check and report the readability level of the code is nearly impossible. Anyway, we would bet the house that even in the quite utopian scenario of having automatic readability-measurement tools available, most people would simply consider them highly unreliable.

We dare say that readability is an attribute of code that developers should learn right at the beginning of their careers and develop and improve over time. Like style and good design, readability should not be reserved for experts and, more importantly, not postponed to when you just have enough time for it.

As a seasoned developer today, you know very well that you are never going to have enough time for anything but just writing the code. That's why good developers manage to write readable code "by default."

A matter of respect

Putting any effort into keeping code readable is primarily a matter of respect for other developers on the team. As a StackOverflow user posted at some point, you should always write your code as if the person who ends up maintaining what you write is a violent psychopath who knows where you live. Less dramatically, aim to make your code editable by any developer while you're offline and hiking in the middle of the Death Valley. In addition, you should not forget that the developer who ends up maintaining your code, one day, might just be you.

There's a nice story we can tell regarding this point.

Some years ago, Dino was looking for content on a well-hidden area of the Microsoft .NET Framework. Google and Bing combined could return only one article from some remote online magazine. The article was not completely sufficient to clarify the obscure points Dino was facing. So, a bit frustrated, Dino started complaining about the author of the article who didn't do that great of a job. But the author, well, it was *him*.

When reading other people's code, a couple of things usually drive you crazy. One aspect that makes reading code hard is the unclear goal of data structures and algorithms used in the code. Another is that strategies developers apply in the code are sometimes not so obvious to readers and not well clarified through comments. It seems the author is trying to kid you, as if she's participating in some obfuscated code contest. This is where good comments are required.

Readability is also about money

Imagine the following scenario. You have a large codebase written in Java and need to port it to .NET. If it sounds weird at first, consider that there are at least a couple of realistic situations in which it can really happen. One is when you try to port a native Android application to the Windows Phone platform. Another is when you are in the process of building a library for various platforms. Suppose you face some code like the following:

```
// Find the smallest number in a list of integers
private int mininList(params int[] numbers)
{
    var min = Int32.MaxValue;
    for (var i = 0; i < numbers.length; i++) {
        int number = numbers[i];
        if (number < min)
            min = number;
    }
    return min;
}
```

And then later on, in the same file, you find something like this:

```
var number = mininList(x, y);
```

As a margin (but not marginal) note, consider that no savvy C# developer would likely write similar code. In C#, in fact, you can rely on LINQ to reduce the code to one line or two. But let's assume that having such code is acceptable. There's more about it that should be said.

First, comes the name of the method. The convention used here is arguable: the name misses a verb and uses a mixed casing logic. Something like *GetMinFromList* would probably be a better name. Second, we reach the most debatable point of the *private* qualifier used in the declaration and the usage of the method within the class. Because it is marked private, the method is used only within the class; it's actually invoked only once and only to return the minimum of two integers. Even without using LINQ, a call to *Math.Min* would have done the trick.

When you encounter similar code, you can't avoid stopping and wondering why that code is there. It's not so much that you want to blame the author; it's only that you want to make sure you're not missing any critical part of it. The code represents potentially reusable pieces of code that can be called from a variety of places in the entire codebase. So marking it as private is total nonsense. However, if the method is used only once, why mark it as public?

Developers know very well the power of the YAGNI rule—*you ain't gonna need it*—and reasonably tend not to expose code that is not strictly needed. So it could be that the author of the code considered the function to be potentially reusable but not at the time it was written. That's why that function was written to be easily turned into a reusable helper function but marked private to be visible only within the host class.

In the end, it is not unlikely that the code resulted from some well-defined strategy. However, the strategy—if any—is hard to figure out for external readers. This is exactly the type of situation where a few lines of comments would clearly explain the motivation behind the decision.

When I encountered that code, it took me some time to first look a lot more carefully at it. Then I felt the need to contact the team to make sure I was not missing hidden points. Then I changed the implementation to use a plain LINQ call. It was quite a few years ago, but I was hired to port the code to .NET. In the end, the company paid for an extra hour of my time.

If you miss adding appropriate comments, you are not being a good citizen in the city of code.

Some practical rules for improving readability

Code readability is one of those topics whose importance is widely recognized, but that it is really hard to formalize. At the same time, without some formalization, code readability is nearly an empty concept. Overall, a sort of rule of the three Cs can be defined to define readability: comments, consistency, and clarity.

Comments

Modern IDEs make it easy to define institutional comments like a descriptive line for the function, parameters, and return value. All you need to do is think of the text to add and let the IDE do the rest. You should consider these comments mandatory, at least for any public piece of code you might have, and make the effort to write significant text for them.

Banning obvious comments is another fundamental point on the way to improved readability. Obvious comments just add noise and no relevant information. By definition, a comment is any explanatory text for any decision you make in the code that is not obvious per se. A good comment can only be an insightful remark about a particular aspect of the code. Everything else is just noisy and potentially harmful.

Consistency

The second "C" on the way to readability is *consistency*. Every development team should have guidelines for writing code, and it's best for such guidelines to be company-wide. The point is not about having good or not-so-good guidelines. The benefit is simply in having, and honoring, guidelines. The value of coding the same thing always in the same way is invaluable.

Suppose for a moment that you are writing a library that does string manipulation. In several places within this library, you need to check whether a string contains a given substring. How would you do that?

In the .NET Framework, as well as in the Java SDK, you have at least two ways of achieving the same thing: using the *Contains* or *IndexOf* method. The two methods, though, serve quite different purposes. The method *Contains* returns a Boolean value and just tells you whether or not the substring is contained in a given string. The method *IndexOf*, on the other hand, returns the 0-based index where the searched string is located. If there's no contained substring, *IndexOf* returns –1.

From a purely functional perspective, therefore, *Contains* and *IndexOf* can be used to achieve the same goals; however, they give a different message to a code reader and often force the reader to take a second look at the code to see if there's a special reason to use *IndexOf* instead of *Contains* to check for a substring. A single second pass of reading a line of code is not a problem, but when this happens on an entire codebase of thousands of lines of code, it does have an impact on time and subsequently on costs—the cost of not having highly readable code.

As a developer, you should aim to write clean code the first time and not hope to have enough time someday to clean it up. As a team leader, you should enforce code guidelines through check-in policies. Ideally, you should not allow check-in of any code that doesn't pass a consistency test.

Clarity

The third "C" of code readability is *clarity*. Code is clear if you style it in a way to make it read well and easily. This includes grouping and nesting code appropriately. In general, *IF* statements add a lot of noise to the code. Sometimes conditional statements—a pillar of programming languages—can't be avoided, but limiting the number of *IF* statements keeps nesting under control and makes code easier to read. Sometimes a *SWITCH* is clearer than many *IFs*. Code-assistant tools often offer to replace many consecutive IF branches with a single SWITCH. It's just a click or two away: you really have no excuses.

Some tasks might require a few lines of code, and it might be inappropriate to perform an "Extract Method" refactoring on it. In this case, it is good to keep these lines in blocks separated with blank lines. It doesn't change the substance of things; it just makes the code a bit easier to read.

These are just two basic examples of things you can do to make your code better from a purely aesthetic perspective. Finally, if you are looking for inspiration on how to style your source code, take a look at some open-source projects. Open-source software is written for many people to read and understand it. It might be a real source of inspiration, and you might want to extract your own guidelines from there.

Short makes it better

Have you ever wondered why newspapers and magazines print their text in columns? Well, there's a reason for that.

The reason is that long lines make it hard for human eyes to read. When it comes to code, you should apply that same principle and limit both the horizontal length of lines and the vertical scrolling of the methods.

But what is the ideal length of a method's body?

Absolute numbers that work for every developer and every project are nearly impossible to find. In general, we say that when you reach 30 lines, an alarm bell should ring. This length suggests it's time you consider refactoring. More generally, a limited use of the scrollbars tends to be a good statement about the style of your code.

Summary

In our opinion, the quality of code is measured against three parameters: testability, extensibility, and readability.

Testability ensures in the first place that the code is well articulated in distinct and interoperating components that are, for the most part, loosely coupled. This statement stems from the fact that you can write tests on your code. If you can do that, your code is componentized and each component can be tested in isolation. Finding bugs, and especially fixing bugs, becomes easier. When it comes to measuring the quality of code, unit tests matter. It's not so much because the code passes them, but because you can write them with ease.

In modern times, any code is written to be extended and improved. Maintaining code is the only known way to write code these days. This means that separation of concerns, loose coupling, and built-in mechanisms for extensibility and dependency injection are concepts every developer should master and apply. As a team leader, you should aim to improve all developers on your team on that count.

Anyone who raises the theme of code quality gets exposed to one common objection: writing clean code is hard and takes a lot of time. In other words, clean code is not a sustainable form of development for many teams. Clean code leads to losing productivity.

Productivity is more than important, but focusing on productivity alone costs too much because it can lead to low-quality code that is difficult and expensive to maintain. And, if it's hard to maintain, where's the benefit?

Finishing with a smile

See *http://www.murphys-laws.com* for an extensive listing of computer (and noncomputer) related laws and corollaries. Here are a few you might enjoy:

- Real programmers don't comment their code. If it was hard to write, it should be hard to understand.

- 90% of a programmer's errors come from data from other programmers.

- Software bugs are impossible to detect by anybody except the end user.

PART II

Devising the architecture

CHAPTER 5

Discovering the domain architecture

Essentially, all models are wrong, but some are useful.
—George P. O. Box

Software definitely stems from mathematics and is subject to two opposing forces: the force of just doing things and the force of doing things right. We like to think that software is overall a big *catch-me-if-you-can* game. Visionary developers riding on the wings of enthusiasm quickly build a prototype that just works. The prototype then becomes a true part of the business; sometimes what originally was just a prototype changes and expands the business. Next, more down-to-earth developers join in to analyze, stabilize, consolidate or, in some cases, rewrite the software as it should have been done the first time, in accordance to theoretical principles.

Software, however, cannot be constrained into too-formal and rigid theorems.

Software mirrors real life, and life follows well-known rules defined in the context of some model. Unfortunately, at some given time, *T1*, we find that our understanding of the model is in some way limited. At some later time, *T2*, our understanding might deepen and we become aware of extended rules that better explain the overall model.

That's how things go in the real world out there; but it's not always how we make things go in real software.

Software architects tend to restrict the solution within the boundaries of a fixed, top-level architecture. We have done it ourselves many times. If we look back, we find it is a common error to start defining some top-level architecture (for example, Client/Server, Layered Architecture, Hexagonal) and then use it everywhere in our business application. That approach might work in the end, but the working solution you reach descends from the wrong approach. It's a sort of technical debt you are going to end up paying at some point.

Because software is expected to mirror real life, as a software architect you should first understand the segment of the real world you are modeling with software. That segment of the real world is the business domain, and it might contain multiple business contexts, each calling for its own ideal architecture.

The real added value of domain-driven design

Domain-Driven Design, or DDD for short, is a particular approach to software design and development that Eric Evans introduced over a decade ago. The essence and details of DDD are captured in the book *Domain-Driven Design*, which Evans wrote for Prentice Hall back in 2003. The book subtitle transmits a much clearer message about the purpose of DDD: *Tackling Complexity in the Heart of Software*.

When it debuted, DDD was perceived as an *all-or-nothing* approach to application design. You were given a method, some quite innovative guidelines, and the promise that it would work. Using DDD was not actually cheating, and we dare say that it really fulfilled the promise of "making it work"—except that it works only if you do it right. Doing it right is not immensely hard; but it's also immensely easy to do it wrong. (See Figure 5-1.)

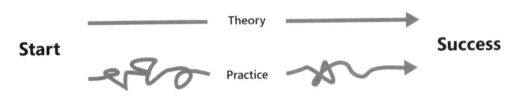

FIGURE 5-1 The DDD road to success is not always as smooth and easy as you expect.

What makes DDD so powerful but also so error prone? We think it's the *context*.

DDD is about crunching knowledge about a given business domain and producing a software model that faithfully mirrors it. The business domain is how a company conducts its own business: it's about organization, processes, practices, people, and language. The business domain lives in a context. Even very similar businesses may live in different contexts.

DDD is easy and powerful to use if you crunch enough knowledge and can model faithfully. DDD is painful and poor if you lack knowledge or fail to turn your knowledge into a model that fits the business domain.

What's in DDD for me?

However you want to frame it, DDD represents a significant landmark in software development. Not coincidentally, DDD initially was developed in the Java space, where the adoption of advanced design techniques (in the beginning of the last decade) was much faster and more widespread than in the .NET space. For many years, the scope and relevance of DDD was not really perceived in the .NET space.

Do we really need it? That was the question we are often asked and have asked ourselves many times.

DDD is not right for every project because it requires mastery and might have high startup costs. At the same time, nothing in DDD prevents you from using it in a relatively simple system. As we see it, the crucial point to using DDD is understanding where its real value lies and learning techniques to take advantage of it. The two biggest mistakes you can make with DDD are jumping on the DDD bandwagon just because it sounds cool, and stubbornly ignoring DDD because in the end you think your system is only a bit more complex than a plain CRUD.

In summary, we think DDD has two distinct parts. You always need one and can sometimes happily ignore the other.

DDD has an *analytical* part that sets out an approach to express the top-level architecture of the business domain in terms of bounded contexts. In addition, DDD has a *strategic* part that relates to defining a supporting architecture for the identified bounded contexts.

The real added value of DDD lies in using the analytical part to identify bounded business contexts. Next, the strategic design might or might not be leveraged to implement any of the bounded contexts.

Conducting analysis using DDD

The analytical part of DDD consists of two correlated elements: the *ubiquitous language* and *bounded contexts*.

The ubiquitous language is a vocabulary shared by all parties involved in the project and thoroughly used throughout the projects, ideally in all forms of spoken and written communication. As an architect, you typically populate the vocabulary of verbs and nouns as you acquire knowledge about the domain. This is the most common approach to starting to populate the vocabulary. More generally, you should also carefully look into adverbial phrases you find in requirements, because they might reveal a lot about the domain, such as events, processes, and triggers of processes.

The ubiquitous language is also the template that inspires the names and structure of the classes you end up writing. The ubiquitous language serves to improve and speed up the acknowledgment of requirements and simplify communication between parties so that they avoid misunderstandings, flawed assumptions, and botched translations when moving from one set of jargon to another.

Initially, there's just one ubiquitous language and a single business domain to understand and model. As you come to understand the requirements and explore the domain further, you might discover some overlap between nouns and verbs and find that they have different meanings in different areas of the domain. This might lead you to think the original domain should be split into multiple subdomains.

Bounded context is the term used with DDD to refer to areas of the domain that are better treated independently because of their own ubiquitous language. Put another way, you recognize a new bounded context when the ubiquitous language changes. Any business domain is made of contexts, and each context is shaped by logical contours. The primary responsibility of a software architect is identifying business contexts in a domain and defining their logical contours.

Context mapping is an expression often used to refer to the analytical part of DDD. Context mapping is a universal technique that can be applied to nearly any software scenario. Context mapping builds a high-level view of the domain from the perspective of a software architect. It shows subdomains and their relationships and helps you make strategic decisions.

Strategic model design

Coupled with context mapping is *strategic model design*. Once you identify the various bounded contexts, your next problem is determining the best architecture for each. DDD offers a recommended architecture in the form of the layered architecture and Domain Model. The term *domain model* here is subject to interpretation and deserves a bit of attention.

In the definition of DDD that Evans gives in his seminal book, the term *domain model* gives a nod to the Domain Model pattern formalized by Martin Fowler: *http://martinfowler.com/eaaCatalog/domainModel.html*. It consists of special flavor of an object model (also known as the domain model or entity model) and a set of domain service classes. More recently, the internal structure of the domain model is being reconsidered within the community. While seeing the domain model as an ad hoc collection of objects is still the most common perspective, a functional vision of it is gaining ground. Functional programming is, in fact, in many ways preferable to object-orientation for implementing tasks and expressing business concepts.

In the end, we can rephrase the whole thing today by saying that DDD suggests a layered architecture designed around a model of the domain. The model is mostly an object model, but it can be other things too—for example, a collection of functions. The persistence of data also depends on the structure of the model. It might require an O/RM tool if the model is a collection of objects; it might even be based on stored procedures invoked from idiomatic wrapper components if the model is, for example, function-based.

In the next chapters, we'll explore in depth the most common scenario for the domain model—when it takes the form of a special object model.

Note According to the original definition given by Evans, DDD is in a way the next natural step for developers versed in object-oriented design (OOD). The first principle of OOD recommends finding "pertinent classes," as you saw in Chapter 3, "Principles of software design." DDD recommends that you model the domain carefully—and that you model the domain carefully by discovering pertinent classes.

The phase of strategic model design consists of evaluating the various architectural options and choosing the architecture for each bounded context. Beyond the layered architecture, with a domain model there are usually other options such as a plain CRUD, a CMS (when the bounded context is expected to be a website), or even more sophisticated things, such as event sourcing (which we'll talk about in upcoming chapters.

Which parameters should drive your choice?

Overall, we think that today there's only one guiding rule, and it's based on the (carefully) estimated lifetime of the software you are about to write. Let's go through a few scenarios.

Fast-food applications

Suppose you are writing a short-term, one-off application such as a survey web application or some analogous set of pages aimed at collecting raw data for your analysts. You know that the expected lifetime is very short and that after the expected data has been collected the app will be bluntly dismissed.

Does it really make sense to invest more than the least amount of time that could possibly make it work? It probably doesn't.

So you can go with the quickest possible CRUD you can arrange, whether it is by using Web Forms, Silverlight, or plain HTML, depending on the skills and the target audience. If you are about to think something like, "Hey, I'm a senior architect, and no boss would pay my time for such trivial problems," well, you are probably just experiencing the power of bounded contexts already. Taken out of context, a fast-food application is undoubtedly a very basic—even silly—example. But it might be just one bounded context of a much larger and more complex domain that you, as a senior architect, helped to map.

Front-end websites

The project you're on requires a web front end. It has a sufficiently complex back end, where a lot of business rules must be taken into account and a bunch of external web services must be coordinated, but at the end of the day the front end is a plain set of read-only pages with zero or limited forms. The most important requirement you have for it is, "It must be shockingly cool and engage people."

Web Forms can be immediately ruled out because of its limited flexibility due to server controls. ASP.NET MVC is a much better option because it allows full control of HTML and can be effectively styled with CSS. Should you really go with an ASP.NET MVC solution from scratch?

Couldn't a CMS be a quicker and equally cool solution?

We can probably hear the same objections—it's a silly example for a book that claims to target software architects. Yes, but a software architect recognizes complexity where she sees it and doesn't create any unnecessary complexity.

You might know that plugins can extend a CMS, like WordPress, to do almost anything you can think of. It's not a far-fetched idea to just get a cool WordPress theme and a bunch of plugins, including custom plugins, to do the job.

Again, it's a matter of opportunity and skills. It's a matter of context.

Any other types of applications

As Thomas Edison used to say, the value of an idea lies in the using of it. So *make-the-code-just-work* is a common approach, especially in these hectic days of emerging ideas and startups. The *make-the-code-just-work* motto is fine if you don't need to touch the code once it's done and it works.

No matter what the customer might say and no matter what the current plans are, there's just one reason that any software avoids further changes: it gets dismissed. If the software is not expected to be dismissed in just a few months, as an architect you better consider a more thoughtful approach than just fast-food code. And Domain Model and the other supporting architectures we're slated to discuss in the upcoming chapters are the best options available for simplifying code maintenance.

 Note This is simply a gentle reminder that, not coincidentally, maintainability is both an OOD design goal and a class of requisites according to ISO 9126.

The ubiquitous language

Requirements are always communicated, but we all know that making sense of user requirements is sometimes hard. In addition, the inability to completely comprehend user requirements is probably the primary cause of misunderstandings between business and development teams.

As a way to mitigate the risks of misunderstandings at any time, Eric Evans suggested the use of a common language that he called the *ubiquitous language*.

Purpose of the ubiquitous language

We write software for a specific business, but we're software architects in the end and we might not be black-belt experts of the specific business domain. Likewise, domain experts might have some working knowledge of software development but probably not enough to avoid misunderstandings and incorrect assumptions.

Developers and domain experts often just speak different languages, and each group has its own jargon. Furthermore, it is not unlikely that different business people involved—say, from different departments—might use different jargon and give the same term different meanings. The language barrier might not preclude business from taking place, but it certainly makes any progress much slower than expected and acceptable. Translation from one language to another must be arranged; jargon expressions must be adjusted and put into context. This not only takes time, but it also introduces the risk of losing details along the way.

The purpose of the ubiquitous language is to define a common terminology shared by all involved parties—managers, end users, developers, and stakeholders in general—and at all levels—spoken and written communication, documentation, tests, and code. A common language reduces the need for translating concepts from the business to the development context, promotes clarity, and minimizes assumptions.

Once defined, the ubiquitous language becomes the official, all-encompassing language of the project.

Structure of the ubiquitous language

The ubiquitous language is not the raw language of the business, nor is it the language of the development teams. Both business and development language are forms of jargon, and both languages, if taken literally, might lack or skim over essential concepts, as well as generate misunderstandings and communication bottlenecks.

Figure 5-2 shows the canonical diagram used in literature to indicate the relationship between ubiquitous language and native languages spoken by domain experts and development teams.

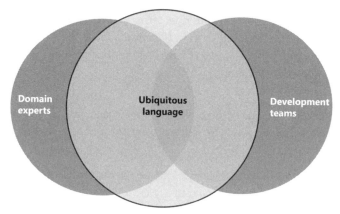

FIGURE 5-2 The canonical diagram that illustrates how the ubiquitous language unifies domain and technical concepts and extends them.

The figure shows that the ubiquitous language is a combination of domain and technical jargon. However, the ubiquitous language is expected to contain, for the most part, words and verbs that reflect the semantics of the business domain rather than technology terms.

It is not limited to the business jargon, however. While technical concepts like caching data, invoking a service, and deleting records of a database should not be part of the language, terms that indicate persistent actions, the response of the system, or notifications sent or received might be necessary to make the resulting language faithfully express the final behavior of the system.

The ubiquitous language exists in the subsoil of the domain. The architect must dig it out at the beginning of the project.

How to define the ubiquitous language

The ubiquitous language is not artificially created in a lab and then submitted for approval to involved parties. Quite the reverse—the language emerges out of interviews and meetings and gets its final shape iteratively along the way. It might take several steps of refinement and adjustment before the language flows as expected and faithfully expresses the reality of the system being built.

The first draft of the language commonly results from acknowledging requirements as architects rewrite and make sense of raw requirements collected during elicitation.

As a technical person, you should expect the language to be rigorous (for example, strictly unambiguous and consistent), fluent, and made of simple elements that can be combined to compose more sophisticated concepts and actions.

As a domain expert, you should hesitate to accept any terms and concepts the language might contain that are unknown in the domain and that are not clearly referring to a process or business concept. Also, as a domain expert, you should ensure that all relevant business terms are defined in the language and, more importantly, are given the right meaning. For example, if the language contains the term *account*, the term must refer to the meaning that *account* has in the domain space.

Note In general, the ubiquitous language contains business terms (nouns and verbs) plus new terms (mostly verbs) that more or less directly map to technical actions, such dealing with databases, cache and security, services and so forth. The number of nonbusiness concepts, however, should be kept to a minimum.

The ubiquitous language is the official language of the project, and the vocabulary of terms is inspired and then validated by domain experts. Everything in the project, from documentation to actual code, is permeated by the language.

How would you physically express and save the vocabulary of the ubiquitous language? In practical terms, it consists of a glossary of terms and expressions saved to a Microsoft Word or Microsoft Excel document or even some UML diagrams. Each term is fully explained in a way that makes it understandable to both domain experts and developers.

It should be the responsibility of the team to keep the glossary up to date throughout the project. The ubiquitous language, in fact, is anything but static. It can change and evolve over time to reflect new insights gained about the domain.

Important There are two main scenarios where the analytical part of DDD excels. One is when there's really a lot of domain logic to deal with that is tricky to digest, distill, and organize. Having a ubiquitous language here is key because it ensures that all terms used are understood and that no other terms are used to express requirements, discuss features, and write code.

Another scenario is when the business logic is not completely clear because the actual business is being built and the software is just part of the initial effort. Startups are an excellent example of this scenario. In this case, the domain logic is being discovered and refined along the way, making the availability of a ubiquitous language a great benefit to understand where one is and where the business can move forward.

Keeping language and model in sync

Naming and coding conventions used in the domain model should reflect naming conventions set in the ubiquitous language. This relationship should not vary during the lifetime of the project.

If the language changes because of a different level of understanding, or a new requirement, then the naming and coding conventions in the domain model should be updated. Also, the opposite is true to a large extent, in the sense that renaming a class or a method is always possible but doing so should require approval if the class or method is pervasive and the change affects a key term of the language. At the same time, it nearly goes without saying that if a given class or method exists only to serve implementation purposes, the constraint doesn't apply and you can rename it without restrictions.

Let's briefly look at an example that refers to the code we'll be examining in more detail in Chapter 8, "Introducing the domain model," and beyond. The domain is an online store, and the use-case we focus on is the placement of an order.

Each order is reasonably associated with a record in a table and with a column that indicates the current state. The order ID is used to track ordered items from another table. Processing the order requires first a check to see if there are pending or delayed payments from the same customer. Next, the process requires a check on goods in store and, finally, a call to the shipping and payment web services and the creation of a new order record.

Here's a more domain-driven way of expressing the same use-case. As you can see, the description is more concise and uses fewer technical details. The terms used should also reflect the jargon used within the organization. Here's an example.

As a registered customer of the I-Buy-Stuff online store, I can redeem a voucher for an order I place so that I don't actually pay for the ordered items myself.

There are a few business terms here—registered customer, order, order items, and voucher. There are also actions, such as placing an order and redeeming a voucher. All these belong to the ubiquitous language glossary. In particular, the term *voucher* here is the term used in the business, and once it is added to the ubiquitous language, nobody will ever think of using synonyms (such as coupon, gift card, credit note and so forth).

When coding the use-case, a developer will likely create a class to access the database table of orders, and instances of the order class will be materialized from the database and saved back there. However, these are just technical details that don't belong in the business context. As such, those details should be buried in the folds of the implementation, limited to technical meetings between developers, and never surface in official communication with business people.

This is the essence of the ubiquitous language.

Bounded contexts

In the beginning, you assume one indivisible business domain and start processing requirements to learn as much as possible about it and build the ubiquitous language. As you proceed, you learn how the organization works, which processes are performed, how data is used and, last but not least, you learn how things are referred to.

Especially in a large organization, the same term often has different meanings when used by different people, or different terms are used to mean the same thing. When this happens, you probably crossed the invisible boundaries of a subdomain. This probably means that the business domain you assumed to be one and indivisible is, in reality, articulated in subdomains.

In DDD, a subdomain in the problem space is mapped to a bounded context in the solution space.

A bounded context is an area of the application that requires its own ubiquitous language and its own architecture. Or, put another way, a bounded context is a boundary within which the ubiquitous language is consistent. A bounded context can have relationships to other bounded contexts.

> **Important** Subdomains and bounded contexts are concepts that sometimes appear to be similar and can be confusing. However, both concepts can be easily understood by looking at the difference between a domain and domain model, which is probably easier to grasp. The *domain* represents the problem to solve; the *domain model* is the model that implements the solution to the problem. Likewise, a *subdomain* is a segment of the domain, and a *bounded context* is a segment of the solution.

Discovering contexts

Without flying too high conceptually, consider a simple booking system. The front-end web site is certainly a subdomain. Is it the only one? Most likely, the system needs a back-office panel to put content on the site and perhaps extract statistics. This probably makes for another subdomain.

In the current draft of the top-level architecture, we have two candidate bounded contexts.

There are two additional aspects vital to investigate: the boundaries of each bounded context and their relationships.

Marking boundaries of contexts

Sometimes it's relatively easy to split a business domain into various subdomains, each representing a bounded context to render with software.

But is it splitting or is it partitioning? There is a huge difference between the two.

In the real world, you don't often see business domains that can be easily partitioned in child domains with nearly no overlapping functions and concepts. So in our experience, it is more a case of splitting than just partitioning. The problems with splitting a business domain are related to marking the boundaries of each context, identifying areas of overlap, and deciding how to handle those areas.

As mentioned, the first concrete clue that you have a new subdomain is when you find a new term used to express a known concept or when the same term is found to have a second meaning. This indicates some overlapping between subdomains. (See Figure 5-3.)

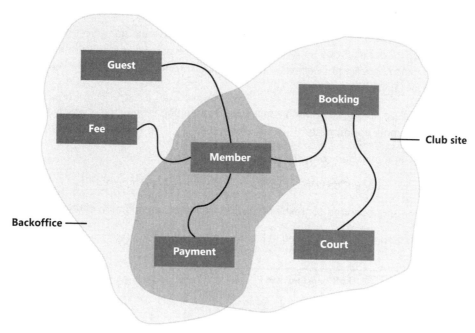

FIGURE 5-3 Two business contexts with some overlapping.

The business domain is made of a subdomain (say, *club site*) that, among other features, offers the booking of courts. The booking of courts involves members and payments. The back office is a distinct but related subdomain. Both subdomains deal with members and payments, even though each has a different vision of them.

The first decision to be made is whether you need to treat those subdomains separately and, if so, where you draw the boundaries.

Splitting a domain into bounded contexts

Working on a single, all-encompassing model is always dangerous, and the level of complexity grows as the number of entities and their relationships grow. The resulting graph can be crowded; entities and related code can become quite coupled, and it doesn't take much to serve up the perfect Big Ball of Mud.

Splitting is always a good idea, especially when this leads you to creating software subsystems that reflect the structure of the organization. The back-office system, for example, will be used by different people than the club site.

Let's say you go for distinct bounded contexts.

How would you deal with overlapping logic? The concept of "club member" exists in both contexts, but in the back-office context the club member has nearly no behavior and is a mere container of personal and financial data. In the club-site context, on the other hand, the member has some specific behaviors because she can book a court or add herself to an existing booking. For doing so, the *Member* entity will just need an ID, user name, and possibly an email address.

In general, having a single, shared definition of an entity will have the side effect of padding the definition with details that might be unnecessary in some of the other contexts. With reference to Figure 5-3, family members are not necessary to book a court from the club site, but they are relevant to calculating the yearly fee.

The fundamental point to resolve when conceptual overlapping is detected is which of the following options is more appropriate:

- A single bounded context that includes all entities

- A distinct bounded context with a shared kernel of common entities

- A distinct bounded context with distinct definitions of common entities

The options are graphically summarized in Figure 5-4.

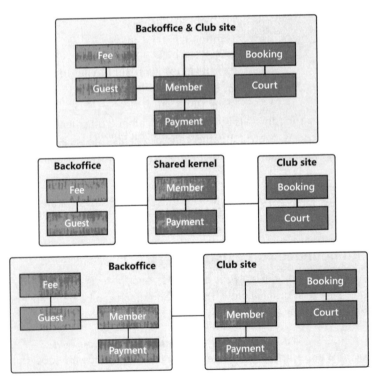

FIGURE 5-4 Resolving the conceptual overlapping of contexts.

There's also a fourth option. Is the entire model entirely inadequate and in need of refinement so that in the end you can have partitions instead of subsets?

That's what it means to mark the boundaries of bounded contexts.

By the way, it's not us dodging the issue by not taking a clear stand on a particular option. It's that, well, it just depends. It depends on other information about the domain. It depends on time and budget. It depends on skills. It also depends on your personal view of the domain.

That's what makes it so fun to mark the boundaries of bounded contexts.

Bounded context and the organization

The number of contexts and relationships between bounded contexts often just reflect the physical organization of the enterprise. It is common to have a bounded context for each business department such as human resources, accounting, sales, inventory, and the like.

Different development teams are typically assigned to each bounded context, and different artifacts are generally produced, scheduled, and maintained.

The overlapping of concepts is quite natural in business domains; speaking in general, the best way to handle such overlapping is to use different bounded contexts, as shown in the third option of Figure 5-4.

Just sharing entities between development teams, as a common kernel, might prefigure risky scenarios, where changes of team 1 might break the code of team 2 and compromise the integrity of the model. Shared kernels work great if an effective shared kernel exists—such as different organizations just using the same entities.

Otherwise, it's the first step toward a true mess.

Context mapping

Bounded contexts are often related to each other. In DDD, a *context map* is the diagram that provides a comprehensive view of the system being designed. In the diagram, each element represents a bounded context. The diagrams in Figure 5-4 are actually all examples of a context map.

Relational patterns

Connections between elements of a context map depict the relationship existing between bounded contexts. DDD defines a few relational patterns.

Relational patterns identify an *upstream* context and *downstream* context. The upstream context (denoted with a *u*) is the context that influences the downstream and might force it to change. Denoted with *d*, the downstream context is passive and undergoes changes on the upstream context. Table 5-1 lists DDD relational patterns.

TABLE 5-1 DDD relational patterns

DDD relational pattern	Description
Anticorruption layer (ACL)	Indicates an extra layer of code that hides to the downstream context any changes implemented at some point in the upstream context. More on this later.
Conformist	The downstream context just passively conforms to whatever model the upstream context comes up with. Typically, the conformist pattern is a lighter approach than ACL and the downstream context also receives data it might not need.
Customer/Supplier	Two contexts are in a classic upstream/downstream relationship, where the supplier is the upstream. The teams, however, work together to ensure that no unnecessary data is sent. This aspect marks the difference with Conformist.
Partnership	Two contexts are developed independently; no code is shared, but both contexts are upstream and downstream at the same time. There's a sort of mutual dependency between the two, and one can't just ignore the other for delivery and change.
Shared kernel	Two contexts share a subset of the model. Contexts are therefore tightly coupled, and no team can change the shared kernel without synchronizing with the other team.

Figure 5-5 is the graphical representation of a context map. Each block represents a bounded context. The Sales block is connected to the upstream External Service block, and an ACL ensures that changes in the service don't force changes in the Sales context. The upstream and downstream contexts are labeled with the *u* and *d* marks.

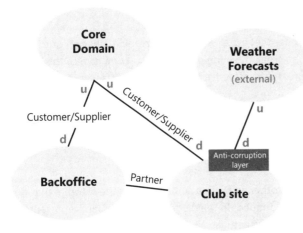

FIGURE 5-5 A sample context map showing some of the DDD relational patterns.

Context mapping is part of the strategic design of the solution. It doesn't produce code or deployable artifacts, but it can be immensely helpful to grab a better understanding of the system.

Note Many DDD experts advise that because software ultimately mirrors the structure of business organizations, a context map should ideally reflect the organization of the enterprise. Sometimes, it turns out that the ideal context map for the system to build doesn't actually reflect the real organization. When this happens—and it does happen— well, things are not going to be easy!

Anticorruption layers

Relationships between bounded contexts pose the problem of how the development of one context influences the other over time. The safest way of dealing with related contexts is by creating an anticorruption layer (ACL).

It's the safest way because all the changes required to keep the contexts in sync when one undergoes changes are isolated in the anticorruption layer, as shown in Figure 5-6.

FIGURE 5-6 The anticorruption layer is an interfacing layer that separates two connected contexts.

The interface that the ACL exposes to the downstream context (the club site in this case) is an invariant. The ACL, in fact, absorbs the changes in the upstream context (Weather Forecasts service in this case) and does any conversion work that might be required. Updating the ACL when the upstream context changes usually requires less work and is less obtrusive than updating the club-site context.

The ACL is particularly welcome when one of the bounded contexts encapsulates a chunk of legacy code or just an external service that none of the teams building the system has control over.

Giving each context its own architecture

Each bounded context is a separate area of the overall application. You are forced to use DDD strategic modeling to implement each bounded context, and not only because you identified the bounded context using a DDD methodology. As an architect, you should validate the context map and then focus on each context separately.

For example, the Core Domain area of the application might be implemented using a Domain Model approach. The club-site context can be an ASP.NET MVC application with a layered back end that uses an application layer on top of MVC controllers. The application layer uses services in the Core Domain context for changing the state of the application. Finally, a simpler subsystem like Back Office can be efficiently given a data-driven design and result in a simple two-layer architecture with only presentation and data access. (Concretely, this could be a Web Forms application using DataGrids.)

Another option might be separating the front end of the club site from, say, the booking module. You could use ASP.NET MVC for the booking module and a CMS (for example, WordPress) for the few pages with news, photos, and static content.

Mixing multiple supporting architectures in the realm of a single system is far from wrong.

Common supporting architectures

The process of identifying business contexts already reveals a lot about the nature of the domain and subdomains. To an expert eye that knows about technologies and frameworks, a good candidate solution appears immediately for a given context.

Just as a quick glossary, Table 5-2 lists the most commonly used supporting architectures you might find in the industry.

TABLE 5-2 A list of supporting architectures.

Supporting architecture	Brief description
Multilayer architecture	Canonical segmentation based on presentation, business, and data layers. The architecture might come in slightly different flavors, such as an additional application layer between the presentation and business layers and with the business layer transformed into a domain layer by the use of a DDD development style. Layered architecture is just another name for a multilayer architecture. We'll be using the term layered architecture instead of multilayer in the rest of this chapter and throughout the book.
Multitier architecture	Segmentation that is in many ways similar to that of a multilayer architecture except that now multiple tiers are involved instead of layers. (More on the possible downsides of a layer-to-tier mapping in a moment.)
Client/server architecture	Classic two-layer (or two-tier) architecture that consists only of presentation plus data access.
Domain Model	Layered architecture based on a presentation layer, an application layer, a domain layer, and an infrastructure layer, designed in accordance with the DDD development style. In particular, the model is expected to be a special type of object model.
Command-Query Responsibility Segregation (CQRS)	Two-fold layered architecture with parallel sections for handling command and query sides. Each section can be architected independently, even with a separate supporting architecture, whether that is DDD or client/server.
Event sourcing	Layered architecture that is almost always inspired by a CQRS design that focuses its logic on events rather than plain data. Events are treated as first-class data, and any other queryable information is inferred from stored events.
Monolithic architecture	The context is a standalone application or service that exposes an API to the rest of the world. Typical examples are autonomous web services (for example, Web API host) and Windows services. Yet another example is an application hosting a SignalR engine.

As we write this chapter, another architectural style is gaining in popularity: *micro-services*. At first, micro-services don't sound like a completely new idea and are not really presented like that. There's a lot of service-oriented architecture (SOA) in micro-services, such as the fact that services are autonomous and loosely coupled. However, micro-services also explicitly call out for lightweight HTTP mechanisms for communication between processes. For more information on micro-services, you can check out the Martin Fowler's site at *http://martinfowler.com/articles/microservices.html*.

The reason why we mention micro-services here is that, abstractly speaking, the overall idea of micro-services weds well with identifying business contexts, discovering relationships, and giving each its own architecture and autonomous implementation. Micro-services, therefore, can be yet another valid entry in Table 5-2.

Layers and tiers might not be interchangeable

Layers and tiers are not the same. A *layer* is a logical container for different portions of code; a *tier* is a physical container for code and refers to its own process space or machine. All layers are actually deployed to a physical tier, but different layers can go to different tiers.

That's precisely the point we want to raise here.

In Table 5-2, we listed multilayer architecture and multitier architecture. Admittedly, they look the same except that one separates blocks of code logically and the other physically. We suggest, however, that you consider those architectures as different options to be evaluated individually to see if they fit in the solution.

The error that many system integrators made in the past was to deploy a multilayer architecture as a multitier architecture. In doing so, they matched layers to tiers one-to-one. This led to segregating in different tiers the presentation layer of a Web Forms application and the business layer using WCF, Web services or even, in the old days, .NET Remoting. It apparently looked like a better architecture, but it created latency between tiers and had a deep impact on the performance of the system. In addition, system maintenance (for example, deploying updates) is harder and more expensive in a multitier scenario.

Tiers are heavy but can be used to scale the application. However, just having tiers doesn't automatically ensure your application is faster. Generally speaking, we tend to prefer the deployment of the entire application stack on a single tier, if that's ever possible.

The layered architecture

In the rest of this chapter, we'll provide an overview of the layered architecture—the multilayer architecture introduced in Evans' book about DDD. The layered architecture is probably the most common type of architecture that results from DDD analysis.

Origins of the layered architecture

In the 1990s, most computing scenarios consisted of one insanely powerful server (at least for the time it was) and a few far slower personal computers. Software architecture was essentially client/server: the client focused on data presentation and commands, and the server mostly implemented persistence. Any business logic beyond basic CRUD (Create, Read, Update, Delete) was stuffed in stored procedures to further leverage the capacity of the insanely powerful server machine.

Over the years, we all managed to take larger and larger chunks of the business logic out of stored procedures and place them within new components. This originated the classic (up to) three-segment model, which is shown in Figure 5-7. Note that the figure also shows a direct connection between the presentation and data layers in memory of SQL data binding.

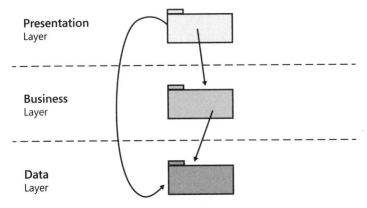

FIGURE 5-7 The classic three-segment architecture.

Note that we're using the term *segment* here as a general way to interchangeably refer to both tiers and layers.

From what we have seen, learned, and done ourselves, we'd say that the largest share of systems inspired by the three-segment architecture is actually implemented as a layered system deployed on two physical tiers. For a website, for example, one tier is the ASP.NET application running within the Internet Information Services (IIS) process space and another was the Microsoft SQL Server service providing data. (See Figure 5-8.)

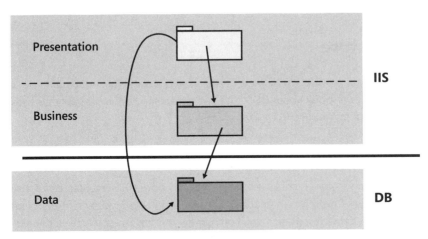

FIGURE 5-8 Common deployment of a multilayer ASP.NET application.

For the most part, the data model of any three-segment architecture is the relational data model of the data store. The growing complexity of applications has led developers to a more conceptual view of that data. As patterns like the *Domain Model* and approaches like Domain-Driven Design (DDD) were developed and exercised, the internal structure of a layered architecture evolved quite a bit. (See Figure 5-9.)

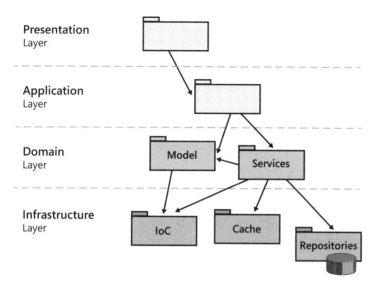

FIGURE 5-9 A more modern version of a layered architecture.

Roughly speaking, the presentation layer is the same in both architectures and the infrastructure layer includes the data layer of Figure 5-7 but is not limited to that. The infrastructure layer, in general, includes anything related to any concrete technologies: data access via O/RM tools, implementation of IoC containers, and the implementation of many other cross-cutting concerns such as security, logging, caching, and more.

The business layer exploded into the application and domain layer. Upon a more thoughtful look, the layered architecture of Figure 5-9 results from a better application of the *separation of concerns* (SoC) principle. In systems inspired by the schema of Figure 5-7, the actual business logic is sprinkled everywhere, mostly in the business logic but also in the presentation and data layers.

The layered architecture of Figure 5-9 attempts to clear up such gray areas.

> **Note** Repositories are generally placed in the domain layer as far as their interfaces are concerned. The actual implementation, however, usually belongs to the infrastructure layer.

Presentation layer

The presentation layer is responsible for providing some user interface (UI) to accomplish any tasks. Presentation is a collection of screens; each screen is populated by a set of data and any action that starts from the screen forwards another well-defined set of data.

Generally speaking, we'll refer to any data that populates the presentation layer as the *view model*. We'll refer to any data that goes out of the screen triggering a back-end action as the *input model*. Although a logical difference exists between the two models, most of the time the view model and input model coincide. (See Figure 5-10.)

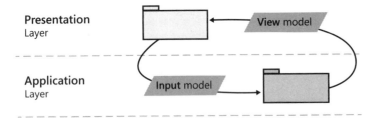

FIGURE 5-10 Describing the data that goes into and out of presentation screens.

Application layer

As we see it, the application layer is an excellent way to separate interfacing layers such as presentation and domain. In doing so, the application layer contributes immensely to the clarity of the entire design. In the past, a typical gray area of many architectures was the placement of the part of the business code that needed to be aware of the presentation.

The application layer is the additional layer that reports to the presentation and orchestrates any further business action. The application layer is where you orchestrate the implementation of use-cases.

Entry point in the system's back end

Each interactive element of the user interface (for example, buttons) triggers an action in the back end of the system. In some simple scenarios, the action that follows some user's clicking takes just one step to conclude. More realistically, instead, the user's clicking triggers something like a workflow.

According to Figure 5-9, the application layer is the entry point in the back end of the system and the point of contact between the presentation and back end. The application layer consists of methods bound in an almost one-to-one fashion to the use-cases of the presentation layer. Methods can be grouped in any way that makes sense to you.

For example, in an ASP.NET MVC application, we expect the application layer classes to go hand in hand with controllers. The *HomeController* class, therefore, will have injected some *HomeControllerService* worker class. Here's a quick sample:

```
public class HomeController
{
    private readonly IHomeControllerService _service;
    public HomeController(IHomeControllerService service)
    {
        _service = service;
    }
    public ActionResult Index()
    {
        var model = _service.FillHomePage( /* input model */ );
        return View(model);
    }
    ...
}
```

The mechanism of injection can happen at your leisure. It can happen via Unity or any other Inversion of Control (IoC) container, or it can be done through poor man's dependency injection, as shown here:

```
public class HomeController
{
    private readonly IHomeControllerService _service;
    public HomeController() : this(new HomeControllerService())
    {
    }
    public HomeController(IHomeControllerService service)
    {
        _service = service;
    }
}
```

In a nutshell, the application layer is responsible for the implementation of the application's use-cases. All it does is orchestrate tasks and delegate work to other layers down the stack.

We think there can be two flavors of an application layer: inside or outside the business logic. Neither is preferable to the other; it's all about how you envision the system.

Orchestrating the business logic

In general, the application layer is bound one-to-one to the presentation with the notable exception of unattended systems. The structure of the layer is driven by the actionable controls in the various user interface screens. With reference to Figure 5-5, this flavor of application layer lives in the club-site context and orchestrates workflows involving components in the Core Domain and external services. Key aspects of this application layer are these:

- It might or might not be consumable by different front ends because, for example, a mobile front end might have slightly different use-cases than the web front end or ends.

- It can be stateful at least as far the progress of a UI task is concerned.

- It gets its input from the presentation and sends a view model back as shown in Figure 5-10.

The application layer holds references to the domain layer and infrastructure layer. Finally, the application layer has no knowledge of business rules and doesn't hold any business-related state information.

As the name suggests, the application layer is just application specific. If our aforementioned booking system must be consumed by a website and a mobile application, we're going to have two distinct application layers—one on the site and one either within the mobile application or exposed as an HTTP service. Are these layers actually different?

Well, they might be different; and if they're different, different layers should be implemented. To continue with the booking example, the application layer of the website might redirect to the credit card site to pay and then proceed with the persistence of the booking data. The application layer of the mobile app might use in-app payment features or just use stored payment information and pass them along in some way to the domain layer.

> **Note** The DDD jargon uses the term *application services* to refer to services that sit atop the domain layer and orchestrate business use-cases.

Domain layer

The domain layer hosts the entire business logic that is not specific to one or more use-cases. In other words, the domain layer contains all business logic that remains once you have compiled the application layer.

The domain layer consists of a model (known as the *domain model*) and possibly a family of services. The nature of the model can vary. Most of the time, it is an entity-relationship model, but it can be made of functions too. Let's stick to what appears to be the most common scenario. So let's say that at the end of the day an *entity model* is an object model.

However, in an entity model, constituent classes usually follow certain conventions. We'll return in detail to domain modeling and DDD conventions for entities in upcoming chapters. For now, it suffices to say that entities in the model are expected to expose both data and behavior. A model with entities devoid of any significant behavior—that is, merely data structures—form an *anemic domain model*.

The ultimate goal of a domain model is to implement the ubiquitous language and express the actions that business processes require. In this regard, exposing some behavior tends to be more relevant than holding some data.

Along with an entity model, the domain model layer features domain services.

Domain services are pieces of domain logic that, for some reason, don't fit into any of the existing entities. A domain service is a class, and it groups logically related behaviors that typically operate on multiple domain entities. A domain service often also requires access to the infrastructure layer for read/write operations. In the aforementioned club-site context, a domain service can be the code to book a court:

```
void BookCourt(Court court, ClubMember member)
```

Court and *ClubMember* are domain entities, and the method *BookCourt* knows how to retrieve and apply due policies.

Infrastructure layer

The infrastructure layer is anything related to using concrete technologies, whether it is data persistence (O/RM frameworks like Entity Framework), specific security API, logging, tracing, IoC containers, caching, and more.

The most prominent component of the infrastructure layer is the persistence layer—which is nothing more than the old-faithful data access layer, only possibly extended to cover a few data sources other than plain relational data stores. The persistence layer knows how to read and/or save data.

The data can reside on a relational server as well as in a NoSQL data store or in both. The data can be accessible through web services (for example, CRM or proprietary services) or live in the file system, cloud, or in-memory databases such as Memcached, ScaleOut, or NCache.

Summary

We dare say that the software industry moved from one extreme to the other. Decades ago, writing software was inspired by the slogan "model first, code later." This led to considerable efforts to have a big comprehensive design up front. There's nothing wrong with an upfront design, except that it is like walking on water. It's definitely possible if requirements, like water, are frozen.

Maybe because of global warming, requirements hardly ever freeze these days. Subsequently, whomever embarks in an upfront design risks sinking after only a few steps.

Mindful of failures of upfront design, architects and developers moved in the opposite direction: code first, model later. This philosophy, although it is awkward, moves things ahead. It just works, in the end. Adopting this approach makes it hard to fix things and evolve, but it delivers working solutions as soon as possible, and if something was wrong, it will be fixed next. Like it or not, this model works. As our friend Greg Young used to write in his old posts, you should never underestimate the value of working software.

What we're trying to say, however, is that some middle ground exists, and you get there by crunching knowledge and deeply understanding the domain. Understanding the domain leads to discovering an appropriate architecture. However, it doesn't have to be a single, top-level architecture for the entire application. As you recognize subdomains, you can model each to subapplications, each coded with the most effective architecture. If it still sounds hard to believe, consider that it's nothing more than the old motto *Divide-et-Impera* that—historians report—helped Julius Caesar and Napoleon to rule the world.

Finishing with a smile

Developers sometimes enter into God mode and go off on a tangent, thus losing perspective on their code. We try to see models everywhere and to see each model as a special case. This makes software design cumbersome at times, and funny. For more tongue-in-cheek examples of Murphy's law beyond the following ones, have a look at *http://www.murphys-laws.com*:

- All generalizations are false, including this one.

- The weakest link is the most stable one.

- Never underestimate the value of working software.

CHAPTER 6

The presentation layer

Design is not just what it looks like and feels like. Design is how it works.
—Steve Jobs

Everybody would agree that the presentation layer manages and makes possible any expected interaction between the user and the system. Much like in a restaurant where a waiter gets and forwards orders to the kitchen staff, the presentation layer picks and dispatches commands to the nearest interfacing layer in charge of processing the command. Just as the waiter at some point serves the ordered dish to the eagerly waiting client, the presentation layer is slated to show at some point any calculated response to the user.

It sounds like the classic chicken vs. egg debate, but it is probably worth raising the question once more: when setting up a new restaurant, which staffing and organizational issues do you focus on first? Is it the serving or kitchen side of the matter?

For a long time in the software world, we started from the back end, and many of us considered presentation the less noble part of the system—just a detail to tackle after the business and data access layers had been completed. There's no question, however, that both the presentation and back end are equally necessary in a system of any complexity. In the past edition of this same book, some five years ago, we wrote the following:

Your attitude, your preferences, and even your skills determine the "priority" you assign to each layer and, subsequently, the order in which you focus on the various layers.

This is a point that today, some five years later, we perceive differently.

Today, most systems are consumed through a wide variety of devices, either smartphones, tablets, laptops, very large or very small screens (such as smart TVs), and wearable devices. The application back end is essentially the same, but the front end might take multiple forms and colors. Each device, in fact, might require its own set of use-cases, and this might lead to an organization of the back end different from the organization you would reckon ideal for one, default type of device.

In addition, years of experience have taught us that requirements tend to continuously change and only a deep understanding of the domain can help smooth the pain and effort. Focusing on the presentation first helps you to gain a better and earlier understanding of the orders to serve and how they should be served. After the presentation layer has defined required scenarios , setting up the back end is far simpler.

User experience first

The most interesting things for an application usually take place in the Domain Model Layer, which is also where you create the engine that gives life and fuels the entire system. Starting the design from the Domain Model Layer is certainly acceptable and also common. Yet, we'd like to push another approach here that might save time and effort, especially when you are relatively new to the domain and the use-cases that are relevant for the users. In some past presentations, Dino called this approach "the Copernican revolution of software development."

Copernicus didn't observe something new that nobody else had seen before. Instead, he just offered a totally different perspective of things and proposed a different explanation for things like day and night that everybody was experiencing.

Similarly, we don't claim to have a new magical potion that will save the world. More simply, we like to share a design approach that puts a lot of emphasis on the presentation layer, focuses on tasks, and has the merit of letting you attack most of the interesting things when the user interface has been already validated by users, refined, and approved. Everything can still change, but most of the presentation wrinkles surely have been ironed out.

Short for user experience first, *UX-first* is what we named this approach to software design that is centered on presentation and user/system interactions.

Focus on interactions

We write software to let customers do their own business the way they like it and that is most effective. Any software exists to produce results, whether it is screens, files, or just database updates. As obvious as it might sound, the more you know about the expected results, the more effectively you can make development plans.

When expected results involve some graphical interface for the user to interact with, focusing on those interactions first sounds like a natural choice. Focusing on interaction leads to a task-based design.

Task-based design

Sometimes the complexity you face is too big for one bite. Starting from the model, then, might be a pretentious and heavyweight approach. A lightweight start focuses on tasks to implement, the input that each task needs, and the output that each task produces.

So you iteratively take a task from the list and start sketching out a possible user interface and, subsequently, a workflow behind it. It's nothing new in the end. This is precisely what the Unified Modeling Language (UML) *use-case* diagram is for.

In UML, a use-case diagram provides a graphical representation of an application's use-cases. A *use-case* describes an interaction between the system and one of its actors. In particular, a *use-case* diagram shows which actors do what. An actor can be a user or any other external system (for example, a database) that interacts with the system being described. An actor cannot be controlled by the system; an actor is defined outside the system itself. Figure 6-1 shows a sample use-case UML diagram.

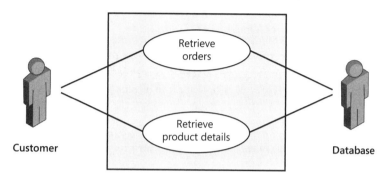

FIGURE 6-1 A sample use-case UML diagram.

The use-case identifies two actions: retrieve orders and retrieve product details. This scenario likely raises the need to have one screen for placing the request and one screen for showing the response. Users won't work directly with the part of the system that retrieves orders or product details. All that the user is interested in is how she specifies the order or the product to retrieve.

The next step is sketching out screens, jotting down ideas for how requests should be specified and how responses should be laid out.

Important The adoption of a task-oriented UI is an emerging trend in the industry that goes hand in hand with separation between the read and write models. In a world that feels the need to separate the domain from data, the transition from data-centric interfaces (Access-style, grid-based) to task-oriented interfaces is just a natural step. This new approach makes it easier to turn requirements into specifications and makes it possible to refine the user interface to turn it into a pleasant user experience. Finally, a task-oriented UI helps simplify the structure of the back end via architectural patterns like Command/Query Responsibility Segregation (CQRS), which we'll start discussing in Chapter 10, "Introducing CQRS."

Aim to find the best way of doing things

Let's say it: for decades, developers didn't pay much attention to the user interface of their applications. The focus was on models and databases and the model behind the presentation was largely ignored and considered to be a pain in the neck. It seemed that ending up with different models for presentation and storage was a sign of bad design.

As a result, the user interface was often more inspired by the entities in the back end rather than by the desired experience and actual tasks performed on the client.

The user interface is the means through which users accomplish their tasks and interact with the system. Any user interface that allows the user to accomplish a task is good; but not all of them are good in the same way. Let's admit it: as developers, for years we faced a mass of forgiving and passive users humbly accepting any user-interface implementations.

Things are becoming different. Now our software more faces a mass of users much less forgiving and often dictating user-interface aspects. As far as we can see, this is already true for consumer applications, and the trend seems defined. It just takes time for it to also become mainstream in the world of enterprise applications.

Continuously refined sketches that focus on interaction rather than data are the way to go. In essence, we think this is where the difference between user interface (UI) and user experience (UX) lies.

A view model class for each screen

In terms of software development, having screens defined and approved is great news and an excellent point on which to start building the rest of the system. A screen is ultimately a collection of input elements and can be easily abstracted to a class.

The class doesn't need to be rich in behavior; a plain data-transfer object (DTO) is more than fine. A DTO is a class used to carry related data across layers and tiers of a system. A DTO indicates what comes out of the screen and gets passed to the application layer for executing the command. Another DTO indicates the data that needs to flow into the form to populate it, for example, with the response of a server action.

Outgoing DTOs form the *input model*; incoming DTOs form the *view model*.

UX is not UI

Some 30 years ago, graphical user interfaces (GUI) changed the rules and both developers and users learned the importance of visual design. Up until a few years ago, and surely before the advent of smartphones and tablets, well-designed visual interfaces were sufficient to ensure a good experience to users of software applications. The road ahead seems to indicate that a good UI is no longer sufficient for delivering a well-designed presentation layer.

To stay on the cutting edge, we have to replace *UI* with *UX*.

So what's UX, and how does it compare to UI? In a nutshell, UX is more than just visual interface design and, in the end, UI is just a part of UX and probably still the most relevant part. What about other aspects of UX? That's where UX experts chime in.

Responsibilities of a UX expert

A UX expert—sometimes called a *UX architect* or even *UX designer*—is an analytical and creative position at the same time. The UX expert analyzes the users' behavior with the purpose of outlining the best possible experience for them to work with and within the system. The four pillars of a user experience are summarized in the following list:

- Information architecture

- Interaction design

- Visual design

- Usability reviews

The order is not coincidental. The first point to look at is the hierarchy of the information and then determine the ideal way for it to show through the application. Next comes the way in which users interact with that information and the graphical tools you provide for that to happen.

All this work is nothing without the fourth point—usability reviews. A UX expert can interview customers a million times—and should do that, actually—but that will bring about only an understanding of the customer's basic needs. This leads to some sketches that can be discussed and tweaked. A high rate of UX satisfaction is achieved only when the interface and interaction form a smooth mechanism that neither has usability bottlenecks nor introduces roadblocks in the process.

For a UX expert, talking to users is fundamental, but it's not nearly as important as validating any user interface live from the field, observing users in action, listening to their feedback and, if possible, even filming them in action.

Usability review is an iterative process that delivers a collection of mockups ready to be translated into any UI formalism supported by allowed technologies. More pragmatically, this means creating things like CSS, HTML, or XAML templates.

Tools for UX experts

The field of UX development is relatively new, though it is growing fast. The art of UX development passes through at least three stages—sketches, wireframes, and mockups—that require ad hoc tools. The fourth possible stage—prototypes—just requires regular coding tools. We want to mention four UX tools. They are described in Table 5-1.

TABLE 5-1 Short list of tools for UX development

Tool	More information	Description
Axure	*http://www.axure.com*	Creates wireframes and mockups, and links them together creating true storyboards with animation and even calculations.
Balsamiq	*http://balsamiq.com*	A rapid wireframing tool that reproduces the experience of sketching on a whiteboard. It provides a toolbox of readymade visual elements you can combine to construct a shareable wireframe. Also, it has the ability to link multiple wireframes together to create quick prototypes.
UXPin	*http://uxpin.com*	More ambitious than Balsamiq, it can be classified as another wireframing tool. It offers a highly sophisticated UI, readymade screen templates, and collaborative options.
Wirify	*http://www.wirify.com*	A bookmarklet you install on a web browser and use to capture wireframes of existing sites. Any captured wireframe can be exported to drawing tools such as Visio and Balsamiq.

In addition, Visio and Microsoft Office PowerPoint are still good at creating quick sketches and wireframes. They're not specific to user interface creation, though. Balsamiq came in to fill that gap. The real challenge as we see it, however, is to go beyond plain sketching and move toward scenarios where UI is mixed with interaction and multiple sketches are connected to produce at least a vague idea of the workflow behind the process. Microsoft's SketchFlow does something in between wireframing and prototyping, but it works only for XAML applications.

Why you might need to spend time on interactions

If UX analysis is the central point of modern presentation layers, usability review is the central point of UX analysis. Here's a brief true-life story that we hope might tell you more than abstract reasoning.

A customer asked for an internal-use quick tool to cherry-pick tweets based on user name and hashtag. All they wanted was a list of tweets to scroll so that they could select those of interest. We offered to create a quick web application based on the following wireframe (created using Balsamiq). They agreed, and we had a deal. (See Figure 6-2.)

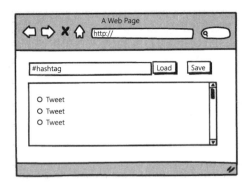

FIGURE 6-2 A sample wireframe created using Balsamiq.

It was a quick gig that involved only a couple of days of work. After the first test, everyone was happy: the application was fully functional. After a couple of days of really intense use, however, we got the first complaints about the overall experience. Dino also used the application personally for a few hours; although he probably wouldn't have complained as a user, he could fully understand the pains of the users. At the end of the day, two key features were missing that apparently everybody ruled out because they considered them to be advanced features and not strictly required initially. One was the ability to select and hide unwanted tweets so that picking really interesting tweets became an easier task. The other missing feature was the ability to hide tweets in the stream that had been already picked.

The lesson we learned is that when it comes to UX, even a super-simple, two-page, CRUD web application might have bad surprise in store. Only by looking at users using the application can you reliably say whether the UX you offer is good or not.

How to create an effective experience

So what should you do to implement a killer UX? Overall, it's a three-step procedure. First, you iteratively outline your ideas, moving sketches to wireframes and finally to full-fledged mockups. Second, you turn views into a working prototype using canned data and working without a back end or with a fake, test-only back end. Third, when the prototype work is done, that's when you get to the hardest part: telling the customer that what he's just approved is only a prototype and not the final app!

> **Note** Before we go any further, it's time we clarify what we intend exactly by terms like *sketch*, *wireframe*, and *mockup*, which are common UX jargon. A *sketch* is a freehand drawing done primarily to jot down ideas. A *wireframe* is a higher level sketch where you focus on functionality, layout, navigation, and info. A wireframe doesn't focus much on UI details. Finally, a *mockup* cares about the actual look-and-feel and is a wireframe with some sample UI attached.

Turning interactions into views

Without a doubt, HTML and CSS, or even XAML, would let you prototype a working view in a matter of minutes. However, the main point here is outlining an interactive model that works for the customer. The customer will probably feel more relaxed and be more open minded if you present sketches and drawings at first rather than colorful screen shots. The risk is that irrelevant details get too much attention at too early of a stage.

So you better work with low-fidelity and stay agnostic with regard to technologies. When sketches are clear enough, you proceed with wireframes and add more details about functionality, layout, and navigation. Tools like Balsamiq help a lot with quick wireframes. Wireframes set up the structure of the screen; mockups are just some graphical ideas developed on top of wireframes.

All you've got up to this point, however, is pure static content with no life and no action in it. Depending on the tool you chose for wireframing, you might want to create true storyboards to demonstrate the flow of UI screens.

Turn views into prototypes

Even after you convince the skeptics, you're far from being done. Keep in mind that even the best and most widely agreed-upon user interface might turn bad when used extensively. So our best recommendation is that you do not stop at first approval; instead, try to convince yourself about the quality of the interaction design you created. If you still have doubts about it, you can go with a prototype and maybe film users using the prototype to get a true indication of their feelings.

In terms of concrete technologies, a prototype can be anything that fits the bill. It can be a set of HTML pages as well as a XAML-based application. It consists only of the presentation layer and uses canned data or just a fake back end to simulate some behavior.

Depending on the level of fidelity you want to offer, creating wireframes and prototypes for an agreed-upon set of sketches is a matter of very few days of work.

Now tell customers it's only a prototype

So the customer likes the prototype and gives the go-ahead to build the application. Having the screen ironed out brings some benefits. You know exactly what the back end of the application has to produce. Each screen can be easily mapped to an outbound class, which becomes the input of the application layer and, in turn, the entry point in the back end of the system. The application layer forwards the input to the back end and that input proceeds down the stack. Any calculated response is carried up the stack to the application layer, packaged in a view model object, and returned to the presentation.

Ideally, each screen should be bound to a view model class that describes the data required to populate the view. In addition, each screen should be bound to an input model class that describes the data that goes out of the screen when an action is triggered. As an example imagine a page in an ASP.NET application that collects the name of two players or teams and returns the list of past matches. (See Figure 6-3.)

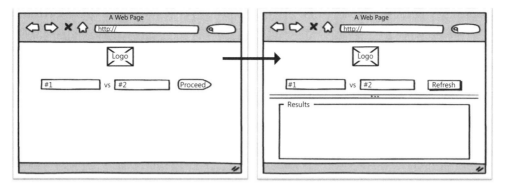

FIGURE 6-3 The screens used to collect names of players or teams and return the list of past matches.

The first screen requires no data to be populated and forwards the data as described by the following C# class:

```
public class H2HInputModel
{
    public Int32 PlayerId1 { get; set; }
    public Int32 PlayerId2 { get; set; }
}
```

The second screen posts the same data as in the *H2HInputModel* class and requires a richer class to be populated:

```
public class H2HViewModel
{
    public Int32 PlayerId1 {get; set;}
    public Int32 PlayerId2 {get; set;}
    public IList<H2HResult> Results {get; set;}
}
```

If it were an ASP.NET MVC application, the input model would result from the model-binding layer, whereas the view model would just be the model being passed to the Razor view engine. The following code snippet shows a possible implementation of the controller method that receives the click from the Proceed button:

```
public class H2HController
{
    public ActionResult Results(H2HInputModel input)
    {
        var model = _service.GetH2HResults(input);
        return View(model);
    }
}
```

With this entire job done, the hardest part that remains to be done is ensuring the customer knows that the application is not already half done. The team has to forget about any prototypes and start building the real thing. Among other things, this means thinking about technologies, planning layers, and identifying tiers. So let's have a look at a few common scenarios and investigate technologies and patterns for organizing a presentation layer.

Important In Chapter 5, "Discovering the domain architecture," we stressed the importance of identifying business contexts that are loosely coupled with others. Most of the time, this produces a minimal diagram with a few blocks and very few relationships. Each block probably can be implemented separately using the most appropriate architecture, design, and technologies.

MVC, MVP, MVVM, and other patterns

Short for Model-View-Controller, *MVC* is a pattern devised in the 1980s to architect the entire application. Applications of the time, though, were essentially monolithic applications, and using MVC as a general pattern totally made sense. The primary goal of MVC is to split the application into distinct pieces—the model, the view, and the controller. The *model* refers to state of the application. It wraps the application's functionalities and notifies the view of state changes. The *view* refers to the generation of any graphical elements displayed to the user. It captures and handles any user gestures. The *controller* maps user gestures to actions on the model and selects the next view. These three actors are often referred to as the *MVC triad*.

The MVC pattern evolved into Model-View-Presenter (MVP), where the presenter element replaced the controller and took more responsibility. This included everything from summing the orchestration of tasks to rendering the view. In MVP, view and model are neatly separated and the presenter mediates between them.

Model-View-ViewModel (MVVM) is just a much more popular name for a pattern that was originally introduced as the Presentation Model. In MVVM, you have a class that incorporates both the commands and view model for the UI. A single class—the view model object—exposes properties to bind to UI visual components and methods to bind to UI events. MVVM is particularly well suited to application scenarios where a powerful bidirectional data-binding mechanism exists. This is especially true for XAML-based applications and Universal Windows applications.

Don't be confused: in the context of layered applications, MVC, MVP and MVVM are all patterns for the sole presentation layer.

Realistic scenarios

Generally speaking, the presentation layer is made of two main components: the user interface and the presentation logic (also often referred to as the *UI logic*). The user interface provides users with the tools to use the application. Any behavior that the application can carry out is exposed to the users through graphical or textual elements in the user interface. These elements—mostly graphical elements nowadays—provide information, suggest actions, and capture the user's activity.

Any gesture a user makes within the user interface becomes input for the presentation logic. The presentation logic refers to all the processing required to display data and to transform user input into a command for the back-end system. In other words, presentation logic has to do with the flow of data from the middle tier to the UI and from the UI back to the middle tier.

As far as the Microsoft .NET Framework is concerned, the range of possible scenarios for the presentation layer of applications includes a web and Windows Presentation Foundation (WPF) front ends as well as Windows Store and Windows Phone applications. Under the umbrella of *web applications*, though, fall quite a few interesting application models, including plain ASP.NET websites, device-oriented websites, and single-page, client-side, responsive applications.

> **Note** When it comes to Windows Store and Windows Phone applications, the *universal application project* allows you to share the same core UI logic project between the Windows Store and Windows Phone application. In the end, you have one project for each platform and the difference is all in the views (XAML, styling, form-factor and other minor stuff); the vast majority of the C# code in the presentation layer is shared.

ASP.NET websites

In a classic ASP.NET website, the presentation layer is split between the browser and the web server. The user interface displayed to the user is rendered on the client device through HTML pages. The presentation logic lives for the most part on the server and is, in most cases, minimal and limited to passing data between user-interface elements and the application layer.

ASP.NET comes in three flavors: Web Forms, Web Pages, and MVC. Frankly, there's no real difference in terms of functionality.

Presentation logic in ASP.NET MVC

In an ASP.NET MVC scenario, controllers are responsible for the implementation of any UI logic. Controllers should not be considered part of the application or business layer and should be kept as thin as possible. The point of thin controllers is not so much for enforcing separation of concerns at all costs; instead, the point is recognizing separation between layers when we find it.

Controllers are tightly bound to the runtime environment and expose the HTTP context as a property. The logic you might need to have here is only any logic that depends on the HTTP context and headers. If an explicit check is required on the user agent, session state, or cookies, those actions belong to the controller. The orchestration of any task requested, though, should be moved outside the controller into the application layer. Here's a code snippet that illustrates the point:

```
public class HomeController
{
    private IApplicationLayer _appLayer;
    public HomeController(IApplicationLayer appLayer)
    {
        _appLayer = appLayer;
    }

    public ActionResult Index()
    {
        // Determine the view name analyzing the user agent
        var request = HttpContext.Request;
        var viewName = "index";
        if (IsSmartphone(request))
            viewName = "index.smartphone";

        // Retrieve session state for further processing
        var session = HttpContext.Session;
        var currentState = session["CurrentState"] as AppCurrentState;

        // Process the request (pseudo-code)
        var model = _appLayer.Index(currentState);

        // Return the view
        return View(viewName, model);
    }
}
```

The application layer receives from the presentation (for example, the controller) whatever it needs in order to process the request, but it has no need to be aware of the HTTP runtime. In this regard, the application layer is fully testable because it runs in total isolation.

What about controllers and testability?

In general, the amount of presentation logic in the controller is *minimal and trivial* and might not even raise the need to test coverage. However, if you think it is important to test that, say, session state is correctly handed out to the application layer, all you do is provide mocks for both the application layer and *HttpRequestBase*. In this regard, ASP.NET MVC lends itself to write tests much more than Web Forms.

Important As you might have experienced, testing a controller mostly means mocking the *HttpRequestBase* object, which has been made as easy as possible but still remains a rather convoluted process because of the complexity of the *HttpRequest* interface. In our vision, this is clearly the heritage of an original design that came about at a time when testability was not a concern. As fans of old horror movies, we paraphrase the popular "Don't open the door" to be "Don't test the controller." In the end, the controller is part of the ASP.NET infrastructure and is only minimally extended by your logic. The need to have tests here is low.

Presentation logic in ASP.NET Web Forms

In ASP.NET Web Forms, there are no controllers. To be precise, there's nothing with the shape and name of an MVC controller, but there's a software entity that plays exactly the same role: *postback handlers*. As emphatic as it might sound, we state that there's no logical difference between button-click handlers and controllers. Both are placeholders for presentation logic, and both should be kept thin by moving out to the application layer the orchestration of any processing tasks.

This is also a statement in favor of testability in ASP.NET Web Forms.

When ASP.NET Web Forms came out, it was the right framework at the right time. And 15 years ago was a time in which rapid application development reigned with nearly no opposition and testability was far from being perceived as an issue. It was no surprise that the design of the framework didn't lend itself to unit tests. But this is not an excuse today to be lazy on separation of concerns. By simply introducing an application layer in a Web Forms site, you make the site a lot more testable.

Application services

Within the context of ASP.NET applications, we design the application layer through classes that match the controller. We also use a naming convention internally for application-layer classes and call them *worker services*. At the end of the day, what we tend to call worker services are known in DDD as application services.

Note We'll be using the term "application service" in the rest of the book. We consider "worker service" and "application service" to be synonyms.

In the end, the *HomeController* class is associated with the *HomeService* class. An instance of the *HomeService* class is injected in *HomeController* either via IoC or poor man's injection. The association between controllers and application services is also reflected in the project structure, as shown in Figure 6-4.

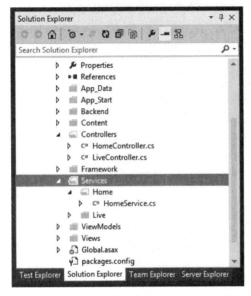

FIGURE 6-4 Using application services in an ASP.NET MVC project.

In our projects, the application layer is the entire content of the *Services* project folder. Moving the application layer to a separate assembly is as easy as creating a new class library out of the *Services* folder. Moving the application layer to a separate tier requires a host application and some wrapping layer to expose endpoints. The host application can be anything—like a Windows Communication Foundation (WCF) service—or, if you are interested only in HTTP communication, it might better to have it be another ASP.NET MVC site or a Web API application.

 Important Our advice is to bet on Web API rather than WCF and step out of WCF over the long term. As we see it, Microsoft is investing a lot in Web API and SignalR, and it just slated WCF to be in a sort of maintenance and support mode for the future. This said, for the time being Web API cannot do everything that WCF can do. For example, Web API is inferior to WCF when it comes to the full range of transportation protocols, security options, transactions, and reliability. Not all developers need these features, so in the end the rule is simple: if Web API does what you need, use it; otherwise go for WCF.

Application service classes contain methods that match one-to-one with use-cases. Each method orchestrates the necessary workflow, starting from the input model and returning a view model. In most cases, the controller logic is as thin as in the *Index* method shown here:

```
public class HomeController
{
    private readonly IHomeService _service;
    public HomeController(IHomeService service)
    {
        _service = service;
    }
```

```
    public ActionResult Index()
    {
        var model = _service.FillHomePage( /* input model */ );
        return View(model);
    }
    ...
}
```

The application service has access to all the layers and tiers down the stack. It is able to query and update data and to invoke, if required, external web services. If you have a domain model, the application service should also be able to access those entities and make use of adapters for translating from the domain model to the view model. (See Figure 6-5.)

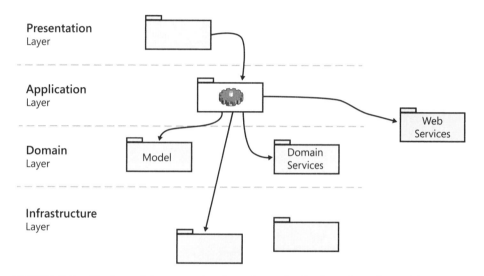

FIGURE 6-5 Ramifications of the connections from the application layer down the stack in an ASP.NET scenario.

User interface in web applications

The user interface of a web application is HTML served to the browser. In ASP.NET MVC, the controller invokes the application layer. When the response has been received, the controller instructs the view engine to generate the HTML markup using the specified view template (mostly a Razor file) and the view model object that the specific view template requires. The view model is often just the response received from the application layer. In other cases, the view model can be the result of some further aggregation process run by the controller itself.

In Web Forms, the request processing takes place within the boundaries of a *Page* object. A *Page* object is built around an HTML template and cannot be decoupled from that. In other words, in Web Forms, users request a page and receive it as it was designed to be. In MVC, there's a lot more flexibility because the component that renders HTML is separated from the component that processes the request to get a response from the back end. This means that in MVC the same request can be easily configured to return different markup under different runtime conditions. In Web Forms, you can achieve the same either by placing a module that rewrites the URL to point to a different page than the originally requested one (for example, default.tablet.aspx instead of default.aspx) or by heavily restructuring the page so that the final template results from the aggregation of user controls selected based on runtime conditions.

> **Note** Today, the amount of JavaScript in web pages is growing. However, unless you organize a website to be a rich client-side HTML5 application, the role of JavaScript in the presentation layer of a web application is minimal. It's mostly used for prevalidating input and to speed up the rendering and refresh of some parts of the page via Ajax calls and client-side data binding. We'll cover JavaScript-intensive client pages as a separate scenario later in the chapter.

Web Forms vs. ASP.NET MVC

In the Microsoft web stack, ASP.NET Web Forms is by far the most well-known and frequently used framework. The majority of remakes of existing sites start from a large Web Forms codebase. When the time for a remake comes, architects pick up their heads after years of hard work on a single system and can clearly see that now ASP.NET Web Forms is a thing of the past—sort of a walking-dead technology.

Architects diligently look around for alternatives but sometimes they find nothing that, to their eyes, is clearly better than ASP.NET Web Forms. More precisely, they sometimes miss a strong business reason for choosing ASP.NET MVC over Web Forms. And for the most part, they're right.

Other architects find that for complex web applications ASP.NET MVC is far more flexible and offers better control than Web Forms.

Who's wrong, then?

Technical and strategic differences

Devised in the thick of the browser wars of the later 1990s, ASP.NET Web Forms introduced server controls to produce user interfaces without learning HTML. It also introduced some ad hoc infrastructure to handle common aspects of web programming, such as session state and authentication and also statefulness. In particular, the Web Forms postback model was the junction point between web and desktop programming. The postback model enabled a programming model similar to what developers did for years: paint the user interface, wait for the user to interact, have the system react to the user's action, and repaint the user interface. Everything took place over the HTTP protocol, making it completely invisible to the developer. That was exactly the purpose; it was not a design flaw.

ASP.NET MVC came 10 years later, when people were demanding different tools—in particular, they were looking for more control over HTML and HTTP. Exactly what designers of Web Forms managed to hide from developers became the primary request of MVC developers. As you can see, there's no room for compromise. It's just two different visions of the same world. It's pointless to determine who's right and who's wrong.

The advent of Ajax and the subsequent change of developers' perspectives are real, but is it also true that Web Forms is now pure junk?

Web Forms didn't fall out of fashion overnight. You can still build successful web applications using ASP.NET Web Forms. You still have plenty of commercial extensions and libraries. You still have a mature and reliable platform that will be maintained for a few more years and supported for the foreseeable future. If it works for you, then it just works. Period.

Another way to look at it is as follows. Web Forms worked well for you in the past decade, and your whole team knows the platform very well. Now, you're about to embark on a significant remake. Is Web Forms up to the task you want it to? If your task is to build a JavaScript-intensive application, you might have a hard time. If you want testable components, you might have a hard time. If you need to ensure full accessibility to any page of the site, you might have a hard time. If it's critical to have SEO-friendly URLs, you might have a hard time.

Facing difficult tasks doesn't mean not being able to do things, however. Following up version 2.0 of ASP.NET Web Forms, Microsoft improved several aspects of Web Forms to minimize exactly the aforementioned aspects. So honestly, there's no compelling business reason to leave ASP.NET Web Forms to embrace other web frameworks.

Does this mean that advocates of ASP.NET MVC are dead wrong?

Most points that MVC advocates make against ASP.NET Web Forms are absolutely true and honest. Except that—in our opinion—they don't make a strong difference businesswise. So the bottom line is that if you don't have a special reason to seriously complain about Web Forms, and if you see a significant effort/cost for your team in acquiring new MVC skills, you can continue on with Web Forms. Regardless of what you might hear, the majority of production sites based on ASP.NET are using ASP.NET Web Forms. You won't be alone out there.

By the same token, ASP.NET MVC is a newer platform and comes closer to meeting the needs and expectations of today. Sticking to the past might be not the savviest choice for your company. But this consideration has little to do with the functional efficiency of the Web Forms platform.

Lack of HTTP endpoints in Web Forms

ASP.NET Web Forms was originally designed to shield developers from the actual structure of the HTML being sent to the browsers. As a developer, you had no control—and only a faint idea—of the ID used to name HTML elements. In these conditions, how could you arrange to replace a grid or a chunk of text with downloaded data? Microsoft addressed this problem already with ASP.NET Web Forms 4, which was released back in 2010, and made DOM manipulation also quite effective in Web Forms.

But that was only the first half of the problem.

Before developers can get to manipulating the DOM dynamically, they have to collect data from some remote HTTP endpoints. In some cases, these endpoints are located on sites outside of your control—for example, RSS feeds, Twitter, or other business partners of yours. The URLs are known and constants. Using JSONP, or other tricks, you can make the calls you need quite nicely.

How can you easily expose, on the other hand, your own endpoints from within a Web Forms application?

Although solutions exist—from ASPX pages returning JSON to ad hoc HTTP handlers up to WCF services bound to the HTTP transportation—the real problem that makes ASP.NET Web Forms feel outdated is the lack of an efficient way to expose HTTP endpoints so that they are easily consumable by whatever JavaScript framework you want to use on the client side.

Important As of today, the official answer to the problem of exposing application-specific endpoints from within a Web Forms application is Web API. Exposing a Web API front end out of Web Forms is as easy as adding controller classes in the *App_Code* folder. Visual Studio 2013 makes this process quite straightforward.

Note Today, Web API is confusingly similar to ASP.NET MVC because it pushes a programming interface that appears to be a clone of ASP.NET MVC. At the same time, up to .NET 4.5 the Web API runtime is completely separated from ASP.NET MVC. This situation will change in a future major release of the .NET Framework, when ASP.NET MVC and Web API will be sharing the same OWIN-based runtime environment.

Mixing Web Forms and MVC together

A common scenario today is that you have no time or budget for a complete remake of the site and you just want to implement a slew of new features using Ajax and libraries like jQuery, jQuery UI, Bootstrap, or perhaps AngularJS or Breeze. Can you do that on top of Web Forms? Can you just bring in some ASP.NET MVC features and leave the rest of the site as is?

Mixing Web Forms and MVC is definitely possible. We did it several times, and it always worked beautifully. We never heard of issues or troubles. And when looking at the underlying architecture, it comes as no surprise. In addition, Visual Studio 2013 specifically supports this scenario and allows you to join the binaries of Web Forms and MVC in one click or two. So the question becomes: should you?

We see two main scenarios for mixing Web Forms and ASP.NET MVC.

Suppose you want to rewrite a website using ASP.NET MVC, but you can't start at full speed on the first day. The site is large, and years of accumulated viewstate and server controls make it hard for the team to bite on the MVC paradigm. So you take one module at a time and rewrite it from scratch using ASP.NET MVC concepts. This means writing routes, controllers, and Razor views; preparing CSS and script bundles; and getting familiar with frameworks and libraries like jQuery and Twitter Bootstrap.

The second scenario is when you just want to add a bit of interaction to some of the existing pages. This mostly means using jQuery to download JSON data from your servers. Given this objective, mixing the existing site with ASP.NET MVC is definitely a possible solution. However, in this scenario, we'd rather go for Web API because it seems to be a cleaner solution.

Is OWIN something we should care about?

If you visit the home page of the OWIN website at *http://owin.org*, you'll find out that OWIN aims to define a standard interface for web servers and .NET client applications to use for interacting with one another. OWIN stands for the *Open Web Interface for .NET*. The design of OWIN—which you can read on the website—was inspired by Node.js and similar frameworks for other environments, such Ruby's Rack and Python's WSGI. Node.js, in particular, allows you to create web servers that operate under your total control. This is also one of the goals of OWIN.

However, the primary goal of OWIN is not to enable you to build your own web server. While that is a possibility, the goal of OWIN is to give the web stack a standard interface and decouple it from any concrete implementation, such as the IIS and the ASP.NET runtime. In a future version of the .NET Framework, OWIN will likely be used on top of IIS. In this regard, OWIN is a very important foundation for the future of ASP.NET MVC, whereas ASP.NET Web Forms will hit a dead end.

You might not see the need to use OWIN in 2014, but it will be a critical pillar for the future once it is fully incorporated in IIS and exposed as a common API.

Adding device support to websites

We bet that in a couple of years all websites will be easy to consume from mainstream devices. Cell phones are a thing of the past, and smartphones are changing too, as devices that are only two years old start are significantly different in terms of capabilities and power from newer ones. In this context, nobody can reasonably afford to stick to websites that get stretched into the device viewport and need users to zoom in and out to read and follow links.

Adding a layer of device-orientation to websites, therefore, is vital. It's not even a simple matter of separating mobile devices from desktop browsers. What's a mobile device today? The term *mobile* means everything and nothing. A wearable device (for example, Google glasses) is mobile in the sense that it moves with the individual, but it can't be compared to a tablet when it comes to content. A smart TV is not a mobile device, but it still requires ad hoc content.

Which strategies should you take to make a website really responsive to the capabilities of the requesting device?

Responsiveness through feature detection

Most developers remember well what a nightmare it was a decade ago to make websites look (nearly) the same on different browsers. As developers, we embarked upon the flaky parsing of user-agent strings and created intricate branches in our HTML code. Not really a pleasant memory. We learned our lesson, though, and when a few years later we started facing the same problem with mobile devices, we opted for something decidedly smarter—*feature detection.*

Feature detection is a concept first popularized by Modernizr—a JavaScript framework that detects HTML5 and CSS3 features in the browser. Modernizr offers an API that checks whether the current browser supports HTML5 input types, local storage, web sockets, CSS gradients, media queries, and much more.

Is the type of the device a feature you can programmatically detect? Not at the moment.

Anyway, a design methodology known as Responsive Web Design (RWD) came to the rescue, mixing together CSS media queries—a CSS3 feature that most browsers support—grid-based layouts, and proportional dimensions. With CSS media queries, you apply different CSS style sheets depending on the size of the current browser window. You define a few breakpoints that require the change of the style sheet, and grid-based layouts and proportional dimensions ensure that intermediate sizes show nicely. Typical breakpoints are placed at 480 pixels to work with smartphones and 800 pixels for tablets.

Devised to render pages responsively as the user resizes the browser, RWD ended up being used to scale down content on mobile devices too. In effect, a 480-pixel-wide screen just requires appropriate rendering regardless of whether it is a resized browser window or full-screen mobile browser.

That's the major strength and major weakness of RWD. To us, these are mostly weakness if we put it in the perspective of providing an optimal device experience.

Pros and cons of responsive web design

If you think it's great that RWD allows you to write one page and adapt via CSS to any window size, we invite you to consider also the following:

- CSS doesn't perform magic; all it does is hide and resize HTML elements. If an image is too large for a small screen, it will simply be resized; however, nothing changes in terms of bandwidth and downloading. And bandwidth is not a secondary point on a device.

- On mobile sites, the 80/20 rule holds true, meaning that only 20 percent of the content is usually relevant for the audience. By using RWD, you risk downloading a lot of content on a mobile device just to hide it in the end because it's not relevant. Or you make it quite slower (and possibly expensive) for the user to read the page.

- User experience is all the rage these days, and it is especially important on devices. With RWD, you just focus on one set of use-cases and adapt it to any window size. In doing so, you can't provide specific use-cases and ad hoc organization of the user interface to users of, say, tablets.

- Some people contrast that prior point by claiming that *mobile-first* design would fix everything. Mobile-first merely consists of thinking of the set of use-cases for a mobile audience first so that you ensure it works well enough on smaller devices first. You then proceed from the bottom up. Unfortunately, this doesn't address the point of performance or the point of usability. As long as CSS is the only tool you rely on to adapt views, all you can do is hide and resize things. To serve content on both small and large screens via CSS, you need to have in place and downloaded all content regardless of the device. The content doesn't change on a per-device basis.

Note Some techniques exist to mitigate the issues of RWD when it comes to performance on devices and the use of bandwidth. In particular, CSS files for a small screen can request different and smaller images.

Taking mobile-first to the extreme, and to some extent moving away from plain RWD, you might decide that with a little bit of extra JavaScript code you download content and style sheets on the fly and possibly on a per-device basis. In doing so, you face another big hurdle. How do you detect the type of the device that hosts the browser?

Responsiveness through server-side device detection

The golden rule to optimize performance and usability on devices is that you need to know their type and intelligently serve ad hoc markup. You maximize performance and usability if you detect the type of the device on the server.

When making the request, each browser identifies itself through the user agent string. Subsequently, a thorough analysis of the user agent string might reveal the identity of the device. Apparently, detecting devices is a boring but not difficult task. A bunch of regular expressions can do it. Well, as usual, it depends. If your purpose is only to identify the operating system and roughly the name of the device, well, that's probably not too hard. If the user agent string contains iPhone, iPad, Windows Phone, or Kindle, you can be reasonably sure what it is. You still don't get details about versions, but that's probably a secondary point for a large share of applications.

What about Android, BlackBerry, and Sony devices? When the only hot keyword you find is *Android*, what can you conclude about the device? It can be anything: a smartphone, tablet, minitablet, legacy phone, or perhaps even a smart TV.

Device detection is a serious matter, and if you need it done seriously, you need expertise. The de-facto standard for device detection is WURFL (*http://www.scientiamobile.com*). WURFL is a cross-platform library—used by, among the others, Facebook, Google, and PayPal—that can detect over 20,000 devices and return over 500 capabilities for each. For the ASP.NET platform, WURFL is available as a cloud solution with an elastic number of capabilities and works as well as an on-premises install you get via a canonical NuGet package.

Note The hardest part of having some logic to recognize devices from their user-agent strings is maintenance. New devices hit the market every day, and that logic and the back-end database must be updated regularly. This entails a significant effort, and it's the primary reason why device description repositories (DDRs) like WURFL are not free, at least for premium users.

A point that is sometimes raised against the server-side approach is that capabilities are kind of *guessed* instead of *detected*. At the moment, browsers don't expose in a common and accurate way the operating system or the more specific aspects of the host device, such as touch support, radio system, SMS, streaming, and so forth. It is not surprising, after all. The browser is not the device, even though we can use the browser agent string to figure out what the device is. As an example, consider that Dino had the incredible adventure of buying a low-cost tablet that clearly runs Android 4.0. The built-in browser, though, keeps on sending an agent string like that of an iPad 3.2. Any automatic software will certainly mistake it for an iPad.

Display modes in ASP.NET MVC

For some reason, a server-side approach is perceived as one that leads to code duplication as opposed to RWD that builds on a single codebase. This is a false perspective of things. In a server-side approach, you provide different views in much the same way you provide different CSS files (or rule sets) in a RWD solution. However, having different views is precisely what maximizes performance and usability. Let's see the steps required to build a WURFL-based adaptive solution in ASP.NET MVC.

The trick that enables a server-side adaptive solution for devices consists of selecting the most appropriate view based on the user agent. Here's some pseudocode to illustrate the point:

```
public ActionResult Index(InputModel input)
{
    // Usual work to process the request
    var model = _appLayer.FillHomePage(input);

    // Find and serve the most appropriate Razor file for the "index" view
    var viewName = SelectAppropriateView("index", Request.UserAgent);
    return View(viewName, model);
}
```

Internally, the *SelectAppropriateView* method will check the user-agent string and, assuming to have multiple versions of the same view, returns the one that best fits the detected device. Starting with version 4 of the ASP.NET Framework, the selection of the most appropriate view is code that can be buried in the folds of ASP.NET MVC thanks to *display modes*.

A display mode is essentially a Boolean expression that evaluates the HTTP context. In addition, each display mode is associated with a unique suffix. Concretely, in ASP.NET MVC, a display mode is an instance of the *DefaultDisplayMode* class, and all currently defined modes are grouped in the *DisplayModeProvider.Modes* global collection. Here's some code that initializes the application from *global.asax*:

```
var modeDesktop = new DefaultDisplayMode("")
{
    ContextCondition = (c => c.Request.IsDesktop())
};
var modeSmartphone = new DefaultDisplayMode("smartphone")
{
    ContextCondition = (c => c.Request.IsSmartphone())
};
var modeTablet = new DefaultDisplayMode("tablet")
```

```
{
    ContextCondition = (c => c.Request.IsTablet())
};
var modeLegacy = new DefaultDisplayMode("legacy")
{
    ContextCondition = (c => c.Request.IsLegacy())
};
DisplayModeProvider.Modes.Clear();
DisplayModeProvider.Modes.Add(modeSmartphone);
DisplayModeProvider.Modes.Add(modeTablet);
DisplayModeProvider.Modes.Add(modeLegacy);
DisplayModeProvider.Modes.Add(modeDesktop);
```

The sample code creates four displays modes, which roughly match breakpoints in RWD. Instead of a media query expression that selects the style sheet, you have a context condition that selects a suffix. The context condition evaluates on the HTTP context and typically checks the user agent. In the sample application that comes with the book, *IsSmartphone* and *IsTablet* methods in the demo are extension methods on *HttpRequest* and use WURFL internally to detect the capabilities of the requesting device.

All this would be nothing without the view engine's ability to evaluate context conditions before rendering HTML. Consider the following controller code:

```
public ActionResult Index(InputModel input)
{
    var model = _appLayer.FillHomePage(input);
    return View(model);
}
```

When the view engine receives the command to render the view named, say, *index*, it then checks all display modes and tries to get a suffix. The suffix is then appended to the view name. So, for example, if the smartphone context condition returns *true*, the actual view employed will be *index_smartphone.cshtml*.

Note that any device-specific view is a full-fledged view that can contain whatever HTML you want it to, including RWD code and media query expressions. This is not a bad idea because, for example, you can rely on RWD to make the view fit nicely in tablets and minitablets or smartphones of different screen sizes. Finally, consider that RWD is still the most effective way of detecting changes between portrait and landscape mode.

Responsiveness through client-side device detection

Yet another option for device detection is calling a remote service to get details about the local device. Based on the received information, you then proceed to tweak the page to adapt it to the specific device.

This approach is sort of a middle ground between RWD and server-side detection. More than RWD, it allows you to increase usability because you can create new HTML elements on the fly to create device-specific use-cases. In a mobile-first perspective, this approach is excellent, because you download the absolute minimum for small devices and download extra content as needed. Relying on a server-side service ensures reliable detection of the device.

Many scripts have been around for a while to make client-side detection happen. The most reliable is a branch of the WURFL project. Add the following script element to your pages:

```
<script type="text/javascript" src="http://wurfljs.com/wurfl.js"></script>
```

You get the following JavaScript object downloaded in your page:

```
var WURFL = {
    "complete_device_name" : "...",
    "is_mobile" : false,
    "form_factor" : "..."
};
```

The *form_factor* property can contain any of the following strings: *Desktop, App, Tablet, Smartphone, Feature Phone, Smart-TV, Robot, Other non-Mobile, Other Mobile.* That gives you the basic information; the rest is up to you. By the way, the *wurfl.js* script is free.

Single-page applications

A single-page application (SPA) is a web application based on one or just a few distinct pages. The building of the interface happens through a series of related calls that progressively download HTML, JavaScript, and CSS. As the user interacts with the application, the user interface is modified entirely on the client. The experience is smooth and fluid, and performance is usually excellent.

The canonical example of a SPA is Gmail. For sites subject to huge volumes of traffic, a SPA might be an attractive option because the amount of work required on the server side is dramatically reduced. Conversely, the insane power of personal computers, and the still-relevant power of tablets and devices, is squeezed out, thus bringing about a better balance of work between the client and server.

Presentation logic in a SPA

A SPA is characterized by thin server architecture and thick client. A large share of the logic that would live on the server in a classic web application is moved to the client. This includes the entire presentation logic and also large chunks of the application logic.

The orchestration of tasks following users' actions might likely take place on the client. The client, therefore, contains logic to coordinate multiple calls to the back end. As a result, the role of the web server in some cases changes dramatically and scales down to be a mere façade for data exchanging.

This is just one possibility though.

Similarly, you can create a task oriented application with logic in the server and sending commands from JavaScript. In this case, the server is not just a mere data publisher. You can have most of the orchestration done on the client, but the core business logic still stays on the server where data will still be validated due to security reasons.

You should note that while the inspiring principles of a SPA are stable and mature, the actual implementations can differ quite a bit for the distribution of application logic between the client and server. In other words, it's OK to have a thin server, but how thin it actually is might be numerically different from one application to another. In implementations where the client is particularly rich, the overall architecture is not really different from the old-faithful client/server architecture of some decades ago. The web client is as rich and smart as Visual Basic clients of the 1990s, and the web front end plays the role of the Microsoft SQL Server database of that time.

The MVC-like organization of the client

The typical workflow of a SPA is summarized in Figure 6-6. The SPA makes its first request to the server just to get some initial HTML. Once some user interface has been presented and the application is fully initialized, any successive interaction takes the form of HTTP requests uploading and downloading JSON data.

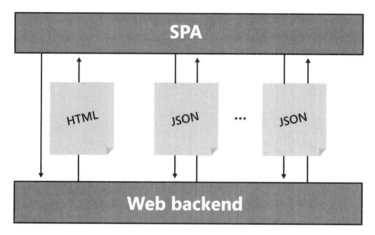

FIGURE 6-6 The typical workflow of a SPA: an initial request for HTML followed by a long list of requests for JSON data.

Requests can be for things as simple as basic CRUD operations on data in a plain REST style or for server-side commands that might trigger transactional tasks.

In general, if you decide to jump on the SPA bandwagon, it's likely because you want to make the most out of the client and get a better user experience. So any changes to the user interface happen via direct modification of the DOM. This means that your JavaScript files might be full of snippets like the one shown here:

```
$.getJSON(url)
  .done(function (data) {
    // Access the DOM here
});
```

Invoking the URL in response to an event is part of the presentation layer; what happens in the *done* function is arguable. If it's simply DOM updates, we can consider it part of the presentation. If it involves linking to other operations, it's orchestration and the whole thing all of a sudden becomes part of the application layer. Anyway, we admit this distinction might be essentially pointless, but ignoring where each piece of code actually belongs is the surest path to building big balls of mud. Let's say that the ugliest part of that code is the direct binding of HTML elements in logic that might not be pure presentation.

In general, single-page applications use comprehensive frameworks such as AngularJS to gain a bit of structure and some conventions. Most frameworks for SPA push an MVC-based pattern for the organization of the client code. Some opt for MVC; others opt for MVVM. In the end, the difference is minimal and, anyway, nothing different from what we stated earlier about server websites: each view is abstracted to a view model, including subviews.

Depending on the specific framework, actions on the view belong to a separate controller class (MVC) or are exposed as methods out of the same view model class (MVVM).

Bidirectional data binding plays a key role in a SPA because it's the way through which downloaded data is bound to visual elements. AngularJS and other frameworks (for example, KnockoutJS) let you use ad hoc HTML attributes to indicate which property of the bound view model links to a particular HTML element. This is the KnockoutJS way of creating a UL looping through the *matches* property of the view model and displaying for each match the value of the *Team1* and *Team2* properties:

```
<ul data-bind="foreach: matches">
  <li>
    <span data-bind="text: Team1"></span>
    vs.
    <span data-bind="text: Team2"></span>
  </li>
</ul>
```

In this way, it's the binding code that goes to the HTML and not vice versa when HTML elements are mixed with JavaScript code.

Transferring data from the server

To build the back end of a SPA, you just need to expose a few HTTP endpoints. This can be done in a variety of ways, ranging from WCF to HTTP handlers, from an ASP.NET MVC site to Web API. In general, no technology is necessarily more favorable than the others. However, we should note that Web API is the leanest of all and also the most recent and well-designed when the concept of SPA was developed. Our guideline, then, is to use Web API unless you have other stronger reasons—mostly legacy reasons—to do otherwise.

When it comes to creating a Web API façade, you can take the REST route or even the RPC route. The REST route means you define one or more resources you'll be exposing over the web through the classic HTTP verbs—GET, POST, PUT, and DELETE. The RPC route means you just expose endpoints for actions and use ad hoc data-transfer objects to move data around.

Yet another option to consider is Open Data Protocol (OData). OData is a protocol designed to expose a data source over the web in order to perform CRUD operations. Originally defined by

Microsoft, the protocol is now being standardized at OASIS. In the end, OData implements the same core idea as ODBC, except that it is not limited to SQL databases and lends itself to interesting uses over the web.

The protocol offers several URL-based options for users to query for metadata, query for flat and hierarchical data, apply filters, sort and, last but not least, page. You might want to check *http://www.odata.org* for more information on the protocol and details about the syntax. As an example, consider the following URL corresponding to a Web API endpoint:

```
/api/numbers?$top=20&$skip=10
```

By enabling OData in Web API, you can have your client place calls that will be interpreted to filter the data being returned. In a way, OData can be seen as a queryable interface over the server data exposed to the JavaScript client. In the context of applications that see the back end mostly as a data server, a bunch of OData endpoints can really cut down the complexity of many use-cases and also the amount of code written and run on the server.

Possible hidden costs of a SPA

What we summarized so far is the theory of SPAs. In principle, it's a great idea, and the thin server and the thick client work together beautifully. At a higher level view, we see that a SPA sits in between the classic world of the web and the classic world of desktop applications. And, at least for the time being, the approach is far from capturing the best of both worlds.

The issues with the SPA model are largely related to the conflict between the old way of using the web and the new way of using the web that a SPA pushes. The SPA model works great if we break up the consolidated practices of the classic web. We mean things like the page refresh, deep linking into the site, tabs, and maybe more. The hidden costs of building a successful SPA are here.

Best practices and specific HTML5 APIs exist (for example, the History API) to smooth out or wipe out these problems. So building a SPA that works and doesn't bring a long queue of complaints is definitely possible. At the same time, in our opinion, embarking on a SPA project on the wave of enthusiasm for a demo application that some guru showed around is risky. You need mastery and expertise to tame the SPA beast.

We want to call your attention on a couple of points:

- Be extremely clear about what you expect out of a SPA, and make it clear with customers that SPA is a new form of using the web. A SPA is closer to a desktop application just built and deployed over the web. Precisely for this reason, it moves from deep *statelessness* to deep *statefulness*. It's not a minor change. Realistically, in an enterprise world, a SPA might require a bit of extra time for syncing up users with interfaces.

- The SPA model doesn't work well in the mobile space. Be skeptical about the possibility of writing a SPA once, running it on a variety of mobile devices, and even turning the app into a native application for all mobile systems of the foreseeable future.

Except for this, everything else works like a charm!

Desktop rich client

Our neat perception is that the number of deployed desktop applications is still very high but the number of new applications is decreasing and are being replaced by rich web front ends (for example, SPA) and native mobile applications. It was not coincidental that this echoes our previous statement about SPAs being halfway between the web and desktop and that it heralds a new web that is envisioned like desktop-style applications that are just deployed as websites.

Whether the rich client is physically built with WPF and XAML and compiled to Windows 8, or as a Windows Store application, or just as a SPA or mobile application, the overall architecture—which is our primary concern here— remains nearly the same.

Classic WPF applications

When the front end of the system is a WPF application, the way to go is already paved. You use the MVVM pattern to model each screen into a class with public properties and methods. Properties represent bindable visual elements, whereas methods represent actions triggered by the user interface. The code in these methods invokes application-layer endpoints. (See Figure 6-7.)

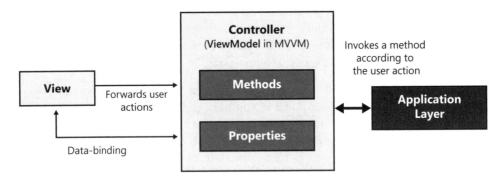

FIGURE 6-7 General schema representing the MVVM pattern as implemented in a XAML-based application.

The deployment of the application layer can take any form, and there are really no globally accepted rules that make a choice stand out. The application layer might be entirely on the server, entirely on the client, or split between the client and server.

The only discriminating factor we like to point out is that the application layer deployed on the client requires a lot more network traffic, because it configures a *chatty* model of interaction between the client and server instead of a sober and plain *chunky* model—make a request, let the server do the job, and wait for results or error message.

Web rich clients

Not that many years ago, Dino would have bet the farm on browser plugins like Silverlight conquering the world, dismissing HTML and JavaScript. Thankfully, that never happened (the betting, actually). Today when you say *rich client over the web*, the only thing that comes to mind is SPA on top of HTML5.

It should be recalled, however, that HTML as we know it today with the wide range of surrounding frameworks (such as WebSockets, local storage, IndexedDB, rich input, SVG, canvas, history and more) is significantly different than the HTML of five or six years ago, at the time Dino was going to bet the farm on Silverlight. The HTML of today is a close relative to Silverlight in terms of additional functionalities over the plain DOM.

Even before Microsoft pushed Silverlight into the corner, the industry trend was to proclaim HTML as the winner. Now the challenge for having successful and rich solutions deployed over the web is finding the right balance between the old and new web, and taking some time to educate customers about the new web, where Back and Forward buttons might not work and deep linking might be optional. Preserving the state of the application over the web is problematic, even though nobody is entirely shooting in the dark and solutions (and ad hoc frameworks) exist.

In terms of architecture, a rich web client is a single-page application if based on HTML and is a Silverlight application otherwise. If it's a Silverlight application, it follows the same pattern of Windows Presentation Foundation (WPF) desktop applications as far as the presentation layer is concerned.

Note Silverlight applications are still supported and, when written, they work. However, choosing between updating an existing large Silverlight application and building a brand new HTML application is a tough call for architects and CTOs. In general, Silverlight is not going to have a brilliant future. For what it's worth, this has little to do with Silverlight itself, and to a large extent the same can be said for Adobe Flash. The change of perspective is due to a change in the devices industry rather than just the quality of plugins.

Native mobile applications

A native mobile application—whether it's running on iOS, Android, Windows Phone, Windows Store, or other platforms—is, architecturally speaking, comparable to a desktop client of a layered system. It communicates with the back end using HTTP services and implements the presentation layer and at least chunks of the application layer on the device.

The organization of the user interface depends on the presentation idiom supported on the platform. That is plain MVC on iOS and MVVM on Windows Phone and Windows Store. Conversely, there's no direct mapping with a recognized pattern in Android even though the inspiration of MVC is clearly visible.

A point we would like to reiterate is that the application layer is the implementation of the use-cases exposed by the presentation layer. For this reason, the presentation and application layers go hand in hand. If the mobile front end requires a different set of use-cases, the application layer should be tailor-made. Having part of the application layer incorporated in the device, and using a chatty model instead of a chunky model, might reduce the amount of code that needs to be written or refactored on the server back end to support a new mobile front end.

Summary

Once upon a time, architects had one insanely powerful computer (the server) to deal with, a few insanely slow personal computers and, more importantly, a mass of forgiving and passive users humbly accepting any user-interface rules from highly respected developers. (The chief architect was usually put just one level or two below God.)

Now it's a different world. The mass of users is much less forgiving and even dictate strict user-interface requirements. So user experience is all the rage today, but for the most part we keep on designing systems the old way, focusing more on storage than users.

UX-first is a design philosophy that suggests you start from the presentation layer and run a preliminary analysis on a double track—collecting business domain data and UX data that can guide you to design interaction models that work for the user before they are made to work for the system. The goal of UX-first is building screens as users love them, and once wireframes and mockups of screens are signed off on, you start defining data workflows from here and domain logic, services, and storage.

In this chapter, we discussed the user experience and the structure of the presentation layer in a few realistic scenarios, including websites, mobile websites, single-page applications, and desktop clients.

Finishing with a smile

A lot has been said about the usability of programs, and we said a lot about the importance of delivering a system that works as expected and, more importantly, provides the features that customers really need. Making jokes about the user interface of computer programs, however, is like shooting the piano man—it can sometimes be way too easy and way too fun. For more tongue-in-cheek Murphy laws beyond the following ones, have a look at *http://www.murphys-laws.com*:

- The only thing worse than an end user without a clue is an end user who has a clue—usually the wrong one.

- When designing a program to handle all possible dumb errors, nature creates a dumber user.

- Build a system that even a fool can use and only a fool will want to use it.

CHAPTER 7

The mythical business layer

> *Any fool can write code that a computer can understand.*
> *Good programmers write code that humans can understand.*
> —Martin Fowler

Since the first edition of this book, some five years ago, we observed a noticeable change in the industry: a shift from data-centric three-tier architecture to more model-centric, multilayer architecture. And another big wave of changes is coming as *event-driven* architecture takes root and developers start experiencing its inherent benefits. As a result, the classic business layer canonically placed in between the presentation and data access morphs into something different depending on the overall system architecture. The only thing that does not change, though, is that in one way or another you still need to implement the core, business-specific logic for the system.

In Chapter 5, "Discovering the domain architecture," we introduced DDD and after this chapter we'll embark on a thorough discussion of a few very popular supporting architectures for layered systems such as Domain Model, Command/Query Responsibility Segregation (CQRS), and event sourcing.

We intend to dedicate this chapter to the facts that justify and actually make the transition from a classic data-centric, three-tier world to a model-centric but still layered world. In doing so, we'll touch on a few other, more basic patterns that can always be used to organize the business logic of a bounded context and common issues you face.

Patterns for organizing the business logic

There's virtually no logic to implement in a simple archiving system that barely has any visual forms on top of a database. Conversely, there's quite complex logic to deal with in a financial application or, more generally, in any application that is modeled after some real-world business process.

Where do you start designing the business logic of a real-world system?

In the past edition of the book, we dedicated a large chapter to the business logic and covered several patterns for organizing the logic of a system. Five years later, we find that some of those patterns have fallen out of mainstream use and might be seen as obsolete. *Obsolete* just means something like "no longer used"; it doesn't refer to something that "no longer works."

For sure, patterns like Table Module and Active Record are not what you should look for now, five years later. Today, the common practice is to use objects to model business entities and processes, but domain modeling might be difficult to do and expensive to implement, and these costs are not always justified by the real complexity of the problem. So, in the end there's still room for something simpler than domain models.

> **Note** A moment ago, we hinted at Active Record becoming an obsolete, no-longer-used, pattern. To be honest, the Active Record pattern is widely used in the Ruby-on-Rails community, where it is part of the foundation of data access. So the true sense of our previous statement is fully expressed by adding "in the .NET space."

The fairytale of CRUD and an architecture Prince Charming

If you're a developer eager to learn new things and compare your best practices with other people's best practices, you might be searching the Internet for tutorials on architecture practices in your technical idiom. So assume you're a .NET developer. You're going to find a lot of resources that claim to teach architecture but use a plain CRUD (Create, Read, Update, Delete) sample application. Well, that's amazing at least and misleading at most. And, look, we didn't say it's *wrong*, just misleading. Except that in architecture *misleading* is maybe even worse than *wrong*.

Forget entry-level tutorials that show how clean a CRUD system might look like once you use objects instead of data rows. If it's a music store that you need, that's fine; but you don't need to waste more time learning about sophisticated things like event sourcing, CQRS, and Domain-Driven Design (DDD). If it's a music store that you need, just write your ADO.NET code or let Entity Framework infer a data model from the database. If you want more thrills, turn Entity Framework Code-first on and immerse yourself in the waters of *unnecessary-but-terribly-hot* complexity. If it's really a CRUD, it has nearly no architecture.

> **Note** OK, just kidding. On a more serious note, our intention here is not to look like the only custodians of absolute truth. The point is you should use the right tool for the job without dragging in pet-technology dilemmas. (See *http://c2.com/cgi/wiki?ArchitectureAsRequirements* for more on the pet-technology anti-pattern.)

Paraphrasing a popular quote from a friend of ours, "Just because it's a CRUD, you don't have the right to write rubbish." Our friend used to say that about JavaScript, but the same principle applies to CRUD as well. Separating the application layer and data layer in a CRUD is all you need to do. If you do so, the result is clean, readable, and possibly extensible. But this is just a matter of using the right tool for the job and using it right.

Through the lens of a CRUD application, you only see a section of the complexity of a real-world system. You might be led to think that all you need is a clean data layer that is well isolated from the rest of the universe. You might be led to think that, all in all, even the application layer is unnecessary and a controller (for example, presentation layer) can coordinate any activity easily enough.

Again, through the lens of a CRUD, that's probably OK, but it shouldn't be generalized.

Complexity is an ugly beast—easy to recognize but nearly impossible to define abstractly. Our goal here is to present general patterns of architecture and software design. We assume a high level of complexity in order to introduce the most layers and functions. No application out there has the same level of complexity and, subsequently, requires the same complex architecture. We expect that you learn the internal mechanics of most architecture patterns—essentially why things are done in a certain way—and then apply Occam's Razor to them when facing a real problem. If you can take out some of the pieces (for example, layers) without compromising your ability to control the solution, by all means do so.

That is what makes you a good architect and also a good candidate to play the role of the Prince Charming of architecture.

The Transaction Script pattern

When it comes to organizing the business logic, there's just one key decision you have to make: whether to go with an object-oriented design or with a procedural approach. In any case, you are choosing a paradigm to design the business logic, so it's primarily about architecture, not technology.

The Transaction Script (TS) pattern is probably the simplest possible pattern for business logic, and it is entirely procedural. TS owes its name and classification to Martin Fowler. For further reference, have a look at page 110 of his book *Patterns of Enterprise Application Architecture*, Addison-Wesley, 2002. We'll refer to this book in the future as *[P of EAA]*.

Generalities of the pattern

TS encourages you to skip any object-oriented design and map your business components directly onto required user actions. You focus on the operations the user can accomplish through the presentation layer and write a method for each request. The method is referred to as a *transaction script*. The word *transaction* here generically indicates a business transaction you want to carry out. The word *script* indicates that you logically associate a sequence of system-carried actions (namely, a script) with each user action.

TS has been used for years, but it's not becoming obsolete any time soon for just one reason: it pushes a task-based vision of the business logic, and that vision is key to increasing the level of user experience as you saw in past chapters.

In TS, each required user action is implemented proceeding from start to finish within the boundaries of a physical transaction. Data access is usually encapsulated in a set of components distinct from those implementing the actual script and likely grouped into a data-access layer. By design, TS doesn't have any flavors of object-oriented design. Any logic you model through a TS is expressed using language syntax elements such as IF, WHILE, and FOR. Figure 7-1 summarizes the spirit of the Transaction Script pattern.

Note A system where the business logic is implemented using TS has a rather compact, layered architecture in which TS coincides with the application layer and connects directly to the data-access layer. The final schema, then, is the same as the classic three-tier architecture, proving once more that the four-layer layered architecture we introduced in Chapter 5, "Discovering the domain architecture," is just a more modern transformation of classic three-tier.

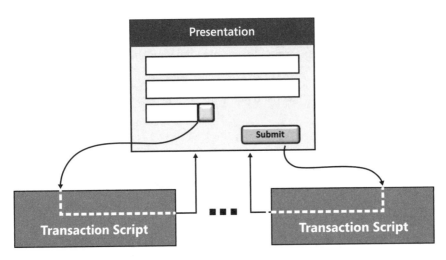

FIGURE 7-1 A bird's-eye view of the Transaction Script pattern.

When Transaction Script is an option

TS is suited for simple scenarios where the business logic is straightforward and, better yet, not likely to change and evolve. More generally, TS is suitable for all scenarios where—for whatever reason, whether it's limited complexity or limited skills—you are not going to use any domain modeling.

 Important We'll provide evidence and make the concept stand out even more in just a few moments, but we want to say right away that domain modeling is not the same as scripting object models quickly inferred from a database. That still might be called a *domain model*, but it is a rather anemic domain model.

For example, TS seems to be the perfect choice for a web portal that relies on an existing back office. In this case, you end up with some pages with interactive elements that trigger a server action. Each server action is resolved by making some data validation, perhaps making some trivial calculations, and then forwarding data to the existing back-office system.

Likewise, TS is an option for a plain CRUD system. Interestingly, it is also a valid option in situations where lack of skills and guidance make domain modeling a risky and dangerous route even for complex domains. In this case, by splitting the system in two parts—command and query—you find it easy to implement the command part via TS and maybe spend more time and effort on arranging an effective model for the sole query section of the system.

> **Note** Simplicity and complexity are concepts that are not easy to measure. More importantly, the perception of what's simple and what's complex depends on a person's attitude and skills. If you've been doing object-oriented design for years and know your stuff well, it might be easier and faster for you to arrange a simple domain model than to switch back to procedural coding. So TS doesn't have to be the choice every time you feel the complexity is below a given universally recognized threshold.
>
> More simply, TS is an option you should seriously consider once you feel you know all about the system, and when it doesn't look overly complex in terms of requirements and business rules. Objects make code elegant, but elegance is a positive attribute only if code works and is done right. There's nothing to be ashamed of in using TS—especially in using TS when it is appropriate.

The pattern in action

When it comes to implementation, you can see each transaction script as a standalone, possibly static, method on a class, or you can implement each transaction script in its own class. In doing so, you end up having a nice implementation of the *Command* pattern.

One of the most popular behavioral design patterns, the Command pattern uses objects to represent actions. The command object encapsulates an action and all of its parameters. Typically, the command object exposes a standard interface so that the caller can invoke any command, without getting the intimate knowledge of the command class that will actually do the job. Here's a quick example:

```
public interface IApplicationCommand
{
    int Run();
}

public class BookHotelRoom : IApplicationCommand
{
    Customer _guest;
    DateTime _checkIn, _checkOut;
    String _confirmationNumber;
    // other internal members

    public BookHotelRoom(Customer guest, DateTime checkIn, DateTime checkOut)
    {
        _guest = guest;
        _checkIn = checkIn;
        _checkOut = checkOut;
    }
```

```
public String ConfirmationNumber
{
    get { return _confirmationNumber; }
}

public int Run()
{
    // Start the transaction
    // Check room availability for requested stay
    // Check customer information (already guest, payment method, preferences)
    // Calculate room rate
    // Add a new record to the Bookings database table
    // Generate the confirmation number
    // Commit the transaction
    // E-mail the customer
    // Store the confirmation number to the local member _confirmationNumber
}

...
}
```

The TS pattern doesn't mandate any data types or formats for data exchange. Providing data to scripts and retrieving data from scripts is up to you. So feel free to opt for the approach that best suits your preferences and design needs. A common practice is using plain data-transfer objects (DTOs).

The Domain Model pattern

Often used in DDD solutions but not strictly bound to it, Domain Model is simply a general design pattern. The Domain Model (DM) pattern suggests architects focus on the expected behavior of the system and on the data flows that make it work. You focus on the real system, ideally, with some good help from domain experts and just try to reproduce it in terms of classes.

Generalities of the pattern

A domain model is *not* the same as an object model made of a collection of related classes. A domain model is a model that faithfully represents a business domain and, especially, the processes within the domain and data flows. If you reduce domain modeling to the transposition of a database structure into C# classes, you're missing the point completely. Anyway, consider that missing the point doesn't mean that you're not taking the project home.

> **Note** At the risk of looking overzealous and sounding pedantic, we want to repeat that you don't need to use successful and popular patterns to write code that works. At the same time, you should not dismiss any popular pattern you hear about as generally useless or impractical. We'll usually be the first in line to yell that some (and perhaps even many) object-oriented patterns are cumbersome and not very practical. However, here we're talking about strategic and architecture-level patterns that might guide you through the twists and turns of the design maze. It's not about being freakily cool; it's about being effective and making the right choices.

When Domain Model is an option

Complexity is the driving force for the adoption of the Domain Model pattern. Complexity should be measured in terms of the current requirements, but to spot indicators of complexity you should also look at possible future enhancements or requirements churn. Working with the Domain Model pattern is generally more expensive in simple scenarios, but it is a savvy choice in larger systems because its startup and maintenance costs can be absorbed more easily.

Note Often the major strength of an approach, when taken to the limit, becomes its most significant weakness. This fact also holds true for the Domain Model pattern. It's really not easy to envision a full system in terms of an abstract model where entities and relationships describe the processes and their mechanics. The major difficulty we've encountered in our careers with domain modeling is not technical, but purely design. Sometimes we spent hours and even days trying to make sense of how a given aspect of the domain was best represented, whether through a method, a combination of properties, or a domain service. And sometimes we also spent considerable time speculating about the right modifier to use for the setter of a class property, whether it was a private, a public, or just a read-only property.

The slippery point is that the domain model is a public programming interface you expose for the application layer and others to consume. In particular, the application layer is bound to a particular client application and new applications can always be written in the future, even outside your direct control. The domain model is just like an API. You never know how people are going to use it, and you should try to make any misuse just impossible. (Impractical is not enough here.) Worse yet, the domain model is not a simple API for some functionality; it's an API for your business. It implies that the misuse of the domain model might lead to misusing the business and running inconsistent and incoherent processes.

Yes, a domain model is a tremendous responsibility and is complex. On the other hand, you need complexity to handle complexity.

Important Sometimes, if you don't feel completely confident or don't get to know the domain very well, you might even want to avoid the domain model and or resort to using far lighter forms of it, like the notorious anemic domain model.

The pattern in action

A domain model is a collection of plain old classes, each of which faithfully represents a significant entity in the business domain. These classes are data containers and can expose public properties, but they also are expected to expose methods. The term *POCO* (Plain Old CLR Object) is often used to refer to classes in a domain model.

More often than not, at this point we get the question, "Which methods?"

It's a fair-enough question, but it has no answer other than, "Your understanding of the domain will tell you which methods each class needs." When designing a domain model, you shouldn't feel like God at work creating the world. You are not expected to build a model that represents all the ramifications of human life on planet Earth. Your purpose is simply to recognize and define software entities that replicate the processes (and related behaviors) you observe in the business domain. Therefore, the more you know about the domain, the easier it will be for you to copycat it in software.

In the real world, you seldom observe models; more likely, you'll observe actions and events. Those actions will help you figure out the behavior to implement on classes. Keeping an eye on actions more than on properties of entities does help. On the other hand, it's the *Tell-Don't-Ask* vector we discussed in Chapter 3, "Principles of software design."

At some point, the classes in the domain model needs to be persisted. Persistence is not a responsibility of the domain model, and it will happen outside of the domain model through repositories connected to the infrastructure layer. To the application's eyes, the domain model is the logical database and doesn't have any relational interface. At the same time, persistence most likely happens through a relational interface. The conversion between the model and relational store is typically performed by ad hoc tools—specifically, Object/Relational Mapper (O/RM) tools, such as Microsoft's Entity Framework or NHibernate. The unavoidable mismatch between the domain model and the relational model is the critical point of implementing a Domain Model pattern.

> **Note** In the next chapter, we'll return to the pros, cons, and details of a domain model when viewed through the lens of a DDD approach.

The Anemic Domain Model (anti-)pattern

The landmark of a domain model is the behavior associated with objects. And "which behavior exactly" is a common objection that boosters of the Domain Model pattern often hear. The Domain Model pattern is sometimes contrasted to another object model pattern known as *Anemic Domain Model* (ADM).

Generalities of the pattern

In an anemic domain model, all objects still follow the naming convention of real-world domain entities, relationships between entities exist, and the overall structure of the model closely matches the real domain space. Yet, there's no behavior in entities, just properties. From here comes the use of the adjective *anemic* in the pattern's name.

The inspiring principle of ADM is that you don't deliberately put any logic in the domain objects. All the required logic, instead, is placed in a set of service components that all together contain the whole domain logic. These services consume the domain model, access the storage, and orchestrate persistence.

Inferring models from the database might cause anemia

The canonical example of an anemic domain model is the set of objects you get when you infer a model from an existing database structure. If you do this with Entity Framework, you get a bunch of classes that map all the tables in the database. Each class is filled with properties that are a close adaptation of table columns. Foreign keys and constraints are also honored, yielding a graph of objects that faithfully represent the underlying relational data model.

Classes that Entity Framework generates are declared *partial*, meaning they can be extended at the source-code level (for example, not through compile-level inheritance). In other words, using Entity Framework in a database-first model doesn't prevent you from having a behavior-rich model. What you get by default, though, is just an anemic domain model in which all classes are plain containers of properties with public getters and setters.

Is it a pattern or an a anti-pattern?

There's a general consensus about ADM: it is more of an anti-pattern than a pattern, and it's a design rule you'd better not follow. We think there's a conceptual view of it and a pragmatic view, and choosing either might be fine. Let's see why it is almost unanimously considered an anti-pattern. The words of Martin Fowler are extremely clear in this regard, and you can read them here: *http://www.martinfowler.com/bliki/AnemicDomainModel.html*. (Note that the article was written over a decade ago.)

In brief, Fowler says that ADM is "contrary to the basic idea of object-oriented design; which is to combine data and process together. The anemic domain model is really just a procedural style design." In addition, Fowler warns developers against considering anemic objects to be real objects. Anemic objects are, in the words of Fowler, "little more than bags of getters and setters."

We couldn't agree more. Additionally, we agree with Fowler when he says that object-oriented purism is good but we "need more fundamental arguments against this anemia." Honestly, the arguments that Fowler brings to the table sound both promising and nebulous. He also says that ADM incurs all the costs of a domain model without yielding any of the benefits.

In summary, the key benefits referred to by Fowler can be summarized as listed here:

- Analysis leads to objects that closely model the domain space and are tailored to the real needs.

- The strong domain perspective of things reduces the risk of misunderstandings between the domain experts and the development team.

- Code is likely to become more readable and easily understandable.

- The final result has more chances to really be close to expectations.

How concrete are these declared benefits? What if the resulting domain model only looks like the real things but leaves a gap to fill? Benefits of a domain model are there if you catch them. In our (admittedly rather defensive and pragmatic) approach to software design, a good anemic model probably yields better results than a bad domain model. In the end, not surprisingly, it's up to you and your vision of things. It depends on how you evaluate the skills of the team and whether you consider the team capable of coming up with an effective domain model.

The bottom line is that ADM is an anti-pattern, especially if it is used in complex domains where you face a lot of frequently-changing business rules. In the context of data-driven applications and CRUD systems, an anemic model is more than fine.

Moving the focus from data to tasks

For decades, relational data modeling has been a more than an effective way to model the business layer of software applications. In the .NET space, the turning point came in the early 2000s, when more and more companies that still had their core business logic carved in the rough stone of mainframes took advantage of the Microsoft .NET Framework and Internet breakthroughs to renovate and modernize their systems. In only a few years, this poured an incredible amount of complexity on the shoulders of developers. RAD and relational modeling then—we'd say almost naturally—appeared worn out and their limits were exposed. Figure 7-2 illustrates the evolution of data-modeling techniques over the past decades.

The figure is neither exhaustive nor comprehensive: it only aims to show changes in patterns and approaches over the years that have been used to produce faithful models.

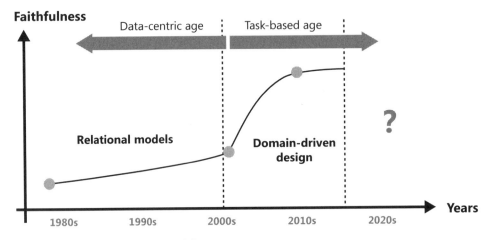

FIGURE 7-2 Trends in application modeling.

The chart measures the faithfulness of the produced models and observed processes. It comes as no surprise that Domain-Driven Design improved faithfulness. The advent of DDD also started moving the focus from data-centric design to task-based design. It was a natural move essentially driven by the need to handle complexity in some way.

The transition to a task-based vision of the world is the ultimate message of the Tell-Don't-Ask principle, which we find generically mentioned more often than concretely applied. Tasks are the workflows behind each use-case and each interaction between the user and the system. From a design perspective, a single layer that contains whatever might exist between presentation and data is a rather bloated layer. In this regard, isolating the orchestration of tasks into a separate layer leaves the sole domain logic to code. Domain logic fits more than naturally either into domain objects or, if an anemic design is chosen, into separate modules.

Let's look at an example to give more concrete form to what we have so far generically called the *application layer*.

Task orchestration in ASP.NET MVC

In an ASP.NET MVC application, any user-interface action ends in a method invoked on a controller class. The controller, then, is the first place where you should consider orchestrating tasks. Abstractly speaking, there's no difference at all between a controller method and postback handler. In much the same way, every savvy developer avoids having full orchestration logic in a *Button1_Click* event handler, you should avoid having full orchestration logic in a controller method.

Controller as a coordinator

Responsibility-Driven Design (RDD) is a design methodology introduced a decade ago by Rebecca Wirfs-Brock and Alan McKean in the book *Object Design: Roles, Responsibilities, and Collaborations* (Addison-Wesley, 2002). The essence of RDD consists of breaking down a system feature into a number of actions the system must perform. Next, each action is mapped to a component (mostly a class) being designed. Executing the action becomes a specific responsibility of the component. The role of the component depends on the responsibilities it assumes. RDD defines a few stereotypes to classify the possible role each component can have. We're not loyal followers of the RDD approach even though we find its practices useful for mechanically breaking up into digestible pieces nuts that are hard to crack.

We think that one of the RDD stereotypes—the *Coordinator*—meticulously describes the ideal of role of an ASP.NET MVC controller. The RDD Coordinator stereotype suggests you group all the steps that form the implementation of the action within a single application service. From within the controller method, therefore, you place a single call to the application service and use its output to feed the view-model object. That's exactly the layout we illustrated Here's the layout again:

```
public ActionResult PlaceOrder(OrderInputModel orderInfo)
{
    // Input data already mapped thanks to the model binding
    // infrastructure of ASP.NET MVC

    // Perform the task invoking a application service and
    // get a view model back from application layer
    var service = new OrderService();
    var model = service.PlaceOrder();

    // Invoke next view
    return View(model);
}
```

The overall structure of the ASP.NET MVC controller method is quite simple. Solicited by an incoming HTTP request, the action method relays most of the job to another component that coordinates all further steps. The call into the *OrderService* class in the example is where the boundary between the presentation and application layers is trespassed.

There's an interesting alternative to the code layout just shown that might come in handy when you don't much like the idea of having a brand new application layer for any new front end. So imagine you have a consolidated application layer and need to add a new front end. The application layer is mostly the same except for some view-model adaptation. In this case, it might be acceptable to add an extra step to the presentation layer, as shown here:

```
// Get response from existing application layer
var service = new OrderService();
var model = service.PlaceOrder();

// Adapt to the new view model
var newFrontendModel = someAdapter.NewViewModel(response);
```

In general, you shouldn't expect the application layer to be fully reusable—the name says it all. However, any level of reusability you can achieve in a specific scenario is welcome. And the more you can reuse, the best. Instead, what is invariably shared and reusable is the domain logic.

Connecting the application and presentation layers

The junction point between application layer and presentation is the controller. In previous chapter, you saw how to use poor-man's dependency injection to implement it. To use a full-fledged Inversion of Control (IoC) pattern like Microsoft Unity, in ASP.NET MVC you need to override the controller factory. Here's a code snippet that shows most of it. In *global.asax*, at the application startup you register a custom controller factory:

```
var factory = new UnityControllerFactory();
ControllerBuilder.Current.SetControllerFactory(factory);
```

The class *UnityControllerFactory* can be as simple as shown here:

```
public class UnityControllerFactory : DefaultControllerFactory
{
    public static IUnityContainer Container { get; private set; }
    public UnityControllerFactory()
    {
        Container = new UnityContainer();    // Initialize the IoC
        Container.LoadConfiguration();       // Configure it reading details from web.config
    }
    protected override IController GetControllerInstance(RequestContext context, Type type)
    {
        if (type == null)  return null;
        return Container.Resolve(type) as IController;
    }
}
```

With this code in place, any controller class can be created without the default parameterless constructor:

```
public class HomeController
{
    private IHomeService _service;
    public HomeController(IHomeService service)
    {
        _service = service;
    }
    ...
}
```

> **Note** Writing your own controller factory to integrate Unity in ASP.NET MVC is not strictly necessary. You can use the Unity.Mvc library available as a NuGet package. For more information, see *http://github.com/feedbackhound/Unity.Mvc5*.

Connecting the application and data-access layers

A similar problem surfaces when connecting the application with the infrastructure layer where data-access code resides. You solve it in the same way—that is, via dependency injection. As you'll see in more detail in the next chapter, a *repository* is a common name for containers of data-access logic in a domain model scenario.

```
public class HomeService
{
    private ISomeEntityRepository _someEntityRepo;
    public HomeService(ISomeEntityRepository repo)
    {
        _someEntityRepo = repo;
    }
    ...
}
```

Interestingly enough, you don't need other changes in the code that initializes controllers and sets up factories. You only need to make sure that repository types and interfaces (one for each significant entity in the domain model) are mapped to the IoC container. All IoC libraries let you do type mapping both through configuration and via a fluent API. The reason why you don't need further code other than configuration is that all IoC containers have today the ability to resolve chains of dependencies in a transparent way. So if you tell the IoC container to resolve the controller type, and the controller type has dependencies on some application service types, which in turn depend on one or more repositories, all of that happens in the context of a single line of code.

Using dependency injection for connecting layers is recommended, but it's not the only solution. If you have layers living in the same process space, a simpler route is direct and local instantiation of objects, whether they are application layer services or repositories. The drawback in this case is tight coupling between the layers involved:

```
// Tight coupling between the class OrderService
// and the class that contains this code
var service = new OrderService();
var model = service.PlaceOrder();
```

At this level, the problem of tight coupling should be noted, but it is not a tragedy per se. It certainly makes the container class less testable, but it doesn't change the substance of code. Also, refactoring to add loose coupling—namely, refactoring to the *Dependency Inversion* principle explained in Chapter 3—is a relatively easy task, and many code-assistant tools make it nearly a breeze.

If layers are deployed to distinct tiers, on the other hand, using HTTP interfaces is the common way to go. You can use, for example, the *async/await* C# pattern to place a call via the *HttpClient* client to a remote endpoint. The remote endpoint can be, for example, a Web API front end.

Orchestrating tasks within the domain

In general terms, the business logic of an application contains the orchestration of tasks, domain logic, and a few extra things. The extra things are commonly referred to as *domain services*. In a nutshell, domain services contain any logic that doesn't fit nicely in any domain entity. When you follow the guidelines of the Domain Model pattern, the business logic is for the most part split across domain entities. If some concepts can't be mapped in this way, that's the realm of a domain service.

Cross-entity domain logic

Domain services typically contain shares of business logic that contain operations that involve multiple domain entities. For the most part, domain services are complex, multistep operations that are carried out within the boundaries of the domain and, perhaps, the infrastructure layer. Canonical examples of domain services are services like *OrderProcessor*, *BestPriceFinder*, or *GoldCustomerEvaluator*. Names assigned to services per se should reflect real operations and be easily understandable by both stakeholders and domain experts.

> **Note** The point of naming domain services so that they are immediately recognizable by experts is not simply to enhance the general readability of code. More importantly, it is to establish a ubiquitous language shared by the development team and domain experts. As you'll see in the next chapter, ubiquitous language is a pillar of Domain-Driven Design.

Let's expand on a sample domain service, such as the *GoldCustomerEvaluator* service. In an e-commerce system, after a customer has placed an order, you might need to check whether this new order changes the status of the customer because she has possibly exceeded a given minimum sales volume. For this check to be carried out, you need to read the current volume of sales for the customer, apply some of the logic of the rewarding system in place, and determine the new status. In a realistic implementation, this might require you to read the Orders tables, some rewarding specific views, and perform some calculation. In the end, it's a mix of persistence, orders, customers, and business rules. Not a single entity is involved, and the logic is cross-entity. A good place to have it, then, is in a domain service.

Finally, operations defined as a domain service are for the most part stateless; you pass in some data and receive back some response. No state is maintained, except perhaps some cache.

Where are the connection strings?

Entities in a domain model are expected to be plain-old C# objects (POCOs) and agnostic about persistence. In other words, an *Invoice* class just contains data like date, number, customer, items, tax information, and payment terms. In addition, it might contain a method like *GetEstimatedDateOfPayment* that works on date and payments terms, adds a bit of calculation regarding holidays, and determines when the invoice might be paid.

The code that loads, say, an *Invoice* entity from storage and the code that saves it persistently to storage doesn't go with the entity itself. Other components of the system will take care of that. These classes are repositories. They are for the most part concerned with CRUD functionality and any additional persistence logic you might need. Repositories are the only part of the system that deal with connection strings.

Should you care about tiers?

Multiple tiers are not generally a good feature to have in a system. A popular quote attributed to Martin Fowler says that the first rule of distributed programming is, "Do not use distributed objects; at least until it becomes completely necessary." Tiers slow down the overall performance and increase the overall complexity. Both aspects, then, affect the overall cost to build and maintain the application. This said, tiers—some tiers—just can't be avoided. So they're sort of evil, but a necessary evil.

For example, an unavoidable barrier exists between the code that runs on the user's machine and the server-side code. Another typical divide exists between the server-side code and the database server. Web applications mostly fall into this category.

In addition, each application might have its own good reasons to introduce multiple tiers. One reason could be the need to support an external product that requires its own process. Another good reason for multiple tiers is the quest for security. A module that runs in isolation in a process can be more easily protected and accessed if it's used only by authorized callers.

Much less often than commonly reckoned, multiple tiers serve as a trick to increase the scalability of a system. More precisely, a system where certain components can be remoted and duplicated on additional tiers is inherently more scalable than systems that do not have this capability. But scalability is just one aspect of a system. And often the quest for scalability—that is, the need for stabilized performance under pressure—hurts everyday performance.

In summary, as a general rule the number of physical tiers should be kept as low as possible. And the addition of a new tier should happen only after a careful cost-benefit analysis, where costs are mostly in the area of increased complexity and benefits lie in the area of security, scalability and, perhaps, fault tolerance. Surely you've seen system integrators creating a crazy three-tier or more system (especially in the early 2000s) and then wondered why the system was so slow even though the right architectural approach was employed.

Moving data across the boundaries

A tier represents a physical boundary to cross, whether it is a process boundary or machine boundary. Crossing a boundary is an expensive operation. The cost is higher if you have to reach a physically distant computer rather than just another process within the same machine. One rule of thumb to consider is that a call that crosses the boundaries of a process is about 100 times slower than an equivalent in-process call. And it is even slower if it has to travel over the network to reach the endpoint.

How does a call travel over the wire and across the boundaries? Does it travel light? Or should it bring along everything and travel overloaded? Choosing the most appropriate way of moving data across the boundaries (logical or physical) is another design problem to tackle in the business segment of an application.

Data flow in layered architecture

Figure 7-3 presents a rather abstract flow of data within a layered architecture. When a command is executed, data flows from the user interface in the form of an input model through the application layer. Depending on the requested action, the application layer might need to arrange instances of domain entities using content from the input model (for example, creating a new order from provided information). In a layered Domain Model system, persistence typically means turning domain entities into a physical—often relational—data model.

> **Note** Especially in DDD scenarios, you find sometimes the term *input model* replaced by the term *command*. The term command is closer to the idea of executing a task.

On the way back, when a query is requested, content read from the data model is first turned into a graph of domain entities and then massaged into a view model for the user interface to render it.

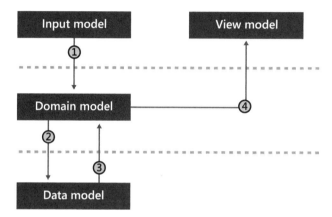

FIGURE 7-3 Abstract representation of data flows across the stack of a layered architecture.

Abstractly speaking, a layered system manages four different models of data. The four models shown in Figure 7-3 are all logically distinct, but they might coincide sometimes. The domain model and data model are often the same in the sense that the domain model is directly persisted to the infrastructure. In an ASP.NET MVC application, the input model and view model often coincide in the GET and POST implementation of a controller action. In a CRUD system, all models might coincide and be just one—that will be the "M" in the Model-View-Controller (MVC) pattern.

> **Important** As we see it, the *model* in the MVC pattern is one of the most misunderstood concepts in the entire history of software. Originally devised in the 1980s, MVC began as an application pattern and could be used to architect the entire application. That was during the time of monolithic systems created end to end as a single transaction script. The advent of multilayered and multitiered systems changed the role of the MVC but didn't invalidate its significance. MVC remains a powerful pattern, except that the idea of a single model doesn't work anymore. *Model* in MVC was defined as "data being worked on in the view." This means that today MVC is essentially a presentation pattern.

Sharing the Domain Model entities

In layered architecture that follows the Domain Model pattern, domain entities are the most relevant containers of data. Is it recommended to let domain entities bubble up to the user interface and serialize them through tiers if required?

Also, in data-driven apps where you propagate the Domain Model to the presentation layer (kind of self-tracking entities), the anemic domain model fits better.

When using a rich-Model (domain model) with methods within the classes, it doesn't make sense to propagate the Domain Entities to the presentation layer, because the presentation layer would be getting access to those methods in the entities. In DDD applications, the presentation layer should have a different *presentation model*, a DTO-model (in many cases a ViewModel) based where the DTOs are designed depending on the screen/page necessities rather than based on the Domain Model.

Domain entities within layers

We don't see any problem in passing domain model classes all around the components and modules orchestrated by the application layer. As long as the data transfer occurs between layers, there should be no problems, neither technical nor design. If the data transfer occurs between tiers, you might run into serialization issues if domain entities form a rather intricate graph with circular references. In this case, it might be easier to introduce some ad hoc, data-transfer objects specifically designed to handle a scenario or two.

> **Note** To be precise, you might face problems even moving domain entities between layers when entities have lazy-loaded properties. In this case, when the layer that receives the entity attempts to read through lazy-loaded properties, an exception is raised because the data has not been read and the storage context is no longer available.

As for letting domain entities rise up to the presentation layer, all previous considerations hold, plus more. The view model behind the user interface doesn't have to match the structure of the domain model used to express the business logic. Quite simply, if the content carried by a domain model entity makes the cut of the user interface, why not use it and save yourself a bunch of other data-transfer classes?

Having said that in principle using domain model entities throughout the various layers and tiers is more than acceptable and, in some cases, even desirable, there are a few possible side effects to consider.

Dangers of using a single model for commands and queries

This is a deeper point we'll properly address starting with the next chapter and even more in Chapter 10, "Introducing CQRS," and Chapter 11, "Implementing CQRS." For now, it suffices to say that referencing domain entities from the user interface might require writing presentation code that fully leverages the behavior built in domain entities. Because the behavior is ultimately domain logic, and domain logic must be constantly consistent with the business rules, we see the potential risk of writing presentation code that breaks up the consistency.

Possible constraints for future extensibility

Modern applications are constantly extended with new, mostly mobile, front ends. Especially with mobile and devices, the likelihood of presenting different use-cases than other front ends is high. This might create the need to bring different aggregates of data into the user interface that just don't exist in the domain model. You don't want to modify the domain model to meet the needs of a particular front end. Adding ad hoc data-transfer objects, then, becomes the most appropriate option.

Using data-transfer objects

It should be clear at this point that seldom does a single solution for moving data across boundaries work within a given system and for its entire lifetime. Sometimes, it might be quick and easy to use domain entities everywhere; sometimes, you want to use data-transfer objects (DTOs). It is important to know that no solution is always preferable over another. As usual, it depends.

Generalities of a data-transfer object

A data-transfer object is an object specifically designed to carry data between tiers. A DTO has no behavior and is a plain bag of getters and setters that is rather inexpensive to create (for example, it needs no unit testing). The reason for having a DTO is that, as a plain container, it allows you to pack multiple chunks of data and transfer all of that in a single roundtrip.

A DTO is an inherently serializable object. Its use is mostly recommended when remote components are involved. However, we like to offer a broader perspective of DTOs and consider also using them between layers.

DTOs vs. domain entities

The typical use of a DTO is when you need, say, to display or process order and customer information at the same time, but the amount of information required for actual processing needs only a few of the properties available on the order and customer entities. A DTO can flatten even complex hierarchies to simpler data containers that contain what's necessary. (See Figure 7-4.)

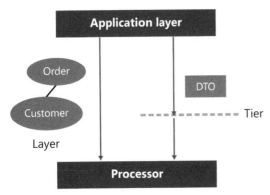

FIGURE 7-4 DTOs vs. domain entities when moving data across tiers and layers.

Sharing domain entities mostly works across layers and is essentially a desirable shortcut to minimize the overall number of classes involved. From a pure design perspective, using DTOs is the "perfect" solution that guarantees the maximum decoupling between interfacing components and also extensibility.

However, a full DTO solution inevitably leads to the proliferation of many small classes in the various Visual Studio projects. On one end, you have the problem of managing and organizing those numerous classes in folders and namespaces. On the other hand, you also have to face the cost of loading data to, and extracting data from, DTOs.

AutoMapper and adapters

The real cost of DTOs is just in filling them with data and reading back from them. This is done by ad hoc components generically called *adapters*. An adapter is a plain C# class; more often, however, it is a repository of static methods. Typically, an adapter copies property values from domain entities to DTOs and vice versa.

As you can see, it's rather cumbersome and even dreary work, and it also takes several lines of code. Finally, you might even want to have some tests around to check whether mapping actually works. Building adapters, therefore, is conceptually simple but takes time and effort. Dealing with this reality led to a tool that largely automates the building of DTOs. The tool is AutoMapper, which you can read about at *http://automapper.org*.

With AutoMapper, you do two basic things. First, you create a map between a source type and a target type. Second, you invoke the mapping procedure to fill an instance of the target type with data in an instance of the source type:

```
Mapper.CreateMap<YourSourceType, YourDtoType>();
```

Once a mapping is defined, you invoke it via the *Map* method:

```
var dto = Mapper.Map<YourDtoType>(sourceObject);
```

The tool also has nongeneric versions of methods that come in handy in situations where you just don't know the actual types involved. AutoMapper doesn't do real magic here and doesn't even read your mind at run time. All it does is use conventions (for example, matching property names) while not denying configuration (for example, for resolving names that don't match or computed properties).

In addition, consider one downside of an automatic tool like AutoMapper. When you ask it to create a DTO from an entity, it can't just avoid to navigate the entire graph of the entity which must be available in memory and therefore materialized from storage. It could be probably much easier and faster to just instruct the domain services to return readymade DTOs.

> **Note** Another option for moving data around is using *IQueryable* objects. As you'll see in more detail in Chapter 14, "The persistence layer," which is dedicated to the infrastructure of the system, a highly debated but emerging practice is returning *IQueryable* from data repositories.
>
> *IQueryable* is the core LINQ interface, and all it does is provide functionality to evaluate a query against a LINQ-enabled data source. One reason to return *IQueryable* from re-positories is to enable upper layers to create different kinds of queries in an easier way. This ability keeps the repository interfaces thinner and also reduces the need to use DTOs, because some DTOs can be anonymous types. Even when DTOs are created out of queries, however, they belong to the specific layer, are isolated in the context of the layer, and can be easier to manage.

Summary

In the previous chapter, we discussed the presentation layer and focused on the user experience. This included looking at how important it is to have user tasks organized around smooth and fluent processes, with no bottlenecks. In this chapter, we discussed the business layer and how important it is to have it faithfully match the real processes in the domain space.

This reminds us of the classic dichotomy between doing the right things vs. doing things right. As you might understand, one doesn't stem from the other, but both are important achievements.

Doing things right is all that the presentation layer should be concerned with. Doing things right is the gist of efficiency: implementing tasks in an optimal way, fast and fluid. Doing the right things is, instead, all that the business layer should be concerned about. Doing the right things is about effectiveness and achieving goals. The ultimate goal of a software system is matching requirements and providing a faithful representation of the domain space.

To make domain modeling more effective, patterns like Domain Model and methodologies like DDD are fundamental. These methodologies sharpen the profile of what was generically referred to as the *business layer* for years. We introduced the application layer and domain layer, and we kept data access isolated in the infrastructure layer, along with other pieces of the surrounding infrastructure (such as email servers, file systems, and external services).

We've been quite generic about the Domain Model pattern here; in the next chapter, we focus on Domain-Driven Design.

Finishing with a smile

A successful business layer requires keen observation and modeling. It also requires an ability to do things in the simplest possible manner. "Do it simple but not simplistically" is one of our favorite mantras. And it is a wink at the first of Murphy's laws that we list for the chapter: if you have anything complex that works, you can be sure that in the past it was something simple that worked.

See *http://www.murphys-laws.com* for an extensive listing of computer (and noncomputer) related laws and corollaries. Here are a few to enjoy for now:

- A complex system that works is invariably found to have evolved from a simple system that works.

- Investment in software reliability will increase until it exceeds the probable cost of errors.

- In theory there is no difference between theory and practice, but in practice there is.

CHAPTER 8

Introducing Domain Model

The model and the heart of the design shape each other.
—Eric Evans

About 10 years ago, a relatively young and fast-growing company hired Dino for ASP.NET training. They said that they mostly wanted some advanced web stuff, but they also wanted to learn more about those emerging patterns that help shape a more conceptual view of the business domain. They asked if they could reserve a day to get an overview of domain-driven design (DDD).

People with at least a smattering of DDD were not numerous at the time. Fortunately, Andrea was one of them and we were already in touch. So Andrea put together a quick primer on DDD that helped Dino immensely to prepare the extra day for the customer. By the way, that customer is now a worldwide leader in its industry, and we can't help but think that their CTO's visionary interest in DDD was very savvy and made it possible for the company to effectively tackle the complexity of a growing business.

DDD was originally defined as an approach to software development that starts from a ubiquitous language, passes through a map of bounded contexts, and ends with a recommended layered architecture centered on an object-oriented model of the business domain. Following the DDD principles, common steps such as understanding requirements, turning requirements into specs, actual coding and testing come easily—or at least, it's the easiest they can come given an objectively high level of business complexity.

This chapter provides you with the rationale of DDD, putting emphasis on the alphabet soup of the domain layer. In the next chapter, we'll see DDD in action applied to a concrete business domain.

The data-to-behavior shift

For a long time, the typical approach to development has been more or less the following. First, you collect requirements and make some analysis to identify both relevant entities (for example, customer, order, product) and processes to be implemented. Second, armed with this understanding you try to infer a physical (and mostly relational) data model that can support the processes. You make sure the data model is relationally consistent (primary keys, constraints, normalization, indexing) and then start building software components against tables that identify the most relevant business entities.

You can also rely on database-specific features such as stored-procedures as a way to implement behavior while keeping the structure of the database hidden from upper levels of code. The final step is finding a comfortable model for representing data and moving it up to the presentation layer.

This approach to modeling a business domain is not wrong per se, and it just works. Nearly every developer knows about it; it's a mature and consolidated practice and, again, it just works. So why should one change it for something that has a more attractive and exotic name—say, DDD—but also represents to many a sort of leap into the unknown?

Rationale behind models and domains

Over the years, the two of us many times have accepted the challenge of explaining the pluses of a domain-driven approach compared to a database-driven approach to software design. And often we just failed. Most of those times, however, we failed because we put the whole thing down as objects versus data readers.

It's not about using objects instead of data readers

Well aware of what data access was before .NET, we recognize that the availability of ADO.NET was a landmark for Microsoft Windows developers. ADO.NET is a relatively thin layer over the infrastructure of a relational database. A data source provider hides the nitty-gritty details of the underlying storage and exposes .NET objects for cursors and result sets. The working pattern is crystal clear and easy: you open a connection, define a SQL command, decide how you want data back—either as a cursor or result set—execute the command, and close the connection. Nicely enough, ADO.NET cursors are also handy objects and result sets are even serializable.

In ADO.NET, you face some trouble only with type conversion and naming is not as strong as it is when you work with classes. To refer to a table column, for example, you must know the name and the name is a plain string. You know only at run time if you happened to type it wrong.

Narrowing the view to the Microsoft .NET Framework, LINQ-to-SQL and Entity Framework offered a quick-and-easy wizard to package up an existing database into a set of easy-to-manage objects. In addition, the burden of dealing with database connections and SQL commands was moved within the folds of ad hoc components that, moreover, were implementing patterns like unit-of-work, query object, lazy loading, and optimistic concurrency.

To cut a long story short, LINQ-to-SQL (now defunct) and Entity Framework were in the beginning Object/Relational Mapper (O/RM) tools with some additional wizardry to infer an object model out of a new or existing relational database.

Well, this is not what it means to take a domain-driven approach to software design.

This is simply writing a data-access layer using handy objects instead of ADO.NET data readers or DataSets. And it is a great achievement, anyway.

A persistent object model is not a domain model

As we discussed in Chapter 5, "Discovering the domain architecture," DDD is an approach that involves much more than just writing data-access code using objects instead of records. DDD is primarily about crunching knowledge of the domain and has ubiquitous language and bounded contexts as the primary outcome. Within a bounded context, you often express the knowledge of the domain through a model. And most of the time—but not necessarily—this model is a special type of an object model and is called a "domain model."

Important Doing DDD is too often perceived simply as having an object model with some special characteristics. As we described in Chapter 5, DDD is especially about mapping contexts and their relationships, and then it is about giving each context an appropriate architecture. The architecture that Eric Evans recommended in his seminal book *Domain-Driven Design: Tackling Complexity in the Heart of Software* (Prentice Hall, 2003) is based on a domain model defined as an object model with special features. A few things have changed since. Today, in DDD context mapping is paramount and modeling the domain through objects is just one of the possible options—though the most broadly used one. We're going with the assumption that the domain model is an object model in this chapter and the next.

In the end, an object-based domain model is just a persistent object model, except that it is decorated by some apparently weird characteristics: the preference of factories over plain constructors, abundant use of complex types, limited use of primitive types, mostly private setters on properties, and methods. All those apparently weird characteristics of the set of classes called a "domain model" exist for a specific reason.

What a model is and why you need one

The Mercator projection is a graphical representation of the world map. Its unique characteristics make it suitable for nautical purposes; in fact, the Mercator projection is the standard map projection used to elaborate nautical courses. See *http://en.wikipedia.org/wiki/Mercator_projection* for more details. Therefore, the Mercator projection is a model.

Is it a model that truly mirrors the real world? Is it both real and ideal?

The Mercator projection is based on a scale that increases as you proceed from the Equator up and down to the poles. Near the poles, the scale becomes infinite. Every square you see on the map represents—regardless of size—the same physical area. The net effect of the scale is that some areas of the world are seemingly larger or smaller than real. For example, if you look at the world layout through the perspective of the Mercator projection, you would say that Alaska is as large as Brazil. The reality, instead, is different, as Brazil takes up as much as five times the area of Alaska.

When you draw a course on a Mercator world projection, the angle between the course and the Equator remains constant across all meridians. This made it easy—already back in the 1500s—to measure courses and bearings via protractors.

The Mercator map is a model that distorts both areas and distances; in this regard, it is not suited to faithfully representing the map of the world as it really is. You don't want to use it instead of, say, Google Maps to represent a city on a map. On the other hand, it's a great model for the (bounded) context it was created for—nautical cartography.

It's all about behavior

The domain model is intended to express, as faithfully as possible, the core business concepts for the application to deal with. The domain model is the API of the core business, and you want domain model classes to be always consistent with the business concept they represent.

When designing the domain model, you should make sure that no incorrect call to the API is possible that might determine, subsequently, that any of the domain objects are in an invalid state. Restrictions on a domain model have the sole purpose of making classes perfectly adherent to the core business concepts and continuously consistent.

It should be clear that to stay continuously consistent with the business you should focus your design on behavior much more than on data. To make DDD a success, you must understand how it works and render it with software. The software you write is primarily a domain model.

DDD is always good for everyone

The analytical part of DDD, as explained in Chapter 5, is good for any project of a significant lifespan. It's about analysis in the end, and it consists of learning the mechanics of the domain and expressing that through an appropriate vocabulary. It's not about coding, and it's not about technologies.

It's just what as an architect you would do in any case—analysis and top-level architecture. However, DDD establishes an approach and introduces the concept of ubiquitous language. Domain modeling is another aspect of DDD closer to software design and coding. And the DDD recipes for domain modeling might or might not work in all cases.

Up until a few years ago, DDD was considered viable only for extremely complex systems characterized by an extremely dynamic set of business rules. The rationale was that the costs of setting up a domain model were too high and easily absorbable only in a long-term project. The final decision results from trading off the need of having a model that mimics the structure and behavior of the system and the costs of having that. Building a successful, all-encompassing object model might be really hard, and it requires the right skills and attitude.

Sometimes, you can just decide that having a domain model is not worth the cost—and it could be both because the return is not perceived to be high and because the costs, instead, are perceived to be too high. When it comes to this, out of your DDD analysis you simply pick up an alternate supporting architecture for each bounded context.

Database is infrastructure

In our experience, one of the aspects that most scares people about DDD is that you end up with a model that has the aura of being database agnostic. How can I effectively design my system and make it perform as expected—many say—if I relegate the database to the bottom of my concerns?

There's a clear misconception here.

All that DDD suggests is that you focus on business concepts and the processes of a given bounded context, learn about them, and plot a system that can faithfully reproduce those business concepts and processes. The resulting system is centered on a model that contains the core business logic.

As long as you are busy designing the model, the database is not your primary concern. Put another way, DDD simply says that domain modeling comes first and the persistence of the modeled domain comes later. But it surely comes. A common way of formulating this same concept is by saying that the database is just part of the infrastructure layer, albeit the most prominent part.

A domain model doesn't have persistence concerns

By design, a domain model is not concerned about persistence. The model is concerned about relevant entities and their relationships, events, and observable behavior. The model just renders such entities through classes and methods. There's no overlapping with databases in this.

The term *persistence ignorance* is often presented as a key attribute of a domain model. But what does this term mean concretely?

Persistence ignorance means that domain model classes should not be given methods to save or materialize instances from disk. Similarly, classes in the domain model should not be exposing methods that require access to the persistence layer to determine things like the total of an order or the status of a customer in the company's reward system.

An application should care about persistence

There's no such thing as a system that doesn't need persistence. The domain model is better if it ignores persistence concerns, but the same certainly can't be true for the rest of the application. All applications need some infrastructure for persistence and various cross-cutting concerns like security, caching, and logging.

DDD applications are no exception.

Furthermore, in a real-world scenario the database is almost always a constraint. Migrating data to a new database is rarely an option; more often, instead, you have some legacy subsystem to integrate and deal with. In this situation, focusing on data design makes even less sense. You are better off focusing on a business-oriented model that is serializable but neatly separated from the persistence layer. First you get the model; next you map it to a new or existing database.

A domain model is serializable if it can be saved to a database. Persistence typically occurs via Object/Relational Mapper (O/RM) tools. If you use an O/RM tool for persistence, the domain model might be subject to some of the requirements set by the O/RM tool. A typical example is when you need to give a domain model class an otherwise unnecessary parameter-less constructor only to let Entity Framework (or NHibernate) materialize the object after a query.

In the end, the domain model should be independent of persistence implementation details, but it often happens that the O/RM technology might place some minor constraints on the model.

Note A domain model class doesn't need dependencies to the O/RM. However, you shouldn't be too surprised if you happen to make some minor concessions to O/RM tools just to be able to serialize the model. An example is having a protected constructor in classes. Another example is having an extra property and a bit of scaffolding to serialize arrays or, in some older versions of Entity Framework, also enumerated types. Let's say that a realistic goal is having a domain model with the absolute minimum dependencies on infrastructure that could possibly work—and it's better if it is zero.

Inside the domain layer

The most common supporting architecture for a bounded context is a layered architecture with a domain model. As described in Chapter 5, on top of the presentation layer, a layered architecture has orchestration code (the application layer) to act on the domain and infrastructure layer. The domain layer consists of a model and services. We assume here that the model is an object model.

Domain model

Overall, one of the most appropriate definitions for a domain model is this: a domain model provides a conceptual view of a business domain. Made of entities and value objects, it models real-world concepts with the declared purpose of turning them into software components.

Inspired by the big picture of DDD you find in the Evans' book, Figure 8-1 summarizes the goal and structure of the domain layer: domain model, modules, and domain services.

Note The term *service* in this context just refers to pieces of business logic, and it has no reference to any technologies (for example, Windows Communication Foundation), architecture (service-oriented architecture), and web infrastructure (web services).

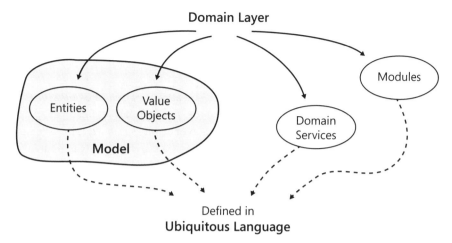

FIGURE 8-1 Terms in the ubiquitous language identify the building blocks of the domain layer.

Modules

When you turn a domain model into software, you identify one or more *modules*. Modules ultimately contain objects and partition the entire domain so that all concerns that surface in the domain model are clearly and cleanly separated. In concrete terms, a DDD module is just the same as a .NET namespace that you use to organize classes in a class library project.

In .NET, you use a namespace to group related types. During refactoring sessions, .NET namespaces can be renamed and change the set of types each contains. Likewise, DDD modules are subject to change over time to better reflect the current understanding of the business domain and actual conceptual contours of the various parts of the model.

If you realize that, at some point, different conceptual contours exist than those currently implemented, you should modify the implementation of the model to reflect that. Conceptual DDD modules and concrete .NET namespaces should be kept in sync all the time.

Within a bounded context, a domain model is organized in modules. Within a .NET project, a domain model is organized in namespaces, and groups of namespaces can be isolated in distinct class libraries. Here's a summary of the cardinalities involved:

- One bounded context has one domain model.

- One bounded context can have several modules.

- One domain model can be related to several modules.

Value objects

A DDD module contains entities and value objects. In the end, both are rendered as .NET classes, but entities and value objects represent quite different concepts and lead to different implementation details.

In DDD, a *value object* is fully defined by its attributes. The attributes of a value object never change after the instance has been created. If it does change, the value object becomes an instance of another value object fully identified by the new collection of attributes. In .NET, DDD value objects are referred to as *immutable* types. The *Int32* and *String* types are the most popular immutable types in the .NET Framework.

Entities

All objects have attributes, but not all objects are fully identified by their collection of attributes. When attributes are not enough to guarantee uniqueness, and when uniqueness is important to the specific object, you have DDD *entities*. Put another way, if the object needs an ID attribute to track it uniquely throughout the context for the entire life cycle, the object has an identity and is said to be an entity.

In his book, Evans uses an example from a banking application to illustrate the difference between entities and value objects and explain why both concepts are relevant to the domain model. How would you consider two deposits of the same amount into the same account on the same day? Are they the same operation done twice, or are they distinct operations that each occur once?

It's clearly the latter.

You have two distinct banking transactions, and the domain requires that you treat each independently. You can always uniquely refer to the transaction later, and the domain must clearly indicate what's required to uniquely identify the object. We'll return to entities and value objects in a moment and discuss in greater detail what it means to create classes for each.

Value objects are just data aggregated together; entities are typically made of data and behavior. When it comes to behavior, though, it's important to distinguish domain logic from application logic. Domain logic goes in the domain layer (model or services); the implementation of use-cases goes into the application layer. For example, an *Order* entity is essentially a document that lays out what the customer wants to buy. The logic associated with the *Order* entity itself is related to the content of the document—taxes and discount calculation, order details, or perhaps estimated date of payment. The entire process of fulfilment, tracking status, or just invoicing for the order are outside the domain logic of the order. They are essentially use-cases associated with the entity, and services are responsible for their implementation.

Persistence of entities

A domain model must be persistent but, as repeatedly mentioned, it doesn't take direct care of its own persistence. Nothing in the domain model implementation refers to load and save operations; yet, these operations are necessary for materializing instances of domain entities and for implementing the business logic.

A special flavor of components—*repositories*—takes care of persistence on behalf of entities.

Repositories are usually invoked from outside the domain model—for example, from the application layer—or from other components of the domain layer, such as domain services. The contracts for repositories are in the domain layer; the implementation of repositories belongs, instead, to a different layer—the infrastructure layer.

The statement that repositories take care of persisting entities is correct given what we have discussed so far. It is inaccurate in the broader perspective you'll gain by the end of the chapter. The bottom line is that repositories persist *aggregates*, a special subset of entities.

Aggregates

As you go through the use-cases found in the requirements and work out the domain model of a given bounded context, it is not unusual that you spot a few individual entities being constantly used and referenced together. In a way, this can be seen as an occurrence of the *data clump* code smell—logically related objects being treated individually instead of being logically grouped and treated as a single object.

An aggregate is basically a consistency boundary that groups and separates entities in the model. The design of aggregates is closely inspired by the business transactions required by your system. Consistency is typically transactional, but in some cases it can also take the form of eventual consistency.

 Note It is a common practice to decompose a domain model in aggregates first, and then, within any aggregate, identify the domain entities.

Devising the aggregate model

In a domain model, the aggregation of multiple entities under a single container is called an *aggregate*. To use the Evans' words, "An aggregate is a cluster of associated objects that we treat as a single unit for the purpose of data changes."

The resulting model is then the union of aggregates, individual entities, and their value objects, as shown in Figure 8-2.

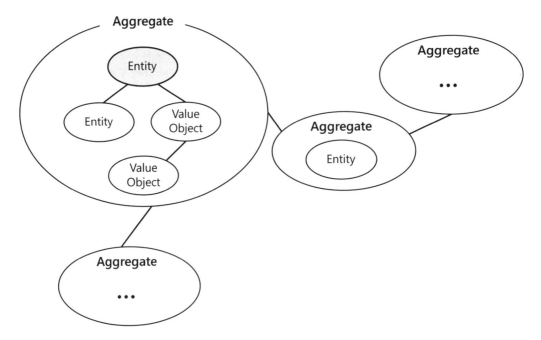

FIGURE 8-2 Representation of an aggregate model.

Entities in the model are partitioned into aggregates. Most aggregates are made of multiple entities bound together by their mutual parent/child relationships. Other aggregates are just made by individual entities that still relate to other aggregates but do not have child entities.

Each aggregate is subject to a logical boundary that simply defines which entities are inside the aggregate. More importantly, an aggregate has a root entity, which is called the *aggregate root*. The aggregate root is the root of a graph of objects; it encapsulates contained entities and acts as the proxy to them.

Using business invariants to discover aggregates

Aggregates are part of the design; architects and developers define aggregates to better reflect with code the ongoing business. In a bounded context, aggregates represent invariant conditions in the domain model. An *invariant condition* is essentially a business rule that is required to be constantly verified in a domain model. Put another way, aggregates are a way to ensure business consistency.

In general, there are two types of consistency: transactional consistency and eventual consistency. *Transactional consistency* refers to the aggregate for preserving consistency after every business transaction (that is, operation) that takes place in the domain. *Eventual consistency* refers to consistency that, at some point, is guaranteed to be preserved but might not be guaranteed after each business transaction. The aggregate is not concerned at all about the consistency and operations taking place outside of the boundary.

When thinking of aggregates, you'll find that the first approximation that often comes to mind is that an aggregate is a graph of objects. You have orders that contain order items, which contain products, which contain categories, and so forth. While an aggregate can contain—and often it does contain—a graph of objects, the cardinality of the graph is typically limited to two or three objects.

> **Important** In a well-designed domain model, only one aggregate is modified in each single transaction. If at some point you find that a given use-case seems to require that multiple aggregates are modified in multiple transactions, you are probably not in an optimal design, although it is acceptable. Instead, when the use-case seems to indicate that multiple aggregates should be updated in a single transaction, that's the clear sign that something is wrong somewhere. Most likely, you're missing an invariant and the decomposition in the aggregate you created is less than ideal for the business.

Benefits of an aggregate model

There are a couple of significant benefits to creating an aggregate model within the boundaries of a domain model. In the first place, the implementation of the entire domain model and its business logic comes easier because you work with fewer and coarse-grained objects and with fewer relationships.

If this benefit seems to contradict SOLID (Single responsibility, Open/close, Liskov's principles, Interface segregation, and Dependency inversion) principles and seems like it might lead to bloated objects, consider the following:

- The aggregate model is a purely logical grouping. The aggregate root class might undergo some changes because of its role, and those changes mostly deal with the management of external access to child entities.

- In terms of code, entity classes remain distinct classes and each retains its implementation. However, you don't want to have public constructors on child entities, because those can break the consistency of the aggregate.

- The aggregate model doesn't necessarily introduce new classes that group the code of logically embedded classes; however, for convenience aggregates often are coded just as new classes that encapsulate the entire graph of child objects. When this happens, it's because you want to protect the graph as much as possible from outsider access. The boundary of the aggregate is explicit in code in this case.

The aggregate model raises the level of abstraction and encapsulates multiple entities in a single unit. The cardinality of the model decreases and, with it, the number of inter-entity relationships that are actionable in code also decreases. Have a look at Figure 8-3, which expands the idea of Figure 8-2 to a realistic scenario.

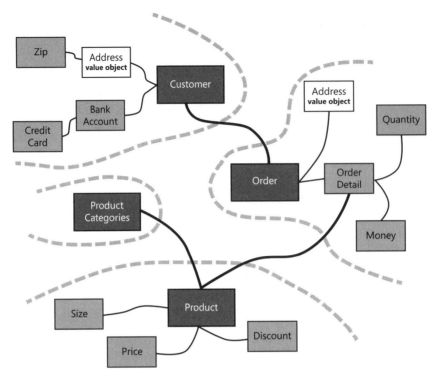

FIGURE 8-3 Partitioning an entity model into an aggregate model.

The other big benefit of the aggregate model is that it helps prevent a tightly coupled model, where each entity is potentially associated with a number of others. As you can see in Figure 8-3, boundaries can identify multiple entities linked to a root or just one entity that is the root of a single-node cluster.

The canonical example is the aggregate rooted in the *Order* entity in an e-commerce system. An *Order* is made of a collection of *OrderItem* entities. Both concepts are expressed via entities with identity and life, but *OrderItem* is a child of *Order* in the sense that the business logic might not require access to an order item outside the context of an order.

> **Important** Obviously, the actual boundaries of aggregates are determined exclusively by looking at requirements and business rules. Although, in general, an order item is expected to be child of an order, there might be a hypothetical scenario where *OrderItem* constitutes the root of a distinct aggregate. An even better example is Address, which could be a value object in some domains and an entity in others, such as utility companies (electricity and telephone).

An *entity* is either an aggregate root or is included in just one aggregate. A good example is the *Product* entity. When you look at orders, it turns out that products are referenced in order items. So the first thought is that *Product* belongs to the *Order* aggregate. However, next you might find out that use-cases exist to treat products outside of orders—for example, for the catalog of products. This makes up for another aggregate rooted in *Product*. The same goes for *ProductCategories*: as long as categories are subject to change (for example, deserve their own table), you need an aggregate and it will likely be a single-entity aggregate.

The final word on the boundaries of an aggregate belongs to the ubiquitous language. If the language says that the order contains product information and quantity, it's clear that *Order* doesn't reference *Product* but a value object instead.

What about value objects? They are definitely part of aggregates because they are referenced from entities. Value objects can be referenced by multiple entities and, subsequently, they can be used in multiple aggregates.

In terms of design, it might be interesting to consider the *Address* concept. We presented *Address* as one of the canonical examples of a value object. In this regard, an address is used to represent the residence of a customer as well as the shipping address of an order.

Suppose now that requirements change or your understanding of the system improves. As a result, you think it's preferable to give addresses an identity and store them as individual entities on a distinct table. That would immediately be reflected in the aggregate model because now *Address* becomes the root of the aggregate itself; likely, it is a single-entity aggregate. Subsequently, two new relationships come into existence: *Customer* to *Address* and *Order* to *Address*.

Relationships between aggregates

Implementing the aggregate model requires minimal changes to the involved entity classes, but it does have a huge impact on the rest of the domain model—services and repositories in particular. Figure 8-4 shows how the use of aggregates reduces the cardinality of objects actionable in code and helps prevent a bloated system.

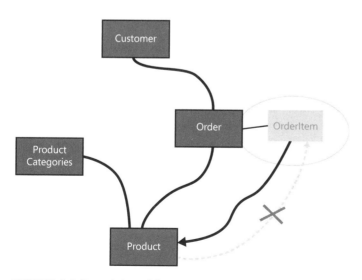

FIGURE 8-4 Collapsed view of the aggregate model laid out in Figure 8-3.

Aggregate root classes hide related classes from callers and require that callers refer to them for any interaction. In other words, an entity is only allowed to reference an entity in the same aggregate or the root of another aggregate. At the same time, a child entity—like *OrderItem* in Figure 8-4—can hold a reference to another aggregate root.

Marking aggregate roots

An *aggregate root object* is the root of the cluster of associated objects that form the aggregate. An aggregate root has global visibility throughout the domain model and can be referenced directly. Entities inside the aggregate still have their identity and life, but they can't be referenced directly from outside the aggregate.

This is the foundation of the aggregate model.

An object (for example, a service) can use, say, the address of a customer or the items of an order. Access to this encapsulated information, though, must always occur through the root. Callers should consider any references to internal objects they get as transient and avoid using them beyond the scope of a single call.

The aggregate root object has relevant responsibilities. Here's the list:

- The aggregate root guarantees that contained objects are always in a valid state according to the applicable business rules (consistency). For example, if a rule requires that no detail of the order can be updated after it has shipped, the root must make this update impossible in code.

- Subsequently, the aggregate root is responsible for the persistence of all encapsulated objects.

- Subsequently, the aggregate root is responsible for cascading updates and deletions through the entities in the aggregate.

- Subsequently, a query operation can only retrieve an aggregate root. Access to internal objects must always happen by navigation through the interface of the aggregate root.

It should be clear that most of the code changes required to support the rules of an aggregate model occur at the level of services and repositories. In terms of code, what does it mean to be an aggregate root?

An aggregate root usually implements an interface commonly called *IAggregateRoot*, as shown here:

```
public class Order : IAggregateRoot
{
    ...
}
```

The interface doesn't strictly require any functionality. It can easily be a plain marker interface that is used only to clarify to the outside world that an entity is actually a root.

```
public interface IAggregateRoot
{
}
```

An aggregate root can also be given a slightly more sophisticated implementation that, overall, can make the implementation of the model more robust:

```
public interface IAggregateRoot {
    bool CanBeSaved { get; }
}
```

By making the property blindly return *true*, you're back to the scenario where *IAggregateRoot* is a mere marker and memberless interface. By adding some logic in the getters, instead, you can validate that the aggregate state is effectively ready for saving or deleting. Here's a possible way to use this variation of the interface:

```
public class Order : IAggregateRoot
{
    bool IAggregateRoot.CanBeSaved
    {
        get { return Validate(); }
    }

    ...
}
```

The aggregate root interface is typically used as a type constraint for repository classes. In this way, the compiler enforces the rule that only aggregate roots have repositories and handle persistence.

> **Note** A simple rule to help developers with a strong database background orientate themselves in the DDD world is the following. Entities are those things for which, in a relational model, you want to have a separate table. Aggregates are the union of tables linked together by foreign-key relationships. Finally, an aggregate root is the unique table in a graph of foreign-key relationships that contain only outbound foreign-key references.

Domain services

Domain services are classes whose methods implement the domain logic that doesn't belong to a particular aggregate and most likely span multiple entities. Domain services coordinate the activity of aggregates and repositories with the purpose of implementing a business action. In some cases, domain services might consume services from the infrastructure, such as when sending an email or a text message is necessary.

When a given piece of business logic doesn't fit in any of the existing aggregates and aggregates can't be redesigned in a way that the operation fits, you typically look into using domain services. So, in a way, domain services are the last resort for logic that doesn't fit anywhere else.

Domain services, however, are not plain, working-class items in a domain model. Actions they implement come from requirements and are approved by domain experts. Last but not least, names used in domain services are strictly part of the ubiquitous language.

Services as contracts

It is common to represent domain services through interfaces and implementation classes. When you use interfaces, most of the time you intend to preserve testability or create an extensibility point in your software.

This is not the case for domain services.

The interface of domain services represents a contract written in the ubiquitous language and lists actions available for application services to call.

Cross-aggregate behavior

The most common scenario for domain services is to implement any behavior that involves multiple aggregates, database access methods, or both. A good example is a domain service that determines whether a given customer reached the status of "gold" customer. Suppose the domain says that a customer earns the status of "gold" customer after she exceeded a given threshold of orders on a selected range of products.

How would you check that?

You can't reasonably have a method *IsGold* on the *Customer* aggregate that calculates the status. Calculating the status requires accessing the database—not the right job for an aggregate to do. A domain service is then the perfect fit. A service, in fact, is able to query orders and products for a customer.

The structure of the model largely influences the number of and interface for domain services.

Consider a booking scenario. You have a club member who wants to book a resource—say, a meeting room. The action of booking requires the application of some business logic steps, such as verifying availability and processing payment. There at least two ways you can do this. You can have a *Booking* domain service that reads the member credit status and checks the room availability, or you can have a *Booking* entity that deals with *Member* and *Room* dependencies. The repository of the *Booking* entity is then responsible for the whole task. Both options are equally valid because they both effectively model the domain.

> **Note** In his book, Evans uses a similar example to illustrate the case for a domain service. He mentions a bank wire-transfer service as an example of a domain service working across multiple entities (bank accounts).

Repositories

Repositories are the most popular type of domain service, and they take care of persisting aggregates. You're going to have one repository per aggregate root: *CustomerRepository*, *OrderRepository*, and so forth.

A common practice is extracting an interface out of these classes and defining the interfaces in the same class library as the core model. The implementation of repository interfaces, instead, belongs to the infrastructure layer. A repository is often based on a common interface like *IRepository*:

```
public interface IRepository<T> where T:IAggregateRoot
{
    // You can keep the interface a plain marker or
    // you can have a few common methods here.

    T Find (object id);
    void Save (T item);
    }
```

Specific repositories are then derived from the base interface:

```
public interface IOrderRepository : IRepository<Order>
{
    // The actual list of members is up to you
    ...
}
```

Note that there's no way to build a repository that is absolutely right or wrong. A good repository can also simply be an interface-based class with a list of members arranged as you need them to be. You can even ignore the *IAggregateRoot* interface and just implement persistence for the entire graph as it should be:

```
public interface IOrderRepository
{
    // The actual list of members is up to you
    ...
}
```

Members of a repository class will actually perform data access—either queries, updates, or insertions. The technology used for data access is up to you. Most commonly today, you use an O/RM like Entity Framework, but nothing prevents you from using ADO.NET, plain stored procedures or, why not, a NoSQL store.

An interesting implementation of the *IRepository<T>* interface consists of marking the interface with a Code Contracts class so that the CLR can inject some Intermediate Language (IL) code into any implementation of the *IRepository* methods:

```
[ContractClass(typeof(RepositoryContract<>))]
public interface IRepository<T> where T:IAggregateRoot
{
    ...
}
```

And here's the implementation of the contract class:

```
[ContractClassFor(typeof(IRepository<>))]
sealed class RepositoryContract<T> : IRepository<T> where T : IAggregateRoot
{
    public void Save(T item)
    {
        Contract.Requires<ArgumentNullException>(item != null, "item");
        Contract.Requires<ArgumentException>(item.CanBeSaved);
        throw new NotImplementedException();
    }
}
```

When the *Save* method is invoked, the *CanBeSaved* method on the provided aggregate is automatically invoked care of the CLR. For the sake of consistency, the check on *CanBeSaved* should happen at the domain service level before the repository is invoked to persist the aggregate and within the repository just before saving. Developers are responsible for writing this code. The contract gimmick ensures that, whatever happens, the CLR checks whether the aggregate can be saved and throws otherwise.

The interface of repositories is usually defined in the assembly where you code the domain layer, but the implementation clearly belongs to the infrastructure layer.

The assembly that contains the implementation of repositories has a direct dependency on O/RMs like Entity Framework, NoSQL, or in-memory databases; external persistence services; and whatever data provider you might need.

To clear up any remaining doubts, we want to point out that a repository is where you deal with connection strings and use SQL commands.

Important So far, we have repeatedly mentioned persistence, but we never focused on physical storage. We'll return to this aspect in detail in Chapter 14, "The persistence layer," which is dedicated to the persistence layer. For now, it suffices to say that a domain model exists to be persisted; to achieve persistence successfully, though, you might need to make some concessions in your domain model and make other compromises.

Note *Repository* is a rather bloated term. If you look around, you might find several conflicting definitions for it and several strongly recommended implementations. We think the same term is used to refer to different concepts. In the context of DDD, a repository is what we described in this chapter—the class that handles persistence on behalf of entities and, ideally, aggregate roots. We'll say more about this in Chapter 14.

Is it a service or is it an aggregate?

As mentioned, we tend to consider domain services to be backup solutions for pieces of behavior that we can't fit naturally—for whatever reasons—in aggregates. However, sometimes we also wonder whether that business action really doesn't fit in the domain model or whether we are just unable to model it right.

When the ubiquitous language seems to present an operation as a first-class concept—for example, transfer or booking—we wonder whether we wouldn't be better off using a new persistent entity instead of a domain service to orchestrate the process.

In the end, however, both options can be made to work.

Domain events

Imagine the following scenario: in an online store application, an order is placed and processed successfully by the system. The payment was made OK, the delivery order was passed on and received by the shipping company, and the order was generated and inserted into the system. Now what? What should the system be doing *when* an order is created? Let's say that the ubiquitous language tells you exactly what to do, and that is some task *T*. Where would you implement task T?

From sequential logic to events

The first option is just concatenating the code for task T to the domain service method that performed the order processing. Here's some pseudocode:

```
void Checkout(ShoppingCart cart)
{
    // Proceed through the necessary steps
    ...
    if (success)
    {
        // Execute task T
        ...
    }
}
```

This code has some problems. In the first place, it is not very expressive. All steps form an end-to-end monolithic checkout procedure. Outside the *Checkout* method, there's no visibility into what might have happened internally. Is this really a problem? Well, it depends. In this case, for example, it might be an indication of some violation of the ubiquitous language.

A few lines earlier, we wrote the adverb "when" in italics. We did so to call your attention to the specific word. Any time you find "when" in the requirements, you likely have the occurrence of a relevant event in the domain. An event registers the occurrence of a fact in some context; the word "when" in requirements indicates that there's some business interest in knowing when a given fact occurs.

Requirements indicate what to do when a given event is observed. If you place the handling code in the domain service method, you have to touch the domain service method in case requirements change or it becomes necessary to perform more actions for the same event. Modifying a domain service class is not dangerous per se, but in general any other approach that minimizes the risk of modifying existing classes is more than welcome.

Raising an event when something relevant occurs

Wouldn't it be better if we just raise an event when a given domain-relevant fact occurs? The event would remove the need to have all handling code in a single place. This brings two main benefits to the table:

- Enables us to dynamically define the list of handlers without touching the code that generates the event

- Enables us to potentially have multiple places where the same event is raised. This means that handlers will run regardless of the actual caller

Let's see how to define an event in a domain model.

Formalizing a domain event

At the end of the day, a domain event is a plain simple class that represents an interesting occurrence in the domain. Good examples are when an order is created or when a customer reaches the gold status according to the fidelity program. If you spend only a few moments thinking about events, you find plenty of examples in nearly any domain model you consider. An event is when an invoice is issued or modified, when a credit note is issued for an outbound invoice, when a new customer is registered in the system, and so forth.

In line with this principle, a domain event can simply be an event member defined on a class. In a Domain Model scenario, however, events are typically represented via a domain-specific class marked with an ad hoc interface.

```
public interface IDomainEvent
{
}
```

Here's a sample class:

```
public class CustomerReachedGoldMemberStatus : IDomainEvent
{
    public Customer Customer { get; set; }
}
```

 Note In .NET, an event is an instance of a class derived from *EventArgs*, and it contains the information that describes the circumstance. In the end, *IDomainEvent* and a base class like *EventArgs* are two different ways of giving the event class a role.

Using *EventArgs* as the base class, the .NET mechanism of raising events might definitely be an option. However, it's a common practice in a domain model to implement an internal event engine, mark events via an interface, and signal significant state changes in the domain entities via an internal publish/subscribe mechanism, as in the following code:

```
public class OrderRequestService
{
    public void RegisterOrder(ShoppingCart cart)
    {
        // Create and persist the new order
        ...

        // Check gold status for the customer who made the order
        CheckGoldStatusForCustomer(cart.Customer);
    }

    public void CheckGoldStatusForCustomer(Customer customer)
    {
        // Get total amount of orders placed in current year
        var totalOrdered = CalculateTotalOrdersForCustomer(customer, DateTime.Today.Year)
        if (totalOrdered > 1000)
        {
            Bus.Raise(new CustomerReachedGoldMemberStatus() { Customer = customer });
        }
    }
}
```

Handling domain events

Raising the event is only part of the job. The next step consists of figuring out a way to define handlers for those domain events. Here's a basic implementation of the class that raises events:

```
public class Bus
{
    private static IList<IHandler<IDomainEvent>> Handlers = new List<IHandler<IDomainEvent>>();
    public static void Register(IHandler<IDomainEvent> handler)
    {
        if (handler != null)
            Handlers.Add(handler);
    }

    public static void Raise<T>(T eventData) where T : IDomainEvent
    {
        foreach (var handler in Handlers)
        {
            if (handler.CanHandle(eventData))
                handler.Handle(eventData);
        }
    }
}
```

As you can see, raising an event actually means going through the list of known subscribers and giving each the chance to handle the event. Any registered handler always gets a chance to handle an event of a given type.

A handler is a small class that contains some logic to run in reaction to a given event. Obviously, you can have multiple classes to handle the same domain event. This allows for the composition of actions, such as when an event occurs, you first do task 1 and then task 2. Here's some sample code for a handler:

```
public class GoldStatusHandler : IHandler<IDomainEvent>
{
    public void Handle(IDomainEvent eventData)
    {
        // Some synchronous task
        ...
        return;
    }
    public bool CanHandle(IDomainEvent eventType)
    {
        return eventType is CustomerReachedGoldMemberStatus;
    }
}
```

Note that if the body of the method *Handle* needs to contain some async operation (for example, sending an email), instead of using events you can use plain messages on some queue. Or, if it is possible given the context, you can just place a fire-and-forget request for the async operation to yet another component invoked from within the method *Handle*.

Cross-cutting concerns

In a layered architecture, the infrastructure layer is where you find anything related to concrete technologies. The layer primarily encompasses data persistence through O/RM tools but is not limited to that. The infrastructure layer is also the place for cross-cutting concerns and encompasses specific API for security (for example, OAuth2), logging, tracing, as well as IoC frameworks.

Let's briefly see how cross-cutting concerns and persistence affect a domain model.

Under the umbrella of a single transaction

Not just because you do smart and cool domain modeling, you don't need to dirty your hands with database connection strings and fancy things like cascade rules, foreign keys, and stored procedures. As mentioned, persistence is not a concern you let emerge through the public interface of a domain. CRUD operations, though, happen and are coded mostly via repositories and combined via domain services and, at a higher level, via the application layer.

Today, most advanced aspects of a CRUD interface are fully handled via the O/RM. When you use, say, Entity Framework, you operate transactionally per units of work that the framework's context object transparently manages for you. The unit of work spans only a single database connection. For multiconnection transactions, you can resort to the *TransactionScope* class. Often, you might need to use this class from the application layer to sew together multiple steps of a single logical operation.

In the end, you isolate data-access code in repositories and use repositories from within the application layer or domain services.

Validation

In DDD, there are two main sentiments as far as validation is concerned. Most people say that an entity must always be in a valid state, meaning that the state must be constantly consistent with known business rules. Some other people reckon that entities should be treated as plain .NET objects until they're used in some way. It's only at this time—the run time—that validation takes place and exceptions are thrown if something is wrong.

As DDD is about modeling the domain faithfully, it should always deal with valid entities—except that honoring validation rules all the time might be quite problematic. Validation rules, in fact, are like invariants; hence, entities should be responsible for fulfilling invariants in their lifetime. Unfortunately, invariant conditions for an entity are often scoped to the domain model (not the class) and often require checking information out of reach for the given entity (for example, database unique values).

This is exactly what makes some situations desirable for making concessions and admitting entities in an invalid state where some of the invariants are missed.

In any .NET class, validation logic can be as simple as an *if-then-throw* control flow, or it can pass through a validation framework such as .NET data annotations or the Enterprise Library Validation Block. While we find that data annotations are great in the user interface and presentation layer, we still aim to keep a domain model as lean as possible. This means that we mostly use *if-then-throw* statements or .NET Code Contracts—mostly preconditions and postconditions.

The simple use of preconditions, however, might not ensure that the object is in a valid state. Because invariants apply at the domain-model level, the entity alone can't realistically be expected to check its consistency at all times. This is where an ad hoc domain service can be created to perform full validation.

> **Important** Classes in the domain model should check whatever they can check and throw ad hoc exceptions whenever something wrong is detected. We don't expect the domain model to be forgiving: we expect it to yell out as soon as something goes against expectations. What about error messages? A domain model should have its own set of exceptions and expose them to upper layers such as the application layer. The application layer will decide whether the domain exception should be bubbled up as-is to the presentation layer, rethrown, or swallowed. The actual error message, instead, is up to the presentation layer.

Security

We distinguish two aspects of security. One has to do with the surrounding environment of the application and touches on things like access-control permissions, cross-site scripting, and user authentication. None of these aspects—relevant in the overall context of the application—apply to the domain-layer level.

The second aspect of security has to do with authorization and ensuring that only authorized users are actually allowed to perform certain operations. As we see it, the application layer should allow only an authorized call pass to reach the domain logic.

It might be hard for the domain service *OrderHistory* to check from within the domain layer whether the caller has been granted the right permissions. Security at the gate is our favorite approach, and we see it implemented by the presentation layer (say, by hiding links and buttons) along with the application layer.

> **Note** Security at the gate in the presentation layer is acceptable in situations in which the granularity of the security matches the use-case. The typical example is when a user within a given role is not authorized to perform a given action. You can achieve that simply by hiding user-interface elements. In general, *security at the gate* means security restrictions are applied as early as possible in the call stack. Often, it is already applied in application services at the beginning of the use-cases.

Logging

The fundamental thing about logging is that it's you who decide what to log and from where. If you decide it's critical to log from within the domain model, you need a reference to the logging infrastructure right in the domain model.

However, you don't want to create a tight coupling between the domain model and a logger component. What you can do to log from the domain model is inject a logger interface in the model classes but keep the implementation of the logger in the infrastructure project.

This said, we believe that in a .NET executable, logging should happen whenever possible through built-in trace listeners, such as the *EventLogTraceListener* class. These classes are built into the .NET Framework and don't require additional dependencies, such as log4net and the Logging Application Block in the Enterprise Library.

Caching

Like logging, the ideal implementation of caching and the placement of the relative code strictly depends on what you really want to cache. Unlike logging, caching doesn't really seem to be a concern of the domain model. However, domain services and repositories might take advantage of caching to improve performance and save some database reads or the invocation of remote services.

From a design perspective, all you do is hide components that are subject to the use of the cache behind a contract. For example, you define the public interface of the repository and then use whatever caching infrastructure you like in the implementation of the repository. That keeps the caching system completely transparent for the consumer of the repository.

For testing and extensibility reasons, you can also abstract the cache API to an interface and inject a valid implementation in the repository or domain service.

Important Caching means serving users some stale data. Even though we recognize that very few applications can't afford data only a few seconds stale, it's not the development team who can decide whether serving stale data is appropriate. It mostly works like this: the domain expert shares his performance expectations, and the development team indicates the costs involved to achieve that, whether it is the cost of hardware or caching. The final word belongs to the domain experts.

Summary

A domain model attempts to model a business domain in terms of entities and value objects and their relationships, state, and behavior. In a domain model, an entity is a pertinent object in the business space; it has an identity and a life. A value object, instead, is simply an inanimate thing within the business space. Some entities are then grouped in aggregates for the sake of code and design.

In this chapter, we mostly focused on the foundation of the Domain Model pattern and looked into its theoretical aspects. In the next chapter, we'll move deeper into the implementation aspects. In upcoming chapters, we discuss other supporting architectures, such Command/Query Responsibility Segregation (CQRS) and event sourcing.

Finishing with a smile

As far as we know, there are no official Murphy's laws for developers. However, we came up with interesting candidates while searching for developer jokes and funny software things on the Internet, and we also invented some on our own:

- If a developer can use an API the wrong way, he will.

- Actual data will rarely reflect your preconceived notions about it. You will usually discover this at the most inappropriate time.

- Those who have the least amount of practical experience usually have the strongest opinions about how things should be done.

- The solution to a problem changes the problem.

CHAPTER 9

Implementing Domain Model

Talk is cheap. Show me the code.
—Linus Torvalds

The quote at the beginning of the chapter, the essence of which we can summarize as "show me the code" (or SMTC for short), is the final sentence in a short answer that Torvalds gave on a Linux mailing list years ago. The original is here: *https://lkml.org/lkml/2000/8/25/132*. Since then, SMTC has been used often to break up potentially endless discussions that are headed toward analysis/paralysis.

While theory is invaluable, theory without practice is of very little use.

We debated at length about what would have been the best scenario to focus on to show the importance of modeling the business domain within a layered architecture. In the end, we went for an online store, disregarding many other scenarios we had the chance to work on in the past. In particular, Dino has interesting domain-driven design (DDD) experiences in the context of management systems, booking reservations, and sports-scoring scenarios, whereas Andrea has been active in banking, enterprise resource planning (ERP), human resources (HR), and publishing.

In the end, we decided that an online store was something that was easy to grasp for everybody, easy to modularize for us, and easy to build an effective learning path on. So in this and the following chapters, we'll build the "I-Buy-Stuff" project and produce three different prototypes based on different supporting architectures: a domain model, Command/Query Responsibility Segregation (CQRS), and then event-sourcing.

And now, without further ado, let us just show the code.

The online store sample project

In this chapter, we'll use a domain model as the supporting architecture. Figure 9-1 presents the home page of the sample application that comes with this chapter.

FIGURE 9-1 The home page of the I-Buy-Stuff sample application.

Selected use-cases

The customer called us to help with the development of an online store. They wanted to build a list of registered online customers and give each the opportunity to buy goods, review existing orders, receive the site's newsletter, and join a customer-loyalty program to get discounts.

For simplicity, but without significant loss of generality, we built the application around the use-cases listed in Table 9-1.

Important The sample application we present is simple enough to require a single bounded context. The online store scenario, however, might be sufficiently complex to require for the sake of the application the use of several bounded contexts. As an example, think of the Amazon system—given its size and complexity, there's no way it can be a single bounded context. The number of bounded contexts depends on the complexity of the scenario and, subsequently, the number of use-cases, expected performance, and other functional and nonfunctional requirements. We'll return to this point later in the chapter after we're done introducing the sample project.

TABLE 9-1 List of supported use-cases

Use-case	Description
Registers to the site	The user fills in the application form and becomes an official customer of the I-Buy-Stuff site.
Log in to start using the site	The user enters credentials and logs in. Credentials can be entered directly to the site or via a couple of social networks.
Subscribe to the newsletter	The user adds an email address to receive the newsletter.
Search an order	The user indicates the number of one of her orders and reviews details such as estimated delivery date, items, and costs.
Place an order	The user fills a shopping cart with a list of products and then proceeds with making payment and entering the details related to delivery.

At first, it might not seem like anything fancy. It looks like just the kind of thing many developers do every day, have been doing for many days, or will likely be doing at some point in the future. The sample application also seems really close to many sample demos you have seen around ASP.NET and Windows Presentation Foundation (WPF) over the years. In particular, we remember the IBuySpy sample portal application built for ASP.NET back in the early days of the Microsoft .NET Framework.

The challenge is showing that there's a lot to do in terms of understanding and rendering the business domain even in a common scenario that has always been handled successfully in .NET with database-centric approaches.

Selected approach

An old but still effective trick to quickly forming an idea about a book, or even a candidate while conducting a job interview, is checking what either might have to say on a topic you know very well.

An online store is something that everybody understands, and nearly every developer might have a clear idea of how to attack it. In this chapter, we'll build it using a Domain Model approach as outlined in the previous chapter. We'll figure out an object model that faithfully represents the business domain and assign each entity a behavior and separate domain logic from domain services.

After an analysis of requirements and defining the ubiquitous language, you should have a clear idea of which entities you are going to have. Built as a separate class library project, the domain model contains the following entities: *Admin, Customer, Order, OrderItem, Product, Subscriber,* and *FidelityCard*. Table 9-2 summarizes the expected content and behavior for each relevant entity we identified in the domain.

TABLE 9-2 Relevant entities in the I-Buy-Stuff business domain

Entity	Description
Admin	Represents an administrator of the site. The administrator is the holder of a user account who's given full access to all the back-office features of the system. In particular, an Admin can enable discounts on products, configure the frequency of the newsletter, generate sales statistics, add new credit cards and shipping partners, and more.
Customer	Represents a user of the site. In this entity, you find both the aspects of a classic user account and a classic customer. To be a customer, you need to have an ID and password, and you need a registered credit card and address. A customer is distinguished by gender and might have a customer-loyalty card and, subsequently, a level of reward (for example, silver, gold, platinum). Read the next note for more details about customers.
Order	Represents an order after it has been created. An order is created from the content of a shopping cart and consists of a list of items. An order has a state that changes over time as the ordered goods are packaged and shipped. An order knows its total value. The order has its ID only when it is created in the system.
OrderItem	Represents a line in the order and is made of a quantity and a product. A collection of items form the content of the shopping cart and are flushed into an order.
Product	Represents a product on sale through the site. It consists of descriptive attributes plus the current stock level and a flag that makes it a featured product, for which the buyer earns special offers and extra discounts. Featured products are displayed in the carousel on the home page. The selection of featured products is driven by business rules.
Subscriber	Represents a simple aggregate that consists only of an email address that the newsletter will be sent to.
FidelityCard	Represents a customer-loyalty card issued by the site. It has a number and accumulated points and is associated with a customer. Based on the points, business rules determine the reward level of the user (gold, silver, and so forth) The points on the card are updated each time an order is placed. The amount of points accumulated with each purchase is determined by business rules.

Note In our example, any customer of the store is a registered customer with a record in the system. In a more realistic scenario, a domain expert will tell you to consider a "customer" to be only a user who actually bought an item from the site at least once. Typically, users are allowed to fill the shopping cart even anonymously, but they are required to register—and become customers—when they check out and pay.

Structure of the I-Buy-Stuff project

In past chapters, we focused on the layered architecture and its role in DDD. Now it's time to see it in action. And it starts from the structure of the solution you build in Microsoft Visual Studio 2013. Figure 9-2 provides two views of the Solution Explorer.

The first view displays only solutions folders.

As you can see, there's a domain layer, infrastructure layer, and site. The I-Buy-Stuff application, in fact, is an ASP.NET MVC website project under the folder Site.

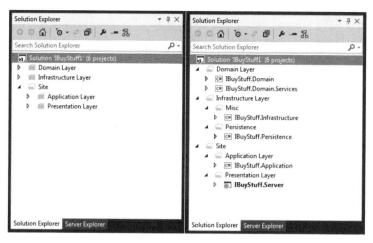

FIGURE 9-2 The I-Buy-Stuff project in the Solution Explorer of Visual Studio 2013.

From the view shown on the left in Figure 9-2, you also can perceive the neat (logical) separation between the back end and front end. The presentation and application layers are part of the front end of the system; the domain and infrastructure layers are part of the back end. The back end is used by as many front ends as you happen to have within the same bounded context, whether the front end is simply yet another user interface (web, WPF, mobile web) or just a separate application with its own use-cases (for example, a mobile app or a WPF client).

The view shown on the right in Figure 9-2 displays the actual projects being created. With the exception of *IBuyStuff.Server*, which is an ASP.NET MVC 5 project, all other projects are plain .NET class libraries.

Important Figure 9-2 presents distinct projects and folders for the web front end and application layer. From a conceptual standpoint, all is good and even extremely clear. However, separating such logical layers in distinct projects might create some wrinkles in the everyday management of the solution. For example, imagine you want to add a new Razor view to the project. The CSHTML file goes in the web project, whereas the view model class belongs to the Application project. The same thing happens when you add a new controller—the controller class goes to the web project, whereas the application service class goes to the Application project. This makes scaffolding a bit more complicated than it should be. In the end, although separation of concerns (SoC) is the timeless foundation of software, the way in which it happens can be adjusted to serve pragmatic purposes. We often have the entire content of the Application project you see in the example under an Application folder within the web project. And we do the same if the project is a Microsoft Windows or Windows Phone application.

Selected technologies

The projects use a bunch of .NET technologies that, for the most part, are incorporated through NuGet packages. As mentioned, the front end is an ASP.NET MVC 5 application that uses ASP.NET Identity as the framework for user authentication. Twitter Bootstrap is used for the user interface. For mobile views, we use Ratchet2 for the user interface and WURFL to perform device detection and ASP.NET display modes to do view routing.

> **Important** The I-Buy-Stuff application is a sort of universal web app—one codebase supporting multiple device-specific views. This is not the same as using cascading style sheets (CSS) media queries to adapt one single piece of content to multiple devices. It's just about serving different web content generated from a single codebase. The site is still responsive but much more intelligent. We'll return to this point in the final chapter of the book, which talks about infrastructure.

The back end of I-Buy-Stuff is based on Entity Framework Code First for persistence. The sample code you get uses a local instance of Microsoft SQL Server to create tables in the *App_Data* folder of the website. Finally, all dependency injection needs within the solution are managed via Microsoft Patterns and Practices Unity.

> **Note** We used to write our own controller factories in ASP.NET MVC to plug into Unity or other Inversion of Control (IoC) containers. Today, as far as Unity is concerned, we plug it in via the Unity.Mvc NuGet package.

Bounded contexts for an online store

The I-Buy-Stuff online store is deliberately simple and small, and the business cases it faces don't require more than just a bounded context. For providing you with an extensive understanding of DDD, it is probably not an ideal example. On the other hand, we thought that a much more sophisticated example would have been too overwhelming.

However, we want to take some time to discuss the online store scenario in a bit more depth because it is likely to appear in a real-word context.

Decomposing the business domain in contexts

In a reasonably simple scenario, you can have three distinct bounded contexts:

- MembershipBC

- OrderingBC

- CatalogBC

MembershipBC will take care of authentication and user account management. OrderingBC cares about the shopping cart and processes the order. Finally, CatalogBC is related to back-office operations, such as updating product descriptions, adding or removing products, updating stock levels, updating prices, and so forth. Figure 9-3 provides a sample context map.

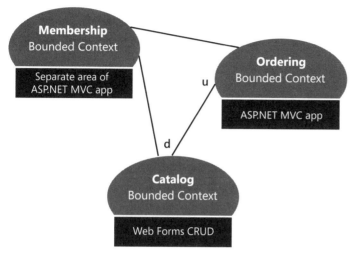

FIGURE 9-3 A sample context map for an online store system that is a bit more complete than the I-Buy-Stuff project presented in this chapter.

OrderingBC can be an ASP.NET MVC application, much like the sample I-Buy-Stuff. The membership part taken out of the main application can physically remain in the same application but configured as a distinct *area*. (ASP.NET MVC areas are a concept similar to a bounded context, but they are specific to ASP.NET MVC. For more information, check out Dino's book *Programming ASP.NET MVC* (Microsoft Press, 2013). Finally, CatalogBC can be a plain CRUD front end on top of the database. CatalogBC is not necessarily related to DDD. It depends on the domain model being used, and it saves data to the database used to persist the domain model.

Making the contexts communicate

How can the OrderingBC bounded context be informed that a product in the catalog has been modified, added, or removed?

If OrderingBC just reads from the database every time it needs to—a quite unlikely scenario—then synchronization is automatic when CatalogBC writes to the database. Otherwise, CatalogBC can use a remote procedure call (RPC) approach and invokes an endpoint on OrderingBC, which invalidates or refreshes the cache of products. The endpoint can, in turn, simply raise a domain event.

In a larger and more sophisticated system, you can even have a service bus system connecting the various pieces of the architecture.

Adding even more bounded contexts

If the complexity of the store grows, you can consider adding bounded contexts. Here are a few examples of contexts you can add:

- **ShippingBC**   This context relates to the domain model to handle any complex logistics. In our I-Buy-Stuff example, this is seen as an external service. We won't get into the details of the interaction, but it could likely require an anticorruption layer to ensure that OrderingBC receives data always in the same way.

- **PricingBC**   This context becomes necessary when pricing is a complex subsystem based on user/product association, personal discounts, fidelity programs, reward points, and so forth.

- **PurchaseBC**   This context relates to the domain model required to manage a purchase system that interfaces multiple payment gateways and possibly supports other forms of payment, such as wire transfer and cash-on-delivery. In our I-Buy-Stuff example, this is seen as an external service. The sample code assumes a single payment mode and gateway, and it provides a mock for the payment in the form of an ASP.NET Web Forms page.

In summary, for relatively simple systems you have a few options:

- Using one large bounded context

- Splitting the domain into several small bounded contexts, with duplicated data, and possibly communicating through a publish/subscribe messaging system

- Isolating some of the larger bounded contexts you identify and exposing them via web services

There's no general rule to determine which option is preferable. It all depends on the context and your skills and experience. And, to a good extent, it also depends on the vision and understanding of the domain you have gained. In some cases, for example, it might be savvy to recognize that querying needs might be very different from writing needs. Subsequently, it can be preferable sometimes to just design separate bounded contexts for queries. This is the essence of CQRS, which we'll discuss in the next chapter.

Context map of the I-Buy-Stuff application

Figure 9-4 shows the context map we're going to have for I-Buy-Stuff.

As you can see in the figure, the I-Buy-Stuff context is an ASP.NET MVC application and will be implemented using the Domain Model architecture. It turns out to be quite a large bounded context because it incorporates membership, ordering logic, and even an extremely simple segment of the purchase context—basically, just the gold status awards for customers.

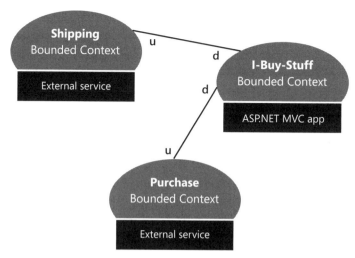

FIGURE 9-4 The context map for I-Buy-Stuff.

The largest share of business logic belongs to the I-Buy-Stuff site. Shipping and Purchase bounded contexts are implemented (mocked up actually) as external services. Both external services end up being upstream to the main site. At least in the demo, for the sake of simplicity, we don't use an anticorruption layer. Had we used that, the implementation probably would have consisted of an extra class receiving the raw information from the external service and massaging data to a known and fixed format.

The noble art of pragmatic domain modeling

The fundamental issue we see in modern software is that too often developers focus on code rather than models. This approach is not wrong per se, but it makes it so hard to manage complexity when you face it.

If you blissfully ignore domain modeling and you still write successful code, are you doing wrong? Not at all, but you might be in trouble when the level of complexity rises. It can be on the next project or on this same project as requirements keep changing and growing.

Behavior is a game-changer

A domain model is, then, a collection of classes with properties and methods. Together they reveal the model behind the business domain. Yet for years nobody really looked into ways to dig such a model out of the darkness. In the last chapter, we outlined the pillars of a domain model and worked out the skeleton of a few classes. That was more or less the theory. When it comes to practice, there are a few aspects to consider:

- Understanding and implementing behavior becomes really crucial for the final success.

- As you need to persist the model, you should be ready to accept compromises.

- The model you work out is the API for the business domain; it must be orchestrated and connected to whatever front end you need to have in place.

As hard as it might sound, we think that everyone willing to enlarge the contours of the "picture" he sees should try to use domain modeling on a domain he knows well—at least as a code kata exercise.

This is the spirit of I-Buy-Stuff.

 Note Taken from the world of karate, a *code kata* is an exercise that refreshes the basics of your skills. In the field of software development, it may consist of rewriting a known algorithm with a fresh mind to see if you can make improvements. For more details about the spirit of code kata, see *http://codekata.com*.

The typical perspective of a .NET developer

Most .NET developers have grown up following the guidelines of the *Table Module* pattern. The Table Module pattern essentially suggests you first create a relational data model that fits the business domain. Next, you identify primary tables in the database and build a module for each. In the end, a table module ends up being just the repository of methods that perform query and command actions against the table (say, *Orders*) and all of its related tables (say, *OrderItems*).

Methods of the table module class are directly called from the presentation layer or the application layer, if you really want to have one. Most of the time, the back-end model you get has the following aspects:

- Two-layer architecture, with the presentation layer calling directly into repositories or table modules.

- Table modules are plain containers of public methods with no state and expressivity limited to their names and parameter list. Extending and maintaining these classes might soon become an issue. Their structure is crystal clear in the beginning but soon becomes quite opaque.

- Unclear definitions of models to be used in code. Should you go with *DataSet* objects? Should you create your own data-transfer objects? Should you leverage Entity Framework and just infer classes that reflect one-to-one the structure of the tables?

The advent of Entity Framework first encouraged the use of designers to infer the database structure so that with a few clicks you could create an object model that mirrors the database. It was easy and effective, and it solved the last point in the preceding list.

Doc, my model is anemic

DDD pundits point out that no model needs to be anemic. As software anemia is generally measured in terms of how much behavior you have in classes, in a model just inferred from a database you have nearly no behavior. Therefore, your model is anemic.

Is software anemia a serious disease?

In humans, anemia results in weariness and is due to lack of red cells in blood. Red cells are responsible for delivering oxygen to the body tissues and bring life and energy. Similarly, in software anemia denotes a lack of energy to face change, but we wouldn't call it a disease. An anemic model can still work effectively as long as the team is capable of managing the complexity of the domain and its evolution.

In the end, an anemic model leaves the sword of Damocles hanging over your code. According to a tale told in ancient Greece, Damocles sat on the throne with a huge sword hanging over him held only by a single hair. This is the right metaphor: all is good as long as the sword continues to hang.

The focus on behavior has two main purposes: creating objects with a public interface closer to the entities observable in the real world. This also makes it easier to perform modeling in accordance with the names and rules of the ubiquitous language.

Location of the business logic

From a more pragmatic view, focusing on behavior is essentially finding a different location for segments of the business logic. Let's consider an *Invoice* class:

```
class Invoice
{
    public string Number {get; private set;}
    public DateTime Date {get; private set;}
    public Customer Customer {get; private set;}
    public string PayableOrder {get; private set;}
    public ICollection<InvoiceLine> Lines {get; private set;}
    ...
}
```

The class doesn't have methods. Is it wrongly written, then? Is it part of an anemic model?

An object model is not anemic if it just lacks methods on classes. An entity is anemic if there's logic that belongs to it that is placed outside the entity class. As an example, consider the problem of calculating the estimated day of payment of an invoice. Input data consists of the date of the invoice and payment terms (immediate, 30 days, 60 days, or whatever).

If you define the method on the *Invoice* class, it ends up with the following signature:

```
DateTime EstimatedPayment()
```

Otherwise, if you prefer to keep all business logic in a single *InvoiceModule* class, it might look like this:

```
DateTime EstimatedPayment(Invoice invoice)
```

The latter receives the entity to be investigated as its sole argument. This is a possible alert that a piece of logic belongs to the entity. Where's the "right" location for this method in a Domain Model design? A simple but effective rule to mechanize decision can be summarized as follows:

- If the code in the method deals only with the members of the entity, it probably belongs to the entity.

- If the code needs to access other entities or value objects in the same aggregate, it probably belongs to the aggregate root.

- If the code in the method needs to query or update the persistence layer or, in general, needs to acquire references outside the boundaries of the entity (or its aggregate), it's a domain service method.

If you ignore these two rules and centralize everything that in some way relates to the *Invoice* in a single service class that does everything—validation, data access, business logic—you're making the entity anemic.

Entities scaffolding

A DDD entity is a plain C# class and is expected to contain both data (properties) and behavior (methods). An entity might have public properties, but it is not going to be a plain data container. Here are the hallmarks of DDD entities:

- A well-defined identity

- Behavior expressed through methods, both public and not

- State exposed through read-only properties

- Very limited use of primitive types, replaced by value objects

- A preference for factory methods over multiple constructors

Let's find out more.

Managing the identity

The primary characteristic of an entity is the *identity*. The identity is any combination of data that uniquely identifies an instance of the entity class. In a way, the identity in this context is comparable to a primary key for the records of a relational table.

An identity serves the purpose of uniquely identifying the entity throughout the lifetime of the application. Developers use the identity to retrieve the reference to the entity at any time. The state of an entity might change, but the identity doesn't. In terms of implementation, the identity is often just an integer property like an *Id* property. In other cases, it can be a numeric string such as a Social Security number, a VAT ID, a user name, or a combination of properties.

The identity just defines what makes two entities the same entity. An entity class, however, also needs to implement equality that uses the identity values to determine whether two entities are the same. Let's start with an *Order* class like the one shown here:

```
public class Order
{
    private readonly int _id;
    public Order(int id)
    {
        // Validate ID here
        ...
        _id = id;
    }
    public int Id
    {
        get {return _id;}
    }
    ...
}
```

Suppose now you have two instances of the *Order* class that refer to the same ID:

```
var o1 = new Order(1);
var o2 = new Order(1);
```

According to the basic behavior of a .NET Framework classes, *o1* and *o2* are different instances. While this is correct in the general domain of the .NET Framework, it is inconsistent in the business domain you're in. In that business domain, what matters is the ID of the order: if the ID matches, two orders are the same. This is not, however, what you get out of the box in .NET and other frameworks.

To implement a custom equality logic that uses identity values, you must override the methods *Equals* and *GetHashCode* that any .NET object exposes. Here's an example:

```
public class Order
{
    private readonly int _id;
    ...
    public override bool Equals(object obj)
    {
        if (this == obj)
            return true;
        if (obj == null || GetType() != obj.GetType())
            return false;
        var other = (Order) obj;

        // Your identity logic goes here.
        // You may refactor this code to the method of an entity interface
        return _id == other.Id;
    }
    public override int GetHashCode()
    {
        return Id.GetHashCode();
    }
}
```

> **Important** Identity and equality are two distinct concepts, but they are related in the context of an entity. *Identity* is just a collection of values that make an entity unique (much like a primary key). *Equality* is class infrastructure that supports equality operators in the .NET Framework. Within an entity, equality is checked using identity values. As you'll see later in the chapter, value objects do not have identity and don't need to be retrieved later to check their state, but they still need some custom logic for equality.

Private setters

An entity has both behavior (methods) and state (properties). However, in the real world it's likely that attributes of an entity are restricted to just a few values. A quantity of products, for example, is not exactly an integer because it is expected not to be negative. At the same time, using unsigned integers is arguable, too, because it could mean you're allowed to place orders for over four billion items.

When designing entities, you should only provide properties that really express the state of the entity and use setter methods only for properties that can change. Also, don't let setters be open to just any value that fits the declared type of the property. Open setters can have nasty side effects, such as leaving entities in a temporarily invalid state.

In general, it's good practice to mark setters as private and expose public methods to let other developers change the state of the entity. When you do so, though, pay attention to the naming convention you use and ensure it matches the ubiquitous language.

Factories and constructors

Constructors are the usual way to create instances of classes and might or might not take parameters. In a domain model, you should avoid classes with parameterless constructors. In addition, each constructor should be able to return an instance whose state is consistent with the business domain. The following code is probably inconsistent:

```
var request = new OrderRequest();
```

The newly created order request lacks any reference to a date and a customer. The date could be set by default in the body of the constructor, but not the customer ID. The following is only a tiny bit better:

```
var request = new OrderRequest(1234);
```

There are two problems here. First, when looking at the code, one can hardly guess what's going on. An instance of *OrderRequest* is being created, but why and using which data? What's *1234*? This leads to the second problem: you are violating the ubiquitous language of the bounded context. The language probably says something like this: a customer can issue an order request and is allowed to specify a purchase ID. If that's the case, here's a better way to get a new *OrderRequest* instance:

```
var request = OrderRequest.CreateForCustomer(1234);
```

Constructors are unnamed methods, and using them might also raise a readability issue. But that would be the least of your worries. By using public constructors, you distract yourself and developers after you from the real reason why that instance of *OrderRequest* is necessary.

Constructors are unavoidable in object-oriented programming languages; just make them private and expose public static factory methods:

```
private OrderRequest() { ...  }
public OrderRequest CreateForCustomer (int customerId)
{
    var request = new OrderRequest();
    ...
    return request;
}
```

A more advanced scenario is when you just arrange a separate factory service for some entities and manage things like object pooling inside.

> **Note** In the next chapter, you'll see that constructors are often marked as protected instead of private. The use of protected constructors has to do with persistence and O/RM tools. When an O/RM materializes an entity instance and fills it with database content, it actually returns an instance of a dynamically created class that inherits from the entity class (for example, a proxy). This allows O/RM tools to invoke the protected default constructor; a private default constructor—as well as a sealed entity class—would make persistence through O/RM tools quite problematic.

Value objects scaffolding

Like an entity, a *value object* is a class that aggregates data. Behavior is not relevant in value objects; value objects might still have methods, but those are essentially helper methods. Unlike entities, though, value objects don't need identity because they have no variable state and are fully identified by their data.

Data structure

Most of the time, a value object is a plain data container that exposes data through public getters and receives values only through the constructor. Here's an example:

```
public class Address
{
    public Address(string street, string number, string city, string zip)
    {
        Street = street;
        Number = number;
        City = city;
        Zip = zip;
    }
    public string Street { get; private set; }
    public string Number { get; private set; }
```

```
    public string City { get; private set; }
    public string Zip { get; private set; }

    // Equality members
    ...
}
```

Methods can be defined, but they must be pure methods that do not alter the state. For example, you can have the following value object to represent the score of a basketball match:

```
public class Score
{
    public Score(int team1, int team2)
    {
        Team1 = team1;
        Team2 = team2;
    }
    public int Team1 { get; private set; }
    public int Team2 { get; private set; }

    public bool IsLeading(int index)
    {
        if (index != 1 && index != 2)
          throw new ArgumentException("index");

        if (index == 1 && team1 > team2) return true;
        if (index == 2 && team2 > team1) return true;
        return false;
    }
}
```

The *IsLeading* method doesn't alter the state of the object, but its presence will definitely make the content of the value object handier to use.

Equality

Using the .NET Framework jargon, we could say that a value object is an *immutable* type. An immutable is any type that doesn't have state and requires new instances every time new values are required. As mentioned earlier in the chapter, the *String* type is the canonical example of an immutable type in the .NET Framework.

You need to override both the *Equals* and *GetHashCode* methods to ensure that within the model objects made of the same data are treated as equal objects. Here's how to check whether two *Address* instance are the same:

```
public class Address
{
  ...

  public override bool Equals(object obj)
    {
        if (this == obj)
            return true;
        if (obj == null || GetType() != obj.GetType())
            return false;
```

```
        var other = (Address) obj;
        return string.Equals(Street, other.Street) &&
                string.Equals(Number, other.Number) &&
                string.Equals(City, other.City) &&
                string.Equals(Zip, other.Zip);
    }
    public override int GetHashCode()
    {
        const int hashIndex = 307;
        var result = (Street != null ? Street.GetHashCode() : 0);
        result = (result * hashIndex) ^ (Number != null ? Number.GetHashCode() : 0);
        result = (result * hashIndex) ^ (City != null ? City.GetHashCode() : 0);
        result = (result * hashIndex) ^ (Zip != null ? Zip.GetHashCode() : 0);
        return result;
    }
}
```

Custom equality logic is *de facto* a mandatory feature in both entities and value objects.

Hash codes and equality in the .NET Framework

The .NET Framework guidelines strongly recommend that whenever you override *Equals* you also override *GetHashCode*. But why is that so?

The *Equals* method is always used when equality is checked explicitly, such as when your code calls *Equals* directly or uses the == operator. *GetHashCode* is not involved in the equality assessment process. Subsequently, its implementation doesn't affect the equality evaluation. Yet, you get a compiler warning if you override *Equals* but not *GetHashCode*.

GetHashCode comes into play only if your objects are going to be stored within hash tables or used as dictionary keys. In this case, the .NET Framework uses the value returned by *GetHashCode* to find the corresponding entry in the hash table or dictionary. Two object instances that are the same object according to *Equals* but return different values according to *GetHashCode* will never be considered equal. As a result, different values will be picked from the hash table or dictionary.

When your objects appear as public objects in a class library, you simply have no guarantee that they will never be used within hash tables or as dictionary keys. For this reason, it is strongly recommended that you override both methods to ensure that two objects that are equal according to *Equals* also return the same *GetHashCode* value. The returned value doesn't matter as long as it's the same. In light of this, why not simply make *GetHashCode* return a constant value in all cases?

When *GetHashCode* returns the same value for two objects, you get a collision and *Equals* is called to ensure the objects are the same. A performance goal, of course, is to minimize the number of collisions by giving each object with a unique combination of values a different hash code.

Finally, note that the hash code should never change during the lifetime of an object. For this to happen, only immutable properties should be used to calculate the code. This rule fits perfectly with the guidelines for entities and value objects.

Operators overloading

Overriding *Equals* doesn't let you automatically use the == and != equality operators on overridden objects. In the .NET Framework guidelines, Microsoft discourages you from overloading operators when mutable properties are used to check equality. This is not the case for entities and value objects. So operator overloading is absolutely safe. Here's an example:

```
public static bool operator ==(Customer c1, Customer c2)
{
    // Both null or same instance
    if (ReferenceEquals(c1, c2))
        return true;

    // Return false if one is null, but not both
    if (((object)c1 == null) || ((object)c2 == null))
        return false;

    return c1.Equals(c2);
}

public static bool operator !=(Customer c1, Customer c2)
{
    return !(c1 == c2);
}
```

We discussed entities and value objects, explored their differences, and now understand equality nuances. But at the very end of the day, when are you going to use value objects in a domain model?

Expressivity

As we see it, the key benefit that value objects bring to the table is *expressivity*. There are two aspects of expressivity: replacing primitive types and replacing data clumps.

Primitive types are sometimes too basic for being used extensively in a model that claims to represent a piece of real-world business. Primitive types are what we actually use when we persist entities; however, at the higher abstraction level of the domain model, primitive types are often elements of vagueness. What does an integer denote? Is it a quantity, a temperature, an amount of money, a measurement? Is it an element of a range?

In the real world, you have quantity, temperature, amount—not plain integers.

While you can still use integers and be happy, using primitive types forces you to validate values any place in the model where an integer is used to mean a quantity, a measurement, an element of a range, and so forth. Not only will your validation code possibly be cumbersome to write, but it is also likely to be duplicated because it applies to the setter rather than to the type itself. Here's how you can more effectively model an amount of money:

```
public sealed class Money
{
    public Money(Currency currency, decimal amount)
    {
        Currency = currency;
```

```
        Value = amount;
    }

    public Currency Currency { get; private set; }
    public decimal Value { get; private set; }

// Add operator overloads
...
}
```

Currency in this example is another value object built around a symbol and a name.

In general, by using value objects, you simplify code and also produce a model closer to the ubiquitous language. In the refactoring jargon, *data clumps* are a well-known code smell. A data clump is when a group of data items are often used together but as independent items. Ultimately, a data clump is just an aggregation of primitive values that could easily be turned into a new object.

A good example is currency and amount in the *Money* value object. In the ubiquitous language, you likely have money, not currency and amount; you have addresses, not individual items like street, city, and Zip code. This is where value objects fit in.

Identifying aggregates

Let's focus now on the entities listed in Table 9-2 and used in the sample application. The I-Buy-Stuff application is meant to be a simple online store, and this is reflected by the limited number of entities and their limited relationships. (See Figure 9-5.) In a site where we just consider a few use-cases like searching and placing an order, *Customer*, *Order*, and *Product* are aggregates and *Customer* and *Product* are single-entity aggregates. The same can be said for *FidelityCard*.

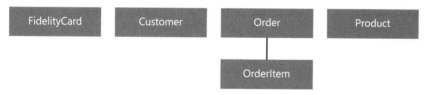

FIGURE 9-5 Aggregates of the sample domain model.

Let's find out more about the aggregates. From the behavior perspective, though, given the order-focused use-cases we're considering, the most interesting aggregate is *Order*. However, some interesting considerations apply to *Customer* too.

The *Customer* aggregate

The customer is characterized by some personal data such as name, address, user name, and payment details. We're clearly assuming that our online store has just one type of customer and doesn't distinguish, for example, between corporate customers and private customers. A corporate customer, for example, might have multiple users shopping under the same customer account. Take a look at Figure 9-6.

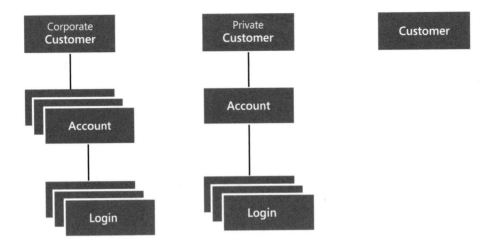

FIGURE 9-6 Three possible ways of organizing the abstract Customer aggregate in an online store application.

The first diagram represents a corporate customer that, under a single financial account, can have multiple users (for example, some of the employees) with different shipping addresses and who log into the system using various credentials. The central graph represents a private customer with a single user account. Finally, the third graph represents the implementation we use in this chapter, where the customer entity represents a single user account and credentials are stored within the *Customer* entity itself.

> **Note** As we said earlier in the note around Table 9-2, for most domain experts of online stores, users and customers will be distinct concepts and entities. This doesn't affect the generality of our example, but it's important to keep in mind to realize the subtlety and depth of domain-driven design.

Another aspect to consider is the login into the system. Should you consider using distinct entities to hold credentials and the rest of the data and behavior? That's probably what you will want to do most of the time. There are two further considerations to point you in this direction:

- Each customer or account can have multiple ways to log in, including credentials stored in the local system and multiple social logins.

- If you use ASP.NET Identity to implement authentication, then, at the current stage of technology you are forced to make user classes implement a fixed external interface (the *IUser* interface). This would reduce the POCO (plain-old C# object) status of the domain.

In the sample application, the customer coincides with the user who logs in. The *Customer* class has the following structure:

```
public class Customer : IAggregateRoot
{
    public static Customer CreateNew(Gender gender, string id,
```

```
                string firstname, string lastname, string email)
{
    var customer = new Customer {
        CustomerId = id,
        Address = Address.Create(),
        Payment = NullCreditCard.Instance,
        Email = email,
        FirstName = firstname,
        LastName = lastname,
        Gender = gender
    };
    return customer;
}

public string CustomerId { get; private set; }
public string PasswordHash { get; private set; }
public string FirstName { get; private set; }
public string LastName { get; private set; }
public string Email { get; private set; }
public Gender Gender { get; private set; }
public string Avatar { get; private set; }
public Address Address { get; private set; }
public CreditCard Payment { get; private set; }
public ICollection<Order> Orders { get; private set; }

// More methods here such as SetDefaultPaymentMode.
// A customer may have a default payment mode (e.g., credit card), but
// different orders can be paid in different ways.
...
}
```

When the customer is created, the *Name* property indicates the login name whereas *FirstName* and *LastName* identify the full display name. Credit card and address information can be added through ad hoc methods. The customer is created through the canonical Register page of most websites, and credentials are stored in the local database. If the user logs in via Facebook or Twitter, a new customer instance is also created if it doesn't exist.

Note You can see that with this extremely simple approach the same individual ends up with two distinct customer records if she logs in via Twitter and Facebook. That makes it necessary to improve the code to support multiple logins for each customer. Ideally, you might want to maintain a table of accounts and establish a one-to-many relationship with customers.

The concrete implementation you find in the sample code uses ASP.NET Identity facilities to do logins and logouts. However, it bypasses ASP.NET Identity entirely when it comes to adding, retrieving, and validating users. The reason is to avoid making the domain model explicitly dependent on the ASP.NET Identity framework. Figure 9-7 outlines a possible adjustment to the model to keep login outside the domain model and link multiple user names to the same customer instance.

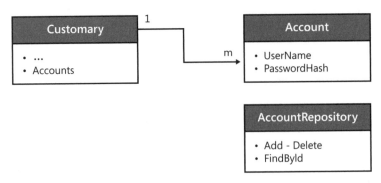

FIGURE 9-7 Keeping the login infrastructure outside the domain model.

The Account entity is a new aggregate. Its repository exposes methods for basic CRUD operations and can retrieve a matching customer when given a user ID. The user ID is what comes out of the ASP. NET Identity login process.

> **Note** Using the schema shown in Figure 9-7, where Account is part of the domain, makes the whole model more flexible and easier to adapt to real scenarios. It doesn't solve, however, the issue of mixing the domain model with a dependency on the ASP.NET Identity *IUser* interface. If you want to leverage the built-in facilities of ASP.NET Identity as far as management of the accounts is concerned, you should keep authentication concerns out of the domain model. If you see *Account* as part of one of the entities, we recommend that you use the account repository to do CRUD instead of the canonical user store object of ASP.NET Identity.

The *Product* aggregate

One of the responsibilities of an entity is carrying data and data stems from the expected behavior of the entity. The *Product* entity must tell the world about its description and pricing. In addition, for the purposes of use-cases, it must possible to know whether the product is currently "featured" on the site and what the current stock level is. The following description is mostly fine:

```
public class Product : IAggregateRoot
{
    public int Id {get; private set;}
    public string Description {get; private set;}
    public Money UnitPrice {get; private set;}
    public int StockLevel {get; private set;}
    public bool Featured {get; private set;}

    // Methods
    public void SetAsFeatured() { ... }
    ...

    // Identity management as for Customer
    ...
}
```

Let's consider the *StockLevel* property. At first, the integer used to define the stock level can be changed into an unsigned integer because negative values are not expected to be valid values for what the property represents. Even better, an ad hoc value object can be created to represent a quantity as a natural number.

As you can see, though, the *StockLevel*, like all properties in the code snippet, has a private setter. This means that the property is read-only and, subsequently, reading it as an integer is fine. Who's going to set the *StockLevel* property? There are two possible scenarios:

- The object is materialized only from the persistence layer.

- The object has a factory method if it's allowed to be instantiated from client code.

Actually, the second option is not credible businesswise, though a factory method might be helpful to have for implementation purposes.

The *StockLevel* property indicates in this simple model the number of items of a given product we have in store. This number is decreased as orders are placed and increased when the store manager refills the stock by placing orders to vendors. Subsequently, a method is necessary to programmatically modify the stock level of a product. The store manager is part of the back office, which is a different bounded context.

The *Order* aggregate

In I-Buy-Stuff, an order is created when processing the content of a shopping cart, which is represented by an *ShoppingCart* class. The skeleton of the class is shown here:

```
public class Order : IAggregateRoot
{
    public int OrderId { get; private set; }
    public Customer Buyer { get; private set; }
    public OrderState State { get; private set; }
    public DateTime Date { get; private set; }
    public Money Total { get; private set; }
    public ICollection<OrderItem> Items { get; private set; }
    ...
}
```

The class needs to have a public factory method because at some point business logic needs to create an order while processing a request. When creating an order, you specify the ID and reference the customer. The date is set automatically, so it is the state of the order.

In the example, we assume that the order is created when the customer clicks to check out. There will likely be a domain service to orchestrate the checkout process; one of the steps is the creation of the order. The factory of the order can be marked internal and can use a nonpublic constructor:

```
internal static Order CreateFromShoppingCart(ShoppingCart cart)
{
    var order = new Order(cart.CustomerId, cart.Customer);
    return order;
}
```

```
protected Order(int orderId, Customer customer)
{
    OrderId = orderId;
    State = OrderState.Pending;
    Total = Money.Zero;
    Date = DateTime.Today;
    Items = new Collection<OrderItem>();
    Buyer = customer;
}
```

To modify the state of the order and add items, you need ad hoc methods. Here are some methods that change the state:

```
public void Cancel()
{
    if (State != OrderState.Pending)
        throw new InvalidOperationException(
                "Can't cancel an order that is not pending.");
    State = OrderState.Canceled;

}

public void MarkAsShipped()
{
    if (State != OrderState.Pending)
        throw new InvalidOperationException(
                "Can't mark as shipped an order that is not pending.");
    State = OrderState.Shipped;
}
```

As you can see, it's not rocket science, but using these methods instead of plain setters improves the readability of the code and, more importantly, keeps it aligned to the ubiquitous language. The conventions used here to name methods, in fact, cannot be arbitrary. Terms like *Archive* and *MarkAsShipped* should be taken from the ubiquitous language and reflect the terminology used within the business.

> **Note** Such methods are often implemented as void methods. This makes total sense because they just represent actions. However, depending on the context it might be interesting to consider a fluent interface. You just make the method return *this*, and it enables chaining calls and makes the whole thing more readable. It's a possibility to consider.

There are a few interesting things to say about the *Items* and *Total* properties. Let's start with bringing up some issues related to having collections in an aggregate. We describe the issues and provide some suggestions. The definitive answer, though, will come in the next chapter and from the use of a different DDD supporting architecture—CQRS instead of Domain Model.

The *Items* property is defined as a collection. This means that any code that receives an *Order* instance can enumerate the content of the collection but can't add or remove items. Unfortunately, there's no easy way to prevent that client code from accessing and updating content within the collection. Even worse, this aspect remains unaltered even if you further restrict the collection to a basic *IEnumerable<T>*. The following code is always allowed and, in addition, you can always use LINQ to select a particular order within the collection:

```
someOrder.Items.First().Quantity++;
```

In our scenario, an order is read-only. It gets created out of the checkout process; it can't be modified, but it can be viewed. So you want the *Items* collection to be consumed as read-only content. How can you prevent changes on the objects within the collection? Unfortunately, even the following won't work:

```
public class Order
{
    private Collection<OrderItem> _items = new Collection<OrderItem>();
    public ICollection<OrderItem> Items
    {
        get { return _items.AsReadOnly(); }
    }
}
```

The *Items* collection is read-only, but you can still retrieve individual elements and change them programmatically.

The definitive solution to this problem comes with the separation between queries and commands and with the provision of different models for reading and writing operations. We'll cover this in the next two chapters.

The *Total* property indicates the total value of the order. How should you deal with that? The property is there to please code that consumes the content of the order. In theory, the total of an order can be calculated on demand, iterating on the order items graph with an ad hoc method:

```
public Money GetTotal()
{
    var amount = Items.Sum(item => item.GetTotal().Value);
    return new Money(Currency.Default, amount);
}
```

This solution, though, has a significant drawback. It forces the *Order* instance to have in memory the entire graph of items. There might be scenarios in which you just want to know the about the total of the order, without all the details. A method like *GetTotal* will force the deserialization of the entire graph and create much more traffic to and from the database.

By having a simple property on the *Order*, you can decide intelligently whether or not to deserialize the entire graph. The *Total* property can be set by the order repository when it returns an instance (which could be a simple SUM operation at the SQL level), or it can be the result of some redundancy in the relational schema of the database. Whenever the order is persisted, the current total is calculated and saved for further queries.

The *FidelityCard* aggregate

The *FidelityCard* aggregate is an extremely simple class that summarizes through the accrual of points the activity of a customer within the site.

```
public class FidelityCard
{
    public static FidelityCard CreateNewCard(string number, Customer customer)
    {
        var card = new FidelityCard {Number = number, Owner = customer};
        return card;
    }
    protected FidelityCard()
    {
        Number = "";
        Owner = UnknownCustomer.Instance;
        Points = 0;
    }

    public string Number { get; private set; }
    public Customer Owner { get; private set; }
    public int Points { get; private set; }

    public int AddPoints(int points)
    {
        Points += points;
        return Points;
    }
}
```

Each order a customer places increases the total points on the card, and those points are then used to determine a reward status the customer can use to get additional discounts. All the logic of discounts and levels is inspired by the business domain and can be as complex and varying as the real world requires.

The content of a *FidelityCard* object is used by domain services to calculate reward levels and discounts.

Special cases

In the context of a domain model, one of the most commonly used accessory design patterns is the Special Case pattern, which is defined here: *http://martinfowler.com/eaaCatalog/specialCase.html*. The pattern addresses a simple question: when some code needs to return, say, a *Customer* object but no suitable object is found, what is the best practice? Should you return NULL? Should you return odd values? Should you make an otherwise clean API overly complex and make it distinguish whether or not a result exists? Have a look at this code. It belongs to the *OrderRepository* class of I-Buy-Stuff and retrieves an order by ID while restricting the search to a particular customer ID:

```
public Order FindByCustomerAndId(int id, string customerId)
{
    using (var db = new DomainModelFacade())
    {
        try
```

```
        {
            var order = (from o in db.Orders
                            where o.OrderId == id &&
                                  o.Buyer.CustomerId == customerId
                            select o).First();

            return order;
        }
        catch (InvalidOperationException)
        {
            return new NotFoundOrder();
        }
    }
}
```

The *First* method throws if the order is not found. In this case, the code returns a newly created instance of the class *NotFoundOrder*:

```
public class NotFoundOrder : Order
{
    public static NotFoundOrder Instance = new NotFoundOrder();
    public NotFoundOrder() : base(0, UnknownCustomer.Instance)
    {
    }
}
```

NotFoundOrder is just a derived class that sets all properties to their default values. Any code that expects an *Order* can deal with *NotFoundOrder* as well; and type checking helps you figure out if something went wrong:

```
if(order is NotFoundOrder)
{
    ...
}
```

This is the gist of the *Special Case* pattern. On top of this basic implementation, you can add as many additional features as you want, including a singleton instance.

Persisting the model

A domain model exists to be persisted, and typically an O/RM will do the job. All that an O/RM does as far as persistence is concerned is map properties to columns of a database table and manage reads and writes. This is only a 10,000-foot, bird's-eye view, though.

What an O/RM does for you

Generally speaking, an O/RM has responsibilities that can be summarized in four points:

- CRUD

- Query engine

- Transactional engine

- Concurrency

The query and transactional engines refer to two specific design patterns: the Query Object pattern (which you can see at *http://martinfowler.com/eaaCatalog/queryObject.html*), and the Unit of Work pattern (which you can see at *http://martinfowler.com/eaaCatalog/unitOfWork.html*).

Today, on the .NET platform nearly all O/RMs offer an idiomatic implementation of the Query Object pattern based on the LINQ syntax. The *Unit of Work* is offered through the capabilities of the O/RM root object. In Entity Framework, this object is *ObjectContext* in its various flavors, such as *DbContext*.

An O/RM is an excellent productivity tool. It doesn't really do magical things, but it saves you a lot of cumbersome and error-prone coding. All that it requires is instructions on how to map properties of objects in the domain model to columns of relational database tables.

When it comes to this, you realize that the database is really important even if you do domain-driven design and build a model that is persistence ignorant and stay as agnostic as possible with regard to databases. In a nutshell, the database and the O/RM are two constraints that typically force you to make concessions and introduce in the model features that only serve the need of persistence.

Making concessions to persistence

The most common concession that you, as a Domain Model architect, have to make to an O/RM is the availability of default constructors on all persistent classes.

```
protected Customer()
{
   // Place here any initialization code you may need
   ...
}
```

The constructor is required for the O/RM to materialize an entity from the database. In other words, it still needs low-level tools to create an instance of that class. Factory methods are an abstraction that serves the purpose of the ubiquitous language. The constructor, on the other hand, is the only known way that compilers in C# (and other object-oriented languages) allow you to create fresh instances of a class.

Nicely enough, though, you can use O/RM tools to hide the default parameterless constructor from public view. When materializing an entity from databases, an O/RM usually returns the instance of a dynamically created class that inherits from the real entity. In this way, the dynamically generated code gains access to the protected constructor.

Beyond this point, other changes you might be forced to do to make the model persistent depend on the capabilities and quirks of the O/RM of choice. For example, up until version 5, Entity

Framework was unable to deal with *enum* types. In version 6.1, it is still unable to handle, at least in a default way, arrays of primitive types.

> **Note** When it comes to arrays, database experts might tell you that arrays do not fit nicely in the world of databases and that you should ideally find a solution that doesn't require arrays. The point is that relational databases don't offer a way to read and write arrays directly. As a result, storing arrays requires workarounds, but it is neither impossible nor particularly hard. Yet, when you think about the model in a database-agnostic way, arrays might be excellent modeling tools for business aspects that require sequences of related data.

All this is to say that first you should strive to get an ideal domain model that matches the features of the ubiquitous language; next, you should strive to make it suitable to the O/RM of choice (notably Entity Framework) to persist it.

> **Note** Entity Framework is certainly not the only O/RM available for the .NET Framework. A popular competitor is NHibernate. The perception, however, is that the fierce debate about which of the two to use no longer matters. And because it is tightly integrated with Visual Studio, Entity Framework is the first option that many consider. In addition, there's a long list of products available from vendors such as Devxpress and Telerik. It's really mostly a matter of preference.

The Entity Framework Code-First approach

Entity Framework is the O/RM provided by Microsoft .NET. It was not even released when we wrote the first edition of this book. It can be considered the most natural choice today for any .NET project—nearly a de facto standard.

Essentially, Entity Framework comes in two flavors: Database First and Code First. There's also a third flavor, called Model First, but it's a hybrid, middle-way approach that uses the visual diagram model and was soon superseded by Code First. The Database-First approach reads the structure of an existing database and returns a set of anemic classes you can extend with methods using the partial class mechanism. The Code-First approach consists of writing a set of classes—for example, a Domain Model, as discussed so far. Next, you add an extra layer of code (or data annotations) to map properties to tables. This mapping layer tells the O/RM about the database to create (or expect), its relationships, its constraints and tables and, more importantly, it tells the O/RM where to save or read property values.

The I-Buy-Stuff example uses the Code-First approach.

Code-First delivers a persistence layer centered on a class that inherits from *DbContext*. Here's an example:

```
public class DomainModelFacade : DbContext
{
    static DomainModelFacade()
    {
        Database.SetInitializer(new SampleAppInitializer());
    }

    public DomainModelFacade() : base("naa4e-09")
    {
        Products = base.Set<Product>();
        Customers = base.Set<Customer>();
        Orders = base.Set<Order>();
        FidelityCards = base.Set<FidelityCard>();
    }

    public DbSet<Order> Orders { get; private set; }
    public DbSet<Customer> Customers { get; private set; }
    public DbSet<Product> Products { get; private set; }
    public DbSet<FidelityCard> FidelityCards { get; private set; }

    protected override void OnModelCreating(DbModelBuilder modelBuilder)
    {
        ...
    }
}
```

The string passed to the constructor is the name of the database or the name of an entry in the configuration file indicating where to read details about the connection string and the data provider. When you install Code First via NuGet, you get the SQL Server engine as the default data provider and the LocalDb engine for storage.

The *DbSet* properties abstract the tables being created, and the initializer class can be used to automate the creation, dropping, and filling of the database mostly for the purposes of an initial setup or for debugging.

Mapping properties to columns

In Code First, there are two ways to map properties to columns. You can use data annotation attributes in the source code of domain classes, or you can use the fluent Code-First API and write configuration classes bound together in the *OnModelCreating* overridable method.

Overall, we recommend the fluent API rather than data annotations. The reason is that data annotations are intrusive and add noise to an otherwise persistent ignorant domain model isolated from infrastructure technologies.

Here's some code you want to have in the mapping layer:

```
modelBuilder.ComplexType<Money>();
modelBuilder.ComplexType<Address>();
modelBuilder.ComplexType<CreditCard>();

modelBuilder.Configurations.Add(new FidelityCardMap());
modelBuilder.Configurations.Add(new OrderMap());
modelBuilder.Configurations.Add(new CustomerMap());
modelBuilder.Configurations.Add(new OrderItemMap());

modelBuilder.Configurations.Add(new CurrencyMap());
```

The *ComplexType* method lets you tell the O/RM that the specified type is a complex type in the Entity Framework jargon, which is a concept close to what a value object is in a domain model. The remaining code in the snippet shows mapping classes each taking care of the configuration of an entity. Note, though, that in case of need you also can have a mapping class for a complex type. It all depends on the instructions you have for the O/RM. Let's look at a couple of examples:

```
public class OrderMap : EntityTypeConfiguration<Order>
{
    public OrderMap()
    {
        ToTable("Orders");
        HasKey(t => t.OrderId);
        HasRequired(o => o.Buyer);
        HasMany(o => o.Items);
    }
}
```

The method *HasKey* declares the primary key, whereas *HasRequired* sets a required foreign-key relationship to a single *Customer* object. Finally, *HasMany* defines a one-to-many relationship for *OrderItem* objects.

The following excerpt, on the other hand, shows how to configure columns from properties:

```
Property(o => o.OrderId)
        .IsRequired()
        .HasMaxLength(10)
        .HasColumnName("Id");
```

The net effect is that the table *Orders* is going to have a column named *Id* mapped to the property *OrderId*. At the database level, the column doesn't accept null values and any content longer than 10 characters. Similar methods exist to make a value auto-generated by the database:

```
Ignore(p => p.Name);
```

Finally, the *Ignore* method is used to tell the O/RM that the specified property shouldn't be persisted. This is what happens, for example, when the property has a computed getter in the C# code.

Implementing the business logic

As it often happens, not all the business logic that is required—whether it is rules or tasks—fits into the classes of the domain model. At a minimum, you need to have persistence logic stored in repository classes. Most likely, you need domain services. In the I-Buy-Stuff example, there are two main tasks—finding an order and placing an order.

Note Before we delve deeper into domain services, let's clarify how the call moves from the web user interface down to the domain layer. As mentioned, our example is an ASP.NET MVC application. This means that any user action (for example, button clicking) ends up in an action method call on a controller class. In Chapter 6, "The presentation layer," we introduced application services to contain any orchestration logic that gets content from the raw HTTP input and returns whatever is required for the controller to produce an HTTP response. Application services, though, don't directly deal with objects in the HTTP context.

Finding an order

Here's the code you find in the controller method that receives the user's request to retrieve a given order. As you can see, the controller method yields to an application service that gets data from the HTTP request and produces a response ready to be transmitted back as HTML, JSON, or whatever else is suitable:

```
public ActionResult SearchResults(int id)
{
    var model = _service.FindOrder(id, User.Identity.Name);
    return View(model);
}
```

The application service method—*FindOrder*, in the example—calls domain services and repositories as appropriate, does any data adaptation that might be necessary to call into the domain layer, and returns a view model.

Another option for organizing this code might be splitting responsibilities between the application service and controller so that the application service just does orchestration and returns raw data that the controller then packages up in a view model.

Important Note that the view model class is a plain container of data that might come in the form of domain entities or data-transfer objects.

Here's the actual implementation of the application service method. Admittedly, in this particular case having an application service is probably overkill because all it does is call a repository method. However, we invite you to consider the underlying pattern first and then apply any simplification that might work. The shortest path is always preferable as long as you know what you're doing and where you really want to go! In general, however, authorization code and even app validations might be additional code for the application services.

```
public SearchOrderViewModel FindOrder(int orderId, string customerId)
{
    var order = _orderRepository.FindByCustomerAndId(orderId, customerId);
    if (order is NullOrder)
        return new SearchOrderViewModel();
    return SearchOrderViewModel.CreateFromOrder(order);
}
```

Note We mentioned repositories in the prior chapter, and we're mentioning repositories extensively in this one. We provide more details about their role and implementation in Chapter 14, "The infrastructure layer."

Placing an order

When the user clicks to start shopping on the site, the system serves up the user interface shown in Figure 9-8. The following code governs the process:

```
public ActionResult New()
{
    var customerId = User.Identity.Name;
    var shoppingCartModel = _service.CreateShoppingCartForCustomer(customerId);
    shoppingCartModel.EnableEditOnShoppingCart = true;
    SaveCurrentShoppingCart(shoppingCartModel);
    return View("shoppingcart", shoppingCartModel);
}
```

The helper application service creates an empty shopping cart for the user and enables interactive UI controls to add or remove items. The shopping cart is saved in the session state for further reference. Note that the actual *ShoppingCart* type is defined in the domain because it carries information that makes up an order request. On the presentation layer, though, the *ShoppingCart* is wrapped in a view-model type enriched with the UI-related properties required to render the HTML page. This also includes the full list of products the user can choose from.

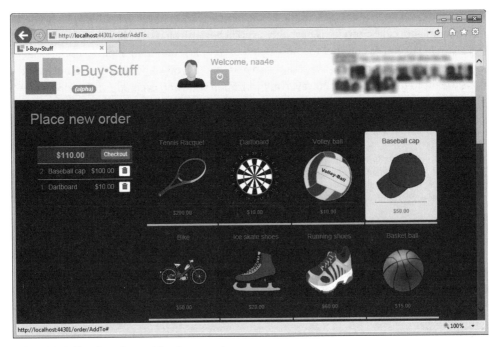

FIGURE 9-8 The shopping cart for the current user.

The shopping page lets the user add and remove products from the cart. Every add/remove action generates a roundtrip; the state of the shopping cart is retrieved from the session state, updated, and then saved back.

```
public ActionResult AddToShoppingCartCommand(int productId, int quantity=1)
{
    var cartModel = RetrieveCurrentShoppingCart();
    cartModel = _service.AddProductToShoppingCart(cart, productId, quantity);
    SaveCurrentShoppingCart(cartModel);
    return RedirectToAction("AddTo");
}
```

The application service adds an element to the shopping cart:

```
public ShoppingCartViewModel AddProductToShoppingCart(
            ShoppingCartViewModel cart, int productId, int quantity)
{
    var product = (from p in cart.Products where p.Id == productId select p).Single();
    cart.OrderRequest.AddItem(quantity, product);
    return cart;
}
```

The *AddItem* method on the *ShoppingCart* domain object contains a bit of logic to increase the quantity if the product is already in the cart:

```
public ShoppingCart AddItem(int quantity, Product product)
{
    var existingItem = (from i in Items
                        where i.Product.Id == product.Id
                        select i).SingleOrDefault();
    if (existingItem != null)
    {
        existingItem.Quantity++;
        return this;
    }

    // Create new item
    Items.Add(ShoppingCartItem.Create(quantity, product));
    return this;
}
```

The checkout button leads to the page in Figure 9-9. Note that the shopping cart is now rendered in read mode and all actionable buttons are not displayed.

FIGURE 9-9 The checkout page of the I-Buy-Stuff site.

Note that the controller method that receives the command to add an item to the cart (or remove an item from it) in the end redirects to the *AddTo* action instead of just rendering the next view. This is done to avoid a repeated form submission if the user refreshes the page. In response to a refresh action (for example, when F5 is pressed), browsers just repeat the last action. Thanks to the redirect, however, the last action is a GET, not a POST.

Processing the order request

When the user finally clicks the Buy button, it's time for the order to be processed and created. At this time, company policies and business rules must be applied. In general, processing the order is based on a workflow that is orchestrated by the application service invoked from the controller. The typical steps of the workflow are checking the availability of ordered goods, processing payment, forwarding shipping details, and storing order data in the database.

Most of these actions can be carried out in silent mode. Payment, though, might require that an external page be displayed to let the user interact with the banking back end. If payment requires its own user interface, you split the processing of the order into two phases: before and after payment. If not, you can implement the processing of the payment and synchronization with the shipping company as two parallel tasks using the .NET Framework Parallel API. Here's how to split checkout into two steps:

```
public ActionResult Checkout(CheckoutInputModel checkout)
{
    // Pre-payment steps
    var cart = RetrieveCurrentShoppingCart();
    var response = _service.ProcessOrderBeforePayment(cart, checkout);
    if (!response.Denied)
        return Redirect(Url.Content("~/fake_payment.aspx?returnUrl=/order/endcheckout"));

    TempData["ibuy-stuff:denied"] = response;
    return RedirectToAction("Denied");
}
public ActionResult EndCheckout(string transactionId)
{
    // Post-payment steps
    var cart = RetrieveCurrentShoppingCart();
    var response = _service.ProcessOrderAfterPayment(cart, transactionId);
    var action = response.Denied ? "denied" : "processed";
    return View(action, response);
}
```

The method *ProcessOrderBeforePayment* on the application service saves checkout information (shipping address and payment details) and checks the stock level of ordered products. Depending on the policies enabled, it might also need to place a refill order to bring the stock level back to a safe value. If something goes wrong (for example, some goods are not available), the response is stored in *TempData* to be displayed by the Denied page across a page redirect.

 Note *TempData* is an ASP.NET MVC facility specifically created to persist request data temporarily across a redirect. This feature exists to enable the Post-Redirect-Get pattern, which protects against the bad effects of page refreshes.

If pre-payment checks go well, the method redirects to the payment page. This is where payment occurs. When done, the page redirects back to the specified URL. In doing so, the payment page will pass the transaction ID that demonstrates payment. (This is a general description of how most payment APIs actually work.)

The post-payment phase might include booking a delivery through the shipping company back end, registering the order in the system, updating the stock level, and updating the records of the fidelity card.

Fidelity card (or customer loyalty program)

Once the order is in the system, a few additional tasks might still be required. In a way, adding an order generates an event within the domain that might require one or more handlers. This introduces the point of *domain events*. In general, a domain event is an event that might be raised within the context of the domain model. Domain events are simply a way for the architect to clean up the design and enable himself to handle situations in a more flexible way.

In particular, the requirements we have for I-Buy-Stuff state that whenever an order is created the system must update the stock level of the products and add points to the fidelity card of the customer.

Both operations can be coded as plain method calls executed at the end of the *ProcessOrderAfterPayment* method in the application service class. It's plain and simple, and it just works.

However, the logic behind the fidelity card is subject to change as marketing campaigns are launched, ended, or modified. The aforementioned implementation might turn out to be a bit too rigid in terms of maintenance and lead to frequent updates to the binary code. A more extensible design of what might happen once the order is created might smooth the work required in the long run to keep the system aligned to the business needs.

Domain events try to address this scenario. A domain event can be implemented as a plain C# event in some aggregate class, or it can be implemented through a sort of publish/subscribe mechanism, where the information is put on a bus and registered handlers get it and process it as appropriate. More importantly, handlers can be loaded and registered using a dependency-injection interface so that adding and removing a handler is as easy and lightweight as editing the configuration file of the application.

Summary

This chapter is an attempt to give substance to concepts and ideas that too often remain confined in the space of basic tutorials or in theory. We didn't just present a domain model where classes have behavior and factories and make limited use of primitive types. We actually presented a multilayer ASP.NET MVC application that proceeds end-to-end from presentation down to the creation of an order in a scenario that is not an unrealistic CRUD.

Along the way, we turned into practice concepts we introduced in past chapters and showed that, while database structure is not a primary concern when modeling, it still is a constraint and concessions are often necessary to make the object model persistent.

We invite you to take a thorough look at the full source code of the I-Buy-Stuff application. The text in the chapter emphasized choices around the domain model; however, the code contains a lot more details and solutions that might be interesting to look at.

Finishing with a smile

StackOverflow.com, TopEdge.com, and other websites contain an endless collection of jokes about developers. In particular, we looked for jokes about developers and light bulbs. Here's our selection:

- How many developers are needed to change a light bulb? None. The light bulb works just fine in *their* offices.

- How many developers are needed to change a light bulb? None. It's a hardware problem.

- How many testers are needed to change a light bulb? They can only assert the room is dark, but they can't actually fix the problem.

- How many Java developers are needed to change a light bulb? Well, the question is ill-posed and shows you're still thinking procedurally. A properly designed light bulb object would inherit a *change* method from a base light bulb class. Therefore, all you have to do is send a light bulb change message.

- How many Prolog developers does it take to change a light bulb? Yes.

CHAPTER 10

Introducing CQRS

Beware of false knowledge; it is more dangerous than ignorance.
—*George Bernard Shaw*

As discussed in Chapter 5, "Discovering the domain architecture," there are two distinct but interoperating parts in Domain-Driven Design (DDD). The analytical part is about discovering the top-level architecture, using the ubiquitous language to dig out bounded contexts and their relationships. The strategic part is about giving each bounded context the most appropriate architecture. A decade ago, the standard architecture for a bounded context was a layered architecture, with a domain layer made of an object-oriented, all-encompassing model and domain services. The effort of developers was then to crunch knowledge about the domain and render it through a web of interconnected objects with state and behavior. The model was unique and intended to fully describe the entire business domain.

It didn't look, in the beginning, like a thing that's far easier to say than do.

Some projects that embraced DDD eventually worked; other projects failed. Success stories can be told too, but many people still believe that DDD is hard to do even though it can possibly deliver significant benefits. The point is that, for many people, the perception that DDD holds benefits is much less concrete than the perception of the damage that might result from using DDD and failing.

Is there anything wrong with DDD?

The analytical part of DDD has little to do with code and software design. It's all about figuring out the top-level architecture while using ad hoc tools like the ubiquitous language. This is an excellent approach to take for just about any project. In complex scenarios, it helps to understand the big picture and lay out modules and services. In simple scenarios, it boils down to having just one context and a single module to build.

The critical part of the original vision of DDD is the suggested architecture for a bounded context. First and foremost, the layered architecture with an object-oriented model and services is just one option, and simpler solutions—for example, Content Management System (CMS), Customer Relationship Management (CRM), coupled CRUD, and two-layer systems—certainly are not banned as long as they fit the needs. Second, even when the layered architecture with a domain layer appears to be the ideal solution for a bounded context, the model doesn't have to be object-oriented, nor does it have to be an all-encompassing model for the entire context.

In this chapter, we introduce a pattern that splits the domain model in two, actually achieving much more than just separation of concerns.

Separating commands from queries

Most of the difficulties that early adopters of DDD faced were in designing a single model to take care of all aspects of the domain. Generally speaking, any actions performed on a software system belong to one of the following two categories: query or command. In this context, a *query* is an operation that doesn't alter in any way the state of the system and just returns data. The *command*, on the other hand, does alter the state of the system and doesn't return data, except perhaps for a status code or an acknowledgment.

The logical separation that exists between queries and commands doesn't show up clearly if the two groups of actions are forced to use the same domain model. For this reason, a new supporting architecture emerged in the past few years called CQRS, which is short for *Command/Query Responsibility Segregation*.

Generalities of the CQRS pattern

Since the days of ancient Rome, *Divide et Impera* has been an extremely successful approach to actually getting things done. Roman ruler Julius Caesar won a number of battles fighting against the entire enemy army, but when things got more complicated, he implemented a strategy of leading his enemy into dividing forces across the battlefields so that he could fight against a smaller army.

Similarly, the CQRS pattern is based on a simple, almost commonplace, idea: queries and commands (sometimes also referred to as *reads* and *writes*) are very different things and should be treated separately. Yet, for a long time, developers—like short-sighted commanders—insisted on having the same conceptual model for both queries and commands in their systems.

Especially in complex business scenarios, a single model soon becomes unmanageable. It doesn't just grow exponentially large and complex (and subsequently absorb time and budget), it also never ends up working the way it should.

Note We wouldn't be too surprised to find out at some point that developers insisted for years on having a single model because having two distinct models might seem like a negative statement about their ability to work out a single, all-encompassing model. Our egos grow big sometimes and obscures a proper perspective on things!

From domain model to CQRS

In a way, CQRS is a form of lateral thinking resulting from the difficulty of finding a well-conceived model for complex domains. If the Domain Model turns out to be expensive and objectively complex, are we sure we're approaching it right? That was probably the question that led to investigating and formalizing a different pattern.

At the end of the day, CQRS uses two distinct domain layers rather than just one. The separation is obtained by grouping operations that are queries in one layer and operations that are commands in another. Each layer, then, has its own architecture and its own set of services dedicated to only queries and commands, respectively. Figure 10-1 captures the difference.

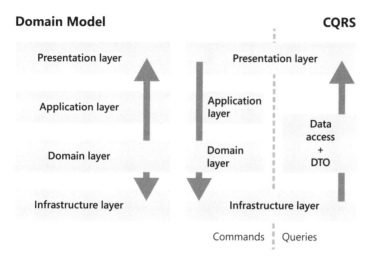

FIGURE 10-1 Visual comparison between Domain Model and CQRS.

In CQRS, it is not a far-fetched idea to have the query stack based exclusively on SQL queries and completely devoid of models, an application layer, and a domain layer. Having a full domain-model implementation in the query stack is not common. In general, the query stack should be simplified to the extreme. In addition, typically a CQRS approach has a different database for each side.

Structure of the query and command domain layers

As surprising as it might sound, the simple recognition that commands and queries are two different things has a deep impact on the overall architecture of the system. In Figure 10-1, we split the domain layer into two blocks.

Are they just two smaller and simpler versions of a domain layer like we discussed in the past two chapters?

The interesting thing is that with the architecture of the system organized as two parallel branches as shown in Figure 10-1, the requirement of having a full-fledged domain model is much less strict. For one thing, you might not need a domain model at all to serve queries. Queries are now just data to be rendered in some way through the user interface. There's no command to be arranged on queried data; as such, many of the relationships that make discovering aggregates so important in a classic domain model are unnecessary. The model for the domain layer of the query side of a CQRS system can be simply a collection of made-to-measure data-transfer objects (DTOs). Following this consideration, the domain services might become just classes that implement pieces of business logic on top of an anemic model.

Similar things can be said for the domain layer of the command side of the system. Depending on the commands you actually implement, a classic domain model might or might not be necessary. In general, there's a greater chance you might need a domain model for the command side because here you express business logic and implement business rules. At any rate, the domain model you might have on the command side of a CQRS system is likely far simpler because it is tailor-made for the commands.

In summary, recognizing that queries and commands are different things triggers a chain reaction that sets the foundation for domain modeling, as discussed in the past two chapters. We justified domain models as the ideal way to tackle complexity in the heart of software. Along the way, we ended up facing a good deal of complexity and thought it was, for the most part, complexity that is inherent to the business domain. Instead, most of that complexity results from the Cartesian product of queries and commands. Separating commands from queries can reduce complexity by an order of magnitude.

Note Just in case you were wondering, a *Cartesian product* is a mathematical operation that, given two or more sets, returns a new and larger set made of all ordered pairs (or tuples), where each element belongs to a different set. The cardinality of the resulting set is the product of the cardinalities of all input sets.

CQRS is not a top-level architecture

Unlike DDD, CQRS is not a comprehensive approach to the design of an enterprise-class system. CQRS is simply a pattern that guides you in architecting a specific bounded context of a possibly larger system. Performing a DDD analysis based on a ubiquitous language and aimed at identifying bounded contexts remains a recommended preliminary step.

Next, CQRS becomes a valid alternative to Domain Model, CRUD, and other supporting architectures for the implementation of a particular bounded context.

Benefits of CQRS

The list of benefits brought about by using CQRS to implement a bounded context is not particularly long. Overall, we think that there are essentially two benefits. Their impact on the solution, though, is dramatic.

Simplification of the design

As our interactions with the Domain Model taught us, most of the complexity you face in a software system is usually related to operations that change the state of the system. Commands should validate the current state and determine whether they can run. Next, commands should take care of leaving the system in a consistent state.

Finally, in a scenario in which reading and writing operations share the same representation of data, it sometimes becomes hard to prevent unwanted operations from becoming available in reading or writing. We already raised this point in the last chapter when we pointed out that it's nearly impossible to give, say, a list of order items a single representation that fits in both the query and command scenarios. Anyway, we'll return to this aspect in a moment with a detailed example.

We stated in an earlier note that the complexity of the Domain Model results from the Cartesian product of queries and commands. If we take the analysis one step further, we can even measure by a rule of thumb the amount of reduced complexity. Let's call N the complexity of queries and commands. In a single domain model, where requirements and constraints of queries affect commands and vice versa, like in a Cartesian product, you have a resulting complexity of NxN. By separating queries from commands and treating them independently, all you have is N+N.

Potential for enhanced scalability

Scalability has many faces and factors; the recipe for scalability tends to be unique for each system you consider. In general, scalability defines the system's ability to maintain the same level of performance as the number of users grows. A system with more users performs certain operations more frequently. Scalability, therefore, depends on the margins that architects have to fine-tune the system to make it perform more operations in the same unit of time.

The way to achieve scalability depends on the type of operations most commonly performed. If reads are the predominant operation, you can introduce levels of caching to drastically reduce the number of accesses to the database. If writes are enough to slow down the system at peak hours, you might want to consider switching from a classic synchronous writing model to async writes or even queues of commands.

Separating queries from commands gives you the chance to work on the scalability aspects of both parts in total isolation.

Note A good example of what it means to treat reads and writes separately is given by a cloud platform such as Microsoft Azure. You deploy query and command layers as distinct web or worker roles and scale them independently, both in terms of instances and the size of each instance. Similarly, when reads are vastly predominant, you can decide to offload some pages to a distinct server with a thick layer of caching on top. The ability to act on query and command layers separately is invaluable. Note also that the investment in Microsoft Azure is focused more on websites, WebJobs, and even mobile services rather than the original web roles and worker roles. In particular, WebJobs is more of a light-weight approach than web roles and worker roles.

Pleasant side effects of CQRS

A couple of other pleasant side effects of CQRS are worth noting here. First, CQRS leads you to a deep understanding of what your application reads and what it processes. The neat separation of modules also makes it safe to make changes to each without incurring some form of regression on one or the other.

Second, thinking about queries and commands leads to reasoning in terms of tasks and a task-based user interface, which is very good for end users.

Fitting CQRS in the business layer

Honestly, we don't think there are significant downsides to CQRS. It all depends in the end on what you mean exactly by using CQRS. So far we just defined it as a pattern that suggests you have two distinct layers: one filled with the model and services necessary for reading, and one with the model and services for commands. What a *model* is—whether it is an object model, a library of functions, or a collection of data-transfer objects—ultimately is an implementation detail.

With this definition in place, nearly any system can benefit from CQRS and coding it doesn't require doing things in a different way. Neither does it mean learning new and scary things.

Noncollaborative vs. collaborative systems

The point, however, is that CQRS also induces some deeper architectural changes that maximize the return in terms of scalability and reduced complexity but that require some investment in learning and performing a preliminary analysis.

In the end, CQRS was discovered by looking for more effective ways to tackle complex systems in which multiple actors—both end users and software clients—operate on the data concurrently and sophisticated and ever-changing business rules apply. The major proponents of CQRS—Udi Dahan and Greg Young—called these systems *collaborative systems*.

Let's try to formalize the landmarks of a collaborative system a bit better.

In a collaborative system, the underlying data can change at any time from the effect of the current user, concurrent users connected through various front ends, and even back-end software. In a collaborative system, users compete for the same resources, and this means that whatever data you get can be stale in the same moment that it is read or even long before it is displayed. One of the reasons for this continuous change is that the business logic is particularly complex and involves multiple modules that sometimes need to be loaded dynamically. The architect has two main options:

- Lock the entire aggregate for the time required to complete any operation.

- Keep the aggregate open to change at the cost of possibly showing out-of-sync data that eventually becomes consistent. (This is often referred to as *eventual consistency*.)

The first option is highly impractical for a collaborative system—the back end would be locked while serving a single request at nearly any time, and the throughput would be very low. The second option might be acceptable but, if the system is not properly fine-tuned, it can end up giving inaccurate results and taking too long a time to respond.

This is the scenario that led to formalizing CQRS.

CQRS to the rescue

CQRS is not simply about using different domain layers for queries and commands. It's more about using distinct stacks for queries and commands architected by following a new set of guidelines. (See Figure 10-2.)

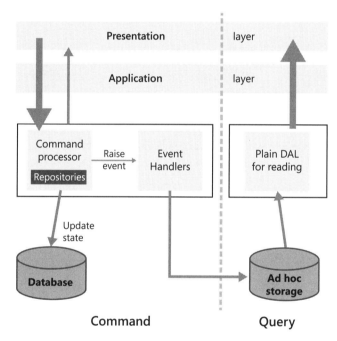

FIGURE 10-2 The big picture of the CQRS implementation of a collaborative system.

In the command pipeline, any requests from the presentation layer become a command appended to the queue of a processor. Each command carries information and has its own handler that knows about the logic. In this way, each command is a logical unit that can thoroughly validate the state of the involved objects and intelligently decide which updates to perform and which to decline. The command handler processes the command just once. Processing the command might generate events handled by other registered components. In this way, other software can perform additional tasks. One of the common tasks is performing periodical updates of a database cache that exists for the sole purpose of the query pipeline.

When the business logic is extremely sophisticated, you can't afford to handle commands synchronously. You can't do that for two reasons:

- It slows down the system.

- The domain services involved become way too complex, perhaps convoluted and subject to regression, especially when rules change frequently.

With a CQRS architecture, the logic can be expressed through single commands that result in distinct, individual components that are much easier to evolve, replace, and fix. In addition, these commands can be queued if necessary.

> **Note** In a CQRS scenario, one-way commands that do not return any response do not conceptually exist. They should be modeled as events fired for one or more event handlers to handle.

The query pipeline is quite simple, on the other hand. All it has is a collection of repositories that query content from ad hoc caches of denormalized data. The structure of such database cache tables (most of the time, plain Microsoft SQL Server tables) closely reflects the data required by the user interface. So, for example, if a page requires the customer name while displaying the order details, you can arrange to have the ID and name readymade in a cache without having to JOIN every time. Furthermore, because the query pipeline is separated, it can offload to a dedicated server at any time.

CQRS always pays the architecture bill

Many seem to think that outside the realm of collaborative systems, the power of CQRS diminishes significantly. On the contrary, the power of CQRS really shines in collaborative systems because it lets you address complexity and competing resources in a much smoother and overall simpler way. There's more to it than meets the eye, we think.

In our opinion, CQRS can sufficiently pay your architecture bills even in simpler scenarios, where the plain separation between query and command stacks leads to simplified design and dramatically reduces the risk of design errors. You don't need to have super-skilled teams of developers to do CQRS. Quite the opposite: using CQRS enables nearly any team to do a good job in terms of scalability and cleanliness of the design.

Transaction script in the command stack

CQRS is a natural fit in a system dependent on collaboration. However, the benefits of command/query separation can apply to nearly all systems.

Most systems out there can be summarized as "CRUD with some business logic around." In these cases, you can just use the Transaction Script (TS) pattern (as discussed in Chapter 7, "The mythical business layer") in the implementation of the command stack. TS is an approach that has you partition the back end of the system—overall, business logic—in a collection of methods out of a few container classes. Each method essentially takes care of a command and provides a full implementation for it. The method, therefore, takes care of processing input data, invoking local components or services in another bounded context, and writing to the database. All these steps take place in a single "logical" transaction.

As Fowler said, the glory of TS is in its simplicity. TS is a natural fit for applications with a small amount of logic. The major benefit of TS is there's only minor overhead for development teams in terms of learning and performance.

 Note CQRS suggests—or just makes it reasonable sometimes—to use distinct databases for reading and writing. When this happens, the adoption of TS in the organization of the business logic raises the problem of figuring out the ideal way to handle eventual consistency. We'll return to this point in the next chapter about CQRS implementation.

EDMX for the read model

What's the easiest way to build a data access layer that serves the purposes of the presentation layer with no extra whistles and bells? Once you know the connection string to the database to access, all you do is create an Entity Framework wrapper in the form of an EDMX designer file in Microsoft Visual Studio.

Running the Entity Framework designer on the specified connection string infers an object model out of the database tables and relationships. Because it comes from Entity Framework, the object model is essentially anemic. However, the C# mechanism of partial classes enables you to add behavior to classes, thus adding a taste of object orientation and domain modeling to the results.

Arranging queries—possibly just LINQ queries—on top of this object model is easy for most developers, and it's effective and reliable. Expert developers can work very quickly with this approach, and junior developers can learn from it just as quickly.

The pragmatic architect's perspective

Taking the point of view of an architect, you might wonder what the added value of CQRS is in relatively simple systems with only a limited amount of business logic.

You set the architecture to define the boundaries of command and query stacks. You pass each developer an amount of work that is commensurate to that developer's actual skills. You still have distinct stacks to be optimized independently or even rewritten from scratch if necessary.

In a word, an expert architect has a far better chance to take on the project comfortably, even with only junior developers on the team.

The query stack

Let's delve a bit deeper into the two pipelines that make up the CQRS architecture. In doing so, another key aspect that drives the adoption of CQRS in some highly collaborative systems will emerge clearly—the necessity of dealing with stale data.

The read domain model

A model that deals only with queries would be much easier to arrange than a model that has to deal with both queries and commands. For example, a prickly problem we hinted at in Chapter 8, "Introducing the domain model," is brilliantly and definitely solved with the introduction of a read-only domain model.

Why you need distinct models

The problem was summarized as follows. The *Order* class has an *Items* property that exposes the list of ordered products. The property holds inherently enumerable content, but which actual type should you use for the *Items* property? The first option that probably comes to mind is *IList<T>*. It might work, but it's not perfect. So let's put ourselves in a Domain Model scenario and assume we want to have a single model for the entire domain that is used to support both queries and commands. Also, let's say we use a plain list for the *Items* property:

```
public IList<OrderItem> Items { get; private set; }
```

The private setter is good, but it prevents only users of an *Order* from replacing it. Any code that gets an instance of *Order* can easily add or remove elements from it. This might or might not be a legitimate operation; it depends on the use-case. If the use-case is managing the order, exposing order items through a list is just fine. If the use-case is showing the last 10 orders, a list is potentially dangerous because no changes to the order are expected.

> **Important** The domain model is the API of the business domain. Once publicly exposed, an API can be invoked to perform any action it allows. To ensure consistency, the API should not rely on developers to use it only the right way. If Murphy (of "Murphy's laws") were a software engineer, he would say something like, "If a developer can call an API the wrong way, he will."

On the other hand, if you expose the list as a plain enumeration of order items, you have no way to create an order and add items to it. In addition, individual items are still modifiable through direct access:

```
public IEnumerable<OrderItem> Items { get; private set; }
```

Things don't change even if you use *ReadOnlyCollection<T>* instead of *IEnumerable*. A Microsoft .NET Framework read-only collection is read-only in the sense that it doesn't allow changes to the structure of the collection. Furthermore, if the read-only collection is created as a wrapper for a regular list, changes to the underlying list do not affect the read-only wrapper. Here's an example where order items are exposed as a read-only collection but methods still make it possible to populate the collection:

```
public class Order
{
    private readonly IList<OrderItem> _items;
    public Order()
    {
        _items = new List<MOrderItem>();
    }
    public ReadOnlyCollection<OrderItem> Items
    {
        get
        {
            return new ReadOnlyCollection<OrderItem>(_items);
        }
    }

    public void Add(int id, int quantity)
    {
        _items.Add(new OrderItem(id, quantity));
    }
}
public class OrderItem
{
    public OrderItem(int id, int quantity)
    {
        Quantity = quantity;
        ProductId = id;
    }
    public int Quantity { get; /*private*/ set; }
    public int ProductId { get; /*private*/ set; }
}
```

However, direct access to elements in the collection is still possible—whether it is gained during a *for-each* loop, out of a LINQ query, or by index:

```
foreach (var i in order.Items)
{
    i.Quantity ++;
    Console.WriteLine(i);
}
```

To prevent changes to the data within the collection, you have to make the setter private.

This would work beautifully if it weren't for yet another possible issue. Is it worthwhile to turn the *OrderItem* entity of the domain model into an immutable object?

Classes in the domain model are modified and made more and more complex because they can be used interchangeably in both query and command scenarios. Using the read-only wrapper, ultimately, is the first step toward making a read version of the *Order* entity.

> **Note** We are not trying to say that having *Items* coded as a list is dangerous; instead, we just want to point out a consistency hole and a sort of violation of the syntax rules of the ubiquitous language. The order displayed for review is not the order created out of a request. This is what CQRS is all about.

From a domain model to a read model

When your goal is simply creating a domain model for read-only operations, everything comes easier and classes are simpler overall. Let's look at a few varying points.

The notion of *aggregates* becomes less central, and with it the entire notion of the domain model as explained in Chapter 8. You probably still need to understand how entities aggregate in the model, but there's no need to make this knowledge explicit through interfaces.

The overall structure of classes is more similar to data-transfer objects, and properties tend to be much more numerous than methods. Ideally, all you have are DTOs that map one-to-one with each screen in the application. Does that mean that model becomes anemic? Well, the model is 100 percent anemic when made of just data. An *Order* class, for example, will no longer have an *AddItem* method.

Again, there's no issue with CQRS having a 100 percent anemic read model. Methods on such classes can still be useful, but only as long as they query the object and provide a quick way for the presentation or application layer to work. For example, a method *IsPending* on an *Order* class can still be defined as follows:

```
public bool IsPending()
{
    return State == OrderState.Pending;
}
```

This method is useful because it makes the code that uses the *Order* class easier to read and, more importantly, closer to the ubiquitous language.

Designing a read-model façade

The query stack might still need domain services to extract data from storage and serve it up to the application and presentation layers. In this case, domain services, and specifically repositories, should be retargeted to allow only read operations on the storage.

Restricting the database context

In the read stack, therefore, you don't strictly need to have classic repositories with all CRUD methods and you don't even need to expose all the power of the *DbContext* class, assuming you're in an Entity Framework Code-First scenario, as described in Chapter 9, "Implementing the domain model," and as it will be used in future chapters.

In Chapter 9, we had a class wrapping the Entity Framework *DbContext* and called it *DomainModelFacade*. The structure of the class is shown here:

```
public class DomainModelFacade : DbContext
{
   public DomainModelFacade() : base("naa4e-09")
   {
      Products = base.Set<Product>();
      Customers = base.Set<Customer>();
      Orders = base.Set<Order>();
   }

   public DbSet<Order> Orders { get; private set; }
   public DbSet<Customer> Customers { get; private set; }
   public DbSet<Product> Products { get; private set; }
   ...
}
```

The *DbSet* class provides full access to the underlying database and can be used to set up queries and update operations via LINQ-to-Entities. The fundamental step toward a query pipeline is limiting the access to the database to queries only. Here are some changes:

```
public class ReadModelFacade : DbContext
{
   public ReadModelFacade() : base("naa4e-09")
   {
      Products = base.Set<Product>();
      Customers = base.Set<Customer>();
      Orders = base.Set<Order>();
   }

   public IQueryable<Customer> Customers
   {
      get { return _customers; }
   }

   public IQueryable<Order> Orders
   {
      get { return _orders; }
   }

   public IQueryable<Product> Products
   {
      get { return _products; }
   }
   ...
}
```

Collections to query from the business logic on are now exposed via *IQueryable* interfaces. We said that the notion of aggregates loses focus in a read model. However, queryable data in the read-model façade mostly corresponds to aggregates in a full domain model.

Adjusting repositories

With a read-model façade, any attempt to access the database starts with an *IQueryable* object. You can still have a set of repository classes, populate them with a bunch of *FindXxx* methods, and use them from domain services and the application layer.

In doing so, you'll certainly run into simple situations such as just needing to query all orders that have not been processed two weeks after they were placed. The *FindXxx* method can return a collection of *Order* items:

```
IEnumerable<Order> FindPendingOrderAfter(TimeSpan timespan);
```

But there are also situations in which you need to get all orders whose total exceeds a threshold. In this case, you need to report order details (like ID, date of creation, state, payment details) as well as customer details (at least the name and membership status). And, above all, you need to report the total of the order. There's no such type in the domain; you need to create it. OK, no big deal: it's just a classic DTO type:

```
IEnumerable<OrderSummary> FindOrdersBeyond(decimal threshold);
```

All is good if the *OrderSummary* DTO is general enough to be used in several repository queries. If it is not, you end up with too many DTO classes that are also too similar, which ultimately also poses a problem with names. But beyond the name and quantity of DTOs, there's another underlying issue here: the number of repository methods and their names and implementation. Readability and maintainability are at stake.

A common way out is leaving only common queries as methods in the repositories that return common DTOs and handling all other cases through predicates:

```
public IEnumerable<T> Find(Expression<Func<T, Boolean>> predicate)
```

In this case, though, you're stuck with using type T, and it might not be easy to massage any queried data into a generic DTO within a single method.

> **Important** We decided to introduce relevant aspects of CQRS starting from a DDD perspective and then discuss issues that arise from using it, as well as what has been done to smooth out the rough spots according to the key guidelines of CQRS.
>
> As far as repositories are concerned, the bottom line is that you don't likely need them in the query stack. The entire data access layer can be articulated through LINQ queries on top of some Object/Relational Mapper (O/RM) classes placed directly in the application layer. Also, a full-fledged O/RM like Entity Framework sometimes might be overkill. You might want to consider a micro O/RM for the job, such as PetaPoco. (See *http://www.toptensoftware.com/petapoco*.)
>
> Looking ahead to .NET, a better option probably is the upcoming Entity Framework 7, which will be a lot more lightweight and aligned with ASP.NET vNext.

Layered expression trees

Over the past 20 years of developing software, we have seen a recurring pattern: when a common-use solution gets overwhelmingly complex and less and less manageable over time, it's probably because it doesn't address the problem well. At that point, it might be worth investigating a different approach to the problem. The different approach we suggest here to reduce the complexity of repositories and DTOs in a read model leverages the power of LINQ and expression trees.

Realistic scenarios

Let's focus first on a few realistic scenarios where you need to query data in many different ways that are heavily dependent on business rules:

- **Online store**   Given the profile of the user, the home page of the online store will present the three products that match the profile with the highest inventory level. It results in two conceptual queries: getting all products available for sale, and getting the three products with the highest inventory level that might be interesting to the user. The first query is common and belongs to some domain service. The second query is application specific and belongs to the application layer.

- **ERP**   Retrieve all invoices of a business unit that haven't been paid 30 days after their due payment terms. There are three conceptual queries here: getting all invoices, getting all invoices for the business unit, and getting all invoices for the business unit that are unpaid 30 days later. The first two queries are common and belong to some domain services. The third query sounds more application specific.

- **CMS**   Retrieve all articles that have been published and, among them, pick those that match whatever search parameters have been specified. Again, it's two conceptual queries: one domain-specific and one application-specific.

Why did we use the term *conceptual* query?

If you look at it conceptually, you see distinct queries. If you look at it from an implementation perspective, you just don't want to have distinct queries. Use-cases often require queries that can be expressed in terms of filters applied over some large sets of data. Each filter expresses a business rule; rules can be composed and reused in different use-cases.

To get this, you have two approaches:

- Hide all filters in a repository method, build a single super-optimized query, run it, and return results. Each result is likely a different DTO. In doing this, you're going to have nearly one method for each scenario and new or modified methods when something changes. The problem is not facing change; the problem is minimizing the effort (and risk of regression) when change occurs. Touching the repository interface is a lot of work because it might have an impact on upper layers. If you can make changes only at the application level, it would be much easier to handle and less invasive.

- Try LINQ and expression trees.

Let's see what it takes to use layered expression trees (LET).

Using *IQueryable* as your currency

The idea behind LET is enabling the application layer to receive *IQueryable<T>* objects wherever possible. In this way, the required query emerges through the composition of filters and the actual projection of data is specified at the last minute, right in the application layer where data is being used to generate the view model for the presentation to render.

With this idea in mind, you don't even need repositories in a read model, and perhaps not even as a container of common queries that return direct and immediately usable data that likely will not be filtered any more. A good example of a method you might still want to have in a separate repository class is a *FindById*.

You can use the public properties of the aforementioned read façade as the starting point to compose your queries. Or, if necessary, you can use ad hoc components for the same purpose. In this way, in fact, you encapsulate the read-model façade—still a point of contact with persistence technology—in such components. Here's what the query to retrieve three products to feature on the home page might look like. This code ideally belongs to the application layer:

```
var queryProducts = (from p in CatalogServices.GetProductsAvailableForSale()
                     orderby p.UnitsInStock descending
                     select new ProductDescriptor
                     {
                         Id = p.Id,
                         Name = p.Name,
                         UnitPrice = p.UnitPrice,
                         UnitsInStock = p.UnitsInStock,
                     }).Take(3);
```

Here's another example that uses the recommended async version of LINQ methods:

```
var userName = _securityService.GetUserName();
var currentEmployee = await _database
        .Employees
        .AsNoTracking()
        .WhereEmployeeIsCurrentUser(userName)
        .Select(employee =>
            new CurrentEmployeeDTO
            {
                EmployeeId = employee.Id,
                FirstName = employee.PersonalInformation.FirstName,
                LastName = employee.PersonalInformation.LastName,
                Email = employee.PersonalInformation.Email,
                Identifier = employee.PersonalInformation.Identifier,
                JobTitle = employee.JobTitle,
                IsManager = employee.IsTeamManager,
                TeamId = employee.TeamId,
            }).SingleOrDefaultAsync();
currentEmployee.PictureUrl = Url.Link("EmployeePicture",
                             new { employeeId = currentEmployee.EmployeeId });
```

As you might have noticed, the first code snippet doesn't end with a call to *ToList*, *First*, or similar methods. So it is crucial to clarify what it means to work with *IQueryable* objects.

The *IQueryable* interface allows you to define a query against a LINQ provider, such as a database. The query, however, has deferred execution and subsequently can be built in multiple steps. No database access is performed until you call an execution method such as *ToList*. For example, when you query all products on sale, you're not retrieving all 200,000 records that match those criteria. When you add *Take(3)*, you're just refining the query. The query executes when the following code is invoked:

```
var featuredProducts = queryProducts.ToList();
```

The SQL code that hits the database has the following template:

```
SELECT TOP 3 ... WHERE ...
```

In the end, you pass the *IQueryable* object through the layers and each layer can add filters along the way, making the query more precise. You typically resolve the query in the application layer and get just the subset of data you need in that particular use-case.

Isn't LET the same as an in-memory list?

No, LET is not the same as having an in-memory list and querying it via LINQ-to-Objects. If you load all products in memory and then use LINQ to extract a subset, you're discarding tons of data you pulled out of the database.

LET still performs a database access using the best query that the underlying LINQ provider can generate. However, *IQueryable* works transparently on any LINQ provider. So if the aforementioned method *GetProductsAvailableForSale* internally uses a static list of preloaded *Product* instances, the LET approach still works, except that it leverages LINQ-to-Objects instead of the LINQ dialect supported by the underlying database access layer.

Using LET is not the same as having a static list, but that doesn't mean having a static list is a bad thing. If you see benefits in keeping, say, all products in memory, a static list is probably a good approach. LET is a better approach if the displayed data is read from some database every time.

Note Crucial to CQRS is the fact that the database you query might not be the core database where commands write. It can easily be a separate database optimized for reading and built to denormalize some of the content in the core database. This approach is often referred to as the "pure CQRS approach."

Upsides of LET

The use of LET has several benefits. The most remarkable benefit is that you need almost no DTOs. More precisely, you don't need DTOs to carry data across layers. If you let queries reach the application layer, all you do is fetch data directly in the view model classes. On the other hand, a view model is unavoidable because you still need to pass data to the user interface in some way.

> **Note** As you might have noticed, we're using different names—DTO and view model classes—for two software entities that can be described using the same words: classes that just carry data. ASP.NET MVC view model classes are actually DTOs, and the reason we're using different names here is to emphasize that one of the benefits of LET is that you can forget about intermediate classes you might need in the classic Domain Model to carry data across layer. In CQRS with LET, all you need is LINQ to query data and a DTO to return data to the presentation. There are no other intermediaries—just LINQ queries and, in ASP.NET MVC, view model classes.

Another benefit is that the code you write is somehow natural. It's really like you're using the database directly, except that the language is much easier to learn and use than plain-old T-SQL.

Queries are DDD-friendly because their logic closely follows the ubiquitous language, and sometimes it seems that domain experts wrote the queries. Among other things, DDD-friendly queries are also helpful when a customer calls to report a bug. You look into the section of the code that produces unexpected results and read the query. You can almost read your code to the customer and quickly figure out whether the reason unexpected data is showing up on the screen is logical (you wrote the wrong query) or technical (the implementation is broken). Have a look at the following code:

```
var db = new ReadModelFacade();
var model = from i in db.IncomingInvoices
                        .ForBusinessUnit(buId)
                        .Expired()
            orderby i.PaymentDueDate
            select new SummaryViewModel.Invoice
                    {
                        Id = i.ID,
                        SupplierName = i.Party.Name,
                        PaymentDueDate = i.PaymentDueDate.Value,
                        TotalAmount = i.TotalPrice,
                        Notes = i.Notes
                    };
```

The code filters all invoices to retrieve those charged to a given business unit that haven't been paid yet. Methods like *ForBusinessUnit* and *Expired* are (optional) extension methods on the *IQueryable* type. All they do is add a WHERE clause to the final query:

```
public static IQueryable<Invoice> ForBusinessUnit(this IQueryable<Invoice> query, int buId)
{
    var invoices = from i in query
                   where i.BusinessUnit.OrganizationID == buId
                   select i;
    return invoices;
}
```

Last but not certainly least, LET fetches all data in a single step. The resulting query might be complex, but it is not necessarily too slow for the application. Here we can't help quoting the timeless wisdom of Donald Knuth: "Premature optimization is the root of all evil." As Andrea repeats in every class he teaches, three things are really important in the assessment of enterprise architecture: measure, measure, and measure. We're not here to say that LET will always outperform any other solution, but before looking for alternative solutions and better SQL code, first make sure you have concrete evidence that LET doesn't work for you.

Downsides of LET

Overall LET is a solution you should always consider, but like anything else it is not a silver bullet. Let's see which factors might make it less than appealing.

The first point to consider is that LET works beautifully on top of SQL Server and Entity Framework, but there's no guarantee it can do the same when other databases and, more importantly, other LINQ providers are used.

LET sits in between the application layer and persistence in much the same way repositories do. So is LET a general abstraction mechanism? The *IQueryable* interface is, in effect, an abstraction layer. However, it strictly depends on the underlying LINQ provider, how it maps expression trees to SQL commands, and how it performs. We can attest that things always worked well on top of Entity Framework and SQL Server. Likewise, we experienced trouble using LET on top of the LINQ provider you find in NHibernate. Overall, the argument that LET is a leaky abstraction over persistence is acceptable in theory.

In practice, though, not all applications are really concerned about switching the data-access engine. Most applications just choose one engine and stick to that. If the engine is SQL Server and you use Entity Framework, the LET abstraction is not leaky. But we agree that if you're building a framework that can be installed on top of your database of choice, repositories and DTOs are probably a better abstraction to use.

Finally, LET doesn't work over tiers. Is this a problem? Tiers are expensive, and we suggest you always find a way to avoid them. Yet sometimes tiers provide more scalability. However, as far as scalability is concerned, let us reiterate a point we made in a past chapter: if scalability is your major concern, you should also consider scaling out by keeping the entire stack on a single tier and running more instances of it on a cloud host such as Microsoft Azure.

Note When you use LET, testing can happen only on top of the LINQ-to-Objects provider built into the .NET Framework or any other LINQ provider that can be used to simulate the database. In any case, you're not testing LET through the real provider. For the nature of LET, however, this is the barrier that exists between unit and integration tests.

The command stack

In a CQRS scenario, the command stack is concerned only about the performance of tasks that modify the state of the application. As usual, the application layer receives requests from the presentation and orchestrates their execution. So what's going to be different in a CQRS scenario?

As shown in Figure 10-1, CQRS is about having distinct domain layers where the business logic—and objects required to have it implemented—is simpler to write because of the separation of concerns. This is already a benefit, but CQRS doesn't stop here. Additionally, it lays the groundwork for some more relevant design changes.

In the rest of the chapter, we drill down into concepts that slowly emerged as people increasingly viewed query and command stacks separately. These concepts are still evolving and lead toward the *event-sourcing* supporting architecture we'll discuss thoroughly in the next couple of chapters.

Getting back to presentation

A *command* is an action performed against the back end, such as registering a new user, processing the content of a shopping cart, or updating the profile of a customer. From a CQRS perspective, a task is monodirectional and generates a work flow that proceeds from the presentation down to the domain layer and likely ends up modifying some storage.

Tasks are triggered in two ways. One is when the user explicitly starts the task by acting on some UI elements. The other is when some autonomous services interact asynchronously with the system. As an example, you can think of how a shipping company interacts with its partners. The company might have an HTTP service that partners invoke to place requests.

The command placed updates the state of the system, but the caller might still need to receive some feedback.

Tasks triggered interactively

Imagine a web application like the I-Buy-Stuff online store we presented in Chapter 9. When the user clicks to buy the content of the shopping cart, she triggers a business process that creates an order, places a request for delivery, and processes payment—in a nutshell, it modifies the state of multiple systems, some interactively and some programmatically.

Yet the user who originally triggered the task is there expecting some form of feedback. That's no big deal when commands and queries are in the same context—the task modifies the state and reads it back. But what about when commands and queries are in separated contexts? In this case, you have two tasks: one triggered interactively and one triggered programmatically. Here's some code from an ASP.NET MVC application:

```
[HttpPost]
[ActionName("AddTo")]
public ActionResult AddToShoppingCart(int productId, int quantity=1)
{
    // Perform the requested task using posted input data
    var cart = RetrieveCurrentShoppingCart();
    cart = _service.AddProductToShoppingCart(cart, productId, quantity);
    SaveCurrentShoppingCart(cart);

    // Query task triggered programmatically
    return RedirectToAction("AddTo");
}

[HttpGet]
[ActionName("AddTo")]
public ActionResult DisplayShoppingCart()
{
    var cart = RetrieveCurrentShoppingCart();
    return View("shoppingcart", cart);
}
```

The method *AddToShoppingCart* is a command triggered interactively, as evidenced by the *HttpPost* attribute. It reads the current state of the shopping cart, adds the new item, and saves it back. The command Add-to-Shopping-Cart ends here, but there's a user who still needs some feedback.

In this specific case—an ASP.NET application—you need a second command triggered programmatically that refreshes the user interface by placing a query or, like in this case, performing an action within the realm of the application layer. This is the effect of *RedirectToAction*, which places another HTTP request—a GET this time—that invokes the *DisplayShoppingCart* method.

What if you have a client-side web application—for example, a Single-Page application? In this case, you use some JavaScript to trigger the call to a Web API or SignalR endpoint. The task completes, but this time there's no strict need for the web back end to execute a second task programmatically to get back to the presentation. The nature of the client makes it possible to display feedback in the form of an acknowledgment message:

```
$("#buttonBuy").click(function() {
    // Retrieve input data to pass
    ...
    $.post(url, { p1: ..., p2: ... })
     .done(function(response) {
        // Use the response from the task endpoint to refresh the UI
        ...
    });
});
```

A similar mechanism applies when the client is a desktop or mobile application, whether it's Microsoft Windows, Windows Store, Windows Phone, Android, iOS, or something else.

> **Important** In the case of an ASP.NET front end, the use of a redirect call to refresh the user interface is doubly beneficial because it defeats the notorious F5/Refresh effect. Browsers usually keep track of the last request and blindly repeat it when the user presses F5 or refreshes the current page. Especially for tasks that update the state of the system, reiterating a post request might repeat the task and produce unwanted effects—for example, the same item can be added twice to the shopping cart. A page refreshed after the task through a redirect leaves a GET operation in the browser memory. Even if it is repeated, no bad surprises can show up.

Tasks triggered programmatically

A system that exposes a public HTTP API is subject to receive calls from the outside. The call merely consists of the invocation of a method through an HTTP request, and the response is just an HTTP response. Here, the fundamentals of HTTP rule over all. Here's a sample Web API template for tasks to be invoked programmatically:

```
public class ExternalRequestController : ApiController
{
    public HttpResponseMessage PostDeliveryRequest(DeliveryRequest delivery)
    {
        // Do something here to process the delivery request coming from a partner company
        ...

        // Build a response for the caller:
        // Return HTTP 201 to indicate the successful creation of a new item
        var response = Request.CreateResponse<String>(HttpStatusCode.Created, "OK");

        // Add the location of new item for their reference
        var trackingId = ...;
        var path = "/delivery/processed/" + delivery.PartnerCode + "/" + trackingId;
        response.Headers.Location = new Uri(Request.RequestUri, path);
        return response;
    }
}
```

In this example, you have a Web API controller that receives delivery requests from a partner company. The request is processed and generates a tracking ID that must be communicated back to indicate the success of the operation.

There are various ways you can do this, and it mostly depends on your personal perspective regarding Web APIs. If you're a REST person, you would probably go with the code shown earlier. If you're more inclined toward remote procedure calls (RPCs), you can just return the tracking ID as a plain string in a generic HTTP 200 response.

Formalizing commands and events

All software systems receive input from some front-end data source. A data source can be any number of things, like a sensor connected to a hardware device that pumps real-time data, a feed asynchronously provided by a remote service, or—the most common scenario—a presentation layer equipped with a comfortable user interface. The input data travels from the front end to the application layer, where the processing phase of the input data is orchestrated.

Abstractly speaking, any front-end request for input processing is seen as a *message* sent to the application layer—the recipient. A message is a data transfer object that contains the plain data required for any further processing. In such an architecture, it is assumed that messages are fully understood by the recipient. Such a definition of a message leaves room for a number of concrete implementations. In most cases, you might want to start with a *Message* base class that acts as a data container:

```
public class Message
{
    // Optionally, a few common properties here.
    // The class, however, can even be a plain marker with no properties.
    ...
}
```

The front end can deliver the message to the application layer in a number of ways. Commonly, the delivery is a plain method invocation—for example, an application service invoked from within an ASP.NET MVC controller method. In more sophisticated scenarios, such as where scalability is the top priority, you might want to have a service bus in your infrastructure that also supports brokered messaging. In this way, you ensure delivery of the message to the intended recipient under any conditions, including when the recipient is not online.

Events vs. commands

There are two types of messages: commands and events. In both cases, messages consist of a packet of data. Some subtle differences exist, however, between events and commands.

A *command* is an imperative message that sounds like an explicit request made to the system to have some tasks performed. Here are some other characteristics of a command:

- A command is directed at one handler.

- A command can be rejected by the system.

- A command can fail while being executed by some handler.

- The net effect of the command can be different depending on the current state of the system.

- A command doesn't generally trespass the boundaries of a given bounded context.

- The suggested naming convention for commands says that they should be imperative and specify what needs to be done.

An *event* is a message that serves as a notification for something that has already happened. It has the following characteristics:

- An event can't be rejected or canceled by the system.

- An event can have any number of handlers interested in processing it.

- The processing of an event can, in turn, generate other events for other handlers to process.

- An event can have subscribers located outside the bounded context from which it originated.

Note The key difference between CQRS and the Event Sourcing architecture we'll cover in Chapter 12, "Introducing Event Sourcing," is this: in an Event Sourcing scenario, messages can be persisted to form a detailed and exhaustive audit log. This gives you a great chance at any later time to look back at what has happened within the system. Once you have the record of all that happened, you can set up a *what-if* elaboration, replay events to figure out the current state, and extrapolate models of any kind.

Writing an event class

In terms of source code, commands and events are both classes derived from *Message*. Dealing with commands and events through different classes makes the design of the system more logical and simpler overall. Here's a sample command class:

```
public class CheckoutCommand : Message
{
    public string CartId { get; private set; }
    public string CustomerId { get; private set; }

    public CheckoutCommand(string cartId, string customerId)
    {
        CartId = cartId;
        CustomerId = customerId;
    }
}
```

Conversely, here's the layout of an event class.

```
public class DomainEvent : Message
{
    // Common properties
    ...
}

public class OrderCreatedEvent : DomainEvent
{
    public string OrderId { get; private set; }
    public string TrackingId { get; private set; }
    public string TransactionId { get; private set; }
```

```
    public OrderCreatedEvent(string orderId, string trackingId, string transactionId)
    {
        OrderId = orderId;
        TrackingId = trackingId;
        TransactionId = transactionId;
    }
}
```

As you can see, the structure of event and command classes is nearly the same except for the naming convention. A fundamental guideline for designing domain events is that they should be as specific as possible and clearly reveal intent.

As an example, consider the form through which a customer updates the default credit card he uses in transactions. Should you fire a rather generic *CustomerUpdated* event? Or is a more specific *CreditCardUpdated* event preferable? Both options lead to a working solution, but which option works for you should be evident and stand on its own. It depends on the ubiquitous language and the level of granularity you have in place. We believe that a finer granularity here is a significant asset.

We generally recommend that the intent of the event be made clear in the name and all ambiguity be removed. If some ambiguity around a single event surfaces, you'll probably find that it's safer to have two distinct events.

Which properties should you have in the base class *DomainEvent*?

We'd say that at a minimum you want to have a timestamp property that tracks the exact time at which the event was fired. Moreover, you might want to have a property containing the name (or ID) of the user who caused the firing of the event. Another piece of data you might want to have is a version number that handlers can use to determine whether they can or cannot handle the event. The point here is that the definition of an event might change over time. A version number can help in this regard.

The implementation of the version number is completely up to the team. It can be a Version object as well as a string or a number. It can be bound to the application build number, or it can even be referred to the version of the event class:

```
public class DomainEvent : Message
{
    public DateTime TimeStamp { get; private set; }
    public DomainEvent()
    {
        TimeStamp = DateTime.Now;
    }
}
```

An event class should be considered immutable for the simple reason that it represents something that has already happened. *Immutable* here means that there should be no way to alter the value of properties. The combination of private setters, no write methods, and a plain constructor will do the trick.

Handling commands and events

Commands are managed by a processor that usually is referred to as a *command bus*. Events are managed by an *event bus* component. It is not unusual, however, that commands and events are handled by the same bus. Figure 10-3 presents the overall event-based architecture of a CQRS solution. This architecture is more standard and is an alternative to the one we mentioned earlier that was based on the TS pattern.

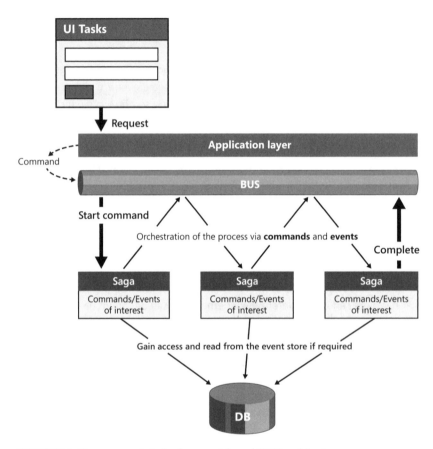

FIGURE 10-3 The command stack of an event-based CQRS architecture.

Any interaction that takes place in the user interface generates some requests to the system. In an ASP.NET MVC scenario, these requests take the form of controller actions and methods in the application layer. In the application layer, a command is created and pushed to some machinery for actual processing.

The bus component

The command bus holds a list of known business processes that can be triggered by commands. Active instances of such processes can be further advanced by commands. Processing a command can sometimes generate an event within the domain; the generated event is published to the same command bus or to a parallel event bus, if any. Processes that handle commands and related events are usually referred to as *sagas*.

The command bus is a single class that receives messages (requests of executing commands and notifications of events) and finds a way to process them. The bus doesn't actually do the work itself; instead, it selects a registered handler that can take care of the command or event. Here's a possible template for a bus class that handles commands and events. We use the interface *IHandles* as a placeholder for actions. The interface has a single void method:

```
public interface IHandles
{
    void Handle(T message);
}
```

The bus uses the interface to handle both commands and events:

```
public class Bus
{
    private static readonly Dictionary<Type, Type> SagaStarters =
            new Dictionary<Type, Type>();
    private static readonly Dictionary<string, object> SagaInstances =
            new Dictionary<string, object>();

    public static void RegisterSaga<TStartMessage, TSaga>()
    {
        SagaStarters.Add(typeof(TStartMessage), typeof(TSaga));
    }

    public static void Send<T>(T message) where T : Message
    {
        // Publish the event
        if (message is IDomainEvent)
        {
            // Invoke all registered sagas and give each
            // a chance to handle the event.
            foreach(var saga in SagaInstances)
            {
                var handler = (IHandles<T>) saga;
                if (handler != null)
                    handler.Handle(message);
            }
        }

        // Check if the message can start one of the registered sagas
        if (SagaStarters.ContainsKey(typeof (T)))
        {
            // Start the saga creating a new instance of the type
            var typeOfSaga = SagaStarters[typeof (T)];
            var instance = (IHandles<T>) Activator.CreateInstance(typeOfSaga);
            instance.Handle(message);

            // At this point the saga has been given an ID;
            // let's persist the instance to a (memory) dictionary for later use.
            var saga = (SagaBase) instance;
```

```
        SagaInstances.Add(saga.Data.Id, instance);
        return;
    }


    // The message doesn't start any saga.
    // Check if the message can be delivered to an existing saga instead
    if (SagaInstances.ContainsKey(message.Id))
    {
        var saga = (IHandles<T>) SagaInstances[message.Id];
        saga.Handle(message);

        // Saves saga back or remove if completed
        if (saga.IsComplete())
            SagaInstances.Remove(message.Id);
        else
            SagaInstances[message.Id] = saga;
    }
  }
}
```

The bus has two internal dictionaries: one to map start messages and saga types, and one to track live instances of sagas. In the latter dictionary, you can typically have multiple instances of the same saga type that are bound to different IDs.

The saga component

In general, a saga component looks like a collection of logically related methods and event handlers. Each *saga* is a component that declares the following information:

- A command or event that starts the process associated with the saga

- Commands the saga can handle and events the saga is interested in

Whenever the bus receives a command (or an event) that can start a saga, it creates a new saga object. The constructor of the saga generates a unique ID, which is necessary to handle concurrent instances of the same saga. The ID can be a GUID as well as a hash value from the starter command or anything else, like the session ID. Once the saga is created, it executes the command or runs the code that handles the notified event. Executing the command mostly means writing data or executing calculations.

At some point in the lifetime of the saga instance, it might be necessary to send another command to trigger another process or, more likely, fire an event that advances another process. The saga does that by pushing commands and events back to the bus. It might also happen that a saga stops at some point and waits for events to be notified. The concatenation of commands and events keeps the saga live until a completion point is reached. In this regard, you can also think of a saga as a workflow with starting and ending points.

Events raised by sagas pass through the bus, and the bus passes them as messages to whomever subscribed to that event. Raising an event from within the saga requires code like that shown here:

```
// Raise the PaymentCompleted event
var theEvent = new PaymentCompletedEvent( /* add transaction ID */ );
theEvent.SagaId = message.Cart.Id;
Bus.Send(theEvent);
```

From the application layer, you invoke the bus as shown in the following example. This example simulates a scenario in which an ASP.NET MVC application is called back from the payment page on a bank service gateway:

```
public ActionResult CompleteProcessOrder(String transactionId)
{
    // Retrieve shopping cart from session state
    var cart = RetrieveCurrentShoppingCart();

    // Prepare and queue a Process-Order command
    var command = new ProcessOrderCommand(transactionId, cart.CartId);
    Bus.Send(command);

    // Refresh view: in doing so, results of previous command might be captured, if ready.
    return RedirectToAction("Done");
}
```

As you might have noticed, the command bus doesn't return a response. This is not coincidental. The refresh of the user interface—wherever necessary—is left to a subsequent read command that queries data from any place—storage, cache, or whatever—where output is expected to be.

What we mostly want from a command bus is to decouple the application layer from the domain services. Doing so opens up new opportunities, such as handling domain service calls asynchronously. Other scenarios that the command bus can simplify are adding cross-cutting filters along the way, such as transactions, logging, and general injection points for optional logic. In any of these cases, all you need to do is change the command-bus class—no changes are required to the application layer and domain services.

> **Important** As battlefield experience grows around CQRS, some practices consolidate and tend to become best practices. Partly contrary to what we just stated about async domain services, it is a common view today to think that both the command handler and the application need to know how the transactional operation went. Results must be known, and if the command needs to run asynchronously, it should be designed as an event rather than as a command.

The combined effect of commands and events

When you write systems based on very dynamic business rules, you might want to seriously consider leaving the door open to making extensions and changes to certain workflows without patching the system.

Think, for example, of an e-commerce website that launches a marketing campaign so that any user performing certain actions through the site will accrue points on some sort of a customer-loyalty program. Because of the huge success of the campaign, the company decides to extend the incentives to more actions on the site and even double the points if a given action (say, buying suggested products) is repeated over time. How would you effectively handle that?

You can certainly fix and extend the application layer, which turns out to be the nerve center that governs the workflow. Anyway, when the business logic is expressed through the composition of small, independent and even autonomous commands and events, everything is much easier to handle. This is a classic scenario for collaborative systems. Let's say you use the flowchart in Figure 10-4 to implement the process of an order being submitted.

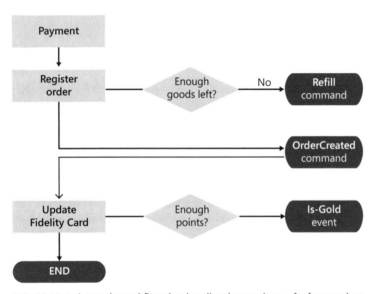

FIGURE 10-4 A sample workflow that handles the purchase of a few products.

Having the entire business logic of the workflow in a single method might make maintenance and testing problematic. However, even in the simple case of having split blocks in the workflow in simple commands, it might be difficult to do things properly. Let's consider the update of the customer's status in the fidelity program after an order is processed.

Instead of having the Register-Order command invoke the Update-Fidelity-Card command, isn't it more flexible if the Register-Order command just fires an event saying that a new order has been created? With this approach, a handler for that event can kick off and check whether the customer is eligible for Gold status and fire another event for other handlers to jump in and update databases.

This would isolate each action, keep each form of validation small and in reusable pieces, and keep the amount of logic in each command to the bare minimum.

> **Note** When it comes to events, we highly recommend that the naming convention reflect the occurrence of something. For example, the generic Not-In-Store and Is-Gold events should be implemented through classes with more evocative names, such as *ItemWasNotInStoreWhenPayingEvent* and *CustomerReachedGoldStatusEvent*.

Sagas and transactions

Looking back at Chapter 8 where we introduced the Domain Model architecture, we can say that a saga is the evolution of the application service concept.

In an application service you orchestrate the tasks that serve a user request. The application service takes care of setting up transactions--possibly distributed transactions--and like a state-machine it coordinates the next step until the end of a workflow is reached. Abstractly speaking, a saga does the same except that it removes the need for a single component to know about the entire workflow and uses events to break an otherwise monolithic workflow into the combined effect of smaller command handlers raising events to coordinate with others.

This makes the entire solution a lot more flexible and reduces the surface of code subject to changes when business changes.

In addition, a saga reduces the need of distributed transactions when long-running processes are involved that span across multiple bounded contexts. The structure of a saga--a collection of rather independent command and event handlers--lends to easily define compensating behavior for each command executed. Thus if at some point a saga command fails, it can execute the compensating behavior for what it knows has happened and raise an event at the saga level to undo or compensate the work completed.

> **Note** In the case of failures, saga methods might receive the same event twice or more. It might not be easy to figure out the event is a repeat. If it can be figured out, methods should avoid repeating action (idempotency)

Downsides of having a command bus

There are contrasting feelings about the command bus. A common criticism is that it just adds an extra layer and contributes to making the code less easy to read. You need to go through some more classes to figure out what happens.

This aspect can be mitigated by using proper naming conventions so that the name of the handler matches the name of the command class being queued to the bus. In this way, you know exactly where to look, and looking into the implementation of methods takes only a few more clicks than with application services, as discussed in past chapters.

With classic application services, you see the call to the method right from controllers and can use a tool like ReSharper to jump directly to the source code. With a command bus, you see the command and know by convention the name of the class in which you need to look.

Readymade storage

Most real-world systems write data and read it back later. Before CQRS appeared on the horizon, reads and writes took place within the same stack and often within the same transactional context. CQRS promotes the neat separation of queries and commands and pushes the use of different stacks. As you saw in this chapter, though, the internal architecture of the two stacks can be significantly different. You typically have a domain layer in the command stack and a far simpler data-access layer in the query stack.

What about databases, then? Should you use different databases too: one to save the state of the system and one to query for data?

Optimizing storage for queries

Many real-world systems use a single database for reading and writing purposes—and this happens regardless of CQRS architectures. You can have distinct command and query models and still share the same database. It's all about the scenarios you deal with.

Our thought is that using CQRS—at least in its lightweight form of using different models—is mostly beneficial for every system because it splits complexity, enables even different teams to work in parallel, and can suggest using something even simpler than a Domain Model for each stack. So CQRS is also about simplification.

However, for most practical purposes, using a single relational database is still the best option. When CQRS is used for scalability in a highly collaborative system, however, you might want to think about a couple of other aspects. (CQRS with a single database is sometimes referred to as *hybrid-CQRS*.)

In the query stack, what you query for has nearly the same schema as the view model. Most likely, these view models come from tables that are largely denormalized and that have very few links to other tables. In other words, the tables you really need are specialized for the queries you need to run.

A question that naturally arises is this: do you actually need a relational database for queries? We say you don't strictly need a relational database, but it's probably the best option you have, even though NoSQL solutions might be handier at times. More importantly—we'd say—you don't strictly need the same database where the state of the system is persisted.

Creating a database cache

If you're using one database to store the state of the system and another database to store data in a format that is quick and effective to query for the purposes of presentation, who's in charge of keeping the two databases in sync?

This seems to be the final step of nearly any command whose action affects the query database. To avoid giving too many responsibilities to each command, the most obvious approach is that any command whose action affects the query database fires an event at the end. The event handler will then take care of updating the query database. The query database doesn't fully represent the business behind the application; it only contains data—possibly denormalized data—in a format that matches the expectations of the user interface. For example, if you're going to display pending orders, you might want to have a query database just for the information you intend to display for orders. In doing so, you don't store the customer ID or product ID, just the real name of the customer, a full description of the product, and a calculated total of the order that includes taxes and shipping costs.

Stale data and eventual consistency

When each stack in CQRS owns its database, the command database captures the state of the system and applies the "official" data model of the business domain. The query database operates as a cache for data readymade for the presentation's needs. Keeping the two databases in sync incurs a cost. Sometimes this cost can be postponed; sometimes not.

If you update the query database at the end of a command, just before the end of the saga or at any point of the workflow when it makes sense, you automatically keep the command and query databases in sync. Your presentation layer will constantly consume fresh data.

Another approach that is sometimes used in the concrete implementations consists of delaying the synchronization between the command and query databases. The command database is regularly updated during the execution of the command so that the state of the application is consistent. Those changes, though, are not replicated immediately to the query side. This typically happens for performance reasons and to try to keep scalability at the maximum.

When the query and command databases are not in sync, the presentation layer might show stale data and the consistency of the entire system is partial. This is called *eventual consistency*—at some point, the databases are consistent, but consistency is not guaranteed all the time.

Is working with stale data a problem? It depends.

First and foremost, there should be a reason for having stale data; often, the reason is to speed up the write action to gain greater scalability. If scalability is not a concern, there's probably no reason for stale data and eventual consistency. Beyond that, we believe that very few applications can't afford displaying stale data for a short amount of time (with "short amount of time" being defined by the context). In many write-intensive systems, writes are sometimes performed in the back end and only simulated on the presentation to give the illusion of full synchronicity. The canonical example is when you post on a social network and the following two things happen:

- The back end of the system is updated through a command.

- At the end of the command, the DOM of the page is updated via JavaScript with the changes.

In other words, what appears as the real status of the system is simply the effect of a client-side command. At some point, however, in a few seconds (or minutes or days) something happens that restores full consistency so that when the page is displayed from scratch reading from the server, it presents aligned data.

Eventual consistency is commonly achieved through scheduled jobs that run periodically or via queues that operate asynchronously. In this case, the saga ends by placing an event to a separate bus, possibly on a persistent queue. The queue will then serve events one at a time, causing the handler to fire and update the query database.

Summary

A decade ago, DDD started an irreversible, yet slow, process that is progressively changing the way many approach software architecture and development. In particular, DDD had the positive effect of making it clear that a deep understanding of the domain is key. And above everything else, DDD provided the tools for that: a ubiquitous language and bounded context.

Initially, DDD pushed the layered architecture with an object-oriented model as the recommended architecture for a bounded context. Years of experience suggested that a single domain model to handle all aspects of the business logic—specifically, commands and queries—was probably taking the complexity up to a vertical asymptote. From that point, there was an effort in the industry to find a different approach—one that could retain the good parts of DDD while making the implementation simpler and more effective.

CQRS was one of the answers.

CQRS propounds the separation between domain layers and the use of distinct models for reading and writing—a brilliantly simple idea that, however, had a far broader scope than first imagined. CQRS is perfect for highly collaborative systems, but it also can serve well in simpler scenarios if you apply it in a lighter form. That's a fundamental point and—as we see it—also the source of a lot of confusion.

CQRS is primarily about separating the stack of commands from the stack of queries. Realizing this architectural separation is not necessarily complex or expensive. However, if you take CQRS one or two steps further, it can really deliver a lot of added value in terms of the ability to manage much more business complexity while making your system much easier to scale out. To achieve this, you need to restructure and largely rethink the command and query sides and introduce LET, command buses, handlers, domain and integration events, and (likely) distinct storage for reads and writes. This flavor of architecture is ideal for collaborative systems, but it can be expensive to use in some systems. In the end, full-blown CQRS is a good solution, but not for every problem.

Finishing with a smile

To generate a smile or two at the end of this chapter, we selected three popular but largely anonymous quotes in the spirit of Murphy's laws:

- To understand what recursion is, you must first understand recursion.

- Before software can be reusable, it first has to be usable.

- Ninety percent of everything is CRUD.

In addition, we saved two funny but deep pearls of wisdom for last, from two people who contributed a lot to the software industry and computer science as a whole:

- If debugging is the process of removing software bugs, then programming must be the process of putting them in. (E. W. Diijkstra)

- C makes it easy to shoot yourself in the foot; C++ makes it harder, but when you do, it blows away your whole leg. (Bjarne Stroustrup)

CHAPTER 11

Implementing CQRS

Computers are useless. They can only give you answers.

—*Pablo Picasso*

The fundamental aspect of a CQRS solution is the neat separation between the command stack and query stack. This means that each stack is designed separately; such a distinct design potentially can lead to having two distinct domain layers and even two distinct databases.

At the end of the day, there are several different flavors of CQRS.

There are CQRS implementations in which the read domain layer is nearly empty and consists only of plain SQL queries run against the database and data-transfer objects used to carry data up to the presentation layer. In other implementations, you have a read domain model that, overall, looks like a subset of a full domain model and a full domain model for the command stack where most of the business logic is contained. The command stack can be lightweight too and sometimes result from a basic implementation of the Transaction Script pattern. In this case, you have no domain layer whatsoever.

More likely, though, the command stack of a CQRS architecture is based on a command bus and handles events on top of a domain model and a database. If two databases exist—one to store the state of the application, and one to contain data in a format highly optimized for reading—then in some way the overall architecture should include a trigger—mostly events—that keeps the databases in sync and updates the read database whenever something is written.

In the end, CQRS is an architectural point. The benefits of the architecture that we listed in Chapter 10, "Introducing CQRS," apply as long as you keep the query and command stacks distinct. In this chapter, we'll first review a few possible CQRS implementations and then proceed with extending the sample application with a CQRS implementation where distinct stacks are used for querying and issuing commands.

CQRS implementations

CQRS doesn't mandate any design choice. Even though the idea of CQRS is often associated with the idea of domain models and Domain-Driven Design (DDD), actually CQRS has just one principle: keep the command and query stacks segregated. Such a core principle can be implemented at least in a couple of ways. One consists of a plain and simple separation of stacks; the other consists of designing the business logic through commands and events.

We feel that a plain and simple CQRS approach is a scenario that often gets overshadowed by the use of command buses and events. Yet it delivers all the architectural benefits of CQRS in terms of simplified design and scalability

Plain and simple CQRS

The architectural benefits of CQRS—primarily the potential for scalability and greatly simplified handling of complex business scenarios—can be delivered even without an explicit focus on domain modeling. As mentioned in Chapter 10, CQRS is not a top-level architectural pattern, but it works beautifully within a bounded context. In a given bounded context, you identify the ideal pattern to express the business logic you have and the ideal pattern to represent any data behind it that gets moved toward the presentation layer for display purposes.

That's all of it—you have two distinct stacks to be maintained and operated separately. Let's review the options you have in case you don't use domain-modeling techniques and the Domain Model pattern.

Transaction script for the command stack

In Chapter 7, "The mythical business layer," we mentioned the Transaction Script pattern as one of the simplest, but not less effective, patterns to handle business logic. The Transaction Script pattern pushes a task-based vision of the business logic. In this regard, it works very well within a stack that focuses only on the execution of commands.

As Andrea experienced in a couple of projects—especially if you're called to help a group of corporate developers finalize a project—you might not want to start using architecture that demands significant development skills. The risk of failing, or just experiencing analysis/paralysis, is too high. Conversely, the command/query separation will deliver the simplicity and scalability that you need.

As a pattern, Transaction Script doesn't make huge demands of developers—it basically recommends they write methods on classes that focus on a task. By carefully choosing names for those methods and classes that closely mirror the language of the business, well, you're surprisingly halfway done.

In a Transaction Script implementation, you have nothing as complex as command processors or domain models. All you have is a screen with command buttons and a method executing requested actions. Each action ends with some database writes. Input data travels from screens down to the methods as plain data-transfer objects (DTOs). All of this is simple and effective, and the reason it is so simple is because the command stack is kept separate from the read stack.

Data-transfer objects for the query stack

In CQRS, the query stack should be as simple as possible and use the simplest technology that could possibly work. In the scenario we are considering, you don't need (or just don't want) a full-fledged data model for the read stack. You return data to the upper layers via data-transfer objects—typically, view model objects if you're using ASP.NET MVC. How do you fill those objects with data?

A common approach consists of calling an ad hoc layer from the application layer that wraps up the database context. The application layer essentially sees a read layer with ad hoc query methods that return any of the following:

- Data-transfer objects that the application layer will later assemble in view model objects for the presentation layer to display

- Data-transfer objects that are already view model objects ready for the presentation layer to display

The first scenario is seldom practical; the second is very convenient. The first approach entails using a tool like AutoMapper, or similar handwritten code, that just maps data from database models to memory object models. The real issue here is not the use of extra code and the processing power required by a tool like AutoMapper; instead, the issue is related to design. In a CQRS scenario, the presence of an object model in the query stack is sometimes just the sign that some of the complexity of the read domain model can be moved to an additional bounded context.

Having the read stack return direct view model objects is the essence of what we referred to as a layered expression tree (LET) in the previous chapter. With LET, view model objects are arranged on the fly in the body of a highly idiomatic LINQ query.

In this simple implementation of CQRS, the read stack is based on a simple data-access layer that just performs queries. Based on the available skills and attitude of the developers, you can code this read layer on top of Entity Framework and LINQ using a LET approach to populate data-transfer objects on the fly. In this case, the read layer internally uses a database context object, except that the database context is not publicly visible outside the read layer. If you don't use Entity Framework and LINQ, the read layer can simply consist of plain ADO.NET or SQL queries and ad hoc data types to bring data back to the client. If you're using an ASP.NET Web Forms front end, using DataSets to carry data might even be an option.

Single database

Depending on the real complexity of the business scenario, in general you can have CQRS with a single database shared by the command and query stacks, as well as distinct databases that are each managed by stacks autonomously. That mostly depends on the complexity (specifically, the nesting level) of the queries you need to execute.

In the case of a shared database, you typically share the database context between command and read stacks, paying attention to keeping the context private in the read stack. In the read stack, you can use code like that shown here:

```
public class ReadStack
{
    private CommandStackDatabase _context;
    public ReadStack()
    {
        _ context = new CommandStackDatabase();
    }

    public OrderDto GetById(int orderId)
    {
        // Use _context to make the query
        // and fill the expected DTO
    }
}
```

If, for query performance reasons, you decide to maintain a separate database, you'll need to have a separate table mapping and a separate database context.

CQRS with command architecture

As more and more people started using CQRS, it became obvious that CQRS is particularly well suited to being coupled with a command-driven strategy and events. By using commands and a command bus, you can split the steps performed in an application service into multiple commands and events sent to the bus.

Orchestrating commands in the command stack

Organizing use-cases and business logic via commands has a number of benefits:

- It makes it easy to map commands to the steps of real business processes. At the end of the day, commands are applied because they exist in the ubiquitous language.

- You can even draw a flowchart out of a process and discuss that with a domain expert.

- It makes far easier to render particularly complex pieces of business logic with events generated by actions that, in turn, generate other domain events.

When you start reasoning in terms of commands, you start feeling the need for another element: events. The execution of a command might generate an event that should be processed by any number of registered handlers. Commands and events go together and represent the real essence of CQRS.

One database or two

When you have two models—one for the command stack and one for the query stack—you need to distinguish whether or not each model refers to its own database. Things are easy to manage if you have distinct databases and rely on architecture like that shown in Figure 11-1.

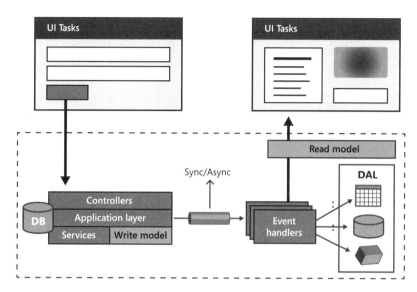

FIGURE 11-1 CQRS architecture with distinct models and distinct databases.

When distinct databases are used to persist the state of the application and for serving the needs of presentation, you need to have something in between the two that ensures synchronization and consistent data. This is generally accomplished in one of two ways. It can be a scheduled job that operates on the write database periodically and copies data to other tables. It can also be an in-process handler that fires after the termination of each command and either synchronously or asynchronously creates read views, which can be relational tables, OLAP cubes or, why not, tabular data.

When the two stacks share the same database and you have models on both sides, you need to manage two database contexts and apply different mappings. You end up with classes analogous to the classes shown next. These two classes belong to different class libraries:

```
public class CommandModelDatabase : DbContext
{
    ...
}
public class ReadModelDatabase : IQueryModelDatabase
{
    ...
}
```

The former database context class inherits directly from Entity Framework's *DbContext* class. The latter class wraps an instance of DbContext and implements a custom interface—arbitrarily named *IQueryModelDatabase*. The interface serves the purpose of restricting the *DbContext* interface to just a few queryable collections so that the *SaveChanges* method, which enables changes to the underlying database, is hidden from view.

The database class for the command model also needs to override *OnModelCreating* to map the content of the database to the physical classes in their own model:

```
public class CommandModelDatabase : DbContext
{
    protected override void OnModelCreating(DbModelBuilder modelBuilder)
    { ... }
    ...
}
```

There are a couple of remarks to make here. First, when implementing the read database class, you might want to choose composition over inheritance. Instead of inheriting from *DbContext*, you can simply create an internal instance. In this way, you prevent undesirable casts to *DbContext* somewhere in the code. Second, the name of the class should closely reflect the actual language of the business. Quite simply, this could be *Database*, indicating (as in the business language) the common name for the container of the business information.

Implementing a query stack

Let's have a closer look at a CQRS implementation that has two distinct models on top of a single database and uses commands for the organization of the business logic.

Creating a read façade

The essence of CQRS is that, as an architect, you mentally separate queries against the back end from actions that you need to write. You should plan to have separate projects for the query and command parts, and you can even have different teams as well. A read façade consists of two main components: a data model and a database context to read data and materialize elements in the domain.

The query model

As mentioned, most of the time you won't have an object model in the query side. If you have one, however, here's more about how to write it. The data model of the query stack has the same structure of the domain model we devised for the entire domain in Chapter 8, "Introducing the domain model," and Chapter 9, "Implementing the domain model." It's the same type of collection of related classes except that the classes are fewer and simpler because they focus only on data and behavior that pertains to rendering queried data.

The read-only domain model is a class library project. Figure 11-2 offers an interior view of the class library project for the sample application.

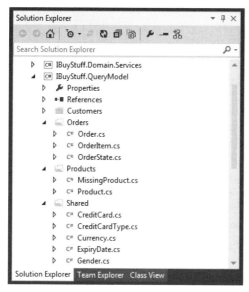

FIGURE 11-2 The QueryModel class library project.

The *Order* class in the read model, for example, doesn't have any behavior and looks like a mere container of data:

```
public class Order
{
    protected Order()
    {
    }
    public int OrderId { get; set; }
    public ICollection<OrderItem> Items { get; set; }
    public Money Total { get; set; }
    public OrderState State { get; set; }
    public DateTime Date { get; set; }
}
```

The *OrderItem* class is nearly the same as in a full domain-model implementation. Also, the *Product* and *Customer* classes are, in our example, nearly the same except that they now lack behavior. Another difference is that in the Orders folder of the full domain model, you find a lot more classes, like *OrderPaymentConfirmation*, that now belong to the command stack.

The read database context

Once you have a domain model, you also have the problem of materializing instances of the classes. Entity Framework does most of the work for you. If you use Code First, as in the example, you access the database using a class derived from *DbContext*:

```
public class QueryModelDatabase : DbContext
{
    public QueryModelDatabase() : base("naa4e-11")
    {
        ...
    }
    ...
}
```

The *DbContext* class provides full, read/write access to the database. To secure the read model and eradicate any chance of allowing write access to the database, you might want to use a private instance of DbContext and implement an interface to close the class. The *QueryModelDatabase* class is implemented in a new class library that implements the persistence layer for the read layer. In the example, we call it *IBuyStuff.QueryModel.Persistence*:

```
public class QueryModelDatabase : IQueryModelDatabase
{
    private DbContext _context;
    public QueryModelDatabase()
    {
        _context = new DbContext("naa4e-11");
        _products = base.Set<Product>();
        _orders = base.Set<Order>();
    }
    ...
}
```

The interface called *IQueryModelDatabase* just lists the collections of interest so that coders of the query stack are given access only to the data they need for read-only operations:

```
public interface IQueryModelDatabase
{
    IQueryable<Order> Orders { get; }
    IQueryable<Product> Products { get; }
}
```

In the segment of the sample application implemented so far, there's no function that queries customers: subsequently, there's no need to have the *Customers* collection in the public interface of the database context. The *QueryModelDatabase* class in the end represents the database to the application's eyes and should expose only data that the application is interested in.

Packaging data for callers

Another difference you might note in a CQRS scenario is that the collections exposed as part of the database context return *IQueryable*. Returning *IQueryable* is not strictly required, but it does help in a few ways, as we discussed in Chapter 10.

Creating LET expressions

Here's the full source code of the database context class in the query stack:

```
public class QueryModelDatabase : IQueryModelDatabase
{
    private DbContext_context;
    public QueryModelDatabase()
    {
        _context = new DbContext("naa4e-11");
        _products = base.Set<Product>();
        _orders = base.Set<Order>();
    }

    private readonly DbSet<Order> _orders = null;
    private readonly DbSet<Product> _products = null;

    public IQueryable<Order> Orders
    {
        get { return this._orders; }
    }
    public IQueryable<Product> Products
    {
        get { return _products; }
    }
}
```

Hiding DbContext and exposing table collections as *IQueryable* removes the risk of finding the *SaveChanges* method available at some point. In addition, an *IQueryable* object is just what its type name says—a queryable collection of data. This enables you to write queries as shown here:

```
using (var db = new QueryModelDatabase())
{
    var queryable = from o in db.Orders
                            .Include("Items")
                            .Include("Details.Product")
                    where o.OrderId == orderId
                    select new OrderFoundViewModel
                    {
                        Id = o.OrderId,
                        State = o.State.ToString(),
                        Total = o.Total,
                        OrderDate = o.Date,
                        Details = o.Items
                    };
    try
    {
        return queryable.First();
    }
    catch (InvalidOperationException)
    {
        return new OrderFoundViewModel();
    }
}
```

The code just rewrites the basic query we considered in one of the use-cases of the sample application in past chapters. The actual projection of data is specified at the last minute, right in the application layer. In this way, you can move around *IQueryable* objects and compile and run the query just when you are going to fill up view model objects. Doing so, also saves you from creating and maintaining a bunch of data-transfer objects.

> **Note** You might wonder why we insist on using the *ViewModel* suffix in the name of classes we use to package data for the caller. At the end of the day, we run a query against some LINQ data layer and copy data into a data-transfer object. We expect the code to run within the application layer and return the object in the context of an ASP.NET MVC application that will be ultimately passed to the view. If you run the preceding code in, say, a Web API method, you might want to use a different naming convention and use the *Dto* or *Model* suffix instead.

Packaging LET expressions in services

You can use LET expressions to call into the database context right from the application layer. To improve readability and adherence to the ubiquitous language, you can also consider having services that return *IQueryable* expressions for you to further concatenate.

The code below shows a sample *CatalogService* class that implements product-related functions:

```
public class CatalogServices : ICatalogService
{
    public IQueryModelDatabase QueryModelDatabase { get; set; }
    public CatalogServices(IQueryModelDatabase queryDatabase)
    {
        this.QueryModelDatabase = queryDatabase;
    }

    public IQueryable<Product> ProductsOnSale()
    {
        return from p in this.QueryModelDatabase.Products
               where p.IsDiscontinued == false select p;
    }

    public IQueryable<Product> Available()
    {
        return from p in ProductsOnSale() where p.UnitsInStock > 0 select p;
    }

    public IQueryable<Product> RelatedTo(int productId)
    {
        var categoryId = (from pd in ProductsOnSale()
                          where pd.Id == productId
                          select pd.Category.Id).Single();
        return from p in Available()
               where p.Id!=productId && p.Category.Id == categoryId
               select p;
    }
}
```

The *ProductsOnSale* method is a plain query that returns all products that haven't been discontinued and are on sale. The other two methods are built on top of *ProductsOnSale* and apply further restrictions. In a service, you can have ad hoc query methods if they are going to be used in several places; otherwise, you can build queries directly in the application layer.

> **Important** You really might not need a layer of services that essentially operate like read-only repositories. Probably a better way to achieve the same level of expressivity and encapsulation at a lower implementation cost is using extension methods on *IQueryable<T>*, where *T* is the type of entity—in the previous example, that would be *Product*.

Experimenting with the true value of LET

One beneficial aspect of LET expressions is that they dramatically reduce the need for DTOs. Building a query model without LET often requires you to define explicit DTO classes and package up data into them. This is a waste of development time and CPU cycles. Here is an example of what you can achieve with LET.

Let's say you're a business-unit manager. You have a dashboard accessible from the home page of your intranet account that allows you to quickly check some accounting information, such as all the unit's invoices that still need to be collected on. You might explain this need using the following wording: *from the list of invoices that the business unit has issued, I want to see all those that are unpaid and past due.*

```
var unpaidInvoices = Database.OutgoingInvoices
                        .PerBusinessUnit(businessUnitId)
                        .PastDue()
                        .Select(i => new UnpaidInvoiceModel() {
                            InvoiceNumber = i.Number,
                            CustomerId = i.Customer.Id
                        }).ToList();
```

The value is all in the fact that the programming language is semantically close to the business language. This is the essence of the ubiquitous language. Interestingly, similar code can be used outside the realm of plain queries to send, for example, a gentle reminder about the invoice:

```
Database.OutgoingInvoices
        .PerBusinessUnit(businessUnitId)
        .ExpiredOnly()
        .Select(i => new {InvoiceNumber = i.Number, CustomerId = i.Customer.Id})
        .AsParallel()
        .ForAll(i =>
            bus.Send(new SendEmailReminderCommand(i.InvoiceNumber, i.CustomerId)));
```

The query returns data ready-made for parallel processing. Next, the *ForAll* method pushes a command to the bus to send an email reminder about the invoice.

Implementing a command stack

As discussed in Chapter 10, the command stack of many CQRS solutions orchestrates the use-cases of the application by having workflows defined in terms of commands and events. Let's find out more details.

Laying the groundwork

Any external input (whether from users or external systems) becomes a command pushed to a bus. Next, the bus dispatches any commands to a registered handler for further processing. Typically, handlers are not stateless components that perform an operation and return. Processing a command, instead, starts a process that is advanced by further commands and domain events. The process that handles commands in the context of a workflow is known as a *saga*.

Domain events might be raised during the execution of commands to notify registered event handlers of specific situations. Integration events are, instead, notifications of occurrences in the command stack that might affect external bounded contexts.

> **Note** Semantically, domain and integration events are the same thing—plain notifications about something that just happened. However, their implementation might be different. Domain events are just messages pushed to the bus. Integration events are custom written. The purpose of integration events is to enable communication between standalone but related bounded contexts. It can be a RESTful API exposed by both contexts, a shared database used as a mailbox, an ASP.NET SignalR infrastructure, or perhaps a commercial service bus.

Devising a saga component

A saga is the logical component in which developers distill pieces of the business logic. More precisely, the saga (in cooperation with the bus) orchestrates all tasks that need be performed to implement a use-case.

Implemented as a plain class, a saga is characterized by the following features:

- ID, to ensure uniqueness of running instances

- Collection of properties, to hold the state of the saga

- List of messages (commands, events, or both) that start the saga

- List of commands the saga can handle

- List of events the saga wants to have a chance to handle

Internally, a saga will typically hold references to repositories and might be able to invoke domain services (if any) or external services. Here's the typical structure of a saga class for a checkout operation, such as the ones used in sample projects we considered in past chapters:

```
public class CheckoutSaga : SagaBase<CheckoutSagaData>,
        IStartWithMessage<CheckoutCommand>,
        ICanHandleMessage<CheckGoodsInStockCommand>,
        ICanHandleMessage<GoodsInStockEvent>,
        ICanHandleMessage<GoodsNotInStockEvent>,
        ICanHandleMessage<CheckCustomerPaymentHistoryCommand>,
        ICanHandleMessage<PaymentHistoryPositiveEvent>,
        ICanHandleMessage<PaymentHistoryNegativeEvent>,
        ICanHandleMessage<PaymentCompletedEvent>,
        ICanHandleMessage<PaymentDeniedEvent>,
        ICanHandleMessage<SendDeliveryRequestCommand>,
        ICanHandleMessage<DeliveryRequestRefusedEvent>,
        ICanHandleMessage<DeliveryRequestApprovedEvent>
{
    ...
}
```

A saga class typically inherits from a base class. At a minimum, the base class must expose an ID property to uniquely identify the saga. The saga base class might look like the code shown here:

```
public class SagaBase<T>
{
    public string ID { get; set; }
    public T Data { get; set; }
}
```

A commercial bus such as NServiceBus, for example, offers a *Saga<T>* base class that also implements some predefined behavior for saga persistence and other features. The type, *T*, you indicate is a plain data-transfer object made of a collection of properties that together define the state of the saga. In our example, the *CheckoutSagaData* class will likely contain the content of the shopping cart and information about the customer.

Designing a saga component

The implementation of a saga is tightly bound to the implementation of the bus. In general, a saga implements two types of interfaces: *IStartWithMessage<T>* and *ICanHandleMessage<T>*. Obviously, choosing names is up to you if you write the bus component yourself. Otherwise, they are mandated by the bus component you use. In NServiceBus, analogous interfaces are called *IAmStartedByMessages<T>* and *IHandleMessages<T>*.

The definition of these interfaces is basic. Here's an example:

```
public interface ICanHandleMessage<T> where T : Message
{
    void Handle(T message);
}
```

From the preceding definition of the *CheckoutSaga* class, it emerges that the class can handle the commands listed in Table 11-1.

TABLE 11-1. Commands supported by the saga

Command	Description
CheckoutCommand	This is a starter message used to begin the checkout process for the content of a shopping cart. This command can be issued when the user clicks the Buy button in the user interface.
CheckGoodsInStockCommand	This command verifies that ordered goods are in stock and the order can be carried out. The execution of this command generates one of two events: GoodsInStockEvent or GoodsNotInStockEvent. Events are listed in Table 11.2.
CheckCustomerPaymentHistoryCommand	This command checks the customer's payment history. Like the previous command, it can be carried out by the same saga or it can be the starter of a new saga. The execution of this command generates one of two events: PaymentHistoryPositiveEvent or PaymentHistoryNegativeEvent. Note that names for events are determined by the ubiquitous language.
SendDeliveryRequestCommand	This command send a message to another bounded context to arrange delivery of the ordered goods. The execution of this command might generate one of two events: DeliveryRequestRefusedEvent and DeliveryRequestApprovedEvent.

Table 11-2 lists supported events.

TABLE 11-2. Events supported by the saga

Event	Description
GoodsInStockEvent	This event is fired if ordered goods are in stock. Reception of this event is handled by placing the CheckCustomerPaymentHistory command.
GoodsNotInStockEvent	This event is fired if ordered goods are not in stock. Some compensation logic will take place here.
PaymentHistoryPositiveEvent	This event is fired if the analysis of the payment history for the customer is positive. Reception of this event is handled by placing a payment request to some bank gateway. Payment will then fire another event.
PaymentHistoryNegativeEvent	This event is fired if the analysis of the payment history for the customer is negative. Some compensation logic will take place here.
PaymentCompletedEvent	This event is fired if the payment completed successfully. Reception of this event is handled by placing a command for delivery.
PaymentDeniedEvent	This event is fired if payment failed. Some compensation logic will take place here.
DeliveryRequestRefusedEvent	This event is fired if the delivery request has not been accepted. Some compensation logic will take place here.
DeliveryRequestApprovedEvent	This event is fired if the delivery request has been approved. Following this event, the saga will actually create the order and fire an OrderCreated event.

The rather interesting thing is that the implementation of the *CheckoutSaga* class closely matches a flowchart, like the one in Figure 11-3.

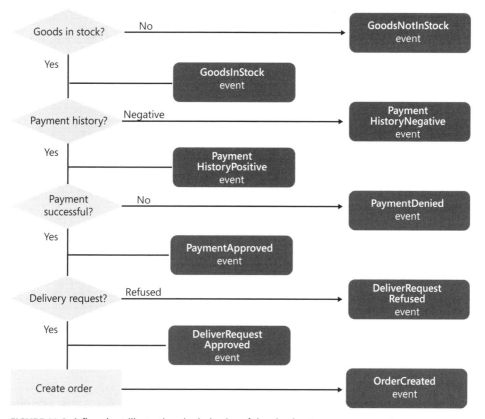

FIGURE 11-3 A flowchart illustrating the behavior of the checkout saga component.

This fact clearly demonstrates the power of the command-based approach: as an architect, you can thoroughly discuss the solution with domain experts using only flowcharts, without writing a single line of code. The flowchart is something that all domain experts can understand, so the feedback you get is appropriate and gives you an excellent starting point for coding business logic. You haven't completed a big upfront design phase, but you're well beyond stabbing in the dark.

Orchestrating use-cases via commands

Now that you laid the groundwork for commands and events to effectively describe the checkout process of the sample I-Buy-Stuff application, let's take a look at the actual source code. You'll see how commands and events make up the saga and how sagas are managed from within the bus.

Starting the saga

When the user clicks to check out and pay, the underlying ASP.NET MVC application receives a request handled by a controller. All that the controller does is prepare an appropriate command and push it to the bus. Here's a sample command class:

```
public class CheckoutCommand : Message
{
    public string CartId { get; private set; }
    public string CustomerId { get; private set; }

    public CheckoutCommand(string cartId, string customerId)
    {
        CartId = cartId;
        CustomerId = customerId;
    }
}
```

The shopping cart is referenced through an ID. The ID can be just the session ID if you're storing the shopping cart in memory. If the shopping cart is persisted to the database, ID is just the cart ID:

```
public ActionResult Checkout(string customerId)
{
    var command = new CheckoutCommand(Session.SessionID, customerId);
    Bus.Send(cmd);
    return RedirectToAction("done");
}
```

Within the bus, processing the command leads to finding the appropriate saga type registered to handle the command. In the initialization code of your application (for example, in *global.asax*) you have code like that shown here:

```
Bus.RegisterSaga<CheckoutCommand, CheckoutSaga>();
```

We described the typical implementation of a bus in Chapter 10. In short, whenever the bus receives a command (or an event) that can start a saga, it creates a new saga object and assigns it a unique ID. A saga declares its (unique) trigger through the *IStartWithMessage<T>* interface; similarly, it declares the messages it can handle through the *ICanHandleMessage<T>* interface.

Inside the saga implementation

The following code shows the startup of the saga. In our example, a new instance of the *CheckoutSaga* component is started when the bus receives a request for the *CheckoutCommand* type:

```
public class CheckoutSaga : SagaBase<CheckoutSagaData>,
                            IStartWithMessage<CheckoutCommand>,
                            ...
{ ... }
```

The *IStartWithMessage* interface has the same contract you saw earlier for *ICanHandleMessage*. The difference between the two is only a matter of semantics. Both interfaces are essentially markers that indicate why a given message is being processed:

```
public interface IStartWithMessage<T> where T : Message
{
    void Handle(T message);
}
```

The primary concern in the implementation of the *Handle* method in a starter command is identifying the unique ID of the current instance of the saga. The most obvious thing you can do is use the ID of the aggregate root you're working with. For example, if the saga involves orders, you can use the order ID as the saga ID. You get a reference to the aggregate root and save its ID in the saga.

In our example case, there's no aggregate root yet. You can use the unique ID that identifies the shopping cart. If you persist shopping carts, you can use the ID of the shopping cart; if not, you can use the session ID or even a generated GUID.

```
public void Handle(CheckoutCommand message)
{
    // Set the ID of the saga using the ID of the shopping cart
    this.Data.Id = message.Cart.Id;
    this.Data.Cart = message.Cart;
    this.Data.CustomerId = message.CustomerId;

    // Begin the saga by requesting a check on goods in stock
    var cmd = new CheckGoodsInStockCommand(message.Cart);
    cmd.SagaId = message.Cart.Id;
    Bus.Send(cmd);
}
```

Note that whenever you create a command (or event), you need a common way to set the ID of the saga so that when the command or event is processed by the bus, the bus can deliver it to the right saga. In our sample code, we assume a common property called *SagaId* on all messages that the bus component is aware of. A commercial implementation of a bus—the NServiceBus product, for example—uses a different approach. It allows each saga component to tell the bus how to recognize it.

In our example, the saga implements the flowchart shown earlier in Figure 11-3. Right after instantiation, therefore, it pushes a command to check whether the ordered goods are in stock. Note that the *CheckGoodsInStockCommand* is placed with reference to the ID of the current saga:

```
public void Handle(CheckGoodsInStockCommand message)
{
    // Check whether goods are in stock
    var instock = ...;

    // Raise an event to notify that all is OK
    var theEvent = new GoodsInStockEvent(Data.CustomerId);
    theEvent.SagaId = message.Cart.Id;
    Bus.Send(theEvent);
}
```

At this point, the event is pushed to the bus and handed over to all sagas that list it in the interface. The bus goes through the list of current saga instances and gives each a chance to handle the event. Here's some code that shows a sample implementation for other commands and events in the flowchart shown in Figure 11-3.

```
public void Handle(GoodsInStockEvent message)
{
    // Order a payment history check
    var cmd = new CheckCustomerPaymentHistoryCommand(Data.CustomerId);
    cmd.SagaId = message.Cart.Id;
    Bus.Send(cmd);
}

public void Handle(PaymentHistoryPositiveEvent message)
{
    // Proceed with payment through the configured bank gateway. This operation is synchronous
    // and may go through an anti-corruption layer or just through a plain web service call.
    var success = ProceedWithPayment(Data.Cart);
    if (success)
    {
        // Raise the PaymentCompleted event
        var theEvent = new PaymentCompletedEvent( /* add transaction ID */ );
        theEvent.SagaId = message.Cart.Id;
        Bus.Send(theEvent);
    }
}
```

The code snippets shown here should be enough to understand how a process triggered by a user action is implemented in a command architecture. For more details, you can have a look at the reference application that comes with the book.

Sagas and persistence

In general, a saga must be persistent and persistence of the saga is a typical responsibility of the bus. In this regard, it might completely be transparent to you if you don't write a bus class yourself. In the sample *Bus* class, we simulated persistence through an in-memory dictionary—whereas, for example, NServiceBus uses SQL Server. For persistence to happen, it is key that you give a unique ID to each saga instance.

If you're not completely convinced about the importance of saga persistence, consider the following scenario. Let's say that the business scenario requires the user of an online store to first pay and then complete the order by specifying shipping details. So the user enters banking details, and the saga completes payment successfully. Before the user regains control of the user interface and receives the page with shipping details, the browser freezes and crashes. The user reopens the browser and is served back the page with the Checkout option. She clicks, and the unique ID of the shopping cart (or the customer ID or whatever you chose to use) makes it easy to retrieve the saga, rebuild its state, and proceed from there.

Granularity of commands

If we were discussing the checkout scenario at a higher level of abstraction, we could say that the checkout scenario is the result of three commands: validation, payment, and completion of the order. In the actual implementation, however, we used plenty of commands and events. So what's the ideal granularity of the command? Should you go with a higher-level flowchart and hide most of the details of checking out inventory and payment history in some generic "validation" command? Or are you better off making every step explicit?

In general, the granularity of the command—defined as the data it carries and the action it takes—is defined at the level of the ubiquitous language. If domain experts talk about saving checkout information and checking the customer's payment history, you should have those logical steps defined explicitly as commands.

Summary

In software architecture, CQRS is the *Columbus egg*—namely, a brilliant and surprisingly obvious solution to a nontrivial problem. Developers and architects spent years trying to understand, justify, and mechanize DDD and Domain Model layered architectures, and they struggled with domain models that could hardly accomplish both query and command scenarios, especially in complex business domains.

CQRS, all of a sudden, made it far simpler. Complex business domains became a lot more manageable, and designing software with CQRS generally results in a solution much closer to the ubiquitous language that emerges out of the requirements. When this happens, requirements get missed less often, and subsequently, writing software becomes a more reliable discipline.

CQRS is applied at an architecture level, even though it's not the top-level architecture. You apply CQRS in a given bounded context and decide among a few options about the details related to the query and command stacks. In this chapter, we reviewed the most commonly used options and evolved the sample online store application of past chapters into a CQRS solution.

This is only the first step, though. CQRS needs to be taken one step further to unleash its true potential. This is precisely what we are slated to do in the next two chapters with the Event Sourcing architecture.

Finishing with a smile

Let's prepare for the next chapter with a laugh at a few of Murphy's laws somehow related to computers and programming. For more laws and details, see *http://www.murphys-laws.com/murphy/murphy-computer.html*:

- A working program is one that has only unobserved bugs.

- No matter how many resources you have, it is never enough.

- All Constants are Variables.

- Constants aren't.

- Variables won't.

CHAPTER 12

Introducing event sourcing

Simplicity is prerequisite for reliability.
—Edsger Dijkstra

The driving force that led to Domain-Driven Design (DDD) was the need to fill the gap between the different views that software architects and domain experts often had about business domains. DDD is a breakthrough compared to relational modeling because it promotes the use of domain modeling over data modeling. Relational modeling focuses on data entities and their relationships. Domain modeling, instead, focuses on behavior observable in the domain.

As a concrete implementation of domain modeling, DDD originally pushed the idea of a whole, all-encompassing object model capable of supporting all aspects and processes of a given domain. But models, especially complex models for complex pieces of reality, face a few challenges. This has led people to investigate alternative approaches, such as CQRS. At the moment you separate commands from queries, though, you are led to think a lot more in terms of tasks. And tasks are tightly related to domain and application events, as you saw when we talked about the Domain Model pattern and CQRS.

Event sourcing (ES) goes beyond the use of events as a tool to model business logic. ES takes events to the next level by persisting them. In an ES scenario, your data source just consists of persisted events. You don't likely have a classic relational data store; all you store are events, and you store them sequentially as they occur in the domain. As you can guess, persisting events instead of a domain model has a significant impact on the way you organize the back end of a system. Event persistence weds well with a strategy of separating the command and query stacks, and with the idea that distinct databases are used to save the state of the application and expose it to the presentation layer.

In the end, ES is not full-fledged, standalone architecture; rather, it's a feature used to further characterize architectures such as Domain Model and CQRS. In fact, you can have a Domain Model and CQRS application full of domain and integration events but still use plain relational databases as the data source. When you add ES to a system, you just change the structure and implementation of the data source.

311

The breakthrough of events

In the real world out there, we perform actions and see these actions generate a reaction. Sometimes the reaction is immediate; sometimes it is not. Sometimes the reaction becomes another action which, in turn, generates more reactions and so forth. That's how things go in the real world. That's not, however, how we designed software for decades. Was it, instead, the other way around?

The next big thing (reloaded)

Overall, we think that events are the next big thing in software development and probably the biggest paradigm shift to occur in the 20 years after object-orientation. And, all in all, we can probably even drop the "next" in the previous sentence and simply say events are a big thing in software development, period. Altogether, bounded contexts as well as domain and integration events, indicate a path architects can follow to deal more effectively with requirements both in terms of understanding and implementation.

Treating observable business events as persistent data adds a new perspective to development. Without a doubt, events play a key role in today's software development. But are events and event sourcing really a new idea? In fact, the modeling problems they help to address have been in the face of developers for decades. So what?

If we look back, we find that approaches similar to what we today call *ES* have been used for more than 30 years in banking and other sectors of the software industry, even in languages like COBOL. So events and event sourcing are a big thing for developers today, but calling that a *new* big thing might be overstating the case. On the other hand, as discussed already in Chapter 3, "Principles of software design," very few things are really new in software.

The real world has events, not just models

A model is an abstraction of reality that architects create from the results of interviews with domain experts, stakeholders, and end users. A model that faithfully renders a given domain might be quite complex to write; a model that is less faithful, however, can be simpler to write but fail to work well, especially in systems with a long life expectation that need a bit of updating every now and then.

While facing this problem, many architects just decide not to have a domain model. In doing so, they lose a lot in flexibility and maintainability. The real world just can't be restricted to models only—or to events only. The challenge is finding the right combination of models and events for a particular domain.

Modeling is a continuous activity, and the waterfall-like methodologies used in the past to handle projects apply now in quite a small number of scenarios. Models might need to be updated frequently as requirements change or are better understood. Whether projects start small or big, they will likely end up being much bigger than expected.

In a way, a model has the flavor of an architectural constraint and might force intense refactoring of the pillars of the system when changes occur. The work of the architect is just making choices that minimize the costs of future refactoring. The fact is, however, that for years DDD was seen, on one hand, as the correct and most ideal approach and that, on the other hand, it was hard to apply successfully.

If you take the approach that every single application's action occurs within a well-orchestrated model, you need to know everything about the model and the domain behind it. Otherwise, the model might not be the right approach. The advent of CQRS is, in this regard, the definitive evidence that a model in a bounded context is much more manageable if it is kept simple and small. Small models, though, might describe only a subset of the domain.

In the end, as the name suggests the model is just a model; it's not what we observe directly in the real world. In the real world, we observe events, and we sometimes build models on top of them.

Moving away from "last-known good state"

When we build a model out of observed events, a model is all we want to persist. A model is typically a cluster of objects. For both the simplicity and effectiveness of modeling and implementation, we identify some root objects in the model (called *aggregate roots* in Domain Model) and manage the storage and materialization of objects through them.

This is what we did for years in both relational data models and, more recently, in domain models.

Event sourcing pushes a form of lateral thinking about software architecture. Summarized, ES doesn't lead you to primarily focus on a model that mimics the entire domain and capture its state to a persistent storage. Instead, ES focuses primarily on the sequence of events you observe. And events are all that you want to capture for persistent storage.

Last-known good state

Think for a moment about the *Order* entity you encountered in past chapters, both in the context of Domain Model and CQRS architectures. The *Order* entity has an associated attribute that indicates its state, either pending, shipped, canceled, or archived. When you read a given order from the storage, all you have is the current state of the order; or, better yet, all you have is the last-known (because persisted) good state.

What if, instead, you need to track down the entire history of the order? What if you need to show when the order was created, when it started being processed, and when it was canceled or shipped?

In Chapter 8, "Introducing the domain model," we introduced domain events. In doing so, we said that any occurrence of the adverb "when" in the requirements is likely the occurrence of a relevant event in the domain. In the previous sentence, the word "when" occurs quite a few times. The creation, processing, and cancelation of an order are all events that change the last-known good state of an order upon occurrence.

In a "last-known good state" approach, though, each new event overwrites the state and doesn't track the previous state. This is hardly an acceptable compromise in most realistic business scenarios. Often, you need to keep track of the order history, and this need leads to adding a mechanism that maintains a history of the changes to orders and does not just maintain the current state of orders. Figure 12-1 shows a possible model.

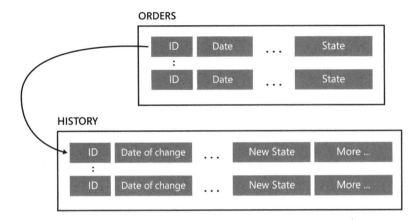

FIGURE 12-1 Tracking the history of an order.

 Note The term *New State* in Figure 12-1 is specific to the example based on orders and refers to changes in the state of the order: approved, canceled, and so on. It doesn't mean that the new state of the Order aggregate is being persisted whenever a new event occurs. Events refer to changes. In a banking scenario, for example, a transfer event will have the amount of the deposit but not the current balance of the account.

The model shown in Figure 12-1, however, just scratches the surface of the real problem we're facing. It works great if your only problem is tracking the change of an order's state. Generally speaking, in the history of an entity there might be events that also alter the structure of the entity. An example is when an item is added to an existing order before the order is processed or even before the order is shipped. Another example is when an order ships partially and missing items are either removed from the order because they are not available or they ship later. Yet another, probably more significant, example is when the entity just evolves over time according to the rules of the business. What if, all of a sudden, you find out that, say, the entity *Invoice* has a new *PayableOrder* attribute that gets a default value on existing instances but is mandatory on any new invoice?

On a relational model, solving the issue involves manipulating production databases and updates to the logic across the entire codebase wherever the *Order* entity is used. With a nonrelational design, the impact of the changes is much less obtrusive on both data stores and code.

The point is that the "last-known good state" approach is good, but it's not necessarily the ideal approach to represent effectively the item's life as it unfolds in a business domain.

Tracking just what's happened

In the real world, we only observe events, but for some reason we feel the need to build a model to capture information in events and store it. Building models out of events is not a bad thing per se. Models are immensely helpful. However, entity-based models serve the purpose of queries exceptionally well, but they do not serve quite as well the purpose of commands.

As discussed in past chapters, separating commands from queries is vital for modern software. If nothing else, it's vital because it makes building the software version of a business domain far easier, far more reliable and, especially, effective.

Event sourcing adds a new level of refinement to the CQRS architecture. According to event sourcing, events are the primary source of data in a system. When an event occurs, its associated collection of data is saved. In this way, the system tracks what happens, as it happens, and the information it brings.

Because the world has events and not models, this is by far a more natural way of modeling most business domains.

> **Note** When someone mentions complex software systems, many think of *Healthcare.gov*. Dino, in particular, is currently involved in the preliminary analysis of a system for the same domain space that never really took off because of the difficulty of designing an effective comprehensive model. Events are giving new lifeblood to an otherwise dead project.

The deep impact of events in software architecture

The "last-known good state" approach has been mainstream for decades. The "What's Happened" approach is a relatively new approach that treats domain events as the core of the architecture. As mentioned, in some business sectors approaches similar to ES are even older than relational databases. ES is just the formalization in patterns of those old practices.

Having events play such a central role in software architecture poses some new challenges, and those attempting to implement that approach might even face some initial resistance to change. The following sections describe some reasons why events have a deep impact on software architecture.

You don't miss a thing

The primary benefit of events is that any domain events that emerge out of analysis can be added to the system and saved to the store at nearly any time. By designing an event-based architecture, you give yourself the power to easily track nearly everything that takes place in the system.

Events are not rigidly schematized to a format or layout. An event is just a collection of properties to be persisted in some way, and not necessarily in a relational database.

> **Note** What's the ideal granularity of events you record? First and foremost, events exist because there's a domain analysis to suggest them and a domain expert to approve them. As an architect, you can modify the granularity of events you want to record and fine-tune such a granularity—for example, by introducing coarse-grained events that group multiple events. For example, you could use a global *Validate* event instead of multiple events for each step of the business-validation process. Grouping events is a controversial practice that tends to be discouraged and is being overtaken by the emerging analytical approach—event storming, which states the opposite: just deal with real domain events at the natural granularity they have in the domain.

Virtually infinite extensibility of the business scenario

Events tell you the full story of the business in a given domain. Having the story persisted as a sequence of events is beneficial because you are not restricted to a limited number of events. You can easily add new events at nearly any time—for example, when your knowledge of the domain improves and when new requirements and business needs show up.

Using a model to persist the story of the business limits you to whatever can be stored and represented within the boundaries of the model. Using events removes such limits at its root, and supporting new and different business scenarios is not just possible but also relatively inexpensive.

Dealing with event persistence requires new architectural elements such as the *event store*, where events are recorded.

Enabling *what-if* scenarios

By storing and processing events, you can build the current state of the story any time you need it. This concept is known as *event replay*. Event replay is a powerful concept because it enables *what-if* scenarios that turn out to be very helpful in some business domains (for example, in financial and scientific applications). The business and domain experts, for instance, might be interested to know what the state of the business was as of a particular date, such as December 31, 2011.

With event-based storage, you can easily replay events and change some of the run-time conditions to see different possible outcomes. The nice thing is that what-if scenarios don't require a completely different architecture for the application. You design the system in accordance with the event-sourcing approach and get what-if scenarios enabled for free.

The possibility of using what-if scenarios is one of the main business reasons for using ES.

No mandated technologies

Nothing in event sourcing is explicitly bound to any technologies or products, whether they are Object/Relational Mapper (O/RM) tools, relational (or even nonrelational) database management systems, service buses, libraries for dependency injection, or other similar items.

Event sourcing raises the need for some software tools—primarily, an event store. However, having an event store means that you have essentially a log of what has happened. For query purposes, you probably need some ready-made data built from the log of events. This means that you probably also need a publish/subscribe mechanism to connect the command and query stacks, a relational store to make queries run faster, and probably some Inversion of Control (IoC) infrastructure for easier extensibility.

For any of these tools, you can pick up the technology or product that suits you—no restrictions and no strings attached. Sure, there are some recommendations and tools that might work better than others in the same scenario. For example, a NoSQL document store is certainly not badly positioned to create an event store. Likewise, a service bus component might be well-suited to enhance scalability by keeping commands and queries separated but synchronized without paying the costs of synchronous operations.

Events and event sourcing are about architecture; technologies are identified by family. The details are up to you and can be determined case by case.

Are there also any drawbacks?

Is it "all good" with event sourcing? Are there issues and drawbacks hidden somewhere? Let's split the question in two parts:

- Are there drawbacks hidden somewhere in the event-sourcing approach to software architecture?

- Does it work for all applications?

The event-sourcing architecture is general enough to accommodate nearly any type of software application, including CRUD (Create, Read, Update, Delete) applications. It doesn't have dependencies on any technologies, and it can be successfully employed in any bounded context you wish and on top of any technology stack you prefer. In this regard, all the plusses listed earlier in the chapter stand. As for painful points, resistance to change is really the only serious drawback of event sourcing. Resistance to change is also fed by the fact that most popular IDEs and frameworks are currently designed from the ground up to scaffold entities. This suggests that scaffolding entities and thinking in terms of entities and their relationships is the ideal way of working.

Event sourcing pushes a paradigm shift that turns around a number of certainties that developers and architects have built over time. To many, it seems that using event sourcing means not saving any data at all. There might not be any classic relational data store around, but that doesn't mean you're not saving the state of the application. Quite the reverse: you're saving any single piece of data that emerges from the business domain. Yet, there might be no classic database to demonstrate in meetings with management and customers.

In our opinion, event sourcing is an important resource for architects. Each architect, though, might need to have his own epiphany with it and use it only when he feels okay and really sees event sourcing as the ideal solution to the problem. Our best advice, in fact, is this: don't use it if you don't see clear and outstanding benefits. Whether you fail to see benefits because no real benefits exist or because you're not seasoned enough to spot them is truly a secondary point.

While event sourcing is a powerful architecture that can be used to lay out nearly any system, it might not be ideal in all scenarios. Events are important in business scenarios where you deal with entities that have a long lifespan. Think, for example, of a booking system for resources like meeting rooms or tennis courts. It might be relevant to show the full history of the booking: when it was entered, who entered it, and when it was modified, postponed, or canceled. Events are also relevant in an accounting application that deals with invoices and job orders. It might be far easier to organize the business logic around events like an invoice issued as the first tranche payment of a given job order, an inbound invoice that needs to be registered, or a note of credit issued for a given invoice.

Events are probably not that useful in the sample online store scenario we discussed in past chapters. Is it really relevant to track down events like searched orders, the creation of orders, and Gold-status customers? These are definitely domain events you want to identify and implement. Their role in the domain is not central as it might be in previous examples. You might not want to set up a completely different and kind of revolutionary architecture just because you have a few domain events.

Our quick rule for event sourcing might be summarized as follows: if you can find one or more domain experts needing for the sequence of events you can produce, then event sourcing is an option to explore further. If events are only useful to concatenate pieces of logic and business rules, then those events are not first-class citizens in the domain and don't need to be persisted as events. Subsequently, you might need to implement an event sourcing architecture.

Event-sourcing architecture

Let's now focus on what you do when you decide to use events as the primary data source of your layered system. There are a couple of fundamental aspects to look into: persisting events and laying the groundwork for queries.

Persisting events

Events should be persisted to form an audit log of what happened in the system. In the rest of the chapter, you'll first see issues related to persisting events to a physical store. Then you'll tackle reading events back to rebuild the state of the aggregates, or whatever business entities you use to serve both the needs of the query side of the system and commands.

An event store is a plain database, except that it is not used to persist a data model. Instead, it persists a list of event objects. As mentioned, an event is a plain collection of properties that could easily fit in a single relational table if it weren't for the fact that an event store is expected to store several types of events. And each event will likely be a different collection of properties.

An event store has three main characteristics:

- It contains event objects made of whatever information is useful to rebuild the state of the object the event refers to.

- It must be able to return the stream of events associated with a given key.

- It works as an append-only data store and doesn't have to support updates and deletions.

Event objects must refer in some way to a business object. If you're using the Domain Model pattern to organize the business logic of the command stack of the architecture, the event store must be able to return the stream of events associated with an aggregate instance. If you're not using the Domain Model pattern, you have some relevant business objects in the model, anyway. It could be, for example, some *OrderTableModule* object if you're using the Table Module pattern. In this case, the event data must contain some key value that uniquely identifies the relevant business object. For example, events that refer to orders should contain something like the ID of the specific order the event refers to.

Events and the overall flow of business logic

Before we go any further with the details of event-sourcing architecture and the event store, we want to make an important point as clear as possible.

Event sourcing is essentially about capturing all changes to an application state as a sequence of events. Events, however, are atomic pieces of information. Imagine the following stream of recorded events:

- Order #123 is created by customer Xyz. The event record contains all details about the order.

- Customer Xyz changed the shipping address for order #123. The event record contains the new address.

- Order #123 is processed.

- Customer Xyz changed the default shipping address. The event record contains the new shipping address.

- Order #123 is shipped.

Each event is a record in the event store, but each event reports about a specific fact that has happened. The current state of the application results from the combined effect of all events. Every time a command is placed, the current state of the system (or just the current state of the involved business entities) must be rebuilt from the stream of events.

Options for an event store

At the end of the day, an event store is a database. What kind of database, however? Generally speaking, there's no restriction whatsoever: an event store can be a relational DBMS, any flavor of a NoSQL database (document, key-value), or even an XML file. This said, really viable options are probably only a couple:

- **Relational DBMS**   An event store can be as easy to arrange as creating a single relational table where each row refers to an event object. The problem here is with the different layout of event objects. There's no guarantee that all event classes you need to store can be massaged to fit a single schema. In situations where this can be done and results in acceptable performance, by all means we recommend you go with a classic relational DBMS. Unfortunately, we don't expect this situation to be that common. In addition, consider that there's no guarantee either that the structure of an event won't change over time. If that happens, you must proceed with an expensive restructuring of the storage. A possible way to neutralize schema differences is using a sort of key-value storage in a relational storage, where the key column identifies the aggregate and the value column refers to a JSON-serialized collection of properties.

- **Document database**   When it comes to persistence, a *document* is defined as an object that has a variable number of properties. Some NoSQL products specialize in storing documents. You create a class, fill it with values, and just store it as is. The type of the class is the key information used to relate multiple objects to one another. This behavior fits perfectly with expectations set for an event store. If you use a document database such as RavenDB (which you can check out at *http://ravendb.net*), you have no need to massage event data into something else. You have an event object and just save it.

  A side effect of most document databases is *eventual consistency*. Eventual consistency is when reads and writes are not aligned to the same version of the data. Most NoSQL systems are eventually consistent in the sense that they guarantee that if no updates are made to a given object for a sufficiently long period of time, a query actually returns what the last command has written. Otherwise, an old version of data is returned. Eventual consistency exists for performance reasons and is due to the combined effect of synchronous writes and asynchronous updates of indexes.

A third option you might want to consider is *column stores*—the most notable example of which is Microsoft SQL Server 2014. A column store is a regular relational table where data is stored using a columnar data format. Instead of having the table composed of rows sharing the same schema, in a column store you have columns treated like entities independent from rows. Columns are related to one another by some primary-key value. In SQL Server 2014, columnar storage is enabled by creating an ad hoc index on a regular table. In SQL Server 2014, the column store index is updatable.

Note Event sourcing is a relatively young approach to architecture. Tools for helping with code don't exist yet, meaning that the risk of reinventing the wheel is high and no ad hoc specialized tools are available. As far as the event store is concerned, a first attempt to create a highly specialized event store is the NEventStore project: *http://neventstore.org*.

Tales from the trenches

An event store is expected to grow to be a very large container of data, which poses new problems regarding performance. An event store is updated frequently and receives frequent reads for large chunks of data.

It's really hard to say which of the three options just presented is ideal in the largest number of business scenarios. If we look only at technical aspects, we'd probably go for document databases. In this regard, RavenDB—a full .NET document database with a few interesting setup models—is worth a further look. Or, at least, RavenDB has worked just fine so far in all scenarios in which Andrea used it.

Dino, instead, has a different story to tell. A customer of his actually decided to go with a key-value relational table after considering both a SQL Server 2014 column store and RavenDB. After a week of performance measurement, the team didn't find in the tested scenario any significant throughput improvement resulting from column and document stores. Anyway, the customer had debated for a long time whether to go with a document database (RavenDB) or a plain SQL Server table. In the end, they opted for a plain SQL Server table because of the ecosystem of tools and documentation existing for SQL Server and the existing skills of the IT department. And in spite of the additional costs of SQL Server licenses, which were a fraction of the overall cost of the product.

Replaying events

The main treat of event sourcing is the persistence of messages, which enables you to keep track of all changes in the state of the application. By reading back the log of messages, you can rebuild the state of the system. This aspect is also known as the *replay of the events*.

Building the state of business entities

Let's consider the Checkout example again. A given user completes a purchase and, at the end of the saga, you might have records in the event store similar to those listed in Table 12-1.

TABLE 12-1. Event log for the Checkout saga

Event	Description	Properties
GoodsAreInStock	For the content of the given shopping cart, goods in stock were sufficient.	None
PaymentCompleted	Payment was completed successfully.	Transaction ID, customer details
ShippingApproved	Shipping company approved the delivery request and assigned a tracking ID.	Tracking ID
OrderCreated	The order has been entered into the system.	Order ID, full details of the order

When the *OrderCreated* event is persisted, it saves all the details of the order—ID, date, shipping date, shipping address, customer name, ordered items, and invoice number. Later on, when the goods ship to the customer, the bounded context taking care of delivery does something that triggers an *OrderShipped* event persisted as shown here:

OrderShipped	The order has been shipped to the customer.	Order ID, Tracking ID, time of delivery

The system contains a detailed log of what's happened, but what about the following two points?

- How could the saga accepting the shipment of the order verify that the operation was consistent and that, say, the order ID marked as shipped was really an order marked as in-delivery?

- How can an admin user know about the current state of a given order?

In a classic scenario where O/RM tools are used to persist a domain model, you probably have an Orders table with a row for each created order. Reading the state of the order is as easy as making a query. How does that work in an event-sourcing scenario?

To know about the state of an order (or a business entity in general), you need to go through the list of recorded events, retrieve those related to the specific order (or entity), and then in some way replay the events on an empty order to materialize an instance that faithfully represents the real state.

What it means to replay events

The replay of events to rebuild the state works in theory, but it is not always practical. The canonical example is a bank account.

How many years ago did you open your bank account? Probably, it was quite a few years ago. This means that some *AccountCreated* event exists in an event store, but it is a few years old. Since then, some hundreds of events might have occurred on the same account to alter its state. In the end, to get the current balance, it could be necessary to replay several hundred operations to rebuild the current state of the account.

Replaying operations poses two problems. One is performance concerns; the other is the actual mechanics of the replay. The event store contains events—namely, memories of facts that happened; it doesn't contain the commands that generated those events. Persisting commands is a different matter; sometimes you do that; sometimes you don't. The execution of a command might take several seconds to complete, and not everybody is willing to wait ages to know, say, the balance of the bank account. On the other hand, if you intend to repeat the same sequence of actions that led to a given state, then events—that is, memories of what happened—might not be sufficient. In a what-if scenario, for example, you might want to know about actual commands and change some parameters to measure the effects.

This means that the replay of events is an operation that must be coded by looking carefully at events and the data they carry. For example, replaying the *OrderCreated* event requires creating a fresh new instance of an Order aggregate filled with all the information associated with the stored event. Replaying the *OrderShipped* event, instead, requires just the updating of some *State* property on the *Order* class.

 Note In many scenarios, however, the performance is not an issue because the replay of events is part of the asynchronous operations. Furthermore, often we're just talking about dozens of events that can be processed pretty quickly. If it is an issue, use data snapshots.

Data snapshots

To make a long story short, projecting state from logged events might be heavy-handed and impractical with a large number of events. And the number of logged events can only grow. An effective workaround consists of saving a snapshot of the aggregate state (or whatever business entities you use) at some recent point in time.

This can be done in either of two ways. You can update the aggregate at the end of each operation, or you can save the snapshot frequently (say, every 100 events), but not every time. In this way, when you need to access an aggregate, you load the most recent snapshot. If it is not already up to date, you replay all subsequent events.

Typically, a data snapshot is a relational table that contains the serialized version of an aggregate. More generally, a data snapshot is any sort of persistent cache you can think of that helps build the state quickly. There might be situations in which it can even grow very close to a classic relational database with cross-referenced tables. In this case, you end up with an event store and a relational database. There's quite a bit of redundancy but, at a minimum, the event store keeps track of the actual sequence of events in the system.

Note, though, that you might need snapshots only for some aggregates. In this way, redundancy will be reduced to just the most critical aggregates.

Data snapshots are essentially a way to simplify development and wed events with the state of business entities. Data snapshots are created by event handlers typically, but not necessarily, within the context of a saga. With reference to our previous Checkout saga example, the state of the created order can be saved to a snapshot right before raising the *OrderCreated* event, or you can have a distinct saga that just captures events and maintains snapshots.

Summary

Events are bringing new ideas and new lifeblood to software architecture. Events promote a task-based approach to analysis and implementation. As obvious as it might sound, any software that focuses on tasks to accomplish can't be wrong and won't miss its goals. Yet, architects neglected tasks for too long and focused on models.

Building a single, all-encompassing model is sometimes hard, and separation between commands and queries showed the way to go to build systems more effectively. Event sourcing is an approach essentially based on the idea that the state of the application is saved as a stream of events. As long as events are sufficiently granular, and regardless of the ubiquitous language, logging events allows you to record everything and, more importantly, start recording new events as they are discovered or introduced.

In event sourcing, the state of aggregates must be created every time events are replayed. Rebuilding state from scratch might be heavy-handed; that's why data snapshots are a valuable resource that can't be neglected.

In this chapter, we focused on the theoretical aspects of the event-sourcing architecture but didn't examine a working solution. That's precisely what we are slated to do in the next chapter.

Finishing with a smile

To generate a smile or two at the end of this chapter, we selected a few quotes we remember reading somewhere:

- If you find a bug in your salad, it's not a bug: it's a feature.

- Computers are like men because once a woman commits to one, she finds out that if she waited just a little longer, she could have had a better model.

- Computers are like women because even your smallest mistakes are stored in long-term memory for later retrieval.

In addition, here are a couple of funny quotes about computers and programming:

- Programming today is a race between software engineers striving to build bigger and better idiot-proof programs and the universe trying to produce bigger and better idiots. So far, the universe is winning. (Rick Cook).

- The trouble with programmers is that you can never tell what a programmer is doing until it's too late. (Seymour Cray)

CHAPTER 13

Implementing event sourcing

It is not about bits, bytes and protocols, but profits, losses and margins.
—Lou Gerstner

Events are a new trend in the software industry, and new patterns and practices have been defined lately to work with events. Events go hand in hand with Command/Query Responsibility Segregation (CQRS) and help model today's complex business domains more effectively. To the application's eyes, an event is the notification of something that happened in the past. Some events are plain, data-less notifications of user actions and system reactions; other events carry additional data.

In some business scenarios, though, events represent more than just notifications and are close to being the true data source of the application. Whenever it makes sense for the business to keep track of "what happened" and not just the "last known good state," event sourcing—namely, logging the sequence of events in the lifetime of the application—becomes a relevant pattern.

In the last chapter, we discussed the theory of event sourcing; in this chapter, we go through a couple of examples. In the first example, we present the classic approach of event sourcing in which logged events related to an aggregate are replayed to build the current state of the aggregate. In the second example, we use a more optimized approach, one that probably builds on top of what a few developers with more gray hair than the two of us used to do in the past without giving it a fancy name like *event sourcing*. In particular, we will record events for tracking purposes, but we will also save the last known state of the aggregates of interest. In this way, rehydrating aggregates for further processing is much faster, because you can skip the replay of events entirely. We practiced this approach in a couple of projects without encountering any issues and, instead, gaining benefits in terms of simplicity and speed.

Event sourcing: Why and when

In past chapters, we worked out an online store example called I-Buy-Stuff. We first designed it around an ASP.NET MVC application and a full Domain Model. Next, we refactored it to CQRS and a command-based architecture. In the definition of the business logic, we identified a few core domain events such as *goods-not-in-stock* and *customer-reached-gold-status*. In a broader perspective, that also includes additional bounded contexts for site administration, shipping, and payment. We could also easily identify integration events to make the site context communicate with external bounded contexts.

This is not enough, however, to say that I-Buy-Stuff needs event sourcing.

> **Note** Recognizing events in the business domain and events for integrating different bounded contexts is not the same as needing and supporting event sourcing. Event sourcing is needed only when you find it beneficial for the expression of the business logic to use events as the real data source of the application. Event sourcing is about persisting events and rebuilding the state of the aggregates from recorded events.

Why event sourcing is a resource

Event sourcing is a relatively new design resource for architects and developers. While the name *event sourcing* is new, the core concepts behind it are not. Event sourcing, for example, is just a more effective way of doing CRUD (Create, Read, Update, Delete).

Going beyond CRUD

Nearly all business applications are concerned with data, and they save and read it. The data of an application describes the state of the application and, as the application evolves, it stores the latest consistent data. In other words, data is continuously overwritten. This is the essence of CRUD.

CRUD is a widely used approach in software and, in most cases, it just works. However, there are a few structural limitations in the CRUD approach. First and foremost, the history of changes is not maintained unless ad hoc countermeasures are taken, such as arranging a custom logging mechanism. Second, especially in highly collaborative applications, data-update conflicts can occur on a regular basis as multiple users possibly work on the same data.

> **Note** It might seem that we're presenting ourselves as those smart guys who, all of a sudden, spotted issues with CRUD. This is not the case, of course. With its pros and cons, CRUD is part of the history of software and widely used in the present day. What we're trying to do is put event sourcing in perspective and guide you to seeing the whole point of it—which is, as we see things, a way to surpass CRUD. In light of today's real-world complexity, going beyond CRUD will surely bring benefits to architects and end users.

Track everything, and rebuild as appropriate

As a design pattern, event sourcing formalizes an approach to data-driven systems that consists of tracking all data operations sequentially in an append-only store. The log of events becomes the primary data source. Any workable representation of data is built (and rebuilt) from the log of events.

Subsequently, event sourcing is a resource for architects and developers because it allows you to track everything that happens around the system and remains flexible enough to let architects extrapolate context and content for the application logic to process. Last but not least, context and content can be rebuilt any time using different business rules without touching the log of events. And the log of events can—with a quick change—start tracking new events.

Today's line-of-business applications

The real world is full of enterprise, line-of-business systems that in one way or another perform audit trails and track every single event around their data entities. Think, for example, of banking applications that don't simply tell you the balance of the account; instead, they list decades of transactions, and the tracked operations are used to replay the state of the account at any given date. Think also of accounting applications that must track all possible changes to invoices (change of date, address, credit note) to the point that printing an invoice can result only from replaying all events that affected the invoice over time.

You can also think of betting applications that, from a list of events, can extract pending bets and easily enable what-if scenarios to make predictions and generate statistics. A few years ago in Italy, a football match was decided by a harshly criticized penalty goal. Probably to gain more visibility, a betting agency decided to pay bets as if the penalty were never awarded. More recently, during World Cup 2014 Uruguay beat Italy. However, some controversial decisions of the referee inspired the same betting agency to also pay bets made on the draw. Rather than because of inspiration, we "bet" they made that decision on the wings of some what-if software simulation.

Event sourcing as a pattern was formalized only a few years ago. All such aforementioned applications existed for decades; some even were written in COBOL or Visual Basic 6. This is to say that event sourcing—in spite of the rather hyped-up name—is not heralding any new concept in software. For decades, each team worked out a solution for the same problem the best they possibly could. Finally, someone formalized it as a pattern.

As explained in Chapter 4, "Writing software of quality," patterns are not the law and are still subject to interpretation, adaptation, and refactoring. Event sourcing as a pattern goes hand in hand with storing events and replaying events to build up some state. This is just the mainstream approach; your way of dealing with these things might be a bit different and still equally effective.

When event sourcing is appropriate

Using events as the primary data source might not be ideal for all systems. Let's briefly think over the I-Buy-Stuff online store. Is it really crucial for all stakeholders to know about products added to and deleted from the shopping cart? Or what the most-viewed products are? Is it crucial to track the gold status of a customer and the entire history of that customer, such as when the status was first acquired, when it was lost, and maybe when it was re-acquired?

The answers are not obvious. They fall into the classic "It depends" category. So let's review suitable scenarios for event sourcing.

Suitable scenarios

The most compelling scenario for an event-sourcing implementation is when the business demands that the intent and purpose of data operations be captured. For example, if you are requested to display the activity of a user within a system—say, all travel-related bookings she made, modified, or canceled and all changes she made to her personal record (address, preferences, or credit card data)—then it is key that you track any operation and save it within the context of an event, such as user-modified-home-address event.

Other suitable scenarios for event sourcing exist too. One is when you need to perform some work on top of recorded events. You might want to be able to replay events to restore the (partial) state of the system, undo actions or roll back to specific points. More generally, event sourcing works well in all situations in which you need to decouple the storage of raw data from materialized models and aggregates built on top of that and strictly follow the business requirements.

As a pleasant side effect, event sourcing also might save you from the burden of controlling conflicting updates to data. All you do in this case is let each concurrent client just record an event and then replay events to build the resulting state of the involved aggregate.

Finally, you might want to use event sourcing when the domain itself is inherently event-based. In this case, storing events comes as a natural feature of the domain and requires minimal implementation effort. This is precisely the case of our first example.

Less-than-ideal scenarios

Event sourcing requires ad hoc software architecture and tools, and it needs architects and developers to do things they don't usually do. In a nutshell, you need a good reason to take the event sourcing route. Our general rule is that you don't need event sourcing unless your scenario matches one of the scenarios in the preceding paragraphs. More in detail, we'd also say the following:

- You don't need event sourcing if a classic CRUD system can do the job well.

- You don't need event sourcing if audit trails, rollback, and replay actions are not strictly required.

Interestingly, event sourcing is also often associated with the idea of *eventual consistency* and, subsequently, many suggest that event sourcing is not ideal for scenarios where you need real-time updates to the views. Based on our experience, we would say, "It actually depends."

Eventual consistency stems from the latency between recording the event and processing it. If synchronous processing of events is arranged, or if latency is kept to a bare minimum, you can happily have event sourcing in the context of real-time systems. Or at least this is what we've done on a couple of projects.

In the end, the key determining factor we recommend for deciding whether to use event sourcing is whether or not tracking events is relevant in the business domain.

Event sourcing and real-time systems

A real-time system is simply a system that must provide a valid response to a request within an agreed-upon amount of time. Failure is not an option for such a system. Failing to provide a usable response in the given interval might have significant repercussions on the business. For this reason, real-time systems are critical systems.

However, a real-time system is not necessarily a system that must provide a usable response instantaneously or in just a few milliseconds. If *real-time* meant just two or three milliseconds of tolerance, probably no implementation would be suitable. Any system constrained to return a response within a fixed amount of time is real-time regardless of the length of the interval.

Dino successfully applied event sourcing in a couple of systems that can easily be labeled as *real-time*. One is the infrastructure for generating live scores of professional tennis tournaments. Every single event for a given match is saved, and the score and statistics are calculated in the background. The calculated score, as well as up-to-date statistics and overlays, are offloaded to a distinct database for live-score clients to consume. We'll see a demo version of a live-score system later in the chapter.

Another example is the software used for monitoring room of wind-power plants. In this case, data captured by hardware sensors flows continually into the system and is just logged. Next, data is processed and grouped in data clumps that are logically more relevant and served to presentation clients.

Event sourcing with replay

There's little value in using event sourcing within the I-Buy-Stuff online store, at least given the limited set of requirements we assumed in past chapters. We could have just forced the demo to use event sourcing with the excuse that all we want, ultimately, is to give a practical demo of how to store and replay events. We decided, instead, to change examples—precisely pursuing the point that event sourcing is a resource and not a must, even for the demos of a book.

Likewise, we don't want to lead you to the wrong assumption: that e-commerce and online stores is not a domain where event sourcing can be successfully applied. It all depends on the bounded contexts you have and their requirements. If it is crucial for all stakeholders to know about the products a given user viewed or temporarily added to a shopping cart, event sourcing becomes the ideal way to implement that part of the system.

Once you determine that tracking events is useful for your application, implementing event sourcing follows the guidelines discussed next.

A live-scoring system

The first example we'll present is a live-scoring system for a water polo game. A live-scoring system generally consists of two distinct stacks: one that collects events taking place in the context of the game, and one that presents the current state of the game to clients such as web browsers and mobile apps.

This is quite a good example of an application that is naturally based on events. Using event sourcing here is straightforward and, given the relatively small number of events, using replay to rebuild the state of relevant aggregates is a no-brainer.

Overall layout of the system

Figure 13-1 presents the overall layout of the WaterpoloScoring sample system. It is based on an ASP.NET MVC application that referees (or, more likely, assistant referees or scorekeepers) use to tally goals. In a more realistic version, the system will also track players' fouls and penalties as well as shots that scored or missed.

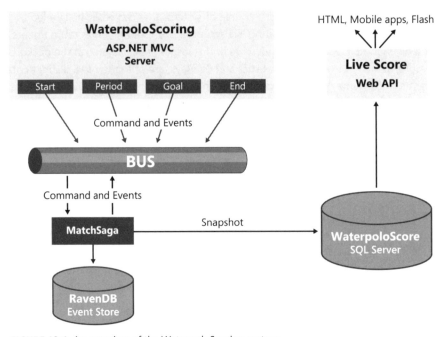

FIGURE 13-1 An overview of the WaterpoloScoring system.

The system consists of two main components: scoring and live-score modules. In the example, however, both components are managed as distinct screens within the same ASP.NET MVC application. In the end, the live-score view just invokes a Web API front end fed by snapshots created on top of recorded events.

Functional requirements

The scoring screen must provide the following functions:

- Start a match

- End a match

- Start a period

- End a period

- Score a goal for either team

- The ability to undo any of the previous actions

Each action generates an event that is saved to the event store. Each action also generates an event that indicates the need to refresh the snapshot database. The snapshot database contains the current state of the match in a format that is suited for live score applications—team names, current score, current period, whether the ball is in play, and a partial score for past periods.

FIGURE 13-2 A mockup for the scoring page of the sample application.

Implementation of the system

The water polo scoring system receives a bunch of UI messages when a button is clicked. Each button click is essentially the notification for a relevant match event, such as start, end, period, or goal. The request generated with the click is dispatched to the application layer and processed. The request is then redirected to the home page.

```
public ActionResult Action(String id)
{
    // We use a dispatcher here only because all buttons belong to
    // the same HTML form; subsequently, the same action is requested
    // regardless of the clicked button. We use this code here to
    // disambiguate.

    var action = MakeSenseOfWhatTheUserDid(Request);
    _service.Dispatch(id, action);
    return RedirectToAction("index", new {id = id});
}
```

The home page just reads back the current state of the match and refreshes the user interface accordingly:

```
public ActionResult Index(String id)
{
    var model = _service.GetCurrentState(id);
    return View(model);
}
```

The current state of the ongoing match is read, all events are replayed, and all of them are applied to a freshly created instance of the related aggregate. Let's find out more details.

The command bus

A scoring system is not rocket science; the most complex part is implementing the scoring rules. For a water polo match, scoring rules are trivial—you just sum up scored goals and that's it. However, a scoring system is hardly limited to just calculating the score. Often, you might want to generate statistics or overlays to be displayed by live clients such as mobile applications, HTML pages, or even Flash video clips displayed on LED walls.

You can easily implement the workflow behind each scoring event with plain, transaction script code. However, in this case, having a command bus and events doesn't really add a lot more complexity and keeps extensibility high. Once you have a command bus, everything comes together easily. For the command bus, we use the same component we discussed in Chapter 10, "Introducing CQRS." Here's the source code:

```
public class Bus
{
    private static readonly Dictionary<Type, Type> SagaStarters =
        new Dictionary<Type, Type>();
    private static readonly Dictionary<string, object> SagaInstances =
        new Dictionary<string, object>();
    private static readonly EventRepository EventStore = new EventRepository();

    public static void RegisterSaga<TStartMessage, TSaga>()
    {
        SagaStarters.Add(typeof(TStartMessage), typeof(TSaga));
    }
    public static void Send<T>(T message) where T : Message
    {
        // Check if the message can start one of the registered sagas
        if (SagaStarters.ContainsKey(typeof(T)))
        {
            // Start the saga, creating a new instance of the type
            var typeOfSaga = SagaStarters[typeof(T)];
            var instance = (IStartWithMessage<T>)Activator.CreateInstance(typeOfSaga);
            instance.Handle(message);

            // At this point the saga has been given an ID;
            // let's persist the instance to a (memory) dictionary for later use.
            SagaInstances[instance.SagaId] = instance;
        }
```

```
        // Check if the message can be handled by one of the existing sagas.
        if (message.SagaId == null)
            return;

        if (SagaInstances.ContainsKey(message.SagaId))
        {
            // Check compatibility between saga and message: can the saga handle THIS message?
            var sagaType = SagaInstances[message.SagaId].GetType();
            if (!typeof(ICanHandleMessage<T>).IsAssignableFrom(sagaType))
                return;

            var saga = (ICanHandleMessage<T>) SagaInstances[message.SagaId];
            saga.Handle(message);
        }

        // Publish and persist the event
        if (message is DomainEvent)
        {
            // Persist the event
            EventStore.Save(message as DomainEvent);

            // Invoke all registered sagas and give each
            // a chance to handle the event.
            foreach (var sagaEntry in SagaInstances)
            {
                var sagaType = sagaEntry.Value.GetType();
                if (!typeof(ICanHandleMessage<T>).IsAssignableFrom(sagaType))
                    return;

                // Give other sagas interested in the event a chance to handle it.
                // Current saga already had its chance to handle the event.
                var handler = (ICanHandleMessage<T>) sagaEntry.Value;
                if (sagaEntry.Key != message.SagaId)
                    handler.Handle(message);
            }
        }
    }
}
```

As you might have noticed, the list of saga instances is not stored in a permanent form of storage; instead, saga instances are kept in memory. This means that, while debugging the application, you won't be able to deliver messages to an existing saga; that works only within the same session.

The bus is the core of the scoring module; it receives messages from the application layer following the user's activity in the browser.

Supported events and commands

The user interface of the scoring application is shown in Figure 13-3. The page contains six buttons for the key events: match started, match ended, period started, period ended, goal scored by home, and goal scored by visitors. In addition, the user interface contains two more buttons: one to undo last action, and one to clear the event store for debugging purposes.

The click on the Zap button doesn't push any message to the bus; the action is handled directly within the application layer. Clicking on the Undo button pushes a command to the bus that the related saga handles. Clicking on any other buttons in the user interface pushes a plain event to the bus. The event is recorded by the bus and then published to registered sagas.

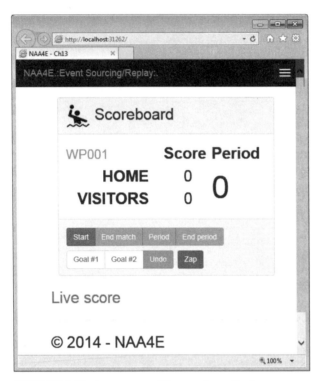

FIGURE 13-3 The home page of the sample application.

Right after each button click, the page collects the current state of the match and passes that to the view. The view looks at the state of the match and its score, and it enables or disables buttons as appropriate. The following code shows the implementation of the saga:

```
public class MatchSaga : SagaBase<MatchData>,
    IStartWithMessage<MatchStartedEvent>,
    ICanHandleMessage<MatchEndedEvent>,
    ICanHandleMessage<PeriodStartedEvent>,
    ICanHandleMessage<PeriodEndedEvent>,
    ICanHandleMessage<GoalScoredEvent>,
    ICanHandleMessage<MatchInfoChangedEvent>,
    ICanHandleMessage<UndoLastActionCommand>
{
    private readonly EventRepository _repo = new EventRepository();
    public void Handle(MatchStartedEvent message)
    {
        // Set the ID of the saga
        SagaId = message.MatchId;
```

```
                // Signal that match information has changed
                NotifyMatchInfoChanged(message.MatchId);
        }

        public void Handle(UndoLastActionCommand message)
        {
            _repo.UndoLastAction(message.MatchId);

            // Signal that match information has changed
            NotifyMatchInfoChanged(message.MatchId);
        }

        public void Handle(MatchEndedEvent message)
        {
            // Signal that match information has changed
            NotifyMatchInfoChanged(message.MatchId);
        }

        public void Handle(PeriodStartedEvent message)
        {
            // Signal that match information has changed
            NotifyMatchInfoChanged(message.MatchId);
        }

        public void Handle(PeriodEndedEvent message)
        {
            // Signal that match information has changed
            NotifyMatchInfoChanged(message.MatchId);
        }

        public void Handle(GoalScoredEvent message)
        {
            // Signal that match information has changed
            NotifyMatchInfoChanged(message.MatchId);
        }

        public void Handle(MatchInfoChangedEvent message)
        {
            SnapshotHelper.Update(message.MatchId);
        }

        private static void NotifyMatchInfoChanged(string matchId)
        {
            var theEvent = new MatchInfoChangedEvent(matchId);
            Bus.Send(theEvent);
        }
    }
}
```

The saga starts when the *MatchStartedEvent* is pushed to the bus. The saga ID coincides with the unique ID of the match:

```
// This message pushed to the bus starts the saga
var domainEvent = new MatchStartedEvent(matchId);
Bus.Send(domainEvent);
```

As you can see from the source code, most messages are plain notifications and don't require much more than just persistence. That's why we coded them as events. For example, here's how the application layer generates a notification that a goal has been scored:

```
// TeamId is an enum type defined in the domain model for the command stack
var command = new GoalScoredEvent(matchId, TeamId.Home);
Bus.Send(command);
```

In addition to plain persistence, the saga method for these events fires another event—the *MatchInfoChanged* event. The *MatchInfoChanged* event causes the saga to trigger the process that updates the snapshot database for live-score clients.

Undoing the last action

When the user clicks the Undo button in the user interface, a command is pushed to the bus instead. The Undo button sends a message through which the user actually tells the system to do something: delete the last recorded action as if it never happened.

```
var command = new UndoLastActionCommand(matchId);
Bus.Send(command);
```

The command is handled by the saga placing a call to the API that wraps up the event store. In general, the event store is append-only; in this case, we remove the last stored item because the undo functionality for the domain just means that the last action should be treated as if it never happened. However, nothing really prevents you from implementing the undo through a logical deletion. Some advanced scoring systems do exactly that to audit the activity of referees and collect usability information.

```
public void Handle(UndoLastActionCommand message)
{
    _repo.UndoLastAction(message.MatchId);

    // Signal that match information has changed
    NotifyMatchInfoChanged(message.MatchId);
}
```

The *UndoLastAction* method uses the storage API (either a classic SQL Server or a NoSQL document database) to retrieve the last event object and delete it. In our example, we use RavenDB for the event store. Here's the code we use:

```
public void UndoLastAction(String id)
{
    var lastEvent = (from e in GetEventStream(id) select e).LastOrDefault();
    if (lastEvent != null)
    {
        DocumentSession.Delete(lastEvent);
        DocumentSession.SaveChanges();
    }
}
```

The *GetEventStream* method is a helper method exposed by the event store application interface to retrieve the entire list of events for a given aggregate. Let's find out more about the event store.

Persisting events

The event store is just a persistent store where you save information about events. In general, an event is a data-transfer object (DTO)—a plain collection of properties. In light of this, an event can be easily persisted as a record of a SQL Server database table or to a NoSQL data store. (See Chapter 14, "The persistence layer," for more information about alternative data stores and polyglot persistence.)

When it comes to event stores, there are two main issues related to relational stores. One issue is the inherent cost of licenses for most popular relational stores. This might or might not be a problem, depending on the context, the business, the costs of software, the financial strength of customers, and so forth. The other issue is more technical: not all events have the same structure and set of properties. How would you go about modeling a table schema for all possible events of an application?

You can probably create a fixed schema of columns that accommodates known events. What if a new event is added or an event's description changes? Another approach entails having a relational table made of a few columns—such as aggregate ID, type of event, and a JSON-serialized dictionary with property values that characterize the event.

Yet another approach is not using a relational store and resorting to a document database such as RavenDB. This is what we did in our example. The following code shows what it takes to persist an event in a RavenDB store:

```
public class EventRepository
{
    private IDocumentSession DocumentSession { get; set; }

    public EventRepository()
    {
        DocumentSession = RavenDbConfig.Instance.OpenSession();
    }

    public void Save(DomainEvent domainEvent)
    {
        var eventWrapper = new EventWrapper(domainEvent);
        DocumentSession.Store(eventWrapper);
        DocumentSession.SaveChanges();
        return;
    }
    ...
}
```

You first initialize RavenDB in *global.asax* at the startup of the application and then use the created engine instance to open a session. Through the interface of the session, you then save and delete objects. Note that you might want to wrap events into a container class—the *EventWrapper* class of our example—so that all stored objects look to be of the same type regardless of the actual type:

```
public class EventWrapper
{
    public EventWrapper(DomainEvent theEvent)
    {
        TheEvent = theEvent;
    }
    public DomainEvent TheEvent { get; private set; }
}
```

Another solution that is gaining momentum is the NEventStore project. (See *http://neventstore.org*.) NEventStore is a persistence library specifically designed to address event-sourcing issues. It offers a unified API to persist events that intelligently hides different storage mechanisms.

Replaying events

In addition to saving events, the other key function one expects out of an event store is returning the full or partial stream of events. This function is necessary to rebuild the state of an aggregate out of recorded events. In RavenDB, getting the stream of events is as easy as in the following code:

```
public IEnumerable<EventWrapper> GetEventStream(String id)
{
    return DocumentSession
            .Query<EventWrapper>()
            .Where(t => t.MatchId == id)
            .OrderBy(t => t.Timestamp).ToList();
}
```

Replaying events consists of looping through the stream of events and applying them to a fresh instance of the related aggregate. In our example, we have a small domain model centered on the *Match* aggregate. The *Match* class has a method for nearly any significant change of state: start, end, new period, end of period, goal, and more.

Materializing an instance of *Match* consistent with tracked events requires the following pseudo-code.

> **Note** We call it *pseudo-code* because it essentially outlines the algorithm being used. The implementation would probably be slightly different and require some ad hoc design in the domain model classes.

```
public class EventHelper
{
    public static Match PlayEvents(String id, IEnumerable<DomainEvent> events)
    {
        var match = new Match(id);
        foreach (var e in events)
        {
            if (e == null)
                return match;

            if (e is MatchStartedEvent)
                match.Start();

            if (e is MatchEndedEvent)
                match.Finish();
            if (e is PeriodStartedEvent)
                match.StartPeriod();

            if (e is PeriodEndedEvent)
                match.EndPeriod();

            var @event = e as GoalScoredEvent;
            if (@event != null)
            {
                var actual = @event;
                match.Goal(actual.TeamId);
            }
        }

        return match;
    }
}
```

This code shows two aspects of event sourcing. First, it tells you that once you have events recorded you can do nearly everything. For example, you can easily enable a *What-If* analysis on your data; more importantly, you can do that at any time. In addition, you can materialize nearly any object out of events. It's just like having a lower level data source that can be used to populate any objects that make sense in your business domain. In this regard, an event data source is likely more powerful than a relational data model because it focuses on domain events rather than on a given data model for a given scenario.

Second, replaying events to build the state of an aggregate every time you need it can be quite a costly operation. It all depends on the number of events, actually. Replaying is not an issue in a scoring system—even in a sport like tennis that is one of the richest in terms of data and most frequently updated. A plain replay of events might not be suitable when the history of an aggregate lasts months or years for system activity, such as for a bank account.

Finally, regardless of the number of events you need to store and manage, the frequency at which you need to rebuild might be a constraint and an aspect to optimize to keep the application lean, mean, and scalable. This is where snapshots fit in.

Before we leap into snapshots, though, let's review a more realistic implementation of the pseudo-code just shown. When you design a domain model to support the replay of events, you typically define a set of *Apply* methods—overloaded—to take an event class parameter. Here's a possible implementation related to the *Match* class:

```
public void Apply(MatchStartedEvent theEvent)
{
    Start();
}
public void Apply(MatchEndedEvent theEvent)
{
    Finish();
}
...
```

Replaying events is then a plain loop that calls into *Apply* and passes the event object.

Creating data snapshots

In event sourcing, data snapshots are just snapshots of the state of an aggregate taken at a given time. You use snapshots to make it faster for an application to consume data that is stored only in the raw format of domain events. You can also see data snapshots as business-specific models built out of raw events.

There are no strict rules as far as data snapshots are concerned. You can decide to have no snapshots at all or multiple snapshots. You are also free of needing to choose the format and the persistence mechanism. A common way of using snapshots is to simplify queries and to expose data comfortably to other bounded contexts. Depending on the business domain, a snapshot can be updated after each operation (as in our example) or periodically through a scheduled job or even via a manual operation.

In our example, we use a SQL Server table to hold data ready for live-score clients that just shows the current state of a given match. Live-score clients don't access the event store; instead, they access a Web API front end that exposes the content of the data snapshot. It is up to you to decide the latency between any writing in the event store and updates to the live-score snapshot. Here's how the sample application updates the SQL Server snapshot database:

```
public class SnapshotHelper
{
    public static void Update(String matchId)
    {
        var repo = new EventRepository();
        var events = repo.GetEventStreamForReplay(matchId);
        var matchInfo = EventHelper.PlayEvents(matchId, events.ToList());
        using (var db = new WaterpoloContext())
        {
            var lm = (from m in db.Matches where m.Id == matchId select m).FirstOrDefault();
            if (lm == null)
            {
                var liveMatch = new LiveMatch
                {
```

```
                    Id = matchId,
                    Team1 = matchInfo.Team1,
                    Team2 = matchInfo.Team2,
                    State = matchInfo.State,
                    IsBallInPlay = matchInfo.IsBallInPlay,
                    CurrentScore = matchInfo.CurrentScore,
                    CurrentPeriod = matchInfo.CurrentPeriod
                };
                db.Matches.Add(liveMatch);
            }
            else
            {
                lm.State = matchInfo.State;
                lm.IsBallInPlay = matchInfo.IsBallInPlay;
                lm.CurrentScore = matchInfo.CurrentScore;
                lm.CurrentPeriod = matchInfo.CurrentPeriod;
                lm.ScorePeriod1 = matchInfo.GetPartial(1).ToString();
                lm.ScorePeriod2 = matchInfo.GetPartial(2).ToString();
                lm.ScorePeriod3 = matchInfo.GetPartial(3).ToString();
                lm.ScorePeriod4 = matchInfo.GetPartial(4).ToString();
            }
            db.SaveChanges();
        }
    }
}
```

In the sample application, we use Entity Framework Code First to create the snapshot. Figure 13-4 shows the web live score client in action.

FIGURE 13-4 The live-score client in action.

Note that the information presented by the live-score client is the current state of the match, but it doesn't reflect the actual data stored in the event store—the data source of the application. The event store only signals that, say, Home scored a goal and that a new period has started. All the details about the current score and current period are figured out while replaying events to build a *Match* instance.

The rebuilt *Match* instance is used to refresh the user interface of the scoring page (as in Figure 13-3). It is also used to serialize a *LiveMatch* object to a denormalized SQL Server database made to measure for just the information required by live-score clients—expanded name of teams, partial scores of periods, the current score, the current period, statistics, overlays, and whatever else your customers can think of.

Event sourcing with aggregate snapshots

The second example we offer uses a different approach for rehydrating instances of aggregates. The system maintains a log of events, and each recorded event has a unique ID that refers to the aggregate. The ID of the aggregate is also used to identify the saga. Whenever an event is tracked that relates to the aggregate instance, a reference to it is added to an internal aggregate collection. In this way, each aggregate instance carries its own list of events. At some point, the aggregate with its current state is persisted and the next time it is requested it will be retrieved from the persistence layer. In this way, there's no need to replay events to build a valid aggregate instance; all you do is materialize the aggregate from an additional persistence layer. In other words, you have a first level of snapshots represented by plain instances of readymade aggregates. These snapshots might be enough to serve the need of the presentation; if not, you add a second level of snapshots specifically designed for the purposes of the read model and presentation layers.

A mini enterprise resource planning system

The primary point of this example is to show an alternate technique for persisting events and rebuilding a valid aggregate instance. Setting up a fully functional, albeit partial, enterprise resource planning (ERP) system is beyond the scope of this chapter.

Managing job orders and extensions

The system is based on a single entity—the *JobOrder* entity—which is characterized by properties like customer ID, name and number, price, date of start, due date, and state. As you start on a project— whatever type of project—it is not unusual that requests for change are made and approved. So from the perspective of the architect of an ERP system, the *JobOrder* has its price change over time and also the due date might be postponed.

Other requirements you likely have on an ERP system are managing payments, installment payments, invoices, and credit notes, In a nutshell, ERP is a good domain to exercise events and the persistence of events. This is because the domain model cannot really be frozen and because the nature of the domain itself supports maintaining entities with its own bag of events that can alter the state.

Modeling a job order

How would you model a job order? The following is probably a good starting point for a realistic *JobOrder* class:

```
public class JobOrder : Aggregate
{
    public decimal Price { get; private set; }
    public int CustomerId { get; private set; }
    public string Number { get; private set; }
    public DateTime DateOfStart { get; private set; }
    public DateTime DueDate { get; private set; }
    public string Name { get; private set; }
    public bool IsCompleted { get; private set; }

    protected JobOrder()
    {
    }

    // Possibly more code here
    ...
}
```

How would you handle changes in the implementation of the job, such as a new due date and a new price? In this case, it is key to be able to track when the extension was requested and the terms of it. Also, in this business domain you must be ready to handle multiple extensions to a job order. Events are ideal.

When a new job order is registered in the system, you log an event with all the details of the order. When an extension is registered, you just log the new due date and price. Let's say the *JobOrder* class has a method like the one shown here:

```
public void Extend(DateTime newDueDate, decimal price)
{
    this.DueDate = newDueDate;
    this.Price = price;

    // Do something here to cause this event to be logged
    // so that the system knows that the current instance of JobOrder
    // was actually extended.
}
```

As you can see, the domain lends itself to having plain instances extended with some events. In this business domain, there's no need for undo functionalities as in the previous demo. When undo is an option, you might want to always replay all events to determine the actual state. When undo is not an option, you can save yourself a lot of work by not replaying events and, instead, saving snapshots of aggregates.

Implementation of the system

The mini ERP sample application is a CQRS system with a command-based architecture. There's a bus that receives commands from the application layer and triggers a saga. Figure 13-5 summarizes the main points of the architecture.

As you can see for yourself, the architecture is similar to Figure 13-1. The main difference is a second database that stores the state of aggregate instances with the declared intent of not replaying all events for the same aggregate. This requires the definition of an ad hoc repository and also some changes to the structure of the aggregate classes.

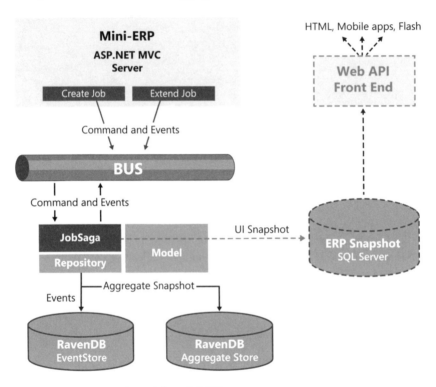

FIGURE 13-5 An overview of the mini-ERP system.

Revised definition of aggregates

Our mini-ERP example uses a domain model in the command stack. The most prominent class in the domain model is *JobOrder*, which is clearly an aggregate. In past chapters, we gave a very basic definition of the *IAggregateRoot* interface used to mark aggregate roots. Let's consider now a revised definition that also incorporates events.

```
public interface IAggregateRoot
{
    Guid Id { get; }
    bool IsChanged { get; }
    IEnumerable<DomainEvent> GetUncommittedEvents();
    void ClearUncommittedEvents();
}
```

In particular, we have a Boolean property to indicate pending changes to the aggregate and a method to return the list of pending events that relate to the instance but have not been persisted and notified yet. Finally, we also need a method to clear the list of pending events. Here's an abstract class that can be used as the starting point for concrete aggregate implementations:

```
public abstract class Aggregate : IAggregateRoot
{
    public Guid Id { get; protected set; }
    private IList<DomainEvent> uncommittedEvents = new List<DomainEvent>();

    Guid IAggregateRoot.Id
    {
        get { return Id; }
    }

    bool IAggregateRoot.IsChanged
    {
        get { return this.uncommittedEvents.Any(); }
    }

    IEnumerable<DomainEvent> IAggregateRoot.GetUncommittedEvents()
    {
        return uncommittedEvents.ToArray();
    }

    void IAggregateRoot.ClearUncommittedEvents()
    {
        uncommittedEvents.Clear();
    }

    protected void RaiseEvent(DomainEvent @event)
    {
        uncommittedEvents.Add(@event);
    }
}
```

Note the protected method *RaiseEvent*, which is used to add an event to the list of uncommitted events of the aggregate. This method will be invoked from within the aggregate to add events internally as methods on the public interface are invoked in sagas.

The *JobOrder* class we mentioned and partially unveiled earlier in the chapter is completed by the following code:

```
public void Extend(DateTime newDueDate, decimal price)
{
    this.DueDate = newDueDate;
    this.Price = price;

    // Raise the JobOrderExtended event and add it to the
    // internal list of uncommitted events maintained by the aggregate.
    var theEvent = new JobOrderExtendedEvent(this.Id, this.DueDate, this.Price);
    RaiseEvent(theEvent);
}
```

When an existing order is extended, the *JobOrderExtended* event is fired. This is a plain domain event and is added to the list of events managed by the aggregate instance. When the aggregate is saved, the event is persisted and notified to all registered listeners, if any.

Revised definition of the aggregate repository

In a CQRS system with a command-stack domain model, you typically have a repository that saves aggregates to some relational store via Entity Framework or any other Object/Relational Mapper (O/RM). When you adopt event sourcing, you typically replace the canonical relational data model with a log of events. As you saw in the previous example, you create an *EventRepository* class to manage the persistence of events in an append-only fashion.

In an architecture like that shown in Figure 13-5, you need an event repository but also a canonical aggregate repository. The aggregate repository, however, needs to have a slightly different structure than in the previous chapters:

```
public class Repository<T> where T : IAggregate
{
    public void Save(T item)
    {
        // Apply pending events to the current
        // instance of the aggregate
        item.GetUncommittedEvents()
            .ToList()
            .ForEach(e => ManageEvent(e));
        item.ClearUncommittedEvents();

        // Persist aggregate snapshot here
        ...
    }

    private void ManageEvent(DomainEvent e)
    {
        // Log the event to the event store
        ...

        // Notify the event via the bus
        ...
    }
```

```
    public T GetById(Guid id)
    {
        // Rehydrate the aggregate snapshot
        ...
    }
}
```

When the saga attempts to save the aggregate, all events attached to the instance are processed, each is logged, and notification is sent to the handlers. Next, the state of the aggregate is persisted as usual. In the end, the persisted aggregate is a snapshot created for the purposes of the command stack.

How sagas deal with aggregates and events

Let's find out how a saga can deal with aggregates and bind domain events to instances. Here are a couple of handlers for commands that create a new job-order and extend it:

```
public void Handle(CreateJobOrderCommand message)
{
    var jobOrder = new JobOrder(
            message.CustomerId,
            message.Price,
            message.DateOfStart,
            message.DueDate,
            message.JobOrderName);
    var repository = new Repository<JobOrder>();
    repository.Save(jobOrder);

    // Sets the saga ID
    this.Id = jobOrder.Id;

    // Notify the "created" event to all listeners
    var theEvent = new JobOrderCreatedEvent(
            jobOrder.Id,
            jobOrder.CustomerId,
            jobOrder.Price,
            jobOrder.DateOfStart,
            jobOrder.DueDate,
            jobOrder.Name,
            jobOrder.Number);
    Bus.RaiseEvent(theEvent);
}

public void Handle(ExtendJobOrderCommand message)
{
    var repository = new Repository<JobOrder>();
    var jobOrder = repository.GetById(message.JobOrderId);

    // This line modifies the state of the aggregate and causes
    // the "extended" event to be added to the aggregate list
    jobOrder.Extend(message.NewDueDate, message.Price);

    // Persisting the aggregate will log/notify pending events
    repository.Save(jobOrder);
}
```

In the previous live-scoring example, the aggregate *Match* was not maintaining the list of related events internally. The event was processed by the saga, saved, and notification was sent outside the aggregate. In this example, we're taking a route that is becoming increasingly popular: giving each aggregate the chance to handle its own events. Both approaches work; choosing which one to use is up to you. Keep in mind that your choice should be made to preserve and improve clarity and readability. And, why not, also performance!

Event replays vs. aggregate snapshots

Event sourcing should be a natural choice—you just use it if it is important to track events and easier to do that and build state from there. When it comes to this, you have two options: replay events to build the state of the aggregate, or persist the aggregate as a snapshot. At the moment, you can read opinions—mostly strong opinions—about either approach. It might seem like replaying events is the only way to go. In the end, replaying events seems like the approach that works in all situations. However, optimizations are often possible, depending on the characteristics of the domain. There's no reason for not pursuing optimizations.

In our opinion, it is desirable to arrive at a point in which any aggregate chooses its own rehydration strategy—replay or snapshots—and to have an underlying repository that behaves accordingly. In general, we tend to recommend snapshots for general event sourcing and event replay when there's the chance in the business domain that something happened to invalidate the persisted state. A good example of this is when some undo functionality should be implemented. Another good example is when you need to build the state of an aggregate until a given date. In these cases, there's no alternative to the plain replay of events.

Summary

Event sourcing is certainly about using events; however, much more than this, event sourcing is about using events as the persistence layer of the system. When you opt for event sourcing, you don't store data according to a canonical, object-oriented or relational model. You just log events as they happen instead.

Next, when business logic should be applied, you need to materialize programmable objects from the event store. How do you do this? You can start from blank instances of aggregates (if you're using a domain model) or plain entities and apply all logged events. In this way, you rebuild the entire history of the application for each and every request. As you can see, this approach might work just fine in some scenarios (for example, in a live-scoring system) but not in others (for example, in a banking application). It all depends on the number of events and how easy it could be to apply their effect to objects. Sometimes, it is also a matter of performance.

Another approach is logging events and snapshots of the key aggregates. In this case, you don't replay events but just deserialize an object from some database—either a NoSQL or relational database. The two strategies can also be mixed by having snapshots up to time *T* and replaying all successive events.

This chapter closes the part of the book dedicated to modeling. In the next chapter, we address persistence and focus on technologies and patterns for saving data. In particular, we'll talk about NoSQL and Entity Framework as well as polyglot persistence.

Finishing with a smile

Events are part of life, and their occurrence is usually considered to be quite an important thing for the people involved. For this reason, getting some fun quotes about events related to programming was not that hard. Here are some we took from here and there on the Internet:

- Give a man a program, frustrate him for a day. Teach a man to program, frustrate him for a lifetime. (Muhammad Waseem)

- The most disastrous thing that you can ever learn is your first programming language. (Alan Kay)

- Programs must be written for people to read, and only incidentally for machines to execute. (Hal Abelson)

- What is the object-oriented way of getting rich? Inheritance, of course. (Anonymous)

- When in doubt, use brute force. (Ken Thompson)

- If brute force doesn't solve your problems, then you aren't using enough. (Ken Thompson)

- Good judgment comes from experience, and experience comes from bad judgment. (Fred Brooks)

- Computers are like bikinis. They save people a lot of guesswork. (Sam Ewing)

Infrastructure

CHAPTER 14

The persistence layer

The possession of facts is knowledge; the use of them is wisdom.
—*Thomas Jefferson*

There was a time in which most of the effort involved in the design and building of a software system was about designing and building a data access layer. The role of the data model was crucial and central to the organization of the rest of the system. The data model—and more often than not, the relational data model—was the first and most important step on the agenda.

Is this step really no longer the most important step today in the building of a software system?

The advent of Domain-Driven Design (DDD) set the ground for a paradigm shift in which it's the business, and no longer the data, that is the foundation of the software design. As discussed in Chapter 8, "Introducing the Domain Model," when you do DDD you're not necessarily using an object-oriented model. For example, you could have a functional model instead. In any case, the introduction of a conceptual model—whether it's object-oriented or functional—makes the persistence of data a secondary aspect.

To the application's eyes, the source of data is no longer the physical database. It is, instead, the logical model built on top of the business domain. For obvious reasons, the logical model has to be persisted. However, this becomes a simpler infrastructure concern, and persistence is not even necessarily strictly bound to relational database management systems (DBMS).

In this chapter, we analyze the persistence layer—namely, the portion of the system's infrastructure that deals with the persistence of data. We'll first define what is expected to be in the persistence layer and then focus on the patterns and implementation details.

Portrait of a persistence layer

At some point, almost all software these days needs to access infrastructure components for reading data, presenting data back to the user, or saving results. With the advent of DDD, the segment of code that deals with reading and writing data that survives sessions has been segregated from the core of the system. The *persistence layer* is the name commonly used to refer just to the segment of code that knows about the nitty-gritty details of data access: connection strings, query languages, indexes, JSON data structures, and the like.

Responsibilities of the persistence layer

Let's start by identifying the responsibilities of a persistence layer. The persistence layer is usually created as a class library and is referenced by the domain layer (specifically, domain services) as well as the application layer. In turn, the persistence layer references any data-access-specific technology, whether an Object/Relational Mapper (O/RM) such as Entity Framework or NHibernate, ADO.NET, a NoSQL database, or even external data services.

Saving permanent data

The persistence layer offers a bunch of classes that, first and foremost, know how to save data permanently. Permanent data is data processed by the application and available for reuse at a later time. Note that not every system today needs to write data of its own.

Sometimes you are called to write just a segment of a larger system—a bounded context of a top-level architecture. It might be that you are just given a set of URLs to get or save data. Yet, the system needs to have a sort of black hole where calls for data persistence end up. This is the persistence layer.

Handling transactions

Especially if you use the Domain Model pattern, you might need to perform write operations in the context of a transaction—sometimes even a distributed transaction. The persistence layer should be aware of the transactional needs of the application. However, the persistence layer should handle in person only transactions that form a unit of work around some data access.

More concretely, this means that the persistence layer should take care of updating multiple tables within the boundaries of an aggregate in a single unit of work. The persistence layer, however, should not be involved in the handling of broader transactions that involve other components and take place within an application service (or a *saga* if you use an event-driven architecture).

In a nutshell, the transactional responsibilities of the persistence layer don't exceed the boundaries of plain data access in the context of a data aggregate. Everything else should be taken care of at a higher level either through the Microsoft .NET *TransactionScope* class, distributed transactions, or just step-by-step rollback/compensation policies within the use-case workflow.

Reading permanent data

The persistence layer is in charge of reading data from any permanent store, either database tables, files, or HTTP services. Especially in a Command/Query Responsibility Segregation (CQRS) scenario, the persistence layer that focuses on reading data might be physically separated from the persistence layer that deals with commands and writes.

For performance reasons, it might be desirable that reading is offloaded to distinct servers and leverages cached data. This is a key aspect for any systems that need to serve millions of pages on a monthly basis. Surprisingly, for such sites (think, for example, of news and media sites or airline and booking sites) caching is far more important than algorithms, *gzip*-ping results, grouping scripts at the bottom, or taking advantage of other tips commonly associated with the idea of improving web performance.

The persistence layer is also the ideal place to centralize some caching strategy for the content of the data source.

Design of a Repository pattern

Today, the persistence layer is traditionally implemented using the *Repository* pattern. A repository is a class where each method represents an action around the data source—whatever that happens to be. This said, the actual structure of the repository classes might vary quite a bit in different scenarios and applications. Let's review the basics of the pattern first.

The Repository pattern

According to Martin Fowler, a repository is a component that mediates between the domain model and data-mapping layers using a collection-like interface for accessing domain objects. (See *http://martinfowler.com/eaaCatalog/repository.html*.) This definition seems to closely match the public interface of the root context object that most O/RM frameworks expose.

A repository is expected to wrap up as collections all persistent data to be managed. Collections can be queried and updated. In a nutshell, a repository is just the interfacing layer that separates the domain model (or, more in general, the business logic) from data stores.

While the definition from Fowler is broadly accepted, it's still a bit too abstract and doesn't drill down into concrete aspects of implementation. A repository impersonates the persistence layer and is expected to have the same responsibility we just outlined. The repository performs data access using one or multiple specific data-access technologies, such as Entity Framework, NHibernate, ADO.NET, and so forth.

Figure 14-1 provides a view of how a repository fits in a layered architecture. Recall, as discussed in Chapter 8, that you should aim at having one repository class per aggregate.

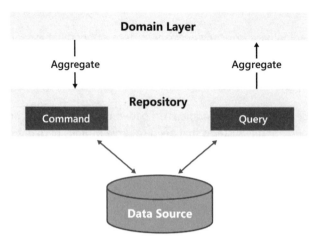

FIGURE 14-1 Fitting a repository in a layered architecture.

Having repositories is a common practice today, though repositories might take slightly different forms in different applications. The benefits of having repositories can be summarized in the following points:

- Achieves separation of concerns

- Reduces the potential for duplicate data-access code

- Increases the amount of testable code in the application and domain layers by treating data-access code as an injectable component

In addition, a set of well-isolated repository classes lays the groundwork for some applications to be deployed with one of a few possible data-access layers targeting different databases.

> **Important** Honestly, we don't think that scenarios where the same application must be able to support radically different data sources in different installations are as common as many seem to think. Sure, there might be applications that need be designed to support Oracle, SQL Server, or perhaps MySQL data stores. Overall, we believe that these applications are not common. It is much more common that applications use just one data source that might change over time as the product evolves. Having repositories surely helps when switching data sources, but this is not an everyday scenario.

The Unit of Work pattern

What's the granularity of a repository? Would you use a single repository class for the entire data source? Or should you use a repository class for each aggregate? (As mentioned in Chapter 8, the term *aggregate* is specific to the Domain Model; however, it is a rather general concept for which you end up having some sort of implementation in most cases, even if you don't use the Domain Model.)

Whether you envision the repository as the persistence layer of a single aggregate or as a single entry point for the entire data source, the implementation must be aware of the *Unit of Work* (UoW) pattern.

UoW is defined as the list of operations that form a business transaction. A component, like the repository, that supports the pattern coordinates the writing out of changes in a single physical transaction, including the resolution of concurrency problems. The definition is taken from *http://martinfowler.com/eaaCatalog/unitOfWork.html*.

At the end of the day, supporting units of work means enabling callers to arrange logical transactions by composing together operations exposed by the repository. A repository built on top of, say, Entity Framework will likely use the *DbContext* object to create a unit of work that will be transactionally persisted by calling the *SaveChanges* method.

Repository pattern and CQRS

Today the design and implementation of repositories is bound to the supporting architecture of choice. If you do CQRS, you typically want to have repositories only in the command stack—one repository class per aggregate. The command stack repository will be limited to write methods (for example, *Save*) and one Get method capable of returning an aggregate by ID. We'll detail the structure of such a command repository in the next section.

In a CQRS scenario, the read stack doesn't typically need a set of repository classes. As discussed in Chapter 10, "Introducing CQRS," and Chapter 11, "Implementing CQRS," in CQRS the query stack is fairly thin and consists only of a data-access layer (for example, based on LINQ and Entity Framework) that returns data-transfer objects (DTOs) ready for the presentation layer. You just don't need the extra complexity of an additional layer like repositories.

Repository pattern and Domain Model

When the supporting architecture is Domain Model, you have a single domain layer with no explicit separation between the command and query stack. We thoroughly discussed this architecture in Chapter 8 and Chapter 9, "Implementing the Domain Model."

In a Domain Model scenario, like the one presented in the Evans' book, you have a single repository per aggregate. The repository class will handle both queries and commands. The implementation of the aggregate repository, therefore, will have methods like *Save* and *Delete* as well as a bunch of query methods (depending on the specific needs of the domain) that return ad hoc DTOs as appropriate.

> **Important** At this point in the book, we wouldn't be surprised to find out that readers are deeply debating the role of the Domain Model pattern. The question we want to raise is, does it really make sense any more to go with a single stack as in the Domain Model instead of a more flexible and lightweight CQRS architecture? We consider CQRS to be the state-of-the-art architecture today for any sort of bounded context that requires a bit of complexity beyond basic two-tier CRUD. In light of this, the only type of repository class you are going to write is what we call here the "command" repository. It's the only repository you likely need today, whether you do CQRS or Domain Model. If you do Domain Model, however, you just add more query methods to the interface outlined next.

The interface of a command repository

Whether you use CQRS or Domain Model, you likely need a repository for write actions to be performed on the aggregates.

A repository is based on a generic interface; the interface is usually defined in the domain layer. The implementation of the interface, on the other hand, usually goes in a separate assembly part of the infrastructure layer. Here's the interface that represents a common starting point for all repositories. Note that it might also be convenient to have a read-only property to access the UoW object:

```
public interface IRepository<TAggregate, in TKey> where TAggregate: IAggregateRoot
{
    TAggregate Get(TKey id);
    void Save(TAggregate aggregate);
    void Delete(TAggregate aggregate);
}
```

We have a few comments to make about this.

First, the *IAggregateRoot* marker interface to identify aggregate types is not strictly necessary, and you can even avoid it altogether if it turns out to be just a marker interface. You can just use *class* or *new()* in the *where* clause.

Second, using an aggregate type is highly recommended, but it is not infrequent to see repositories built for individual entities. This happens either because of a simple model that just doesn't have significant aggregate boundaries or because the designer can't see boundaries and ends up treating every domain entity as an aggregate.

Third, the *Delete* method seems to be an obvious requirement for a repository interface. However, this is true only if you look at repositories through the lens of CRUD and with a largely database-oriented mindset. In a real-world business domain, however, you don't delete anything. So if you really design your system paying full respect to the ubiquitous language—and build a ubiquitous language that faithfully reflects the business domain—you don't need a *Delete* method in all repositories. You likely have forms of logical deletions that end up being a variation of the *Save* method at the repository level.

Fourth, mostly the same can be said for the *Save* method, which encompasses the role that an *Add* method would have in a classic CRUD interface.

Finally, it makes sense to have a *Get* or *FindById* method that takes the aggregate ID and returns an aggregate instance.

Implementing repositories

The overall structure of a repository can be split in two main parts: query and update. In a CQRS solution, you might have two distinct sets of repositories (and for the query part probably no repositories at all). Otherwise, the same class incorporates both query and update methods. As mentioned, you will generally have a repository class for each aggregate or relevant entity in your system.

The query side of repositories

Built around an aggregate type, a repository might return an entire graph of objects. Think, for example, of an *Order* type. When you implement the *FindById* method, what are you going to retrieve and return? Most likely, the order information—all details and information about the customer and products. Maybe not in this case, but this approach in general lays the ground for a potentially large graph to retrieve and return to upper layers.

What could be an alternate approach?

Options for prototyping query methods

The first option that comes to mind is having multiple query methods that address different scenarios, such as methods that return a different projection of the same data (fewer properties, fewer calculated properties, or both) or an incomplete graph of objects.

This option makes up for a rather bloated repository class, at least for some of the aggregates. To cut the number of methods short, you can have a single method that accepts a predicate through which you specify the query criteria. Here's an example:

```
IEnumerable<TAggregate> FindBy(Expression<Func<TAggregate, bool>> predicate);
```

A deeper analysis, however, reveals that the major problem of building the query side of a repository is not getting query criteria but is in what you return. Unless you choose to have individual methods for each scenario, the best you can do is return *IEnumerable<TAggregate>* as shown earlier.

The point is that in general there's no guarantee that once you've called a repository query method you're done and have exactly the data you need to present back to the users. When complex business logic is involved, more filters might need to be applied to reach the desired subset of data for a given use-case. In doing so, and also depending on the structure of your code, you might need to create and maintain multiple data-transfer objects (DTOs) on the view to the presentation layer.

Using DTOs also means using adapters and mapper classes to copy data from entities to DTOs, which means more complexity, at least as far as the number of classes (and unit tests) is concerned.

There's also a subtler point that goes against the use of predicates that return collections of aggregates. As an architect, you learn about the system to build from the *semantics* of the ubiquitous language. The ubiquitous language, though, also has a *syntax* made of specific verbs and names. When the domain expert says that the system must return all inbound invoices for more than $1,000 that have not been paid yet, she is actually referring to "inbound invoices" that are *then* filtered by "amount" and *then* further filtered by "payment state."

The following LINQ expression renders it clearly:

```
from invoice in Database.InboundInvoices
                        .NotPaid()
where invoice.Total > 1000;
```

The preceding code snippet is a plain description of the query to write, and it is fairly expressive because it is based on a number of custom extension methods. The preceding code snippet has neither multiple database queries nor multiple LINQ in-memory queries built on top of a single database query that initially returns all invoices.

What you see is an abstract query that can be built in a single place—a repository method—or across multiple layers, including repositories, the domain layer, and the application layer. The query finally gets executed only when data is actually required—typically, in the application layer.

In short, we see two main options for building the query side of a repository class:

- Use a repository class with as many query methods as required and prototyped as appropriate. This option has the potential to introduce some code duplication and, in general, increases the size of the codebase because of the DTOs you might need to create at some point.

- Have very few query methods that return *IQueryable<TAggregate>* objects for the upper layers of the code to close the query by indicating the actual projection of data. This would define the actual query to run against the database. This approach minimizes the database load as well as the number of DTOs involved and keeps the overall size of the codebase to a minimum.

Our personal sentiment is that there's little value in having repositories for the query side of the system.

Note Returning *IQueryable* types is what we have defined in past chapters as *LET*, or *Layered Expression Trees*. In particular, you can refer to Chapter 10, for the pros and cons of LET.

Asynchronous query methods

Starting with version 6, Entity Framework supports asynchronous query operations. The *DbContext* class is enriched with a list of async methods, such as *ToListAsync*, *FirstOrDefaultAsync*, and *SaveChangesAsync*. Therefore, you can query and save using the popular *async* and *await* keywords that were introduced with .NET 4.5. Here's an example:

```
public async Task<IList<ExpenseCategoryV2DTO> GetExpenses()
{
    using (var db = new YourDataContext())
    {
        return await db.ExpenseCategories
                        .AsNoTracking()
                        .OrderBy(category => category.Title)
                        .Select(category => new Models.ExpenseCategoryV2DTO
                        {
                            Id = category.Id,
                            Title = category.Title,
                            DefaultAmount = category.DefaultAmount,
                            Version = "Version 2"
                        }).ToListAsync();
    }
}
```

Note The *AsNoTracking* method configures the LINQ query so that entities returned will not be cached in the unit of work object, because that happens by default when Entity Framework is used underneath LINQ.

Async database operations can be applied when long-running operations or network latencies might block the application. Async database operations are also an option when you—just to reduce blocking—manually create multiple threads to carry operations separately. In this case, however, you might end up with a large number of threads and a large memory footprint. Async operations hard-coded at the .NET level make use of system threads to wait for operations to complete and do not penalize the application itself.

Important The *DbContext* class you use to control query or save operations (sync or async) is not thread-safe. To avoid issues and apparently weird exceptions, you should have only one operation per *DbContext* running at a time. You can still run multiple database operations in parallel as long as you use distinct instances of the *DbContext* class.

Returning *IQueryable* types

Returning *IQueryable* types from a repository instead of the results of an actual query against the database will give a lot more flexibility to the callers of repositories. This is a gain as well as a pain.

It's a gain because it's the actual consumer of the data who takes the responsibility of narrowing results to what's actually needed. The idea is that you build the query by adding filters along the way and generate SQL code and execute the query only when it cannot be further deferred.

This approach can also be a pain in some situations. Repository callers are actually given the power of doing nearly everything without control. They can certainly use the power of *IQueryable* to add filters and minimize database workload while keeping the repositories lean and mean. However, they can also overuse the *Include* method and grow the graph of returned objects. Repository callers can implement very heavy queries against the database and filter results in memory. Finally, you should consider that the composition of queries occurs within the LINQ provider of the O/RM of choice. Not all LINQ providers have the same capabilities in terms of both performance and the ability to manage large queries. (In our experience, the LINQ provider in Entity Framework is by far the most reliable and powerful.)

The risk of running into such drawbacks is higher if the team writing repositories is not the same as the one writing upper layers and, of course, it is also a matter of experience.

A repository centered on *IQueryable* types can have the following layout:

```
public interface IRepository<TAggregate>
{
    IQueryable<TAggregate> All();    // Really worthwhile?
}
```

As you can see, however, the query side consists of just a single method. Ultimately, you rarely have a strict need for repositories in the query stack. This means you can avoid *IRepository<T>* entirely and build your queries starting from the data source context class (*DbContext* in Entity Framework). The data source context class offers as *IQueryable<T>* the full list of data objects to filter further.

Some don't like *IQueryable* at all

In the community, there's a lot of debate about the use of *IQueryable* in repositories. As mentioned, an approach based on *IQueryable* gives upper layers of the system more responsibilities about the query being built. Also, the query side of the system is tightly bound to LINQ providers. This latter point alone seems to be the major argument raised by those who don't like *IQueryable* in the repository.

The *IQueryable* interface is not responsible for the actual execution of the query. All it does is describe queries to execute. Executing queries and materializing results is the task of a specific LINQ provider. LINQ providers are bound to the actual technology being used for data access.

As long as you use Entity Framework with Microsoft SQL Server, relying on LINQ for queries is not a problem at all. The same can be said if you use a different database, such as Oracle, whether through the official Oracle provider or the third-party DevArt provider. We used the NHibernate provider a few years ago, and it wasn't very reliable at the time. But it likely has improved along the way.

Another objection to using *IQueryable* is that it puts a dependency on the LINQ infrastructure. Determining whether this is a problem or not is up to you and your team. The syntax of LINQ is part of C#, so having a dependency on it is not a problem at all. The point is something else—a dependency on the syntax of LINQ for database queries poses a dependency on some LINQ provider for that data source. We do recognize that in general there's no guarantee you can find reliable LINQ support for every possible data source. In this regard, a solution based on *IQueryable* might face serious problems when you have to switch it to a different data source.

But is this really going to happen? If it's only a theoretical possibility, in our opinion you'd better ignore it and take advantage of the benefits of *IQueryable* for its level of performance and code cleanness. However, we like to suggest a test. What is your stance regarding the following statement?

A repository should offer an explicit and well-defined contract and avoid arbitrary querying.

If you have a strong opinion about that, you also have the best answer about the whole *IQueryable* story.

Persisting aggregates

Because the repository is also responsible for the persistence of aggregates, a common thought is that the command side of a repository must mimic the classic CRUD interface and offer *Add*, *Update*, and *Delete* methods.

As mentioned earlier, instead, in a realistic business domain you hardly have anything like *Add* or *Delete*. All you have is *Save* because "save" is a sufficiently neutral term that can be used for nearly any aggregate and is also familiar to developers. Most business jargon doesn't have a "save" verb; rather, you'll find something like "register," "issue," or maybe "update." However, by using *Save*, you'll likely stay close enough to the ubiquitous language and simplify development. It might be, instead, that on a specific repository class—not the base interface—you can have business-specific methods that logically correspond to delete and insertion methods. You always *save* the order, for example, whether it is a new order or an update to an existing order. You hardly ever *delete* the order, at least in the sense of removing it from the system. Instead, you likely *cancel* the order, which consists of setting a particular value on a particular field—in the end, an internal call to the *Save* method.

Implementing the Unit of Work pattern

A repository class needs to have a dependency on some concrete database technology. If you use the Microsoft stack, the database technology is likely Entity Framework. Let's have a look at the common implementation of a repository class:

```
public interface IOrderRepository : IRepository<Order>
{
    // Query methods
    ...

    // Command methods
    void Save(Order aggregate);
    ...

    // Transactional
    void Commit();
}
```

The concrete repository might look like the code shown here:

```
public class OrderRepository : IOrderRepository
{
    protected Database _database;
    public OrderRepository()
    {
        _database = new Database();
    }

    public void Save(Order order)
    {
        _database.Orders.Add(order);
    }

    public void Commit()
    {
        _database.SaveChanges();
    }
    ...
}
```

The *Database* class here is a custom class that inherits from *DbContext* and represents the entry point in Entity Framework. Having an instance of *Database* scoped at the repository level ensures that any action performed within the scope of the repository instance is treated within the same physical database transaction. On the other hand, this is the essence of the UoW pattern.

You should also have a *Commit* method to attempt to commit the transaction at the *DbContext* level.

Atomic updates

In some simpler scenarios and, in general, whenever it works for you, you can have atomic updates that basically use a local instance of the database context scoped to the method rather than the class:

```
using (var db = new Database())
{
    db.Orders.Add(aggregate);
    db.SaveChanges();
}
```

The only difference between atomic and global methods is that atomic methods trigger their own database transaction and can't be joined to other, wider transactions.

Storage technologies

An interesting change that occurred in recent years in software engineering is that more and more systems are using alternate storage technologies in addition to, or instead of, classic relational data stores. Let's briefly recap the options you have. These options are relevant because they are the technologies you would use in the repository classes to perform data access.

Object/Relational mappers

Using O/RM tools is the most common option for repositories. An O/RM is essentially a productivity tool that greatly simplifies (and makes affordable for most projects) the writing of data-mapping code that persists an object-oriented model to a relational table and vice versa. For a system based on the Microsoft stack, today an obvious choice is Entity Framework. Another excellent choice—for a long time, it was the primary O/RM choice—is NHibernate. (See *http://community.jboss.org/wiki/NHibernateForNET.*)

Entity Framework and NHibernate are only the two most popular choices; many other O/RM choices exist from various vendors. A quick list is shown in Table 14-1. A more comprehensive list can be found at *http://en.wikipedia.org/wiki/DataObjects.NET.*

TABLE 14-1 A list of O/RM tools for Microsoft .NET

O/RM	More information
LLBLGen Pro	http://www.llblgen.com
Data Access (formerly, Open Access)	http://www.telerik.com/data-access
XPO	http://www.devexpress.com/Products/NET/ORM
Genome	http://www.genom-e.com

Choosing the O/RM to use can be as easy as it can be hard. Today, Entity Framework is the first option to consider. In our opinion, Entity Framework is not perfect but it's really easy to use and understand; it has tooling and a lot of support and documentation. Beyond this, Entity Framework is like any other O/RM: you need to know it to use it properly. A developer can still create a disaster with Entity Framework. Among the mistakes we've seen (and done) with Entity Framework are using lazy loading when it is not appropriate and loading object graphs in memory that are too large without being aware of that. And, more than anything else, complaining about Entity Framework and its performance when it was, in the end, our own very fault.

When it comes to choosing an O/RM, we suggest you consider the following points: productivity, architecture, and support.

Productivity mainly refers to the learning curve necessary to master the framework and how easy it turns out to be to maintain an application. *Architecture* refers to the capabilities of the framework to map domain models and the constraints it might impose. In addition, it refers to the set of features it supports, especially when it comes to performance against the underlying database, testability, and flexibility. Finally, *support* refers to supported databases, the ecosystem, the community, and the commitment of the vendor to grow and maintain the product over time.

Entity Framework and NHibernate are the most popular choices, and the saga about which of the two is the best O/RM in town is a never-ending story. We have successfully used both products. We used NHibernate extensively in years past, and we find ourselves using Entity Framework with both SQL Server and Oracle quite often now. If we drew a line to find a set of technical differences, we'd say that Entity Framework still has room for improvement and that the lack of batch commands, the lack of a second-level cache, and especially the lack of custom-type support are the biggest differences we're aware of.

Are those differences enough to determine a winner?

No, we don't think so. Those differences exist and can't be denied, but honestly we think that they don't dramatically affect the building of a persistence layer.

External services to read and write data

When a layered solution is mentioned, it is natural to think that the solution is the entire system. More often than many think, instead, architects are called to write layer solutions that are only one bounded context in a larger system.

In this scenario, it is not surprising that you have no access to the physical database and that sometimes you don't even see it. You know that data is somehow written and read from some place in some remote cloud; all you have is a set of URLs to call.

In this case, your repository doesn't include any *DbContext* object, just some .NET API to arrange HTTP or network calls. Such calls might be atomic or chained, synchronous or asynchronous; sometimes multiple calls might even go in parallel:

```
var tasks = new Task<Object>[2];
tasks[0] = Task<Object>.Factory.StartNew(() => _downloader1.Find(...));
tasks[1] = Task<Object>.Factory.StartNew(() => _downloader1.Find(...));
await Task.WhenAll(tasks);
var data1 = tasks[0].Result as SomeType1;
var data2 = tasks[1].Result as SomeType2[];
```

In the repositories, you use downloader and uploader components and run them asynchronously on separate threads using synchronization when required. Caching is even more important in repositories based on external services because it can save HTTP calls. Similarly, caching at the HTTP level through front-end proxy servers can increase performance and scalability for large and frequent reads.

> **Note** Probably the most common situation in which repositories are based on external services are mobile applications and single-page web applications. In particular, in single-page web applications you can use ad hoc JavaScript libraries (for example, *breeze.js*) to connect to a tailor-made Web API front end and perform reads and writes with minimal configuration and effort.

OData endpoints

OData, short for *Open Data Protocol*, is a web protocol that offers a unified approach for querying and manipulating remote data via CRUD operations. In addition, OData exposes metadata about the encapsulated content that clients can use to discover the type information and relationships between collections. Originally defined by Microsoft, the protocol is now being standardized at OASIS.

OData implements the same core idea as Open Database Connectivity (ODBC), except that it is not limited to SQL databases. You might want to check *http://www.odata.org* for more information about the protocol and details about the syntax. To form a quick idea about the protocol, consider the following URL:

```
/api/numbers?$top=20&$skip=10
```

The URL gets whatever the *numbers* endpoint returns—assumed to be a collection of objects—and then gets 20 items, skipping the first 10. OData defines the query string syntax in a standard way. This means that a server-side layer can be created to parse the query string and adjust the response.

In terms of repositories, OData helps arrange queries on top of remote services. In other words, if the remote service supports the OData protocol, you can send HTTP requests that build custom queries on top of exposed collections so that a filtered response can be returned as well as custom projections of data.

With ASP.NET Web API, you can easily create an OData endpoint around a data set. All you need to do is mark the method with the *Queryable* attribute and make it return an *IQueryable* type:

```
[Queryable]
public IQueryable<SomeType> Get()
{
    var someData = ...;
    return someData.AsQueryable();
}
```

OData supports several serialization formats, including JSON.

Distributed memory cache

A repository is the place where you use caching if caching is required. This means that caching technologies are also part of the architect's tool chest. There are many easy ways to cache data. In an ASP.NET application, you can use, for example, the built-in *Cache* object. This object works beautifully except that it is limited to a single machine and Internet Information Services (IIS) process.

More powerful memory caches are available that work across a distributed architecture. The most prominent example is Memcached, but several other commercial and open-source products exist, such as NCache, ScaleOut, and Redis. When it comes to using a cache—distributed or not—the pattern followed by the repository code is fairly common:

- Try to read from the cache.

- If no data is found, access the back-end store.

- Save data in the cache.

- Return the data.

For updates, the pattern is similar: you first update the back-end store and then the intermediate cache, although in some scenarios of extreme scalability it is acceptable that things occur in the reverse order.

NoSQL data stores

Yet another storage technology for (some) repositories are NoSQL data stores. Such data stores are designed from the ground up just to store huge amounts of data—any data, of any size and complexity—across a possibly huge number of servers. They don't follow any fixed schema, meaning that they don't face any rigidity and let you evolve the system with great ease. The key benefit that NoSQL provides can be summarized as follows:

- Ability to deal with unstructured data

- Ability to support eventual consistency scenarios, which cuts off writing time and makes a write-intensive system easy to scale

- Independence from query language

- Natural sharding that doesn't require balance and predesign analysis of the involved tables and partition of data

A NoSQL data store requires a team to develop new skills, and it poses new challenges for the team both on the development side and with the setup and administrative part of the work. As we see it, NoSQL data stores are definitely an option to consider for some segments of the persistence layer. In smaller, simpler, or just specific bounded contexts, NoSQL storage can even be the primary storage technology. More often than not, though, we see NoSQL used in conjunction with more traditional forms of storage. This form of persistence has been given the quite fancy name of *polyglot persistence*.

Why should you consider nonrelational storage?

At present, cracks are starting to show in the otherwise solid granite wall of relational stores. The cracks are the result of the nature of a relational store and of some applications and their data. It's becoming increasingly difficult to fit real data into the rigid schema of a relational model and, more often than not, a bit of redundancy helps save queries, thus making the application faster. No hype and no religion—it's just the evolution of business and tools.

In our opinion, calling relational stores "dead" and replacing them tout-court with the pet NoSQL product of choice is not a savvy move. There are moments in life and business in which you must be ready to seize new opportunities far before it is clear how key they are. If you're an architect and your business is building applications for clients, NoSQL stores are just another tool in your toolbox.

It's a different story, instead, if your business is building and selling tools for software development. In this case, jumping on the NoSQL bandwagon is a smart move. NoSQL stores are useful in some business scenarios because of their inherent characteristics, but smart tooling is required to make them more and more appealing and useful. This is an opportunity to seize.

If you're an architect who builds software for a client, your responsibility is understanding the mechanics of the domain and the characteristics of the data involved and then working out the best architecture possible.

Familiarizing yourself with NoSQL

For the past 40 years or so, we used relational data stores and managed to use them successfully in nearly all industry segments and business contexts. We also observed relational data productively employed in systems of nearly all sizes.

Relational data stores happily survived the advent of object-orientation. Presented as a cutting-edge technology, object-based databases did not last long. When objects came up, relational stores had already gained significant market penetration to be seriously threatened by emerging object-based databases. Quite simply, development teams found it easier to build new object-oriented artifacts in which to wrap access to relational data stores and SQL queries. For decades, the industry didn't really see a need for nonrelational storage.

Are things different today?

Not-Only SQL

Originally, the NoSQL movement started as a sharp and somewhat rabid reaction to SQL and relational databases. At some point, the NoSQL movement and products hit the real world. The NoSQL acronym was then reworked to a more pragmatic "Not Only SQL." In a nutshell, a NoSQL store doesn't store data as records with a fixed schema of columns. It uses, instead, a looser schema in which a record is generically a document with its own structure. Each document is a standalone piece of data that can be queried by content or type. Adding a field to a document doesn't require any work other than just saving a new copy of the document and maybe a bit of extra versioning work.

With NoSQL, there's no need to involve the IT department to make changes to the structure of stored data. NoSQL allows you to write a data-access layer with much more freedom and many less constraints than a traditional relational environment.

Is the increased agility in writing and deploying software a good reason to abandon relational stores?

Where are NoSQL stores being used?

As a matter of fact, an increasing number of companies are using NoSQL stores. A good question to ask is, "Where are NoSQL stores being used?" This is a much better question to ask than, "How can we take advantage of NoSQL stores?" As we see it, examining realistic technology use-cases to see if they match your own is preferable to blindly looking for reasons to use a given technology.

NoSQL stores are used in situations where you can recognize some of the following characteristics:

- Large—often, unpredictably large—volumes of data and possibly millions of users

- Thousands of queries per second

- Presence of unstructured/semi-structured data that might come in different forms, but still needs the same treatment (polymorphic data)

- Cloud computing and virtual hardware involved for extreme scalability needs

- Your database is a natural event source

If your project doesn't match any of these conditions, you can hardly expect to find NoSQL particularly rewarding. Using NoSQL outside of such conditions might not be wrong, but it might just end up being a different way of doing the same old things.

Flavors of NoSQL

There's not just one type of NoSQL data store. Under the umbrella of NoSQL, you can find quite a few different classes of data stores:

- **Document/Object store**   This store saves and indexes objects and documents in much the same way as a relational system saves and retrieves records. Stored data can also be queried via associated metadata. The big difference with relational systems is that any stored object has its own schema made and can be abstracted as a collection of properties.

- **Graph store**   This store saves arbitrarily complex collections of objects. The main trait of these systems is that they support relationships between data elements.

- **Key value store**   This store works like a huge dictionary made of two fields—key and value. Store data is retrieved by key. Values are usually serialized as JSON data.

- **Tabular store**   This store is based on concepts similar to relational stores. The big difference is the lack of normalization you find in tabular stores. Tabular data usually fulfills the first normal form of the relational model (which is about repeated groups of data) but not the second form (which is about giving each data element a primary key). For more information, refer to *http://en.wikipedia.org/wiki/First_normal_form* and *http://en.wikipedia.org/wiki/Second_normal_form*.

NoSQL stores offer quite different sets of capabilities. Therefore, various segments of the application might need different NoSQL solutions. Examples of a key-value store are in-memory data containers such as Memcached. Examples of a document stores are products often associated these days with the whole idea of NoSQL, such as CouchDB, MongoDB, and RavenDB. Let's find out more about document databases.

What you gain and what you lose

Relational databases have existed for at least 40 years, and everybody in the software industry is used to them. A few well-established relational databases exist and take up the vast majority of the world demand for data storage, dwarfing any NoSQL solution. Far from being a dead-end technology, classic SQL technology improves over time, as the new column store feature in SQL Server 2014 demonstrates.

Yet, some new business scenarios emerge that push the power of relational databases to the limit. The challenge for architects is to resist the temptation to use trendy tools—and, instead, to use them just when, and if, appropriate for the particular business.

Downsides of the relational model in some of today's scenarios

The major strengths of relational databases can be summarized as follows:

- Supports a standard data-access language (SQL)

- Table models are well understood and the design and normalization process is well defined

In addition, the costs and risks associated with large development efforts and with large chunks of data need to be well understood. Gaining expertise in design, development, optimization, and administration is relatively easy, and an ecosystem of tools exists for nearly any necessity.

On the downside, really data-intensive applications treating millions of rows might become problematic because relational databases are optimized for specific scenarios, such as small-but-frequent read/write transactions and large batch transactions with infrequent write access.

In general, it is correct to say that when relational databases grow big, handling them—reads and writes—can become problematic. However, how big should it grow to become so expensive to handle that you want to consider alternative solutions? They should grow fairly big indeed. Relational tables certainly don't prevent scaling-out, except that they introduce the extra costs of data sharding.

In a relational environment, the issues with massive reads and writes are mostly related to the cost of managing indexes in large tables with millions of rows. Relational databases also add overhead even for simple reads that join and group data. Integrity, both transactional and referential, is a great thing, but it can be overkill for some applications. Relational databases require the flattening of complex real-world objects into a columnar sequence of data and vice versa. The negative points can be summarized as follows:

- Limited support for complex base types in both reading and writing via SQL (need of O/RM).

- Knowledge of the database structure is required to create ad hoc queries.

- Indexing over a large number of records (in the order of millions of rows) becomes slow.

In general, a relational structure might not be the ideal choice for serving pages that model unstructured data that cannot be reduced to an efficient schema of rows and columns and to serve binary content from within high-traffic websites.

Relational databases still work great, but in some very special scenarios (lots of reads and writes, unstructured data and no need for strict consistency) different choices for storage are welcome. It's easy to map those aspects to social networks. If you're building a social network, you definitely need to look into polyglot persistence. When heterogeneous storage is taken into account, NoSQL storage is likely one of the options—and the most compelling one.

Eventual consistency

There are two major features of a NoSQL store: the ability to handle schemaless data and eventual consistency. Together these features offer a persistence layer that is easy to modify, supports CQRS scenarios well, and facilitates scalability. Eventual consistency is a critical attribute from a pure business perspective.

Eventual consistency is when reads and writes aren't aligned to the same data. Most NoSQL systems are eventually consistent in the sense that they guarantee that if no updates are made to a given object for a sufficient period of time, a query returns what the last command has written.

In most cases, eventual consistency isn't an issue at all. You generally need to be as consistent as possible within the bounded context. You don't really need any level of consistency across bounded contexts. As the system grows, despite the technology, you can't expect full consistency. Within the bounded context, though, there are business scenarios in which eventual consistency is not acceptable. As an example, consider a banking application that lets a user withdraw an amount of money from an account. If two operations for the same amount occur, you must be able to recognize them as distinct operations and take no risk that the second is taken as a repetition of the first. Without the full ACID consistency of a relational store, this could be a problem.

There's a simple test to see whether eventual consistency is an issue. How would you consider a scenario in which a command writes some data, but a successive read returns stale data? If it's absolutely crucial that you're constantly able to read back what has just been written, you have two options:

- Avoid NoSQL databases.

- Configure the NoSQL database to be consistent.

Let's see eventual consistency in action in a sample document database such as RavenDB.

Eventual consistency in RavenDB

Consider the following code snippet, which assumes the use of RavenDB—a popular .NET NoSQL database. For more information, visit *http://ravendb.net*.

```
// You store an object to the database
DocumentSession.Store(yourDocument);

// Try to read back the content just saved
DocumentSession.Query<SomeDocumentType>().Where(doc => doc.Id == id)
```

The effect of eventual consistency—the default configuration in RavenDB—is that what you'll read isn't the same as what you've just written.

As far as RavenDB is concerned, writing on the store and updating indexes used by the query engine are distinct operations. Index updates occur as scheduled operations. That misalignment doesn't last more than a few seconds if there are no other updates to the same object taking place in the meantime.

Scared? Just worried? Or thinking of dropping all the wicked NoSQL stuff for the rest of your career? Well, there are programmatic tools to control eventual consistency. Here's a possible way to force ACID consistency in RavenDB:

```
var _instance = new EmbeddableDocumentStore { ConnectionStringName = "RavenDB" };
_instance.Conventions.DefaultQueryingConsistency =
    ConsistencyOptions.AlwaysWaitForNonStaleResultsAsOfLastWrite;
```

When you do this, though, that read doesn't return until the index has been updated. A trivial read, therefore, might take a few seconds to complete.

There are better ways to wait for indexes to update. For example, you can determine the type of consistency a query needs at query time, as in the following example:

```
using( var session = store.OpenSession() )
{
    var query = session.Query<Person>()
                .Customize(c=> c.WaitForNonStaleResultsAsOfLastWrite())
                .Where( p => /* condition */ );
}
```

In this example, the *WaitForNonStaleResultsAsOfLastWrite* query customization is telling the server to wait for the relevant index to have indexed the last document written and ignore any documents hitting the server after the query has been issued. This helps in certain scenarios with a high write ratio, where indexes are constantly stale.

There are many other *WaitForNonStaleResultsXxxx* methods in RavenDB that solve different scenarios. Another possibility is to fully embrace eventual consistency, ask the server if the returned results are stale, and behave accordingly:

```
using( var session = store.OpenSession() )
{
    RavenQueryStatistics stats;
    var query = session.Query<Person>()
                .Statistics( out stats )
                .Where( p => /* condition */ );
}
```

In this example, you ask the server to also return query statistics that inform you whether or not returned results are stale. You then take the best possible action based on the scenario.

> **Note** From this, you see that NoSQL stores fill a niche in the industry. They do pose challenges, though. NoSQL addresses some architecture issues while neglecting others. Eventual consistency is an excellent example of trade-offs in the software industry. You can happily concede to eventual consistency to gain performance and scalability. And you can probably do that in more situations than one might think at first. But if you need full ACID consistency, you should not use NoSQL at all.

Polyglot persistence by example

Today there are at least two options for a persistence layer: classic relational storage and polyglot persistence. *Polyglot persistence* is a fancy term that simply refers to using the most appropriate persistence layer for each operation.

Let's consider a polyglot-persistence scenario for a generic e-commerce system. In such a system, you reasonably might need to save the following information:

- Customers, orders, payments, shipments, products, and all that relates to a business transaction

- Preferences of users discovered as they navigate through the catalog of products or resulting from running business intelligence on top of their transactions

- Documents representing invoices, maps of physical shops to find the nearest one to the user, directions, pictures, receipts of delivery, and so on

- Detailed logs of any user's activity: products he viewed, bought, commented on, reviewed or liked

- Graph of users who bought the same and similar products, similar products, other products the user might be interested in buying, and users in the same geographical area

Saving any such pieces of information to a single relational or NoSQL store is possible, but probably not ideal. Polyglot persistence consists of mixing together various stores and picking the right one for each type of information. For example, you can store customers and orders to a SQL Server data store and access it through Entity Framework or any other O/RM framework. Entity Framework, in particular, can be used also to transparently access an instance of a Microsoft Azure SQL Database in the cloud.

User preferences can go to the Azure table storage and be accessed through an ad hoc layer that consumes Azure JSON endpoints. Documents can go to, say, RavenDB or MongoDB and be consumed through the dedicated .NET API. The user's history can be saved to a column store such as Cassandra. Cassandra is unique in that it associates a key value with a varying number of name/value pairs. The nice thing is that any row stored to Cassandra can have a completely different structure than other records. The effect is similar to having a name/value dictionary where the value is a collection of name/value pairs. Cassandra can be accessed from .NET using an ad hoc framework like FluentCassandra (*http://fluentcassandra.com*). Finally, hierarchical information can be stored to a graph database such as Neo4j through the .NET client.

The overall cost of polyglot persistence might be significant at times. For the most part, you end up working with .NET clients that are relatively straightforward to use. Yet, when a lot of data is involved and performance issues show up, heterogeneous skills are required and a shortage or lack of documentation is the norm rather than the exception.

Planning a sound choice

Eventual consistency is the first relevant factor that might cause you to rule out the use of NoSQL products. Another factor is when the data to represent is so intricate, large, growing, and frequently updated that a relational table would grow too fast, posing other issues such as sharding and caching.

When you have to make a decision, which other aspects and parameters should you consider?

The "why-not?" factor

To put things into perspective, let's clean up any bias and try to honestly answer the following simple question: "In the context of the project, are you satisfied with relational storage?" Here's a table of possible answers.

TABLE 14-2 Are you satisfied with relational storage?

Answer	Follow-up decision
Yes	It's a no-brainer question. You just stick to using whatever relational data store you used to this point, or use analogous and better products.
No	You stop using relational stores and start investigating alternatives. Most likely, today you will look into the various flavors of NoSQL, but also consider big storage in the cloud.
No, but ...	This answer probably means that constraints exist to keep you bound to the status quo. You realize the current approach might not be ideal, but you have no energy, budget, or appetite to turn elsewhere.
Yes, but ...	You're OK with the state-of-the-art; you worked hard on it, and it works quite well. But you are familiar with the word "progress," and you are constantly open to change. But not change for the sake of change, just for the sake of building better artifacts that work. And you're not scared of little-known innovations. (In software, you should always be scared of the "unknown" peripheral toy/pilot projects.)

Relational vs. NoSQL is definitely an architectural choice; it's a choice that's hard to make, critical, and not to be indefinitely delayed. As we see things, the "Yes, but" answer is the sole answer that opens up a whole new world of opportunities without flying the project away from sane pragmatism.

But where does that answer lead the project?

The "Yes but" answer indicates that, overall, relational storage works for you, but the sound of the engine is not completely clean. You perceive that some grains of sand are left in the gears. Should you consider moving away from the consolidated, well-established, and comfortable relational world? And why should you change? Compelling reasons wanted!

Beyond the aforementioned discriminants, a compelling reason is represented by the hefty license fees you (or your customers) are asked to pay for most relational databases. Beyond this, we don't think there are compelling reasons to choose NoSQL as the sole approach for storage.

NoSQL is gaining ground and momentum. At the moment, though, there's no clear perception of why this is happening. But it is happening. We're led to believe that it's a mix of curiosity and love for innovation—a sort of "Why-not?" factor—to push more and more companies to try out a NoSQL store in a real-world system. The mechanics of NoSQL, therefore, are that by trying it out an increasing number of companies figure out that in more and more scenarios they can drop relational databases in favor of NoSQL.

This is slowly eroding the pillars of a world that couldn't have looked more solid and untouchable only a couple of years ago.

If you're clueless about what to do, we suggest you look into three parameters that relate to the nature of the data you handle: characteristics, volatility and growth.

Characteristics of the data

Is the data the application will handle homogeneous? In this context, *homogeneity* refers to the degree at which conceptual data can be partitioned in formal tables of homogeneous entities. You should be aware that not all entities captured in requirements can be always and easily constrained within a tabular model and expressed as combination of rows and columns.

This is a general point—things have always been like this. However, for some reason and for many years, architects preferred to normalize (actually, flatten) data to tabular schemas rather than look into, say, object-based stores. We believe that the primary reason has been the lack of (commercially) valid alternatives, which are now available.

The relational model is more than adequate if the data is naturally homogeneous or if it lends itself well to be flattened within a tabular schema. The second scenario, though, opens a window for alternate solutions that the savvy architect should be ready to catch and investigate further. Having to work with data that is hard to bend into a table scores a point in favor of NoSQL, even though architects have been able to massage nontabular data into tables for years.

Volatility of the schema

How often is the schema of data expected to change over time and across installations of the system for different customers? If the requirements churn of the system introduces new data types to persist, you must ensure that the database can support them as well.

A NoSQL store is much better suited than a classic relational store to handle originally homogeneous data that, at some point, turns into more heterogeneous data. In a relational model, such adjustments can be accomplished only by altering the structure of the (production) tables. As you might understand, this is never a small change.

Growth of the data

A data store might grow in size to address new requirements or just because of an increased number of users. When this happens, a relational database might encounter serious performance issues, especially when the rate of reading and writing is quite high. In this context, the more the data is tabular in nature, the more the application delays indicate its getting into trouble.

When the amount of data grows to a point that it might become a problem, the database must be scaled up in some way. The simplest option is vertical scaling, except that it has the drawback of just moving the bottleneck forward without removing or definitely fighting it. Another option is horizontal scaling through clustering.

Most commercial relational databases do offer horizontal scaling, but these solutions can be very complex to set up and quite expensive. Modern NoSQL products have been designed to address specific issues of horizontal scaling and performance issues related to intensive read and write operations.

Summary

There's no application and no reasonable bounded context that doesn't have to read and/or write data. These tasks are performed by the persistence layer, which is ideally the only place in the application where connection strings and URLs are known and managed.

A lot has changed in recent years as far as persistence is concerned. First and foremost, reads and writes might not take place over the same data store. Second, the data store is not necessarily a database. If it is a database, there's sometimes no necessity for stored procedures and a separate database-level layer of SQL code to access data.

The final aspect that has changed is the nature of the database, whether it has to be relational, NoSQL, or polyglot. Ultimately, the point isn't to pronounce relational stores dead and replace them with the NoSQL product of choice. The point is to understand the mechanics of the system and characteristics of the data and work out the best possible architecture. In our opinion, the most foreseeable concrete application for NoSQL stores is as an event store in the context of an event-sourcing architecture.

For systems where there isn't a simple yes or no answer to whether or not you should use relational stores, the best you can do is consider polyglot persistence. Instead of forcing a choice between NoSQL and relational databases, you could look into a storage layer that combines the strengths of the two. This type of storage system tackles different problems in the most appropriate way.

Within the context of an enterprise, you should use different storage technologies to store different types of data. This is especially true in a service-oriented architecture. In this case, each service might have its own storage layer. There would be no reason to unify storage under a single technology or product. Polyglot persistence does require that you learn different storage technologies and products. As a training cost, though, it's a reasonable investment.

Finishing with a smile

To generate a smile or two at the end of this chapter, we resort to rephrasing a few popular sayings. To start, we'd love to resurrect the popular Maslow's hammer law. Nearly everybody knows it, but few people connect it to Abraham Maslow. In its commonly-used short formulation the law sounds like "If all you have is a hammer, everything looks like a nail." Here is a really profound way of rephrasing it:

> If all you know is SQL, all data looks relational.

Lily Tomlin (an American actress and comedian) said, "If love is the answer, would you please rephrase the question?" We think this can be applied to data access as the following:

> If too many records are the answer, would you please rephrase the query?

The popular Murphy's law can also be rephrased for databases:

> If you design a database such that a developer can put incorrect data into it, eventually some developer will do that.

Index

A

Abelson, Hal, 349
abstraction, 273
acceptance tests, 31, 94–96
accessibility, 10
actions
    in Behavior-Driven Design, 95
    in Domain-Driven Design, 121
    execution through components, 177
    implementing as classes, 174
    objects representing, 171
Active Record pattern, 168
adapters, 186
ADO.NET, 192
aggregates, 199–205, 266
    aggregate root objects, 200, 204–205, 344–346
    boundaries of, 202–203
    cross-aggregate behavior in domain services, 206
    data snapshots, 323, 340–348
    event handling, 347–348
    identifying, 235–243
    locking vs. keeping open to change, 260–261
    modeling, 199–200
    persistence, 199, 347, 357, 363–364
    rebuilding state, 328, 339
    repository for, 346–347. *See also* repositories
    snapshots vs. replaying events, 348
Agile development, 15–17
    Extreme Programming, 17
    Scrum methodology, 17
    training and practice, 41
    unforeseen events, 37
Agile Project Management with Scrum (Schwaber), 17
agility in architecture, 4, 11–12
Ajax, 152–153
Alexander, Christopher, 75
American National Standards Institute/Institute of Electrical and Electronics Engineers (ANSI/IEEE) standard 1471, 5
analysts, 18, 22
Anemic Domain Model (ADM), 63, 134, 174–176, 226–227

anticorruption layers (ACLs), 126–127
anti-patterns, 175–176
Apple's organizational culture, 35
application layer, 132–134, 177–180, 257
    connecting to data-access layer, 179–180
    connecting to presentation layer, 178–179
    in CQRS, 257
    event notification from, 336
    extending, 284
    front ends, 178
    messages delivered to, 277
    security concerns, 213
application logic, 198
application persistence, 195–196
application services, 134, 149–151, 248–251, 285
architects, 17–24
    as analysts, 21–22
    code writing, 23–24
    and developers, boundary between, 12
    flowcharts, use of, 305
    misconceptions about, 21–24
    openness and transparency, 32
    as project managers, 22
    responsibilities, 18–20
    roles, 4, 20–21
architectural patterns, 19. *See also specific pattern names*
architecture, 5
    agility in, 4, 11–12
    of bounded contexts, 127–129
    classic three-segment, 129–130, 167
    early decisions, 12–14
    emerging, 16–17
    event-based, 315–318
    implementation, 7, 12
    layered, 130–131, 167. *See also* layered architecture
    process of, 14–17
    requirements, 7. *See also* requirements
    single-tier, 129
    tasks, responsibility for, 14
    upfront, 15
    vision of, 7

About the authors

Dino Esposito is CTO and cofounder of Crionet, a startup providing software and IT services to professional tennis and sports companies. Dino still does a lot of training and consulting and is the author of several books on web and mobile development. His most recent books are *Architecting Mobile Solutions for the Enterprise* and *Programming ASP.NET MVC*, both from Microsoft Press. Dino speaks regularly at industry conferences, including Microsoft TechEd and DevConnections, and premiere European events, such as Software Architect, DevWeek, SDD, and BASTA. A technical evangelist covering Android and Kotlin development for JetBrains, Dino is also on the development team of WURFL—the ScientiaMobile database of mobile device capabilities that is used by large organizations such as Facebook.

You can follow Dino on Twitter at @despos and through his blog: (*http://software2cents.wordpress.com*).

Andrea Saltarello is CEO and founder of Managed Designs (*http://www.manageddesigns.it*), a company providing consultancy services related to software design and development.

A solution architect, Andrea is eager to write code in real projects to get feedback related to his architectural decisions. Andrea is also the lead developer of MvcMate, an open source project aimed at providing useful extensions to the ASP.NET MVC toolkit.

As a trainer and speaker, Andrea had several speaking engagements for courses and conferences across Europe, such as BASTA! Italia, DevWeek and Software Architect. He has also taught "Operating Systems" during the "Master in Editoria Multimediale" class organized by the University "Politecnico of Milan."

In 2001 Andrea co-founded UGIdotNET (*http://www.ugidotnet.org*), the first Italian .NET User Group, of which he is President and leader.

Andrea is passionate about sports and music, and grew up devoted to volleyball and to Depeche Mode, which he fell in love with upon first listening to Everything Counts.

You can follow Andrea on Twitter at @andysal74 and through his blog (*http://blogs.ugidotnet.org/mrbrightside*)

Now that you've read the book...

Tell us what you think!

Was it useful?
Did it teach you what you wanted to learn?
Was there room for improvement?

Let us know at http://aka.ms/tellpress

Your feedback goes directly to the staff at Microsoft Press,
and we read every one of your responses. Thanks in advance!

 Microsoft